MATRIMONIAL HONOR

Daniel Rogers

Edification Press
Warrenton, VA

Matrimonial Honor
Copyright © 2010 by Edification Press

Edification Press
Warrenton, VA
www.edificationpress.com

This edition is based on *Matrimoniall Honour* published in 1642. The text has been revised to reflect modern spelling, and a few words and phrases have been modernized. Minor modifications have been made to the grammar and punctuation, but the majority of the original has been retained. Every effort has been made to make the work more accessible to the modern reader without altering the intent of the author.

ISBN 978-1-936473-00-7

Matrimonial Honor

or

The mutual crown and comfort of

godly, loyal, and chaste marriage

Wherein

The right way to preserve the honor of marriage
unstained is at large described, urged, and applied:
with resolution of sundry material questions
concerning this argument.

Also

An appendix, added to the treatise, describing the
just and terrible judgments of God upon all
that dare violate the honor of marriage

To which is added an alphabetical table, very
necessary for the reader's understanding, to find
each several thing contained in this book.

Set forth for the good of all such as either are to enter, or are already entered into this honorable estate.

By D.R. Batch. in Divinity, and Minister of the Gospel.

---

1 Thess. 4.4
*And, that every man may know how to preserve his vessel in
holiness and honor*

To the Right Honorable, and his
very good Lord, Robert Earl of War-
wick, Baron of Leez, etc.

The author of this treatise
wishes all health, honor,
and happiness.

Right Honorable:

When I first intended this discourse (being some years since) I thought I felt in myself a desire of some intermission from former arguments of deeper exercise, and more spiritual nature: as conceiving that a moral theme might, another while, both revive my wearied spirits and perhaps delight the reader with variety. Hereupon I considered what object in this kind might most fitly sort with my thoughts; and after some inquiry, both the many complaints of the married and daily questions moved unto me by such as intended marriage. As also secondly, those notorious errors and corruptions which (through sin and Satan) have insinuated, even pierced the very internal parts of this state; and lastly (which is worst of all) those infinite pollutions of body and mind, in all degrees of men both natural and unnatural, moved me with resolution to fasten upon this argument. But notwithstanding the pregnancy of these inducements, the theme seemed so weighty that I was forced to search what furniture I had stored up for such a work. And at last I found the case to stand with me as it does with two friends, who through discontinuance or absence, have waxen strange to each other; until by some fair occasion of meeting they happen to renew their acquaintance. So stood the case between myself and these meditations, which gave the first draft of the treatise ensuing; which since my first preaching thereof lay long by me, as half forgotten; but now seemed to present themselves to my view with double appetite and savor, as promising to be material and useful for the bettering of public manners and helping to redress the corruptions of the time. Accordingly therefore shaking off the dust and soil of my papers, I have bestowed some pains to contrive them into some such order and expression as might (if not satisfy the curious, yet) profit the desirous of counsel and resolution in cases of this nature.

You see (Right Honorable) how bold I am to draw you from your deeper occasions to listen a while to these private notions of mine: which I presume (out of your facility to give best construction to things) you will not disdain to do. To proceed then: alas! How evident is it, by men's practice that although all confess they ought to be religious (and who now-adays is otherwise?) yet few will admit the yoke of God upon their neck in the wise undergoing of those relations wherein they stand obliged? Among which this of marriage is a rooted and fundamental one, as being in order before the rest; and such a one as either affords influence and sap to them (family, polity, and church) or else infers a blemish and aspersion upon them all. So that if men would derive the savor and power of godliness into this estate of life, seasoning it with the graces of self-denial, faith, and holiness; they should (doubtless) enjoy it in a far more sweet and contentful sort than they do now, while they detain this truth in unrighteousness, separating the thing which God has united.

Men tell us they will hear preachers (while they keep their bounds) while they teach them only faith and repen-tance; but if they must meddle with a more close and near search of their lives and relations, their callings, companies, trading, and liberties; or if they will pry into their more re-tired ways, their closets, chambers, and marriages then, as he who raged against Elisha for the discovering and defeating of his plots to the King of Israel: so these recoil at the minister, and threaten that they will give him over. They tell him that they can teach him as good passages and rules of experience as he can. So far are they from standing to God's bar in these points and say, they knew them before he knew what his books meant; they are nearer a kin to that lascivious poet, who being told of his unchaste epigrams, answered thus, It is true indeed,

2 Kings 6.13

it is meet that the poet himself is chaste, but as for his verses, let them have their course, to show the author's wit and skill, it matters not what they are. So say these, We grant all that we must be honest folk, but that our marriage actions should run in the stream of religion we deem it overly scrupulous, and more than is necessary. Subtle men (we say) float aloft and dwell in universals, but bring them to the particular, show them Rhodes, and the stage whereon they should dance, and then they are at a set, their great skill suddenly fails them.

Cattull. Epigr. Castum esse decet, & pium Poetam, Ipsum : versi culos nihil necesse est.

Howbeit, if we look into the Scriptures we shall meet with some whose very marriages have been cast into the mold of obedience. Not to urge the rules which Paul gives to husbands and wives, both for their entrance upon and cohabitation in that condition; we read of Zechariah and Elizabeth, both which were just, walking before God in all his commands without reproof: that is, they practiced piety, righteousness, and soberness in the state of marriage. How could they walk in all commands, balking the fifth, which urges religion in our particular state of life? But what say men to this? Surely as the Papists tell us, assurance of salvation belongs to Peter and Paul, and such as had special revelations, but it is no ordinary man's case. So say these, such as Zechariah and Elizabeth were eminent persons, masterpieces, above the common size: objects of admiration rather than imitation. But alas! This mist is not thick enough to escape in: all of us under the gospel are under the same law which they were. We are a royal priesthood tied to as strict a rule as ever they were, of chastity and holiness.

Luke 1.6

I doubt not (Right Honorable) if the question might be decided by your voice, but you are of this mind and desire to be of the same practice. Now yet why I devote this treatise to your name, many may wonder, as deeming many other subjects more worthy and proper to present your lordship with. But (my good lord) such is the estate of fragile flesh in this veil or misery that there is no condition of life, whether ministry, magistracy, single, or married state wherein counsel may not do well for the rectifying of such errors as through human infirmity break into all. Each state has its several temptations, and a well ordered course in marriage (as long experience of a double marriage can teach you) is no easy theme. Again that sweet and mutual accord which God has granted between your Honor and your worthy consort may serve to turn my dedication into a congratulation. And indeed, though the book is much under the value of such a personage as yourself (a man not only of noble descent but of great and deserving acts both for our church and commonwealth, both formerly and of late), yet I presume that if a draught of muddy water presented in the crown of a hat was so welcome to a potent monarch: then doubtless your honorable spirit will not reject a scholar's mite, offered with as deep respect unto you as that was. You will not despise small things, since there may be a blessing therein. Not always in a great thing there is good, but in a good there is ever great, and that which may agree with greatness, as one tells us out of a Greek poet. All helps shall one day cease, yet every book of use may serve as a little walking-staff to further us in our travel home.

Acts 24.2

Moreover it may become the best scholar of us all to learn that lesson which Paul, and from him my book urges; *The time is short* (wrapped and folded up, as the text is). *Let them that possess, be as if they possessed not, such as weep, as if they wept not, such as rejoice, as if they rejoiced not, such as marry, as if they married not, such as use the world, as if not using it: for the fashion of it passeth away.* A time for all things, and so a time for the married to embrace, and a time to be far from embracing. Seek therefore that place where all these relations shall cease (for so I think, though some think otherwise), where there shall be no marrying, nor giving in marriage, for the spouse shall be wholly spiritual, like her husband, at least like the angels of God. In which desire I rest, craving a blessing from heaven upon your Honor, your virtuous and Noble Lady, and posterity: as also upon the perusal of this your book: and so humbly take my leave, resting.

1 Cor. 7.29, 30
Eccles. 3.1 &
chapter 5

Mat. 22.30

At your Honor's command
in the LORD,

DANIEL ROGERS

To the
R E A D E R,
all health.

Judicious and religious reader, this wheel of our conversation, whereof this book treats, (marriage I mean) including many lesser wheels in and under it, all subject to the motion thereof, and each of them requiring a due order and direction that both might be regular and according to knowledge; how should I think any other but that I have lighted upon this point of marriage by a special, careful guidance of providence? Desirous we are sometimes that the matter we have by us in readiness might be seasonable also for the times wherein we live: but, when indeed the manners of our present age seem to give a life to that which we have before prepared (for you know occasion is the life of a thing), then doubly it appears seasonable, truly as apples of gold and pictures of silver. Howbeit further musing of the matter, sundry other smaller cords concurred to draw me on to this endeavor: whereof I will make you a partaker (as counting it none of the smallest mercies that I may give an account to the church of God for the improving and redeeming of my seasons) in these sad times; wherein that good God, who allows us any the least protection and liberty, requires that we spend it not in vanity and froth, but to the best advantage, if not as we would (for he is wiser than man, even his foolishness and weakness exceeds the best wisdom and strength which is in us) yet as we may for the better making up of our reckoning at his coming, when the use of our talents shall be examined.

1 Cor. 1.25

First then, I observed that religious consent between couples did not only fashion the family relations, the children and servants, much more orderly; but also extended itself to the church and commonwealth; causing those services which

1.

concern public communion of worshippers to proceed more fair; as also the duties of common life to pass more comely than otherwise they would. One godly and harmonious couple, I have noted, to dispatch more good service to God, to themselves, and to their brethren than some ten couples unequally yoked. So true a maxim of Machiavelli and his master the Devil it is, He that would bear rule, let him sow discord and division. This one wheel then being of so main importance; what need is there that the spokes and staves of it be sound and well compact, according to the rule of the sanctuary? This was one motive.

Si vis imperare, divide.

2.

I observed moreover, that as barren as the world is of good persons and good couples, yet here and there are scattered many of a tractable and docile disposition to do well, and to order their marriage course aright. Only their principles lying rather in a moral way of good affections, zeal, and duties than in the particular relations of life in which they live, as of marriage. Indeed, being ignorant of that which should either inform their judgment, or order their will thereunto; alas, they never attain the tithe of comfort and contentment which this estate might afford them. How great a pity was it then to defraud such people of directions, who if they might enjoy it, would not be lacking to improve it? How many full of knowledge, yet live (and in marriage especially) as if they had none? By so much the more it is a pity that such should lack it as would gladly enjoy the fruit of it. And considering, that without knowledge the heart is not good; and that good intentions without rule are as a good coach without a skillful driver; I conceived I should do them acceptable service, and some glory to God, in casting this platform of direction for them, out of God's Word. This seemed another inducement.

Psal. 50.end

3.

Besides these, as we see a great deal of ground vanishes in a narrow map, which in a larger lays open; so I have noted, that in sermons or short touches upon the fifth commandment (wherein the preacher only following his text, meets with no such occasions of inquiry) much instruction about particular duties of marriage are concealed, which yet in a treatise appointed for the occasion will offer itself fitly to be discussed. They that are in a crowd must get through as they can; but the door standing open freely, one by one may pass through with ease. So is it here; a treatise has this advantage, to reach in many things which a general handling passes over: and satisfaction to a doubtful mind is more easily given this way than by some other means of more weighty nature: each ordinance of God serving specially for that end, which another does not. A poor star may in her use exceed the sun when it is dark and night season though the sun exceeds all stars in her light. This was a third respect.

But above all others, I considered that the woeful   4.
overflow of sin and of lust by name, in this our age, which reigns as in her element, through disdain or violation of the ordinance of marriage seemed to need some check and affront from heaven, which might remain as a witness against our debauchery, and which might cause men to flee their uncleanness. Unto this work, though I know myself the most unfit of many, yet as one having more leisure than they (as sometime a looker-on may see what a gamester oversees), I dare not wholly decline that task, so far as this vice offered itself, or came within the bounds of my treatise. The contempt of long light, having begot those spiritual penalties of a secure, unbelieving, and impenitent heart with apostasy from the truth: how should it be otherwise, but the Spirit of grace must straiten itself exceedingly, both in removing of many helps, and a fruitless living under such as remain? And what then must follow save a formal, empty profession of that truth, the power whereof is woefully wanting! Now we know, hypocrisy cannot long continue within her own bounds, but she must quickly discover herself to be openly profane. When was hearing and worship (in the memory of man) accompanied with so much   2 Tim. 2.3-5
wickedness? Or when had Popery better color to traduce our gospel for a doctrine of licentiousness? And while men have leisure enough for every other thing, who looks at reforming of ill manners? And how justly does God leave men who will not be as they ought (as with Hazael) to prove worse than they seemed? What argues this, that men living in a practice of drunkenness and uncleanness, dare press upon a minister of Christ for comfort to their souls, as imagining it to belong to them? Is it not a sign of a spirit of giddiness reigning in the world, out of deep doting upon their prayers and hypocritical worship? Has such a Balaamish conscience ever appeared,

and as commonly as now it does in all places? Dare usury, drunkenness, covetousness, and swearing (which are more infamous and hated) openly proclaim their shame and do we think that more secret sins, which love the dark, are not much more generally practiced, as sodomy, fornication, and wantonness? For which sake the wrath of God justly comes upon the children of disobedience! And this fourth was my strongest reason.

Now then as my endeavors lack not due motives, so it lies in you for whose sake I have written, to look to yourself, lest it be undertaken in vain! If there is little hope that my medicine (not mine, but God's) will work any great cure, yet I wish it may prove preventing to such as yet remain untainted. What the success is like to be, lies not in me or you to determine! At least this I desire, that they who are entered, or are to enter the estate of marriage, may find these rules somewhat advantageous to further them in their choice, or to guide them in their course! I shall be happy in my design if either of these are obtained: to the effecting whereof, I commend all to his grace, who has by his providence brought this treatise to an end, both for me to publish and for you to peruse.

Yours in the Lord,

D. R.

A table describing the several contents of the chapters of this treatise, and the appendix thereto.

Matrimonial Honor

OR

A TREATISE OF MARRIAGE

HEBREWS 13.4

*Marriage is honorable, and the bed undefiled: but
whoremongers and adulterers God will judge.*

CHAPTER I
*The analysis of the text. The first point handled, that
marriage is honorable.*

The scope of
the text.

What the peculiar aim of Paul in this epistle might be, in the interlacing of a solemn praise of marriage between the fourth and the sixth verse of this chapter (which are of another garb and nature) may perhaps seem questionable to a reader that is not observant of the circumstances of times and persons. Sure it is that the apostle's scope is very orderly and familiar. For having in the former chapter propounded the doctrine of justification in the causes thereof, both matter and form; and having also very effectually built thereon that great exhortation, to believe and to live by faith. In the chapter before this he proceeds to the urging of obedience and holiness, in the general: and in this thirteenth chapter he proceeds to particularize and instance in some special, and some personal offices and acts of Christian practice. But for the question moved, what should cause the apostle to think this argument of marriage as weighty as the rest, and to equal it to other doctrines handled in this place; may be supposed, not to be from a common notion, swimming with other things in his mind, and uttered by course: but probably from some occasion of real and present necessity moving him. I will propound what seems to me the truth. There were at the time of writing this epistle two sorts and

Chapter 12

practices of men very rife, and that of contrary intention; the one of heathenish profaneness, the other of Jewish superstition. The heathens, as they thought single fornication no sin at all (as appeared by their common practice of it) and adultery itself, none of the greatest sins; so they slighted all denunciations of God's wrath and judgment against either; and snorted securely in the practice of both. The Jew, on the contrary extreme, comes in with his superstition, as thinking there is no way to control this impiety except by maintaining a flat contrariety unto it, namely that marriage itself is unlawful. Paul himself taxes such false teachers, *forbidding to marry*, that is, crossing God's own ordinance that is provided for the safeguard of chastity. Much like the Papists at this day, sundry of whose positions favor of no other strain than to oppose one error by a far worse. As, because they see men's lives very barren of good works, they have no other way to draw men to be forward in well-doing than by a false doctrine, that works are meritorious. Likewise, finding fault with men's backwardness to mortification; in policy, they devise such penances of the flesh as God never ordained, to whip themselves with cords beset with needles and sharp pricks, or to stand up naked to the chin in cold water, or to fast from all kinds of flesh, to go barefoot on pilgrimage, to renounce the world, sell all, and live in a cloister. This mystery of iniquity wrought early, even here in the minds of superstitious Jews and false teachers, who found no way to allay the flame except by quenching the fire: and therefore, to quash heathenish contempt of marriage by whoredom, or the corrupting thereof by adultery, they affirm no marriage or carnal knowledge at all to be allowed to Christians; which remedy is much worse than the disease; as if the life of devils (adultery) could be overthrown by the doctrine of devils, which is, defiance of marriage. We see that this stopping of the stream has in all ages doubled the rage of all kind of uncleanness. Here therefore, the apostle, that he might oppose both these extremities: first, the superstition of the Jew, tells him, *Marriage is honorable*; and therefore an ungodly thing to disannul an ordinance. *And the bed is undefiled*: there is no necessity of making ourselves eunuchs to avoid unchasteness. And on the other side, to the heathenish, or lately converted from pagan profaneness, this he adds, *but whore-*

Jew confuted in his conceit of marriage. 1 Tim. 4.3

1 Tim. 4.1-3

Heathens' opinion of fornication.

mongers and adulterers God will judge. Let no man strengthen himself in his adultery or filthiness under pretext of the lawfulness of carnal knowledge: for why? Whether men go to common harlots, and defile virgins more openly, as *whoremongers*; or go to work more covertly, shrouding their sin by the married estate; although for a time they may defile or be defiled without fear or check: yet they must know that the God of marriage and pureness will one day in person sit upon them, and show his detestation of such ways by plaguing them, be they great or small, high or low, princes or peasants. As once Latimer, that holy martyr, upon a handkerchief with a book wrapped up in it, and presented to a king, wrote this very text for a posy, *fornicatores and adulteros judicabit Dominus.*

The words then contain in them a discretive proportion, which divides itself into two truths; either an assertive or denouncing truth: only there must be conceived to be a secret defect of the words in them both, which must be supplied for the making up of a full meaning. Touching the assertion first, it is twofold; the one concerning the ordinance itself, *marriage is honorable*; the other respecting the use of it; *and the bed is undefiled* (for so I read it according to the text and scope). The second truth denouncing, divides itself into two parts; either a threat or the object thereof: the threat is against the corrupters of marriage, *God will judge them.* The object is double; first, fornicators, such as mixed unlawfully with the single, either harlots or virgins, making these whores, or nourishing them that are so, in their trade. Or else adulterers, who (although either of the parties married, cause adultery) yet being married, do link themselves with other men's wives, for the concealment of their villainy, and so of bastardy. Both these, the one for his manifest and open, the other his subtle and close uncleanness, shall be judged by God himself. The conceived defect of the sentence lies in the opposition of the parts, thus, namely, *marriage is honorable, the bed is undefiled, and blessing is upon all that so preserve it. But whoremongers and adulterers are dishonorable, debauched ones, and God will curse and plague them.* I will go through both the parts, God assisting: and first of the first.

Marriage is honorable: and that for four respects: first, in the parts of it: secondly, in the nature of it: thirdly, in the use

The analysis of it.

The first point.

of it: fourthly, in the quality or sacredness of it. For the parts of it, if the marriage is best where the parts of it are so (*in concreto* at least) the wife and the husband are both precious pieces. Of the wife we have sundry Scriptures for her honorableness: she is called *the gift of God*: it is the use of the Holy Ghost to style excellent things, God's things, as *the mount of God, the city of God, the house of God, the garden of God*: because excellency cannot own anything which is base: God's greatness gives no common gifts, so that a wife is no common blessing: she is God's woman, not only made by God, as she is his creature alone (so by sin she both lost her own and her husband's royalty also). But, as she is made up again by God's grace to a better image than she lost; and so, honorable by a second creation: indeed, restored to man with advantage, much better than she was when first brought unto him in Paradise. By this means, she becomes a help instead of a snare, a true gift of God, an excellent piece, which a man may bless God while he lives. This, I say, in the first place, as the chief ground of her honor: and yet this is not all; she is called the crown of her husband, both by Solomon (using that word) and by Paul, calling her *his glory*, who before was his utter shame. *Crowns*, we know, are very precious things and honorable, serving to grace things of chief eminency, emperors, kings, and princes: crowns are made of the purest gold, embellished with the costliest pearls, set in with curious workmanship. So again her price is said to be far above *rubies*: truly, *Wisdom herself* and a good wife are not far different in their descriptions; no jewel is to be compared to her, far above silver, even the choicest gold. Happy is he upon whose head such a crown is set, to whom heaven has given such a gift. The other party is the man; we know the man does especially resemble the image of God, and in that respect is the wife's head: and although by her sin, he came to lose his honor, yet if he is a good man, he is a man of understanding, and of an excellent spirit; indeed, better than his neighbor. Not a Ruben any longer, whose dignity is gone, but as Nebuchadnezzar, restored again to his former, even greater glory; as Job, whose latter life was better than the former; in whom the majesty, authority, and wisdom of God does shine. Conclude then, if both the members of this body are so honorable, what must the whole be? If each of them

Marriage is honorable. How? In four respects. The first respect.

Woman honorable. Prov. 19.14

Marriage is from God, even in innocency, and he still orders it: see Psal. 68.6. God sets solitary ones in families. Prov. 12.4

Prov. 31.10

Man honorable. 1 Cor. 11.7

Prov. 17.27

Gen. 49.3

Dan. 4.34
Job 42.12

is so precious, what is the compound? If a ring alone is rich, what is it with a richer pearl enclosed in it? As we see when a prince and heir of a crown marries a princess do wager, how glorious is their union? How honorable their concurrence? This may serve for the first of the four.

But, lest any should allege that the text speaks not of those that make marriage honorable; but says, marriage (as such an ordinance) is honorable: therefore let the parties go, and come to the nature and kind itself of marriage. The Greek word here used is the same which is used in 2 Peter 1.1, and may as well be translated *precious*, or of worth and value, a costly thing: and so it well befits marriage; for why? It is precious in the nature of it. A prince is a precious piece in himself;

Thou art worth ten thousand of us (say the people to David) without any other respects; he is the delight of his subjects, an object of natural contentment and esteem. The light of the sun (though considered apart from the use), a pearl, gold, and skill and cunning in arts have a peculiar splendor, grace, and nobleness of nature in them, and do eminently exceed other things. So marriage in the nature of it (although never so much stained with the unjust aspersions of Popery and their comparisons with virginity) is a precious ordinance in her nature. How men by their sin make it, is not the question (for a crown may be cast into the dirt) but how it is. I speak not now, how general consent and opinion has settled it in worth, graced it with privileges, disgraced single life (which yet I approve not), and granted immunities to marriage far above it, both in war and peace (as the Roman's law of the claim of three sons shows), but I speak of God's own institution of it; for that is only honor which a king gives, who himself devised it; truly, and that not as a relief of man fallen, but an addition of perfection to his creation, before ever sin entered: for the order of it, after all other creatures were made to entertain and grace their lord and lady, indeed, the guard of heaven to usher them

into Paradise; even the Father, Son, and Holy Ghost consenting to propagate man created, and not ceasing to create till the woman was created: more especially, the Lord Jesus himself (when he needed it not) yet would grace it by being the son of a married virgin, and choosing to be Joseph's reputed son: not to speak of that honor he cast upon it when he did yield to do

his first divine miracle at a marriage. Now that which a God John 2.5
of pureness ordains by a perpetual decree of pureness, in an
estate of pureness, how can it choose but to have an engraved
character and formal nature of preciousness and honor in it?
This for the second.

The third respect is yet more for the honor of it. We Third respect:
say it bears *prick and price*, which contains sweet and good, the use of
price and use in one. For why? The very pleasing pure luster marriage.
of a pearl would make it precious of itself, though it had no
virtue or quality for use in it. Marriage then is also honorable
for the use of it. If the sun is excellent for her pureness, what
is it then for his influence and life, the very heat and vegetation
of the creatures? What should the world be, save a dungeon
without it? And what is it but an emptiness and vanity without the usefulness of marriage? If light is so precious for the
pureness of it, what is it for the useful direction of it to do the
world of work which it daily affords? If a prince is so honorable for his nobleness, what is he for the use, to be a father
to his people, to rule them with all godliness and honesty, to
feed them in Jacob and Israel? Usefulness is the varnish and
luster of honor, grounding and establishing it as colors set in
oil. Now then what is equal to marriage, for the being or wellbeing of life? I say, the being, ornament, or defense of it. It is
the prop of mutual content, the aid of nature, the perfection
of health, wealth, beauty, learning, honor, and experience of
youth, manhood, and old age, whereof none is sweet where
marriage supplies not the lack. It serves not only for the necessity of generation (for how can there be warmth to one, but
if two *lie together, they have warmth?*) but for the relief of such
as are past it, looking at the safeguard of the stock and comfort
of life. Marriage is the *preservative of chastity, the seminary
of the commonwealth, seed-plot of the church, pillar (under
God) of the world, right-hand of providence, supporter of laws,
states, orders, offices, gifts, and services: the glory of peace, the
sinews of war, the maintenance of policy, the life of the dead, the
solace of the living, the ambition of virginity, the foundation of
countries, cities, universities, succession of families, crowns, and
kingdoms*; truly (besides the being of these) *it is the wellbeing
of them being made,* and whatsoever is excellent in them, or
any other thing, the very furniture of heaven (in a kind) de-

pending thereupon.

The fourth re-
spect of honor,
namely, the
sacredness.

Fourthly, it is also honorable for the solemn sacred-ness of it; I mean not hereby spirituality; for I know it is a civil ordinance; and, although for the better witness, our marriages are finished in churches, yet marriage properly is no sacra-ment. But I mean, that God generally has planted a reverend esteem of it in man, and put a deep awe of it into our minds (as all those laws do testify, which have so strictly maintained the repute of it), but especially that divine sanction by which

1 Cor. 3.17

pure marriage is blessed: and all that dare defile and dishonor it, the Lord threatens to dishonor and destroy them. Him who defiles the temple of God, by the pollution of this ordinance, God will also destroy. The anointing of a king, though it is not properly a divine spiritual act, yet it is sacred, and the con-secration of him, an act of solemn and high reverence, most

Rom. 13.5
Psal. 105.15
1 Sam. 26.9

religiously obliging the subject to all due service, as to his liege lord, for conscience sake. *Touch not mine Anointed, and do my prophets no harm*: and therefore David trembling at Abishai's bloody motion to kill Saul, (though a tyrant) says, *God for-bid I should lay mine hand upon the Lord's anointed*, lest God should lay his hand upon him with vengeance. Even so sacred

Prov. 6.29

a thing is this marriage: not in the jealousy only of reveng-ing man (whose heart cannot be pacified with gifts, in case of such violation, which argues a sacred depth of thoughts upon such an injustice) nor only in the punishments inflicted by hu-man laws thereupon (some whereof make the wronged party his own jury, judge, and executioner). But especially the just hand of the God of marriage, going out against all offenders in this kind, against chastity (which should be kept in this sacred cabinet) and not only against the party offending himself, but also his name and posterity. As the text itself adds, and we shall prosecute in the end of this discourse; *but whoremon-gers and adulterers God will judge*. Sum up therefore all these respects in one and conclude, if marriage is so solemn and precious in her parts, nature, use, and sacredness then doubt-less it is true both in the nature and use of it that *marriage is honorable, and the bed is undefiled*. So much for the opening of this first point. I come now to the use.

Use 1.

First then, is marriage so honorable? Woe then and terror to all such as directly or indirectly, by doctrine or practice, openly or secretly, by thought, word, or deed dare violate marriage; whatsoever they are, Epicures, Papists, Protestants, unmarried men or married, do deface marriage, either really or occasionally, casting their dung upon it, they are all guilty. First, here let all Papists, Jesuits, Priests, or others, with all their fomenters and adherents tremble and be ashamed, who have dared so many times to dishonor marriage, and so many ways to defile it. Their clergy, indeed, are all cut off at one blow from it, truly, though it is a sacrament. How just is it that such should be left to the spirit of giddiness, that they should with the same mouth be compelled to magnify that with most holiness, which yet they debar their most holy order of priest-hood from? Or rather secretly confess, what a polluted order it is, which disdains the use of that which (though erroneous-ly) they call a sacrament? The state of marriage is with these impure ones an estate of such as live in the flesh. Better is it (says their champion Bellarmine) for a priest to defile himself with many harlots than to be married to one wife. When the trumpet gives so certain an alarm and sound of defiance to marriage, who should dare venture upon it? These children of the purple whore scorn that their great revenues should serve to maintain the honorable offspring of marriage; therefore God leaves them to be filthier, and to let such a filthy offspring maintain none except the children of fornication. Marriage was honorable in the church, not among laymen only, but (in the Old Testament) with the high priest and all his tribe (which yet were typical of the pureness of Christ himself) and Moses himself, a man who was conversant with God, and spoke to him face to face, was married: after Christ, with the apostles themselves, notwithstanding their travels, Peter their grand patron (and Paul had the same power) with the evan-gelists, and many religious bishops and overseers of Christ's flock, from their times to many generations following. Till the mystery of iniquity, which long before had been laid as leaven, and began to work, was grown at length to open doctrine of devils, in rejecting of marriage, and practice of devils, in play-ing the sodomites and whoremongers; for generally this taint has run through them all (if histories may be believed) from the head to the foot. And although I deny not, but many vota-ries among them abstain from uncleanness, some more, some

Terror to all the dishonor-ers of it.

1. Against Papists.

Papists have personal sac-raments.

1 Tim. 4.2

See our learned writ-ers. Centur.

2 Tim. 2.17less; yet their doctrine frets like a canker to defile and dishonor this honorable ordinance. Away you hypocrites, and vanish at the light and luster of this truth! Your works in secret are such that it is a shame only to name them, the sun blushing at them: your cloisters of both sexes, vaults, privies, fishponds, and the like have witnessed sufficiently (by the confession and sanction of a great Pope and proctor of your own) what hellish abominations do swarm under the shroud and veil of your defiance of marriage.

The life and practice of Papists justly judged by God.

How justly has the Lord (by giving over such, both to sins unnatural and unlawful) disabled them of credit and ability to dishonor that which they so abhor so that their words against marriage, which they nickname, a living in the flesh, are no slander to it? For as the proverb says, Clodius accuses whoremasters and Catiline Cethegus to be a traitor. This error of theirs, never passed without contradiction, from first to last in the church, notwithstanding their violence has brought it to this. As Paul of those Jews, so I of these, God they opposed, and man they disregarded; hateful and hated of all men. God has said, *It is not good for man to be alone*, for snare's sake. They say, It is not good to be married, for devotion's sake; abusing that text, *It is not good for a man to touch a woman*. As Augustine said between Donatus and himself, Whether of the two believe you? So say I between God and these. And, man they control; for here the text calls *marriage honorable* among all, poor and rich, simple, learned, noble, base, minister, people; all men. What then are these? Men, or beasts in their likeness, with women's faces, lion's qualities, or rather devils in the flesh. That which they raise up as high as a sacrament among men, they beat down and anathematize to hell among themselves. But I leave them to the discovery of their own sect sometimes, Luther and others, who upon the experience of them, loathed them; and therefore (though at their parting Satan foamed and raged), even out of horror of conscience, departed from them. No wonder; for who could endure the society of such thieves as have robbed the earth of men, men of honesty, and heaven of saints, as a learned man speaks.

As for their deifying of virginity above marriage (which partly they color over with Jerome's preposterous zeal

1 Thess. 2.15
Rev. 18.2
Gen. 2.18
1 Cor. 7.1

against Vigilantius) let me answer with that wise town clerk of Ephesus, speaking to the tumultuous people, Who knows not that virginity is precious? But grant it is so. What? Can it not be praised without the disgrace of marriage? Is the eye of the one evil because the other is good? Can no oblation pacify the one, but the honor of the other depraved, and a sacrifice of the heads of married men? Does she not cut down the bow she stands on; even break her own neck in destroying marriage? To be sure, none are so unfit to commend or defend her as they who confute marriage by the same uncleanness whereby they defile virginity. Virgins, I confess, have their honor, even those eunuchs who have made themselves spiritually so for the kingdom of God are praiseworthy. And, as that demoniac said, *Jesus we know, and Paul we know, but who are ye?* So we, Marriage and true virginity we admire, but as for you, what, or from where are you? If you speak a good word for it, it is meet (as they at Athens were wont in the senate to do) to take it out of your unvirginlike, unseemly mouths, and put it into the mouth of more honest persons. Praise stinks in the mouths of such as do reproach more by deeds than their mouths can commend. As the poet once said of the cold poetry of them who commended fasting with their bellies full: so may I say of you who praise virginity, yourselves having bodies debauched with uncleanness; your breath is not sweet enough for this work, nor your words strong enough to make you believed. None but orators can praise eloquence, nor any save chaste virgins, single life, whether married or unmarried. One once said of the great Turk's horse, that no grass grew after where he had once trod; so, neither did ever virginity thrive upon your praises. As locusts eat up all before them, so does your unbridled lust; and the more by how much it is veiled with the vow of that chastity, which becomes the greatest snare of uncleanness to them that make it. Thus much for the first branch.

But to leave these, I would also apply this truth to a second sort of men for their dishonoring of marriage. Such I mean, as do (though not by Popish, yet) by their unclean lives and practice deflower and disgrace this ordinance. The most real and chief offenders in this kind, who by their manners do not only impute, but infuse (in a sort) a blot and shame into

Popish magnifying of virginity confuted.
Acts 19.35

Mat. 19.12

Acts 19.15

2.
Terror against all profaners of marriage.

marriage, causing it to stink by their sin, which God has honored and blessed. And these are the successors of Hophni and Phinehas, whose open and shameless pollutions by whoredom and adultery do corrupt it. A course in these days so common that not only among the viler sort it is thought nothing (for there are of the ignorant and baser sort of people who are free from it) but even of them of the better fashion also (where grace rules not) of whom in the end of this treatise I shall speak more. But besides these, how do the lives of such as live in this estate of marriage cause men to vow the grossest uncleanness rather than they would be so married? As once a heathen said, If this is the practice of Christians to eat their God, and to kill their king, let my soul be with the philosophers. So say I, The base cursed life of many professors, who brawl, scold, fight, and live at defiance with each other, causes many ungodly ones to prefer a single life, though besmeared with all sorts of lusts contemplative, practical, natural, unnatural, with wives, harlots, or as they can, rather than to marry! That is to say, Let my soul be with the adulterers. I say to such married persons, stumbling-blocks and eye-sores; perhaps you may be guiltless of this sin yourselves; but verily, many by your occasion are as deeply tempted to uncleanness as others are by the enticements of harlots and companions of harlots. Well, as odious as you are, yet is *marriage honorable* in herself: you do as much as in you lies (and shall answer for it, as well as if it were in your power) to defile it; but yet you cannot defile that which God has stamped with honor.

To see some married couples, how they bring up their brats to all filthiness of manners: to see Ahabs and Jezebels both combining together in villainy: to see the woeful confusion of bad wives with good husbands, or them with as bad wives, drawing in a most unequal yoke: Nabals and Abigails, Moseses and Zipporahs; would it not cause men to stop their noses at the stench of marriage? Should this be if men kept the honor of marriage unstained? If they were jealous to suffer any eye to behold their unseemliness lest marriage should be dishonored? To see the separation of such in the country of all sorts, as depart from their yokefellows, abandoning each other by law, or lawless divorces, from bed, board, and affection (I mean by willful separating themselves); would it not

1 Sam. 2.23

1 Kings 21.25

1 Sam. 25
Marriage abhorred by the base life of some couples.
Exod. 4.25

cause men to irk marriage? To behold scoundrels and monsters openly, and in the face, and defiance of courts and laws, without penance or due pursuit and punishment, to do as Num. 25.6,14 Zimri and Cozbi did (though with contrary success) to bring their whores and the bastards they have begotten by them, not only into their houses and under their wives' noses, but to lay them in their beds, to force them to afford them like nursery and equal terms with their own: would it not make heathens themselves to spew us out? To see great men to relinquish and cast up their chaste and well-deserving ladies, (whom they at first loved and sought with the greatest ambition) and to give themselves to vagrant and libidinous courses; would it not fray men from marriage, and say as they did, If the case stands so, it is not good to marry? To conclude, to see but the base marketplace that is now made of marriages, how men look only at the prize and the best game, how they may take in, or put off their children, in and at the best vantage (as cattle in a market) for wealth and portion, be they ever so debauched, drunkards, or light, worthless women; would it not provoke men to vomit such marriages? A worthy wife cannot be suf- Prov. 31.10 ficiently prized, a man cannot tell what to ask for such a pearl; and a bad one deserves no price, being the worst of wares: the one is above this line, the other is under it, neither ought to be bought and sold: I say, these, and other similar abuses, as the perpetual jealousies between some couples (not the worst persons, yet bad in marriage) their sinister conceits, melancholy distempers, how do they make this commodity of marriage, indeed and a better too, even religion itself (which too many such profess) to be badly spoken of. But in the meantime, by these rents and disorders the innocent ordinance hears ill; as if, by her default such evils were committed.

I proceed to a second use of admonition; and that is, Use 2. Admonition to prevent the dishonor of marriage. to all such as shall upon trial find out their errors, or else can prove their endeavor to preserve this honor of marriage entire and unstained. Sundry are the fears and grief I know of the weak (though religious couples) when they look back to their beginnings: some to consider how unprepared they entered into this condition at first, and since having found God to be more gracious to reclaim them home, or the husband and wife that before was averse: yet when they also think how unthankfully they have requited God for it, waxing light, wanton, worldly, and loose; they cannot choose, but they must be in bitterness for it. Others, although they have entered into this estate with much zeal, resolution, and consent of heart to honor God to their uttermost in it: yet alas, when they come to weigh seriously how many days, months, and years are come over their heads in a most unprofitable sort; gray hairs being upon them without any impression of fruit and growth in good; able to say little for themselves, either for religion, walking between themselves, praying for and with each other, joint care in education of their children; even that they have humored each other in their base corruptions, bolstered each other in worldliness (which has eaten up their stock) not suffered grace to revive but to decay; serving their turns of each other only for common and vanishing ends of their own: spent Sabbaths carnally, and little delighted in them for God's cause, fruitless in hearing and family duties: oh! Much cause of grief must be to such. Be therefore admonished; slight not the care of maintaining of religion in your marriage with all solicitous carefulness, shunning that which might weaken it, the honor and comfort of it. Crowns of honor are fickle things; and look whatsoever it is that has much honor put upon it, has with it much care, anxiety, and burden annexed. Beware then: scum not off the fat and sweet of the honor and content of marriage; but as for the burden and service of it, to seek God, to worship him jointly, to shun all occasions of ease, carnal occasions of jollity, and unchaste company, you are loath to take the pains: surely, you shall find at last that repentance will be the best fruit of such slightness. It is strange how little this is believed at first till experience has taught it: but men think marriage to be a buckler to fence off all blows: so long as they love one another (as they thank God that they do heartily, though with a rotten love) that will hold them in as the cornerstone does the sides of a house. Others take marriage to be an estate of loose liberty, to live as they desire, and therefore observe no caution, nor fear any danger, till at last they bewail their folly when they see how by their rash improvidence they have brought a snare of poverty upon themselves: others, a habit of pleasures and expense till time, thrift, and heart is all lost and past recall.

Others there are who by their froward, peevish car-

Marriage no buckler to fence ourselves in bad courses.

riage have provoked each other to weariness, impatience, and discontent. Others have drowned themselves in lust, and led each other by base example to follow them; and instead of complainers of each other, to be as deep in and overshoes therein as the other, thereby heaping diseases and needless sorrow upon their heads. And whereas for lack of mature regard and prevention they have pierced through themselves with the fruit of their sin; then they cry out too late, wishing they had been wiser to keep this crown entire from stain and dishonor! Kings and emperors have so slighted the due care of their crowns that they have brought ruin and misery upon themselves by running into excess of contempt: as in the example of Rehoboam. But whereas for their loose, exorbitant ways they have come to see those sad effects which have followed, they have wished their crowns again, upon condition of improving their honor with ten times more temperance and wisdom. How much more then have married persons cause to abhor their carelessness in this kind, and to prop up the honor of this ordinance if they will enjoy the quiet fruit of righteousness by their good behavior? If a minister or magistrate, having more honor put upon them in their places than others, should carry themselves the more disdainfully, and bear themselves so upon their places that they care for no man, nor balk any bad courses, do they not look for their honor to bear them out? Should not God say to them, *Those who honor me, I will honor*; but such as reproach me, I will make vile? If private persons excelling others in gifts will not attend to humility and fear of themselves, shall not their glory end in their shame, their gifts in barrenness, and their profession in revolt? Even so is it here; such as care not, regard not their demeanor in marriage, to God, themselves, and their families by shunning offences, jealousies, losses, or alienation of affections; but think it will always be a honeymoon, and a merry world with them, is it not just that their unseasonable ruins should teach them repentance too late? Therefore let all that are married once be warned hereby, to be sober, heedful, advised, moderate in their affections, loves, and liberties; rather walking on this side of the brink than otherwise: always fearing a change and saying, What if my follies breed in my wife (by God's secret vengeance) a loathing of me; a fire of conten-

1 Sam. 2.30

Conclusion.

tion in my bosom; a continual dropping upon my head, my contentment at home, and my reputation abroad? God keep me within such bounds of marriage as I first vowed to keep at my entrance. Thus much for the admonition.

Next, I proceed to comfort all such godly couples as have labored to enhance and uphold the honor of this ordinance. Try yourselves then; no doubt you will meet with uncomfortable thoughts for your manifold failings: and no doubt you think few religious marriages so ill managed, and so poorly carried as your own! The many breaches and flaws of your marriages do cause you to mourn and complain, saying, If indeed I had so inured and acquainted myself and my wife to prayer and close worshipping of God; if I had wisdom and understanding enough to be God's voice to my wife to guide her: if I had abstained from the snares and occasions laid in my way by Satan to overthrow me and my peace; had I preserved both body and soul in that chastity and honor that was meet, nourishing love and amity, abhorring all occasions to the contrary, I might behold the face of God with comfort! But now my burden is increased by my errors in marriage; namely that with a slight, heedless, and regardless heart I have carried myself in a business of such consequence; upon which the well or ill fare of my life depends. Well, there is no doubt, but as in all other, so in this part of the wheel of our conversation, namely of marriage; we all sin many ways, and our errors are infinite. But now, sift yourself more narrowly, and leaving your faults, examine yourself in intentions, in all the wanderings and swerving of your course. Can you say that as in all others, so in this part of your course, you have sought better to be informed what that good and accepted will of God is? And accordingly, with simplicity of heart have you quit yourself to your companion, not for your own base ends and ease, but that marriage might have her honor preserved, offences might be prevented, God worshipped within, and honored without doors; a peaceable life in all godliness and honesty preserved? I ask not whether there has been staggering, weariness of the yoke, and desire after more liberties (for who is there that sins not? as Solomon said), but I ask this, Have you denied yourself, and curbed your base heart to stoop to God in drawing this yoke; not sought your ease, fleshly content, letting

Comfort to good couples, who honor marriage.

Wants of weak and religious couples shall be pardoned. Rom. 12.2

1 Kings 8

the honor of God to sink or swim? Have you humbly bowed your neck and stooped to the ordinance, acknowledging how much it has changed from the first creation, and by sin filled with sundry sorrows, distempers, and bitter-sweets, hardly to be avoided? I say, Have you under all these abased yourself before the Lord, craved pardon of your stout heart and proud stomach, loath to yield, and your impotency of your passions, desiring to testify your obedience in bearing these annoyances as justly inflicted for sin? Have you acknowledged the Lord most wise, in so ordering the matter for you, that because your heart is haughty and insolent, therefore he has tamed you by this bridle; and has by it exercised your faith and patience, and brought you to the bent of his bow? So that for the avoiding of far worse snares, and for the comforts and liberties accruing by marriage, you can willingly yield obedience to the rules and duties thereof, not dividing burdens from privileges. And you can correct all your licentiousness in seeking fleshly contentment only in marriage. Surely, if in some comfortable sort you can speak thus in the ears of God, begging a pardon of all wants, and a release of all deserved penalties; then I say (according to infirmity) you have sought the honor of marriage; and to prevent the just stain and aspersions thereof by your watchfulness; truly, you have sought the honor of the ordainer thereof for your singular comfort, which you might ill have wanted.

What remains therefore, but that I comfort you from God, and encourage you by his promise, not only against the fear of your dishonoring God, but also towards a heartier endeavor to honor him further. Surely, you have need of no less. Your journey is long, your obedience difficult! It is not for a day or a month, but for life; it is not for a soldering up of breaches for a while, to break out so much the worse after: it is no work of an outside, to set a good face upon the matter abroad, nourishing still the disease within; God is not mocked, and sins in this kind are like oil in the hand, which cannot be hid. But this obedience is a perpetual, yet an ingenuous, humble, and holy subjection to the will of the subjecter; who by it tries men, and shows them all which is in the heart: so that, I dare say, a true obedient in marriage, is a good servant in all. Therefore, as you need encouragement from

Application of the comfort.

Marriage is no loose or idle way of service.

Encourage-
ment to reli-
gious couples.
God (as who does not in difficult duties) so, take it into your bosom as your own, chew upon it and digest it: it is the Lord's will that you should; I say unto you, that as the Lord has put honor upon this ordinance, so you have sought to maintain it, and who so honors God shall be honored of God. God can and will turn all the impediments and encumbrances of this estate into blessings: you shall find this estate made honorable to you; you shall find acceptance with God in all your suits; success in enterprises, honor, and esteem among his people: he shall crown you with old age and good report in the way of righteousness. Your wife shall be a blessing, no snare; your liberties shall be pure unto you, and you shall visit your habi-

Job 5.24
Job 20.17
Prov. 17.6
Psal. 138.3

tation without sin, as Job speaks; you shall drink of the floods of milk, butter, and honey. Your children shall honor you in the gate and shall be your crown in your age; they shall stand about your table as olive plants; truly, although any of them should prove irregular, yet that should not condemn your in-nocence. In a word, God shall bring upon you all the blessings promised to such as honor his ordinance, even to love you for

Isa. 59.21
Ezra 9.8
Psal. 128.6

many generations. His Word shall not be taken from you and them forever: he will continue you a name upon earth, and a nail in his temple, and peace upon Israel.

Furthermore, I add that your very obedience alone in itself shall be a blessing unto you. Do you preserve your body in holiness and honor? You shall avoid hereby those in-

Miseries
shunned by
good couples.

finite woes and miseries, which befall the unchaste, as poverty, baseness, a rotten body, a worse soul, a ruined estate, both in this world and in the world to come. Do you nourish love and amity between yourself and your wife that so the peace of God thereby may the better rule your heart and mind? Be-hold, how infinite many disturbances and miseries you avoid of wrath, debate, envy, railings, quarreling, and discontents,

Married
couples must
serve God in
their time.
2 Sam. 19.24
Amos 6.6

which bad marriage causes. But can you say, that besides these ordinary duties of the married estate, you and your wife have also closed with God in the special service of the time, and (with good Uriah and Mephibosheth) moderately used the comforts of this life (during the sorrows of the church), and been married, as if not; remembering the afflictions of Jo-seph, making them the due and daily matter of your humili-ations and requests before God? Have you often, with Joel's

bridegroom and bride, come out of your feasting chamber to
hide your head in your fasting chamber (as our Savior tells us,
when the bridegroom shall be taken away, they shall mourn
in those days) the husband apart, and the wife apart, for sincerity, or both together for fervency? Or with the Psalmist,
do you desire your tongue cleave to the roof of your mouth,
except the joy of Jerusalem is above all your joy, even marriage
joy itself (which yet is allowed to be great). Surely then, I say,
you have honored marriage indeed, and as your share in the
duty has been greater, so shall it be in the blessing: the Lord
shall give you a hiding place in the day of evil, and because you
have kept the word of his patience in bad times, he shall also
deliver you in that hour of temptation, which shall come for
a trial upon all flesh. He shall uphold you in six troubles, and
the seventh shall not come near you: the floods of great waters,
with all those plagues which God has denounced against these,
shall not come near you. Be cheerful in the Lord therefore,
and still, you and your wife, cleave and cling to him; deny your
own wills and carnal reason, and trust to his eternal strength;
buckle with the work of God faithfully, and walk in his ordinance humbly, till he comes; and then he shall bring healing
in his wings at last; and in the meantime, he shall cause a voice
to sound behind saying, *This is the way, walk in it.* He shall
order your paths, resolve your doubts, prevent dangers, and so
preserve the souls of his saints that thousands shall fall at your
right hand, and ten thousands at your left, you going safe in
the midst, and so be brought safe and well through all extremities at last. So much for comfort, and for this first chapter.

Joel 2.16

Isa. 26.20

Luke 5.34

Zech. 12.12

Psal. 137.6

Isa. 4.end

Rev. 3

Psal. 32.6

Isa. 26.3

Mal. 3

Isa. 30.21

Psal. 91.7

CHAPTER II

*More full explication in what the honor of marriage consists
(being the ground of the treatise ensuing), namely
entrance and continuance. Entrance first, in
marrying in the Lord, handled.*

Question.
How may
married
couples obtain
this honor?
Answer. By
two things;
first, by good
entrance:
secondly, con-
tinuance.

B ut because there are many more uses to be made of this
point, before I come to them, I desire further to open this
truth, and in particular to show what the honor of this marriage is, and in how many things it consists. Honorable we see
it is, by that which has been said; but the question is, how married couples may attain this honor? To which I answer, by two
main duties: first, procure it: secondly, preserve it. Procure it
first, by laying the foundation of it in honor; for as the root is,
so will the branches be, either honorable or reproachful. Seek
therefore to enter into that estate according to God and his
rules. And then secondly, having entered well into it, manage
it well also, nourish the honor of it carefully and warily, for it is
no bit less a virtue to keep well than to seek aright; and many
begin with great show of honor, who yet end in shame.

The former
part: to marry
in the Lord.

Entrance
requires
goodness and
aptness.

To marry
in the Lord,
what?
2 Cor. 5.20

Touching the former of these, there is a double rule
of the word; first, to marry in the Lord: secondly, to marry
aptly in the Lord. This is the ground of an honorable marriage, when you are content to be taught by him who first put
honor upon it, to maintain it. For the former, to marry in
the Lord is to use our uttermost discreet diligence to seek out
such companions as (in charity and likelihood) are either already espoused to the Lord Jesus, their husband by faith; and
in token thereof, sit close to him in obedience; or an endeav-
orer thereto; that is, such as are in a fair and hopeful way of
inclining to it. These two (I confess) differ; but beware lest you
attempt any marriage in which neither of these can be perceived. To open myself a little; they that are indeed actually
married to Christ have been truly drawn to him by his Eliezer
and spokesmen, by whose embassy God has treated with them
about this spiritual union between himself and them. They

have well digested the offer, and with Abigail (when sent for to Marks of it.
1 Sam. 25 be David's wife) confess themselves to be so far from worthiness to be his consorts, and to taste of his marriage contents and benevolence that they are unworthy even to be fellow-servants with his children, doorkeepers in his house, or to wash and wipe the feet of his household. So vile God has made them The first: sight of unworthiness of this favor. in the sight of their own eyes; showing them by his pure law, the baseness of that conversation of theirs wherein they have walked (as the door always rolling one way upon her hinges) so they always living in the same vices, soaked upon their old dregs; that hereby he empties them of themselves, dashes that pride and vanity which puffed them up before: so that alas, they rather think that he is throwing them out of his presence forever than marrying them in faithfulness to himself. By this The second: they sue a reconciliation. humiliation they come to be further acquainted with his pleasure. That even to such woeful ones who have defiled their Father's bed worse than Reuben, even defaced his image; yet to these most forlorn harlots and children of adulterers he is willing to be reconciled, truly, to seek them out as that Levite did Judg. 19.3
Jer. 3.1 his concubine even after just cause of divorce, Jeremiah 3.1,2, to admit them to his bed again; themselves seeking no favor, but fleeing from him, as she from her Lord. By this unheard of The third: their hearts are broken hereby.
Zech. 12.10 love, he has broken their whorish hard heart and forehead of brass, melted them into tears, to see his bottomless and causeless compassions, as Zechariah in chapter 12 verse 10 calls them: especially while they by rejecting or slighting it, even shutting him out and abhorring his love, deserved to have his heart hardened, and love to turn jealousy against them. And now, they consult whether they were better to perish in their desolate courses, or venture upon his love for a second reconciling. At length, seeing his scope to be, to get himself a name The fourth: they being convinced of God's ends, believe it. in turning a harlot's heart (as bad as Mary Magdalene) to her husband again (a thing which no man can do to a whorish wife). Indeed, to make her more loyal and tender to him than she ever was before she forsook him. I say, at length, she is convinced, and casting herself down at his feet as one that is loath to dishonor that love which she so much abused; with a trembling and self-despairing heart begins to touch the hem of his garment to apprehend him to speak as he means, and so becomes one again with him, nearer in covenant than ever;

The fifth: from hence they are encouraged to obey.
Psal. 45

Eph. 6

Marks of a lower degree.

Job 33.23

Zech. 9.9

Song of Sol. 3

bone of his bone, and flesh of his flesh. Striving from that second renewing of love towards him, to draw mighty encouragement and resolution, not only never to be faithless to him in her conjugal affections anymore; but also to return the fruit of his dear love into his bosom again, to walk in all subjection to his teaching and will, to delight in denying herself that so she may be well pleasing in his sight, whether in doing or suffering for him. Thus abiding faithful to him in the uttermost service she can do, she waits patiently for his coming that he may find her in peace and well occupied at his coming, and then makes her glorious, and like himself, without spot or wrinkle.

This is a short description of a spouse of Christ, and a son or daughter of Abraham: and such a one (in measure more or less) is each soul married to Christ: and of such no question needs to be made, but they are (in this first respect) meet husbands and wives for each other. But lest my words prove snares to any who come short of these, and yet are loath to be debarred from marriage: I add, that there is a lesser degree of grace under this, only appearing in the seed, tender and weak; and that is of such as (although they reach not so far) yet have their eye towards this bridegroom, counting him one of ten thousand, comparing themselves with such as are married to him, think themselves far inferior, wish their case were so happy; abhor their own treachery, count the feet of such beautiful, as woo them to Christ, think highly of the offer, love to be such friends of the Lord Jesus, and children of his bride chamber, full of tears, affections, and desires after it. Even these are not to be excluded, there is hope of such that they may come to be married to Christ in due time; therefore it is unequal that for mere lack of time and training they should be rejected: rather, if better fail (in ordinary providence) there being sufficient ground to hope that their little is in truth: I dare not deny, but a contract with such may be lawful, and the Lord may cover defects in mercy; especially if the more forward party is industrious to improve a little to a greater measure, in the other, if the weaker party is teachable, and in either of both there is a self-denying heart (if God cross their hopes) to lie down meekly at his feet, humbled for sin (the cause thereof) and patiently taking up and bearing their cross, till God amend it.

By all this it appears that marrying in the Lord requires good consideration; and that they who so marry have laid the foundation of future honor beforehand. And who doubts but it had need be so? For what hope is there that they who never sought it before should ever light upon it after? Honor requires good breeding, and it is a stud, which except it subsists upon a good ground-cell, will soon lie in the dust. Rash and sudden attempts in this kind do but make way for shame and reproach; only marrying in the Lord prepares the soul for the work: it has her tools in readiness to fall to the trade, whereas the contrary is still to seek. Truly, the very method of the apostle in this epistle shows no less, for he speaks of no marriage business before he has fully opened the doctrine of faith, he lays that for the bottom, and then comes in and tells such, their marriage is honorable. Faith then is the hand and wheel, which must frame a vessel for honor, prepared, as for all other, so for this work of marriage. And in truth, as it is all religion (upon point) so it is the marriage ring, which makes the soul one with the Lord; and this ring is beset with many rich jewels, all of them serving for the honor, that is, the well carrying and discharge of marriage duties. One jewel is humility and self-denial, whereby the heart is tamed and humbled to this work with all subjection, and freed from that rudeness and rebellion of spirit, which makes it fit for nothing but its own will and ends, but this grace levels it to the obedience of this ordinance. Another jewel is peace, whereby the soul is so calmed and pacified within itself, in the point of pardon and God's favor, that it can bear any affronts: even as the shoes or brass boots of the soldier can walk upon rocks or pikes, and feel no hurt; so a heart well pleased in the Lord is calm and able to clear the coast of all distempers; and to go through discontents and crosses such as an unquiet spirit cannot. A third is purity, which cleanses the soul of many bad humors, very unequal for marriage; self-love, pride, disdain, wrath, heart-burning, jealousies, and conceits, and makes a man much fitter for marriage. A fourth (the last which I will name) is righteousness; that is, the fellowship with Christ's holy nature, by which the soul partakes the properties of Christ, qualifying it with wisdom, influence, strength, meekness, patience, holiness, cheerfulness, long-suffering, and compassion; which graces,

Reasons of this first branch.

The first: rash matches unblest.

The Jewels of the marriage ring.
1. Faith and humility.
2. Peace.

3. Purity.

4. Righteousness.

as they make him a meet head and husband for the church, so they make married couples meet heads and helpers for each other. Faith, I say, does draw from Christ all such abilities and graces as may prepare the soul to all the services which the marriage estate calls for. Even as the spokes or staves of the wheel strengthen it for the good motion of it, so does faith strengthen this great master-wheel of conversation, which is marriage.

Reason 2.
Trials of mar-
riage, many.

Again, except the honor of marriage is laid down beforehand in the entrance, when the mind is free and impartial, how should it be like to be provided for in marriage itself? Alas! Marriage has her hands full of trial, what grace is already wrought in the soul; marriage will find a gracious heart work enough at the best; for it is given to exercise grace. It is not given to work grace (without singular mercy do occasion it) but to exercise it; for what abundance of other distractions do there fall out in this estate, which (as the apostle tells us)

1 Cor. 7.33-35

keep off the soul from sitting close and comely to God? The necessities of marriage-occasions are such as compel the parties to please each other in the matters of this life. So that, except single persons have well considered themselves, and fitted themselves with a stock to live upon, they will find it a hard thing to act a true part on this stage upon the sudden: rather they are likely to find (except God alter it) marriage to pull them from God, to carry their spirits to worldliness, unsettledness, cares, fears, temptations, and lusts, sometimes on the right hand by baits to carnal ease and jollity; and another time on the left to snares and distempered passions of anger and impatience, neither of which extremity favors religion, but kills and damps it; taking up all the time and leisure of the soul from attending the best things, or at least causing it to attend them less; as good never a whit (as we say) as never the better.

Reason 3.
God is seldom
found out of
his own way.

Besides these reasons, what hope have we that when we forsake God's way, he will be found of us, in ours? How just is it for him to forsake us and give us over to our own by-ends and respects in our marriages, and to suffer us to defile ourselves more and more that as we entered badly, so we should live worse, and end worst of all? As Paul says, The wicked wax

2 Tim. 3.13

worse and worse, deceiving, and being deceived; so may the

Lord plague ungodly marriages by themselves, and scourge
them with their own whip; so that the husband should be deceived with the bad qualities of the wife, and she by his; one
defiling the other more, and neither doing any good to the
other. We see it thus daily, unclean men do but teach their
wives their trade that they might match them in their kind;
carnal, proud, and bad wives draw their husbands to the like
evils, one must please another by concurring with their humors, and all for a penalty upon such as slighted God's ordinance, to marry in the Lord: that so the thing they sought
might be a snare unto them. True it is oftentimes, the Lord
orders it otherwise (for the elect shall be brought home by one
means or another, be they ever so ill married); the Lord can
turn poison into a medicine if he pleases, and sin to good.
But it is ever best to seek God in his way: the question is not
what God can do, but what he does, or will do ordinarily. Sure
it is, ordinarily, these doubtful, irreligious, and clandestine
matches are as basely carried as entered upon; repentance
itself being hard to get for the sin at first much less amendment of errors, but rather a hardened heart, an unsavory going
through-stitch, swallowing up much sorrow, and none to pity
them that pitied not themselves, in hasting sorrow upon them.

Lastly, marriages are full of disproportions. Now religion is fittest to level and equal them of all other. I confess
it to be the way of God that such equality as possibly can be
attained, should be in this condition, as of years, education,
disposition, breed, estate, and the like (as in the next point
shall appear). But what is more common than disparity in
all? Young are married to old, rich to poor, untaught to well
trained, harsh to amiable, and the like. How shall this be lev-
eled? Surely no way except religion will compound it. I do
not always say it can; for religion itself has no warrant to enter
upon unequal marriage, howbeit, if it is so, religion can best set
all straight and even, or else nothing can. It is not her wealth
which can procure contentment with a profane, froward wife;
it is not a good nature which will purchase love to a wasteful,
improvident, wanton woman; that plaster is not broad enough
for the sore. No outward complement can ease or level an inward inequality; only grace can do it, if it may prevail. Grace
will say thus, Your wife was but poor, but she is loyal, chaste,

Reason 4.
Grace levels
all dispropor-
tions.

wise, provident, and saves her portion in seven years: that which makes her thus, shall go for her portion. Your husband is but a plain man, has no great learning, is none of the sweetest tempers, but harsh and rough. But religion shining through these clouds makes the best of a hard bargain: both of them, perhaps, are passionate and sudden, but because God's bridle is presently in their mouth, their wants are the more easily endured. And, as I say this of marriage in general, so in particular of second matches; wherein, either encumbrances by former marriage, children, or the world frowning, or suspicion of fraud either way; or, in a word, unsuitable success to expectation; if in the throng of these, religion steps not in to mediate and moderate the controversy, how endless may the breaches be?

Objections and doubts answered.

But for all this, truth cannot lack cavils or queries: for first, do we not (say some) see very many couples do very well who never observed any such strict course, but happened by better chance than good skill upon one another? I answer: you have lighted so, perhaps rather in a negative way that you are free from many evils which pester others who are in a holy positive way of grace: or if so, it is rather a lot of mercy than any good forecast of your own. If it is as you wish, thank God who has borne with your sinful tempting of his providence, and swerving from his way: howbeit, one swallow makes no summer, neither ought it to prescribe a precedent unto others: ten miss where one hits well. And secondly, I say, all honor and success in marriage must not be esteemed by outward league and peace together; Ahab and Jezebel accorded, but how? They accorded in mutual combining for wickedness and idolatry. Still swine eat up all the draff sometimes: and, if outward peace attended with wealth, ease, and welfare cannot hinder a profane heart, contempt of the ordinances, Sabbaths, and ways of God, what advantage is it for a good marriage? But it is objected, suppose a hypothetical case that God converts them to himself? I answer, his mercy is the greater, but yet so free that it cannot certainly be rested upon. The grace of God which turns all to their good, whom he has eternally loved, must be no pretext for sin.

1 Kings 21.25

Objection 2.

Again, others come in and cavil; disapprove, why must you be so precise, grace may come in due season, no time past, and when it comes it never comes amiss? I answer: grace is precious at all times, after marriage as well as before, if a man were sure of it; but what ground have any to presume of it without some word for it, much more being against it? God may be patient and say, No time past: but neither is he tied to it; and besides, they that tempt him are most unlike to speed well. Walk in his way, and then indeed, no time past: God may, truly, and will convey his grace to a poor soul that waits for him.

But it is further objected; the best (by their leave) have failed in their godly attempts, and found worse wives than they sought. I answer: yet, they may have peace in this, that they have sought God to the uttermost. He has hidden himself from them in this particular, as the prophet said to the Shunammite: but they have peace in their endeavor, and therefore have no cause to give God over, but to hang upon him still to find mercy in another way, that is, in the bush burning and not consumed: that is, that by your prayers. God has reserved mercy for them, and means to grace their enterprises at last, doing that for them in marriage, which he did not before. If the Lord pleases to hear them at last, it shall be well; and to such this free grace of his belongs, who though they have been disappointed a while, yet it is in their obedience, and so includes a hope of further audience and supply from heaven. But I conclude, if any careful ones have yet miscarried; surely, ten times more have done so for lack of it. *(Objection 3.)* *(2 Kings 4.27)*

But many religious ones may have perilous qualities, and so dishonor marriage. I answer. If this is done in the green tree, what shall be done in the dry? What shall become of such as without restraint, even out of the abundance of their evil heart, bring forth such fruit with full purpose? Add to this, their evil qualities come not from religion, but because they are not religious enough to bridle and mortify their lusts. It is because they drown the power of their religion in their own sensuality and will; detaining the truth in unrighteousness: and no doubt such would be much worse if religion did not now and then step out to moderate. *(Objection 4. Luke 23.31)* *(Mat. 12.35)* *(Rom. 1.18)*

But if you tie us to such strictness, to marry only in the Lord, what shall become of those persons that are not in the Lord. I answer. Take no thought for them, take thought *(Objection 5.)*

rather how (in the swarm of such) you may shun them, and light upon such as are the Lord's. As for these, you shall not need to take thought for them; our rules will not much hinder their marriages, like will to like, do we what we can, and the

Luke 9.60

dead will bury the dead, the world will love their own, and that to their mutual sorrow; and all to teach us to love such the rather whom the Lord loves. What have we to do to judge them that are without? No, we speak to no other but the will-

1 Cor. 5.12

ing people, Psalm 110.3, who will stand to be judged at God's bar.

Objection 6.   But I have cast my affection already upon such a one, and am snared. I answer. Then forbear a while, till all means are tried for the party's bettering, and so venture upon them. There is an objection. But I cannot so far deny myself. I answer. Thank yourself; God forces no such necessity upon any, if they will be ruled. If not, their snaring themselves with a needless necessity cannot make God's command of no effect. If you can make to yourselves such a necessity as must break a charge of God, then try how well you can endure the fruit of it, when sorrow, repentance, and shame shall come upon you as the necessity of an armed man. Is it not good reason that

Prov. 24.34

you digest this mouthful as that the Lord digest the other? Yes surely.

Objection 7.   But when all is done, perhaps we shall miss of our choice desired because there are so few to be found in this woeful barren world, of such that are religious, and those who are but merely civil are counted puritans, and those precise whose manners are not debauched. I answer. Set not God's providence and his command together by the ears as if he charged you to marry only in the Lord, and yet debarred you from it in practice; so that either you must be forced to marry with all sorts, or else must not marry at all. No: God puts no such snare upon any: look to yourselves that you are such as you go for, and the Lord will not deceive you; he has good in store for the good. It is one of heaven's works to make good

2 Chron. 19.11

marriages: and he who has bad women in store for sinners that they may fall by them; he has also good ones for the good

Eccles. 7.26

that they may honor marriage and him thereby: indeed, and he has wisdom, discerning of spirits, of the subtle shows and guises of all sorts, both hypocrites and other bad ones, so that

(as subtle as the world is) they who loathe to be cheated by
their dice-play shall not want wisdom to judge, and savor to
relish the good in the midst of the bad; they shall hear a voice
behind them saying, *This is the way*: and withal, giving them
an ear to hear, and a heart to obey and walk therein.

Eph. 4.14

Isa. 30

But to conclude, we have met (say some) with good
companions, by providence, yet still are we hindered; for our
parents and friends (at least of one side) will not consent. I answer. Perhaps you seek among the good, and find better than
yourselves for some sinister end, the beauty or the portion of
the party; otherwise unworthy to speed: and what wonder if
a wise parent will not consent to bestow his child upon you?
But you object: yes both of us being both religious and consenting, yet parents cross us. I answer. If indeed it is so, tarry
till I come to the next chapter, and there I shall fall into that
argument of the parents' duty, and therefore I will not prevent
myself. We have answered objections enough, and more will
occur after, enough therefore is said here. Let us hasten to
some use of the point, wherein more satisfaction will be given
to other questions.

Objection 8.

First, this is terror and reproof to the marriages of this
degenerate age; wherein this duty of marrying in the Lord is
cast off at large. As Rehoboam's juveniles carried that weighty
business of his kingdom, and overthrew it: so do the unruly
and rebellious humors of most youth miscarry this. They knit
and combine themselves together as if they were right grave
counselors, wiser than their parents and ancients, disdaining
that any should overrule their rash and rebellious appetites;
and so with rash resolutions and fury of undeniable passions,
they rush themselves upon the pikes of eternal misery. If once
their parents are dead then most of these impetuous persons
have made sure enough for the honor of marriage: for by that
time they come of years (if not before) most of them have
embezzled their inheritances. But if not, yet in this point of
marriage this is their resolution: Give me her, for she pleases
me well. She may please well for a moment, though she is a
prick in the eye and a goad in the side forever after. And so
for a vanishing satisfaction, to a vain humor, what do such but
enthrall themselves to a wanton, wasteful, and willfully ungodly companion? And as the heathen said of a bad bargain,

Uses of the
point.
1. Terror and
reproof.
Branch 1.
Profane scorn-
ers to marry
in the Lord,
terrified.
1 Kings 12.10

Judg. 14.3

it vexes the foolish buyer more with the continual upbraiding than the loss of the money, so may I say of this: and as
Sampson found this at leisure, for the willful mind he bore
to have Delilah: so do these. But alas! There is no season for
such as he was, to believe it being intoxicated with the cup of
enchantment, disabling them from taking better counsel. But
why then do I speak this? Surely, because I see religion among
young couples, for the most part, is the first of those respects
which are last thought of. Desperate and stolen waters are
sweetest to such; like those of the Benjamites, who rushing
into a company of dancers, in their jollity, snatched up each
man his wife, as she came to hand, prove well or ill, for better
for worse: for why, they sought wives, not good ones, and that
anyway, so they had them. What a merry world would it be
for our debauched drunken youth in these our days, if they
might choose their wives in such a lottery. To catch (among
a drove) each one his own companion in a wild and reckless
manner: oh what a brave thing were it? There is a pleasure
in doing that which is forbidden to our cursed nature, even
because it is so: and if it were not so, they would die upon
a sword's point before they would attempt it. And notwithstanding the woe of such marriages, against God's word, law
of reason, consent of parents, and even the general experience
of such that have gone before them; yet, who may speak to
such? Surely such matches are made in hell, like are fallen
upon like by the Devil's spokesmanship: as I confess, better
one house troubled with such than two. But what a sad thing
is it to think, what a cursed posterity such are like to hatch: I
say such, as whereof one or two might poison a whole neigh-
borhood? Drunken meetings, marriages, reveling, markets,
fairs, taverns, and alehouses are the places wherein such persons choose their companions. But of this enough.

A second sort coming here to be reproved are not so
debauched as these, and yet reproved for their carelessness to
marry in the Lord. Many, not grossly profane, yet because but
civil, trusting to their wit and policy alone, thinking themselves secure enough, although they go not so spiritually to
work, as to marry in the Lord, are to be taxed by this doctrine. So long as they can marry morally, such as are free from
gross crimes, uncleanness, riot, alehouse-haunting, and the

Prov. 9.17
Judg. end

As Gen. 6.2,3

2. Branch of
terror.
Marriages with
them that are
only civilized,
unsafe.

like: such as are of a sweet carriage, fashionable, and complete, brought up well to a pleasing and outwardly graceful behavior. Especially if there are any means to live competently in the world, good husbandry and housewifery; oh, they think their choice is excellent; even when children themselves stagger for conscience sake at such offers, yet their parents are earnest for the match and vex themselves to see their children so precise. And indeed it is no wonder, when morality (in these Gen. 6.2 times) is counted preciseness. And yet, tell me, what difference is there between those Benjamites I spoke of and those children of God marrying the daughters of men, the posterity of Seth with idolaters? What woeful imps proceeded from such a mixture? And the truth is, even such as profess religion are grown to make such matches without any check. The common question now, not only among great ones, or among profane ones, but even among the ordinary sort, and such as profess religion, is: What shall she have? What is she worth? Psal. 4.6 What dowry can he make? Who will show us any good? As if men were selling of cattle in a market. Not in this manner: What is the woman? How was she brought up? How qualified with knowledge, love of God's church, meekness, modesty, or other fruits of faith and the spirit? They yet are the only ornaments of wealth and beauty, truly, more in price with God than all they possess, who enquire so little after them. But by that time, some of these, by bad example, and for want of the fear of God, grow to be bad companions, others become unclean, others spendthrifts, and the like; then their parents (who so shunned religious ones before) can wish they had matched them with religious ones too. But it is just that they pierce themselves through with cares, who seek religion out of season, rather out of their own ends than for herself. Hence it is that such solemn marriages in the world, as begin with great hopes and honor; yet within a few years turn to misery, beggary, imprisonment, and defiance of each other to the pit of hell. Why? Surely because they sought other things as chief such as money, and beauty, and the like, but not religion; just it is with God to forsake them and leave them destitute, not only of what they sought not, but also of that which they chiefly coveted. Not to speak of those base and wicked shifts, which some of them are faint to come to, as flattery of their betters, unclean relations, bankrupt-like ways, and to borrow what they can and leave men in the lurch. Ill marriages are one cause of bankrupts, though not the only; for many streams there are that cause this bank to overflow so excessively nowadays. So much of this.

Branch 3.
Reproof.
Of such in
which either
party is bad.

Thirdly, this is reproof, and that of two sorts: first, such as whereof neither party is religious: secondly, whereof only either of the two is such. Touching the former, we see a woeful pattern of Ahab and Jezebel, of whom neither was better (though perhaps the one less ill) but conspired together, and set forward each other to mischief. And indeed so it commonly falls out, that if both are bad, the woman proves to be the worst. It is much what, in this sex, as in the inferior natures of creatures, the she-bear, lioness, or wolf is the most savage and fierce: so here, the impotency and unbridledness of the sex makes her more subject to rage, unrighteousness, revenge, and wickedness than a man: not to speak of the natural persuasiveness of such, incensing to evil forcibly, ever since Eve tempted Adam; Jezebel provoking Ahab to be far worse than himself, by saying, *Art thou now King of Israel and liest thou upon thy bed as a fool? Come, and I will give thee the vineyard of Naboth, etc.* The corruption of best is worst; and when she who by her kind should have been the most modest, becomes bold, she commonly keeps no bounds of immodesty. Two are better than one (says Solomon) and woe to him that is alone: but here we may sadly invert the words, and say, One is better than two; and woe to those couples who are both bad. Better had it been for such to have lived in the mountains, to bewail their virginity, even to dwell with the foxes and wild beasts in extreme solitariness (where no other then misery can be looked for) than to enter into a hoped condition of welfare, to double and triple their own sorrows, sin, and judgment; making each other much more the children of Satan than before.

1 Kings 21.25

1 Kings 21.7

Eccles. 4.9

Judg. 11.38

Mat. 23.15

And verily, it is the usual destiny of most families to be pestered with such couples, whereof neither is religious, but both rude and profane, and studying who should excel the other therein. If the one dare lie, the other dare swear to it: if the one slander, the other will avow it; if one is bad, the other will be worse. And this pleases him that brought them together, on life; that by their vying and outvying each other in evil they should approve their gratitude and service unto him: joining to moral sins, the omitting or despising of God's worship and ordinances within doors or without, as Word, sacrament, prayer, and duties. Alas! Suppose that bad couples are not combined in open ungodliness and malice, but only in a mere, civil, formal, and sapless religion, keeping of Sabbaths barrenly, or mutual complacence in each other for the raking up of money, making great portions for their children, ill brought up, and like to spend it as prodigally, and mock them for their labor (as one lately did, who after his father's death, having found out his hoard of money, cried out, Oh faithful drudge!) and so waste it out in bravery and fashions, pride *A villainous* and pomp of life. Or suppose they live in a mere harmlessness *speech.* of course, spending out their days in working, eating, sleeping, neither doing good nor gross evil, welcoming and visiting neighbors, and living courteously (which I confess is the best of such) yet alas! What a miserable life is this in comparison of the true gain and sweet of a marriage religiously carried? But yet the worst is behind.

For why? Rarely do we see couples thus married to *Admonition to* repent themselves of their course; but wither away like shad- *such.* ows, except they die like beasts, without sense; and even as they have entered basely, and lived worse, so the last act of their life is worst, and they die impenitent. Oh then! In God's fear, let me speak unto you, and be admonished before it is too late (before either the one of you is swept from the other, or both to destruction) to consider your sin at the first, humbling your soul for it, and much more for the long thread of your former course, which you have spent amiss. And if neither of you will at all profit, by either Word or works of God, while you live together, but go on hardened in your mutual wickedness; yet when God shall separate the one from the other by death, crying out lamentably of his or her sinful course; oh, let the survivor be yet scared out of his den, and with that third captain of fifty cry out to God and say, Although you have parted us Lord, and my companion is dead in sin, yet *2 Kings 1.13* *let my life* (I pray thee) *be precious in thy sight*: unsettle me from those dregs upon which I am settled (for want of rolling) that I may break off my long profane, fruitless conversation and seek thy face, and recover myself before I depart and be *Psal. 39.13* seen no more! Oh! It were better (I grant) if the Lord were so pleased that as both of you have been partners in sin, and one corrupt flesh; so you might both together repent, and become one spirit in the Lord, both of you might be roused by his terrors out of your dead sleep: that the one being humbled might alarm his fellow and say, husband, wife, do you not see that God's hand is out against us, and his wrath is upon us; we are under all adversity, our bodies, souls, children, and affairs,

Job 20.11

nothing prospers: oh, we have made use a long time of each other for the Devil's vantage, till our bones are full of the sin of our youth. Except we return in time, God will be avenged on us, and send us to our place and long home of misery: Alas! We have never honored marriage as other holy couples have done; it is strange patience that yet we are on this side of hell: let us now join together and turn to the Lord that, if possible, all may be forgotten and forgiven. Oh! Happy you are if ever you should live to see that day! Happy are your poor children and family, whose souls you should snatch out of the fire, and be instruments of pulling them out of that misery unto which you have bred them. But I forbear.

Branch 4.
Admonition
to the religious
married to the
irreligious.
Branch 1.
Luke 1.6
1 Sam. 18.27
1 Sam. 25
Job 1.8,9
Deut. 22.11
2 Cor. 6.15

But there is a fourth sort of marriage, whereof only one party is religious. These also are to be humbled for their ungrounded attempt, the one for venturing upon an irreligious yokefellow; the other for irreligious entrance. Zechariah and Elizabeth are commended that they were both just; therefore it is a stain to such marriages, as wherein either party is good, the other opposite to it. Examples whereof we have in Scripture are David and Michal, Nabal and Abigail, and Job and his wife. The Lord who forbade to sow one field with diverse seeds, or to wear a garment of linen and wool, much more abhors that the marriage bed should be defiled with persons of diverse religions; for we know no opposition is so strong as that which is spiritual; and how then should there be amity and love where the seeds of greatest enmity abide? What a tempting of God is it, to draw the yoke of God with one that draws in the yoke of the Devil? Or as Paul speaks in the like case: What fellowship is there between Christ and Belial, the believer and the infidel? What is such a union, save a monster compounded of diverse natures, by an adulterous mixture? What a noisome thing would it be for a lively and healthy body

to walk with a dead carcass bound to it, back to back? How
long could it continue? How should it avoid decaying? As
appears by the manner of that punishment, in some cases inflicted, among the heathens; as that image of Nebuchadnezzar,
which had the body made of metals and the feet of clay, could   Dan. 2.32
not abide long without dissolution; so neither can that temper which consists of such contraries. And besides add that,
which one well observes, that when good and bad are joined
together, seldom is the worse bettered by the good, but often
the better is marred by the worse party. The brown bread in
the oven will be sure to fleece from the white, not that from
it. How can it otherwise be in this so near a knot of marriage,
since it is seldom seen, but it is so in all other fellowships?
When the one party is patient, devout, meek, sober, a lover of
the Word, conscionable in Sabbaths, and the use of means; the
other is careless, froward, unchaste, intemperate, and profane.
What a corrosive must the one needs be to the other, and instead of a helper, what a continual dropping? Was it a savory
thing (think we) to Job to hear his wife bid him *Curse God and*   Prov. 19.13
die? Himself being so armed with patience as to say, *Shall we*   Job 2.9-12
receive good things of God, and not evil?

When David danced before the Lord, and in the
height of zeal brought home the ark of God, was it a pleasing thing to hear Michal to call him a fool for his labor? And   2 Sam. 6.23
although they are not so gross as to scoff at their husbands or
wives, yet what a cross it is to have such lying in our bosoms
as are of a diverse mind? What complaint is so usual in these
days as to hear the complaints of good husbands, of ill wives,
and wives of husbands, through this disparity? Some making
their moan for the churlishness, straightness, maliciousness,
and restraint from use of means; others, for other eyesores, of
which sort unequal marriages are infinitely fruitful. So rare
are those couples, of whom it may be said, They draw mutually   Luke 1.6
and equally in one yoke; as Zechariah and Elizabeth, both just,
diligent hearers, zealous worshippers, lovers of God, of good
men, and the like! And hence it is that there is oftentimes
little difference between those families in which both are bad,
and those in which only either party is good; because commonly the better party makes himself but a prey to the other.
Religion must always be the disadvantage of the party, and the

Luke 15.28
irreligious must bear the chief sway: even as the elder brother will dominate over the younger, because of his birthright; so, the better party must ever look to be the underling. As we say of a syllogism that the conclusion ever follows the weaker part: so here. Alas! Where both parties are as they ought, how little good is done? So many crosses, business of the world, debts, and temptations by sin and Satan come between that even the comfort of such marriages goes near together. What good is like to be done when the one is always thwarting the other in the duties of the family, or lesser occasions? I say, when the main is unsound, how shall the rest be soldered? But enough of these.

Branch 2.

    To pass therefore to another sort of couples: how many husbands are of this rank, disaffected to their religious wives, and yet for some by-respects and ends of their own will tolerate them in their profession of religion and use of means? But alas! Full ill is it against their wills, if by any counsel,

Diverters of their wives from religion to other matters, reproved.
benefit, or persuasion they could be withdrawn from it, how glad would they be? Moreover, if they could divert their affections from this way to any worldly way of feasting, jollity, and companionship, how much rather would they choose to be at double or triple cost to maintain it rather than at a single one to nourish the other? So that if they permit them not their religion with ridicule and scoffing them openly, yet with a secret disdain. If (say they) our wives must be precise, let them: why? Is it because you love it in them? No: for then they should have your company, and you would be like them (whereas now you suffer them by a kind of connivance, winking at them, and looking between the fingers). But why? Per-

Connivers only at the religions of their yokefellows, not approvers thereof, taxed.
haps they being men of a more indifferent and gentle nature, and convinced by the secret grace which breaks out in their wives, which they cannot smother; and now and then (especially in the time of their fear of death) acknowledging their state to be better than their own. Besides, beholding sundry graceful qualities in their wives, which tend to their own honor and credit in the opinion of others, beholding them to be in esteem with some of their betters; and themselves accepted the better for their sakes: sometimes also stirred in conscience to desire they were as they are, though when their pangs are over, their lusts do again overtake them. I say, by such second

motives many men (not being Nabals and base blocks) being persuaded better of their wives than others are; as seeing their estates to be the more prosperous by their frugal, housewifely, and wise managing thereof; they grow more indifferent towards them, and especially their persons and sweet innocent behaviors gracing them in their eyes. And by such means many women unequally yoked live at better terms than others do.

But alas! How few of such husbands are drawn to God (as the apostle says) by the conversation of the wives, or wives by such husbands? But put it off with a trick; you see (say they) what our wives affect, they must have their wills, we must not cross them, for then all were out of order; let them alone and run their course as poor silly women may do: but as for us, who are wiser, and have greater affairs to look after; we must play the good husbands at home, and hold in matters together. Well, take heed you wise fellows lest you be taken in your own snare, beware lest God pull you not down from that pride and jollity, by which you look over religion as a mean thing, under your worth and employment. The wisdom of man is but foolishness with God, and when the glory of this world shall be abased, and bid you farewell, then God's matters will bear some price, and Mary's portion may happen to be wished. Oh therefore (as Paul says) *what knowest thou*, O man, whether God has appointed your wife to occasion your conversion? Oh, it is death to many a bad man to think that a woman should bear stroke or sway with him in the cause of God. They will not yield so far as to grace their wives with such a victory. It is well if her ornament proves not her greatest detriment, and she has not much sour sauce to digest her sweet meat. But as for following her steps to heaven, oh, it is too great honor to the wife! Well, you shall wish you had esteemed it your own greatest honor! Meantime, the greater shall her thankfulness be to God, by how much her religion has cost her the setting on: if she suffers not her zeal and grace to quail by any discouragements, till she see better things at last, after her long patience, to be wrought in her husband. Oh you unequal husband! Are you content to pocket up all the commodities and contents of a good wife, and to take all which religion affords you in your wife, for your own ends,

Commenders of religion in their wives for other respects, not for religion, blamed.

1 Pet. 3.1

1 Cor. 1.25
1 Cor. 7.16
Luke 10.42
Scorners to be drawn by their wives' religion, faulty.

never looking whence this mast falls? Will you love the daughter thrift, modesty, subjection, sobriety, and teaching of your children, and do you not care for the mother, religion, which bred them all? How base is it to love the effect, and to dislike the cause? To desire that these good qualities were in a wife without religion rather than by them to behold the beauty thereof? Take heed, resist not the light, and stop not your eyes from beholding that sun whose beams you are so much beholding too.

Counsel for such as draw in an evil yoke. Gen. 41.9

1. Rip up your state to God.

2. Redeem old errors, and pray for pardon.

Gen. 17.18

Deut. 5.28
3. Pass by ordinary faults.

1 Pet. 3.1

I conclude this fourth branch (being a very material one) with an admonitory caveat to such persons, whose wisdom will be (as I take it) to make a virtue of a necessity, either in drawing the backward party to a better pass, or themselves to a more patient bearing of their burden. First therefore, let such say with Pharaoh's butler, I remember my sin this day, the sin of rash entrance into marriage, my sensuality and yielding to my appetite without consulting with God. These and other sins of your youth, open before God, that he may cover them. Redeem your former neglect by present diligence, in humbling your soul, and praying to God for pardon; it is never out of season to do so if the fruit is not as you desired, yet it shall be some supply of your lack of good marriage, and an ease of your sorrow. As for your companion, pour out your soul to God for him as Abraham for Ishmael, Oh that he might live in thy sight! If conscience moves you not, yet let self-love do it, for you are desirous to enjoy the good. And with spiritual means join suitable practice, commend whatsoever is praiseworthy in your companion (for the worst have some good parts) that it may appear that you art loath to bury good under the mass of evil, and would be glad to commend for somewhat: for so God himself does, Deut. 5.28, etc. Infirmities pass by, and mark not; for who speaks of a scar when the body is crooked? Grosser evils so observe, as waiting your season to reprove them, and that with all mercy and meekness, lest you exasperate instead of mending; join especially a convincing and winning conversation, for this glass will say more than all your words; even (if Peter may be believed) more than the Word itself sometimes. And they are neither men nor women, whom such a carriage will not win in time. But in the event God still answers not your desires: fret not

against your lot, which is God's providence, nor by compari- 4. Fret not at your lot.
Luke 21.19
Isa. 26.20
son of worse folks' better success. But possess your soul with
patience, bear this indignation a while, till the evil is past;
you drink of no other cup than that which you have filled for
yourself. Moderate such pangs and melancholic passions of
discontent as do attend such a condition, and be not froward
with the froward, knowing that the Devil is seldom outshot in
his own bow. Especially you woman (if it is your lot) beware
of it, let not fly against either marriage or procurers thereof,
lest religion bear the reproach of your folly. No man puts new Luke 5.36
5. Conceal grievances so long as possible.
cloth into old garments, lest the breach be worse. And (if I
might advise) I would wish such rather to conceal their grievances than to open them much, especially to strangers: and
it requires great wisdom to do it to any, most of all with ripping up all grievances before witnesses: for hereby, as secrets
become reproaches, so that which might have been healed, is
quite made incurable by over-deep search and exasperating.
However the issue proves, wax not desperate, still hope; the Heb. 12.13
Prov. 18.10
name of the Lord is a strong tower, the righteous flee to it and
are preserved. You are not alone in your grief, live by that
faith whereby Job, Abigail, and others lived and do live, and
you shall see what end the Lord shall make; keep still your
humility, care, and diligence. The way of the Lord is straight Prov. 10.29
to him that walks uprightly, though there is no other. Above
all, beware of justifying your base heart under color of your 6. Justify not your own er- rors, by others.
companion's more apparent sinfulness: play not the hypocrite
as many do, who promise great matters if free of the cross,
who yet being set at liberty, discover themselves to be wanton,
worldly, and carnal: sometimes stumbling at the same stone
which before gave them a fall, and becoming worse in good
marriages than they were at the first in bad. And thus much
for this first use, with the cautions thereof.

The second use is instruction: teaching us by com- Use 2.
Instruction.
What the best object of the married is.
parison to esteem and judge what is the most excellent object
for the married to behold in each other. And that must be
sound religion; very heathens could say so of their virtue that
she is desirable for herself: how much more we of this? No
other things are so; they have their desirableness, yet for that
they are in order serving to better ends, rather than for what 1. Respect.
is comely in themselves. And as wisdom itself is usually in

Job 28.18
Prov. 8.11

Scripture spoken of in this kind, that she is better than rubies, the topaz, the treasures of the East, no gold is like her: so is a good woman furnished with this grace, more precious than all pearls. Even as also a husband is: birth, education, means, and wealth greatly conduce to a completeness and contentment of marriage: but as for making it happy and honorable, they reach it not: only religion can do that. They are as the second sort of worthies of David, which attained not to the first.

2 Sam. 23.19

Many daughters have done well, but you have the birthright, and surmounted them all. There is an honor of complement, and there is an honor of substance: the former may stand in externals; the latter only in religion. Solomon's words will express the point; That which is desirable in a man is his goodness: no man is praised for that which is out of him, but for that which is within him. Secondly, there is no comparison between the graces of the mind, with outward abilities; for the one is of absolute necessity, the other not. It being not absolutely necessary that a man should be well bred or wealthy: but it is necessary that he is religious: without the one he may live and maintain the honor of marriage (though in the other there is usefulness), but without the other he cannot. Lastly, in respect of the absence of either: better lack a pound of the one (if want must be) than a pinch of the other. Wealth and parts will not recompense the lack of religion (for they are under it in their kind), but she can supply theirs with a hundred fold. The conclusion is, we learn to settle our judgments solidly upon this truth; that so our eye is not blurred with the false and erroneous opinions of the world; which (as in all other respects, so) in this point, forsake the rule of God for vain shadows and emptiness; and having embraced them all their lifetime, seeking in the creature that which is not there to be had: (for as apparel cannot feed, nor meat clothe, nor anything exceed his own sphere; so neither can beauty reach beyond that is in her, nor riches above that is in them) they cry out at last, taught by experience of fools, we have lost the body for the shadow, embraced vanity and forsaken mercy: *All is vanity*! So it was at the first, but you saw it not.

Prov. 19.22

2. Respect.

3. Respect.

Jonah 2.8

Use 3.
Admonition

Thirdly, let this admonish us to shun all delusions and errors in this kind, which might destroy the honor of marriage. Imagine not that profit and pleasure can do the work of honoring marriage. A heathen could say, these are but by-respects in a lower contract of friendship: how much more here? When sweet and profit are once worn off, as the nap from the fine cloth, nothing remains behind except bare threads: as when the leaves are blown off the rose, nothing is left except the prickle. Not so here: for although she begins with some sourness, yet she is durable and outlasting. Secondly, be not duped with the rashness of such brainsick idiots, as think marriage to be magic, that look what defect soever there is in couples, yet marriage will accommodate all suddenly. Marry them (says one) and all will do well enough. Can marriage make all errors vanish? Is any man so mad as to think that because he has a great sum to pay, therefore he may convey twenty slips into it, and not be discarded? Shall not each piece come to the weights? Surely that which in the several is nonexistent, cannot do well in the compound. Once (as our English story mentions) there was in the English court a very sweet lady, called Jane-makepeace; which no sooner perceived any little difference among the nobles or courtiers, but she would accord them presently. But this office is only in religious marriage, not marriage only: no, rather marriages ill entered upon are commonly so far from sweet accord that rather afterward they prove worse; for then does the Devil present more baits of liberty to an unbridled heart than before. The old speech is, magistracy makes not the man, but discovers what mettle is in him. Be not deceived, God is not mocked: as a man sows, so shall he reap; of wheat, wheat; of ryegrass, ryegrass; and he is mad who would look for other. Thirdly, neither let any think that in unequal marriages the religious husband (as the stronger) may better adventure upon an irreligious wife than a Christian woman upon a husband of that strain: for my part, I have seen small odds in the bargain; Solomon's words prove too true here, *Victory is not always to the strong*: it is ill grappling by strong hand with a headstrong woman. She should be the weaker vessel, but when she is perverted, she proves the stronger in mischief. The sum of all is, let none that fear God venture upon those that do not: and let all seek for their parts, to be in the Lord, before marriage. Above all, let second marriages beware of adventuring in this kind, upon each other for advantage's sake (an error very rise in this kind); for en-

against some errors herein. The first.

The second.

Gal. 6.7

3. Branch.

Eccles. 9.11

hancing themselves for jollity, and a braver and fuller life than formerly they were content with: for it falls out commonly that by one attendant or other; as charge of children, perfidiousness in the valuing of their estates, costliness of diet or apparel, or by some unexpected canker, wasting the apple at the core, God cuts their comb, fills their new hopes with new sorrow, and makes them wish that they were but as they have been, forfeiting all their felicity for nothing. So much for this.

Use 4. Exhortation to marry in the Lord in 3 branches.

The last use is exhortation, to excite and persuade all to marry in the Lord: an exhortation at all times necessary: but so especially necessary in these deceitful and cheating days, that who so should reject this counsel is worthy to give it himself too late, upon costly experience. And truly I less blame them who are of good estate, fearing God, for their buying good wives by forsaking greater worldly contents: which commonly are joined with greater peril (for great portions commonly go with great stomachs, high spirits, costly fashion, and great expenses). They therefore who can deny a little pomp may buy much peace, and redeem both their own and their children's safety with a little self-denial in outward respects, whereas they are sure to gain it in spiritual. But I digress not.

Three branches of it.

Still I press the point, marry in the Lord: concerning the which, I would commend three duties to the well-affected. The first concerning youth before their entrance into this estate. The second more closely concerning such as purpose to change their estate. The third concerning them upon their contract.

The first. Youth must redeem her golden season for this end. Eph. 4.19

Touching the first, the duty of young ones growing up towards this estate is this, that they redeem their golden opportunity of youth and single life: improving all such helps either public or private; all such counsels of their ancients; all examples of such as are commendable in this kind, especially any such motions of the Spirit in the ordinances, whereby they are inclined to seek the Lord to be their portion, in pardon and grace. Remember this is your season of getting about you such a stock of provision as may hereafter stand by you. This is your golden time; each period following will prove worse downward, even brass, iron, and clay. Mark how the greater sort of youth dally out their precious time, never setting their

Eccles. 12.1

hearts to *Remember their Creator in the days of their youth*: but to lick up the common foul remains of the times, to learn fashions, complements, carriage (which avail little for the main) to stand upon their great births, portions, or hopes, and so to live bravely. But how to be fit for such a solemn change, I speak not of death for that is out of thought, out of season for youth, but of marriage if God brings them to it; that so out of the treasure which they have gotten, they may bring forth direction, how to order themselves, or make their estate honorable and comfortable, it is furthest from their thought. What? Do you hear that the chief way to honor marriage is entering with the Lord? And do you not conclude that so weighty a matter will cost you a great deal of preparing? What should you then do beforehand? Surely, as your parents are busy about providing your portion (which is their work), so you should be busied a better way, about that one thing necessary, to get the pearl in the field, to seek the Lord while that he may be found. Heathen poets bring in virgins upon the stage, professing that they take no thought for their matches. They look at modesty and good report. The less you are busied about things less needful, the more you may attend that one thing, which shall never be taken from you. Except in these days of your youth, wherein each thing is sweet, the main work is thought of, the days are coming (and that perhaps long before old age) of which you shall say, you have no pleasure in such objects: there may come a day of uncomfortable marriage, losses of estate, death of husband, of wife, sorrow of heart for your ill matching, and then how will you do? Is it not just to such, as set the chief things behind? Yes verily.

Mat. 12.35

Luke 10.42

Eccles. 12.1

Remember our Savior's words to Peter, *When thou wast young, thou girdedst thyself, and went whither thou wouldst; but when thou art old, another shall gird thee, and lead thee whither thou wouldest not.* You may meet with an unpleasing girdle; your great charge of children, calling for your care and maintenance; the world frowning upon you, and not answering your hopes; a riotous and spend thirsty husband, or waspish and untoward wife (for so it may be, when you have sought the greatest prevention of it, if God will so try you), debts, diseases, and reproaches pursuing you: in the midst of all these, little leisure to wait upon the ordinances, which should infuse the grace of support into you: and perhaps (which is worst) as small a heart after it. Then, when all these have made your

John 21.18

Single life not like marriage in point of troubles, but more free.

life unpleasant and your conscience coming upon all, with a worse stream, and causing an overflow of sorrow unto you; what shall you do? God has dealt righteously in it, because you contemned all helps in your youth, and therefore in your trouble, sends you to your idol beauty, money, and will, laughing at your misery: how will you then wish you had but that former liberty granted you, to marry in the Lord? Oh! How eagerly are things loved out of their season? Alas! The Spirit blows where it lists, time and tide must not stay upon you; you had them and would not use the watchwords thereof wisely: why should the Spirit any longer strive with you, but rather suffer your sails to stand still for ever? If this then is the time of girding your loins with grace for time to come, gird them with that precious girdle of knowledge, sincerity, self-denial, faith, patience, and the like: learn to wear the yoke of God from your youth, and it shall not pinch you in your age. By this girding of your own soul, you shall be fit to admit of God's unpleasing girdles for time to come, crosses (if they come) shall befall you in your innocency, so as you shall know how to defray them, and the Lord shall be afflicted with you in your afflictions, and teach you how to pass your marriage with comfort. But if this counsel will do you no good, but perhaps you have learned to do as the world does, that is, to wallow in your sorrows, and to bear them off with head and shoulders so that you can go on through a second, or a third marriage (if it so fall out) with as graceless an heart as through the first. Certainly, there remains nothing for you, except that your end proves worse than your beginning, because your troubles brought you not upon your knees for your former sin, but rather you walk on still in the obstinacy of your heart.

I proceed to a second duty, when you intend a change; that is, be sure you do nothing rashly, but use all possible wisdom, that as you have sought the Lord, so he would bring you to a suitable companion. A great work, I grant, and you will ask how it may be effected. I will labor to satisfy your desire with these advices following. First, deny yourself, renounce that carnal wisdom, presumption and will of your own, which ascribes so much to itself, as if it needed no advice: submit yourself to the Lord, do not at first rush yourself upon marriage by a necessity of nature, or by custom of the world, or

Read Prov. 5.11,12.

John 3.8

Gen. 6.2

Lam. 3.27

Isa. 63.9,10

Isa. 57.17

The second branch of exhortation in many particulars.
Duty 1.
Self-denial and trial what God's mind is about our estate.

because years require it, or out of base ends, to give way to
your lust: but let it be your care to preserve your vessel in holiness and honor: abstain from all provocations to lust, be much
in prayer for a sanctification of every age and condition of life,
perhaps the Lord has appointed you a single life, which may be
much better for you than marriage to honor God in; perhaps
you are not a meet man for marriage; but it would prove in-
commodious for you: however, it is your duty to try what God
has for you in store, and many repent for their yielding to the
first pangs of unbridled youth, and wish they had not given
way so soon to an impotent humor. Furthermore, many who
at the first intended no other save marriage, yet by their more
wary and temperate diet, company, and by subduing their
flesh by fasting and prayer, meditation, and close attendance
of study, calling, or the ordinances of God have obtained such
a gift of chastity, that they see it is rather the way of God, they
should not marry*. There are some (says our Savior) who are
eunuchs born: marriage was a snare to such (notwithstanding
their frothy concupiscence) and some have made themselves
so for the kingdom of heaven. Chastity is a peculiar gift of
God, all will grant; and God will have it appear in some, that
grace has more strength than nature has, as against lusts, so
above lawful liberties: and he who advises continence to some,
in times of danger, especially in which marriage might prove
an obstacle; and otherwise also for a more close cleaving to
God, without marriage distractions; there is no doubt, but he
has grace suitable to frame some men and women for this very
purpose. And sure it is, where such a gift is, God is highly honored with the pure and undivided spirit of such as serve him in
that condition. Therefore all due means must be used for the
attaining of it, till the mind of God is known in this kind; and
no man ought to anticipate providence in that respect: weigh
well your strength or your weakness in the balance, lay before
yourself the burdens and service of marriage; your bodily or
spiritual abilities or imperfections, play not the part of a fool,
to say after marriage, I never thought it such a state, I see now
I am not meet for it: that should have been thought of before:
inform yourself duly of the conveniences and inconveniences
of each condition, the single and the married; and when all is
done, if God inclines you to a private state, reserve yourself

Mat. 16.24
1 Thess. 4.4

Mat. 17.21

*All receive
not this gift.

Mat. 19.12

1 Cor. 7.8

1 Cor. 1.5
Continency
being a gift of
God, must be
sought for.
1 Cor. 7.35

No vows of single life warranted.

to it; I say not to you, vow it, for who knows but your mind and body may alter, and require a change? But so long as by your abstinence from all provocations, and watchful eye over yourself, you can keep yourself chaste, and prove it by the contentment of your spirit, without perniciousness and neglect of the duties of your place: you may gather the will of God by the sign, and so you are to yield yourself to a single life; wherein although there cannot but fall out some petty discommodities (in some kind) yet they ought to be digested meekly, for the avoiding of worse, and the attaining of the benefit of a single estate. For when God is in a condition that shall be tolerable to one, which would be burdensome to another; and there is no state wholly free from trouble in this world, only that is to be embraced (as near as we can) which is free from the most. And having once understood the way of God, go not out of it willfully, nor dally with him in such weighty purposes. If it pleases him to alter your mind, you shall understand it by signs easily, and may without sin follow him, so your sin is not accessory. So much for the first counsel, which I desire may be conceived of discreetly, and not mistaken.

The second. Sound judgment, and

subduing of a rebellious heart.

Then secondly, if notwithstanding this trial, you shall find, that God has allotted marriage to you, know, it is a lawful condition of life, be resolved it is so, be not snared with fear, melancholy, or any distemper; although it is joined with many troubles, yet they shall be the lesser when God tells you, it is best, and your gain shall be above your loss; cast yourself upon the ordinance in such a case, to make it sweet. And therefore prepare yourself for it; deny your own rebellion, pride, passions, will, and lust. Know that marriage is no state (as many think) of licentiousness, to live at ease, and as a man desires. They, who are of that mind, need no other plague than their own error to vex them when they meet with the contrary. No,

Job 39.9,10

no, this estate is not for an untamed heifer: you may as soon force a unicorn to plow with your oxen, as your rude spirit to draw in your yoke of marriage. Learn therefore self-denial early (it is as essential for a married life as for a single) humility and wisdom, and how hardly this hard theme will be handled, till the heart is subdued and meekened before. For

1 Cor. 7.38
Luke 23.31

all unbroken ones are likely to find sorrow in the flesh, double and triple. If it is so in the green tree, how much more in the dry? If it is unavoidable to the best, how much more to them who seek it? So much for the second.

Thirdly, be warned against the common disease both of error and practice, which has overflowed the world, and so blurred the eyes of men that they can see nothing except the outside of things. Suffer not beauty, breeding, portion, personage, and education, with complementary behavior, fashionableness, and the like, so to bribe your judgment, and lead your affections that religion should come too late, and be thrust out from consultation. Beware of covetousness, pride of life, and jollity, ambitious and aspiring thoughts, to count none suitable for you, save such as are transcendent. The world is nowadays become a great snare; each young one, scarce out of the shell, tickles himself with the proposal of great hopes to himself, and telling him, his fortunes are great, and he may marry in so and so high a degree, and what is so high but his hopes may equal? And thus, not looking at his base beginnings, and unlikelihood of anything, but puffing up himself with offers, with conceit of his own worth, he grows to think the world too narrow to choose in. And never, I think, was the spirit of the male sex so vast, as in this age, wherein the multitude of the female sex, and the contempt thereof, has brought it to pass that every boy new out of his apprenticeship values himself by the scores and hundreds, although scarce worth a cent besides his occupation. And most men deem none, be they ever so religious (which in our Fathers' days would have been counted rich matches), fair, or good enough for him except beauty and wealth in a higher degree than common make them so. In so much, that except parents overstrain and half exhaust themselves to dowry their daughters, be they otherwise ever so well brought up and deserving, they lay by as nobody.

Duty 3. Error of the time to be abhorred.

But what? Will some say, Do you envy our lot to be better now than in former times? Or is it unlawful to marry wealthy ones, and our betters? I answer. If God lays out a portion for you (without your politic ambitious seeking) and such a one, as whose portion in grace equals her estate, even such as in judgment desire you for your religion, although you are inferior otherwise, I deny not, but (friends consenting) it is lawful. God has brought such an advantage to your hands.

Question.

Answer.

But what is this to men's covetous and proud desires? As one once said of his second match, I will now have a gallant, whatsoever it cost me; and so he had such a one as he fancied. But by that time he had wintered and summered her a while, his bladder was so pricked that he sadly wished he had one of his former wives' stature and fashion, as plain as he then thought her to be. I conclude thus, think not too highly of yourselves when there is little worth in you to equal the lowliest women, or husbands; but moderate your spirits, and marry in the Lord. Nothing hinders, but the Lord and outward means may concur (as the case may stand) and then the question is ended. But if it is so, that a match of five hundred pounds is offered with the Lord, and another of seven or eight hundred without him, or at least without any apparent hopes of him, what then shall be done? I answer. Other conditions being concurrent in any tolerable proportion, despise the greater offer, and take the lesser, counting the loss of your gain happy, and the gain of her grace with that loss, happier. Buy your wife in such a case, if you are wise, and let it appear that God's oracles are no ties with you. If her price is above pearls, I trust, you who will not part with a little gold or silver for it, are well worthy, for your betraying her for a little wealth, to betray yourself to sorrow; and to have bag and baggage and all. Tell me, in what market could you traffic so well as to game a pearl for a little silver? Doubtless, your silver would not recompense your loss, if you should choose it, with a far less bargain. The times have been wherein the man was to bring a dowry to the woman (though I think they held not long). I am sure Christ's marriage is such to his beloved. Think yourself to be the man, and ask yourself, if not what you would give, yet what you would forgo for a good companion? I think the days were never so rare for marriages in this kind, as now: and yet the sorrowful fruit of the contrary should bring this choice into date again. It is a custom (we know) for men ambitious to buy honor, rather than lack it, truly glad they are, if they can so come by it. Do you so. Marriage is honorable: buy it whatsoever it cost you, and be glad you can get it so. Let bad customs be no prescriptions, and set a good one against a bad.

Fourthly, let the Lord be much solicited by prayer both ordinary and extraordinary for this blessing: beg hard

Grace must be preferred to wealth, in marriage.

1 Sam. 25.18

Good marriages must be bought.

The fourth:

for it, rather than want. I said before, pay for it, and now I add, pray for it, pay and pray too, and think it worth it. Let the Lord see that your soul is deeply in love with it, and will not be denied, seek to honor him forever for it, and count it not every man's case; and you shall see what answer he will make you. If prayer will not get it, try if importunity will prevail: come for a wife as she (Mat. 15) came for her daughter, and refuse any denial, this is the way to get it: God will grant it you, rather than be wearied (and yet he loves it) with importunity. Either God will hear you, or else give you a reason which shall satisfy you: which I add because I believe that exceedingly good marriage is not good for some that seek it; it would puff them up and hurt them; they rather need exercising marriages. But know this God will not part with his jewels so easily, as not to be sought to for them: this blessing is like to that, Ezek. 36, which the Lord so promised to give his people, as yet he would be sought too by them for it. Commit your way to Jehovah, and he shall effect it. If your wife is to you as Samuel was a son to Hannah, a wife of prayer, you may the more rejoice in her, and say with Jacob, *Lo the wife which the Lord in mercy has given his servant.* To the pure all are pure: each gift is sanctified by prayer: else, if you do only happen well by accident, as Nabal upon Abigail, she shall be but a dry morsel to you, without savor or favor: you shall find her as he did, a snare to you, a helpless helper (God depriving you of the staff of bread, the true good of a good wife) not only a dry pit, but even an increase of your judgment. It is said Abraham called Eliezer his servant in this weighty business of choosing a wife for his son Isaac, bidding him to put his hand under his thigh (a solemn adjuration) for assurance that he would not choose him a heathen wife, but one of Terah's family (the best which then could be had, though not as it ought) beyond the river. How much more ought you to put your hand under the Lord's, in this case of your own marriage, vowing, that if he will provide a Rebecca for you, and make your voyage prosperous, you will discern as real a providence as Eliezer saw in meeting of her at the well. Is there not a wife for you (said the parents of Sampson) but you must go among the uncircumcised? Vow it, that if God will entrust you with one that is religious, although another should be laid against her, yet your lodestone would

pray hard for good marriage: pay and pray too.

Mat. 15.28

Ezek. 36.end

Psal. 37.5
1 Sam. 1.27
Gen. 33.5
Tit. 1.15

1 Sam. 25.1

Judg. 14.3

draw the former.

Duty 5.
Advice of the
most judicious
and impartial
friends requi-
site for good
marriage.

  Fifthly, add hereto the advice of the most judicious and impartial friends that you can come by: for though two eyes are too few, yet he that will advise in this case must only judge with one, that is, a single eye, and look but one way. Such is the subtlety of suitors nowadays that though their merit is ever so small, yet they will so go to work that their credit shall be good; hindering the truth by their interest, either in a good minister, or man of note: if they are but moral, they will engage them by gifts: if religious, by seeming devotion, to think well of them. It is sad thing to think what bad matches have been made by the mediation of the best men; being first deluded. Alas! How easy it is to make charity and credulity to be on men's sides? The best have been deceived about this business. But the third person (who neither sows nor mows by the bargain) is more fit to judge of this game than the parties are. And be assured that true intelligence is not easily come by in these interblending days: yet, as I have

John 15.14,15

said, you have a promise that God will hide no secret from you if you are his friend; so that you do not pervert your own way, and stumble at the offence which you lay before yourself:

1 Sam. 16.6

to think with erring Samuel that the anointed of the Lord is before him, when it is no such thing, but your carnal conceit. We easily believe that to be, which we would have to be. The judgment of the church either is infallible in this kind, or else it is safer erring with it than hitting well without it. Great is the cozenage of dissembling parties when they set themselves to sale by religious semblance. Machiavelli's maxim is all in all, namely soundness of religion is difficult to be had, and quits not the cost in the world's esteem: shows are easy, and will serve the turn even as well. Hence it is that few walk humbly and plainly, most are content with shows. As that scholar of Cambridge said, If I may get my degree, I have that I came for; let learning go where it will: so these, I am now upon sale hill, if I am once sold, I have enough. And I should offend many honest hearts if I should discover what I know touching the humors of some malcontents in this kind, especially of the female sex, basely pretending that their conscience is the ground, whereas it is but a decoy, serving to twist themselves into some good opinion for marriage: whereas, their turns not

being served, but their ends crossed, they have betrayed themselves in their colors to be but counterfeits. A spirit for the
present time is needful in this discerning work; therefore let
inquisition be narrow and wise, among them that are neither
nearest the blood, nor to the advantage, by such a match.

Sixthly, be very observant and careful in your mutual
discussions together to mark the spirits of each other, having
first begged of God an understanding heart. The ear (says Eli-
hu) tries words, as the furnace does metals; the fool believes
everything, but the wise ponder sayings. So do you. And as
I said of the help of other men's eyes and wits: establish your
thoughts by counsel, for in the multitude of counsellors there
is peace: so I say to yourselves, trust not so to others, as to
put and dash out your own eyes and brains; but consult with
wisdom's oracle, and ask it of him who gives and upbraids not.
There is a spirit in man, but the inspiration of the Almighty
gives understanding: as Paul says, the spiritual man judges of
all things, and is judged of none: so here; only add this, they
who have been very wise in and for others, yet in their own
case, and this of affection especially, have failed much; and the
proverb is verified here, once, all men have doted. Put difference therefore between smooth words and neat passages of
wit, or conceits that come only from the brain, and between
sound grounds planted in the heart. Out of the abundance of
the heart the mouth will speak, to a wise hearer. It is hard for
a barren heart to dissemble fruitfulness, or for a well-seasoned
to seem unsavory. Question each with other, not concerning
persons, but things: not about preachers or sermons, or duties of religion, or circumstances only of abuses and corruptions of time: (for who is not up to the ears in this nowadays?)
but concerning the real work of the Word by name, how the
law has quelled a proud heart, and stopped the course thereof
in evil: how it is brought so low and to such a tameness, as
to crouch to God for the crumbs that fall from his table: to
be low in herself, and lay aside all her ornaments, glad to be
equal to them of low degree, and the like. Look not at the
gifts of each other, but try whether a mean opinion of ourselves increases as knowledge increases: ask each other, what
the nature of a promise is, wherein the nature and life of faith
consists. Also, how faith purifies the heart, kills the strongest

Duty 6.
Observing the
spirits of each
other, meet for
such as would
marry in the
Lord.
Job 34.3
Prov. 15.22
Jam. 1.5
Job 32.8
1 Cor. 2.15

Exod. 33.6

Rom. 12.16

Acts 14.15

Prov. 17.24

Objection.
Answer.

lusts and passions, quickens the heart by a principle to all holiness, meekness, patience, and mercy to the distressed, and
sorrow for the sins of others. If these seeds are planted in the
spirit, they will subdue it unto God; indeed, they will set a
new frame within, and make the countenance to shine. And
whereas it is objected, few can so fully satisfy themselves in
the degrees of each other's grace. I answer. Try the substance,
and let degrees appear in time, it is well if grace in youth can
creep, though it cannot go (though the more advanced it is the
better). If in the lack of great measure, yet the savor of these
things break forth out of the cloud; and where bashfulness and
modesty is the veil to cover some graces, their uncomely parts
are clothed with the more honor. I know no better care-marks
to choose good couples by than humility and modesty. Despise not a little, if these two are present, for as the prophet
says, there is a blessing in it. Observe also how providence
sways your minds to or against each other; observe each other's disposition, parts, natural guises, and behavior; that which
one thinks comely another distastes, and some disproportion
and unsympathetic herein may cause religion to be meanly
thought of. And to end, remember that this business borders
much upon the outward man; beware therefore that neither
outward defects do weaken, nor their abilities do prevent your
judgment either way, from the due weighing of the best things
in the balance, here or there. Slight defects will soon be supplied by religion, where love is entire, but want of religion is
not easily recompensed with externals: be wise not to stumble
too much at the former; neither let heat of affection snare and
deceive you in the latter. So much for the means to be used for
marrying in the Lord.

Conclusion
of this second
duty.

The man has
the leading
hand, there-
fore ought to
be wary.
Women woo-
ers threatened
with woe.

And to this issue pertains all this discourse: therefore
still I so conclude as I began. And because no bad marriage
befalls any, where the husband's sin is not chief, either because
he is bad or errs in judging the wife (the woman having only
a refusing voice, not a choosing, but the man having the prerogative of choice as the leader of the business). Therefore let
the man especially look to himself. It is not for the modesty of
the woman's sex to play the suitor, to put forth herself towards
the man, but to wait till God offer her an object of consideration: and I seldom have noted matches very successful in

this kind. I remember the answer of a wise man to a gentle-woman, which told him, she could love him before any man: he answered her, but of all others, I dare not venture upon you for my wife. He considered that such pangs in that humorous sex cannot come from judgment, because they thwart an ordinance: and as a sudden torrent of passion or heat causes them, so they suddenly fall as fast, and leave the channel dry: when the humor is over, then cool blood succeeds, and checks the party for rashness, works a dislike of the choice, and a very indifferent spirit to the husband; thinking him to be too mean for them; and so little joying in him, waxing dark, and far from that sweet temper of amity and subjection which a wife should demonstrate. Therefore you husbands be not deceived with easy matches; they are not so easy to relinquish as to get: the furthest way about is the nearest way home. There is a pleasantness in show, to be fancied by a woman, to be offered that estate which I could never have expected: but when all is said that can be, it is too easy to prove happy: what it may prove I cannot say, but since it is not of God, and is against the modesty of that sex, I can see no great hope of it. I end my counsel with a two-fold question. One is this: if (say some) we wait until these choice marriages are offered to us, we may wrong our hopes, passing the time of our virginity and youth vainly away. To whom I say (I speak to none in this kind save to the religious; let the rest move in their own sphere) commit your way to Jehovah and he will effect it. Where there is truth of grace, it cannot lie hid; some way or other the Lord shall provide, and the labor of your love shall not be concealed: fear not the world's fears, cry not a confederacy, where they cry it; but wait, and there will always be some men who will be as jealous as women, to plunge themselves into a cross marriage, as glad of you as you of him: it is a reciprocal case, and he who believes makes no more haste than good speed. Your worth shall break out as the light, and your patience and modesty as the noonday.

Another question is, where should we go to find out such? For we see the families of such as had name of religion, are now degenerate and empty of such choice. None do more degenerate to pride, vanity, and profaneness than the children of many ministers and professors, which have been religious;

Marginal notes:

Touching marrying in the Lord: three questions answered.
1. Question answered.
Psal. 37.5

1 Pet. 3.15

Psal. 37.6

2. Question answered.

truly, many towns anciently of note for such, yet are now become as barren as any other. To whom I answer: when the
people came and told Samuel that his children walked not in
his ways, it was not so much from any offence at their sin, as
for their own ends, to make them a king. Many upbraid good
families because they are willing to refuse them, and to look
elsewhere. I am sure that families are not so lacking of good
matches as the good matches who are in them are disregarded. But further, it is true, God's rules are slighted in all places
nowadays, and religion was never thicker sown, nor come up
thinner than now. What wonder, if sin carry this duty down
the stream of contempt, as well as others? Yet I say, religion is
gone quite out of all families. Though it is entailed to no one,
yet cannot free grace plant itself where it desires? If it leaves
one, can it not choose another? Religion (for all I see) may lie
long enough, except excess of portion smell her out. Oh! Follow not the stream, conform not to the fashion of this world:
God is tied to no places, families, or congregations, he is no
accepter of persons; but in all places where his name is feared
and called upon, there will he bless. Such shall not need to
distrust God: he makes none a son of Abraham, but he makes
a daughter of Abraham also meet for him. Use means to find
them out, and having so done, prefer pearls before pebbles,
and the Lord shall bring the good to the good, for he is a God
of order, not of confusion.

Question 3.   But will some say, perhaps we have found out a jewel,
but it is in a dunghill: a good husband or wife, but the parents
bad, the kindred bad, and no encouragement to proceed. I
answer: as a bad wife is never the better because graced with a
good: so neither ought a choice either wife or husband be too
much sullied by a bad family. It is their ill lot to be so, but that
grace that made Lot eminently good, Noah excellently righteous in their sinful times, does even more abundantly requite
that blemish, with the select religion of someone among them.
I blame no man, if with a good wife he would be glad to marry
to a good family and stock: but in another respect, I would account that grace which is unstained with so much ill, being in
the midst of it, more approved and tried with the touchstone
than that which grows up together with the grace of a family,
for company. It is some grace to a lily to grow among thorns;

1 Sam. 8.5

Acts 10.34

1 Cor. 14.33

Gen. 7.1
Gen. 19.1

and a rose looks the more beautiful among thistles: contraries set one against another, are the more orient. I should not refuse a truly virtuous companion for the cause. And this is said of the second main rule, for such as are upon entrance of marriage. I go to the third.

The third duty concerns the two parties, after their contract, namely to spend that space between it and marriage (as a more due and solemn season) for a preparation of themselves to the estate and conversation of marriage to come. But because I foresee that the reader will expect that somewhat be said in this treatise touching a contract: I will therefore suspend this third advice till I come to that argument in the fifth chapter, at the end thereof. Thus much for this chapter.

The third duty: preparation between the contract and the marriage, necessary.

CHAPTER III

The second requisite unto a good entrance, which is aptness or suitableness.

The second
general for
entrance is to
marry aptly.

Now then I come to the second general thing, pertinent to good entrance, and that is, to marry aptly in the Lord; that is, to join all circumstances of equality and suitableness to religion. And in this (as I conceive) as well as the former, consists the entry upon a happy and honorable marriage. It is not for nothing that the Lord brought Adam a meet helper for him; that is, not only one created in the same image of holiness as he; but made of himself, flesh of his flesh, and bone of his bone: woman of man, equal to him in dignity; not of his head, nor his feet or lower parts, but of his sides and ribs, in token of one that was to side with him and agree with him in the married estate. The apostle uses a phrase about husband and wife, which is translated in this manner, *For that which is comely.* The original word is an equal siding, or sitting close to the side, with comeliness: so should it be with the married. There should be such an aptness in the choice (so far as may be) that the one might seem to be a true fellow in the yoke, well met (as we say) and suitable each to other. Hence marriage is called a match to signify that couples should be peers, and like each other, true matches. Otherwise, a manifest disproportion causes not only a fulsomeness in the judgment of others, but to the affections of each other. And this the Lord would have us take notice of, as foreseeing the inevitable inconveniences, which must follow upon mismatched couples. Cattle of uneven size and stature, strength and proportion draw very poorly in one yoke, and untowardly. This I add, lest any should mistake my former speech, namely that religion is the true level of all other inequalities. I meant this, that if it is the lot of any to enter marriage unequally then there being religion to moderate, it will make a better level than any other thing can when religion is absent. I did not justify inequality but accommodate it, when it is. Here I add moreover, that

1 Cor. 7.35

when other conditions and respects are unequal in any great degree, religion can do no more than she can do. Marriage consists of a carnal piece one way, as well as a religious another way; and we may say of it as of the belly, she has no ears. When I say, the inequality of couples is apparent, it is as the clashing of a glassy body against a grosser metal. When a poor party meets with a rich, a well-bred one with a rude and illiberal, a courteous with a froward, a bountiful with a miserly, a noble with a base; one from the court with another from the cart or the shop; a proper and personable with a deformed, crooked, or dwarf, what a disproportion does it cause, and a kind of loathsomeness? We say of the same body that it is an uncomely sight to behold a sweet face and a crooked back: if it is such a jar in the same, how much more in two persons, who can better view each other behind and before than the same eye can see her own crookedness? But especially when two religious ones meet, the one whose disposition lies on the left and to forwardness, melancholy, sullenness, and peevishness in an eminent degree; the other's is to meekness, courtesy, and amiableness; what a continual vexation is it? What a discord of sounds does this cause? An instrument out of tune, unapt to play upon, distempers each lesson, and displeases every ear.

But here arises a question, how we shall judge of unaptness? None are so unapt, but they can allege one thing or other for themselves. Old women marrying young men, justify themselves by this, that they will maintain their husbands, and that shall make up the flaw, and levels that valley. Deformed ones marrying fair or personable allege they are penny white: and kitching-maids marrying gentlemen may say that they are good nurses, and deny themselves as much another way. To all which I answer and affirm that none provide for the honor of marriage except those who provide against the stain and dishonor of unapt marriage. And yet I must add that when I urge aptness, I urge it not in so arithmetical and strict a proportion, and in every point of aptness, as if else it might be no marriage. There is a dissimilitude in the same kind, which is no disproportion in a diverse kind: and there is a discord of tones in the most exact music, making it most pleasing, because still it is within the kind. I judge not one unequal to another in birth because the fashion of the one is a

Question. Who are unapt?

Answer.

little lower; but by disproportion of degree, when gentle marry base; noble, honorable, worshipful marry ignoble, and under themselves in the whole kind. Else, as the roundness of the each recompenses this or that particular unevenness; so may marriage level petty inequalities. And to this, that inequality does not always follow some contrarieties of temper, except they are such as infer a natural distaste of each other: as for

Exceptions against the rule of general aptness, many.

example, nothing hinders why there may not be sweet accord between a very provident wife matched with an improvident husband, when the husband counts that gift a supply of his defect; because it is only a defect in accident or quality, not real. Difference also in estates may cause a kind of necessity of disproportion. It falls out that some impair or crack of brain lessens the repute of a gentleman well descended; this disables his hopes of any great marriage. Shall one defect infer a worse, a deprival of marriage wholly? No verily, a woman much inferior to him in birth and means, or years, should yet be thought a very good, truly apt match for such a one, and that with reputation and honor to her humility if she is faithful. Again, a man has by a former venture a great charge of children, which are like to lay upon the hand of a second wife, both for education and attendance; in such a case, a woman of a hundred or two hundred pounds worth, who is willing to requite that defect with love and painfulness (being otherwise competent for her honest parentage and fashion of life) may be as equal a match as perhaps one of a thousand pound estate without that encumbrance. Again, in the judgment of men, defect of honor may sometimes be recompensed with wealth and estate: as if a man nobly descended, yet grown to mean estate, has need of such a supply, though perhaps he fail of some degree of the other: I say, if both concur, it is best; but if the defect does lie in honor, it may be equaled with estate; and it is a shame for honor to quarrel with such a wife for inequality; for then may she say, she has bought her honor at a sad rate and upon dear terms.

More exceptions.

Besides, it falls out that two marry, the one a man whom present honor and favor with his prince has advanced beyond the rank of his family; or perhaps, honor has gone along with swifter pace toward him than with some other house, who yet may be as honorable in times past, and more ancient than they are presently, though not with such titles: if now the one match with the other, shall present honor contest with such a one as inferior? Certainly not; if the root is as good, the match is not unequal. Lastly, in case of persecution for religion, or of going voyages of hazard by sea to foreign plantations: in which cases, strict equality is not to be mentioned. Now in such cases, the woman being to fly or transplant, needs the aid of a wise head, or the man the help of a discreet woman. They cannot match themselves in their due ranks, as otherwise they might; therefore looking at the main point, that is, at religion and integrity of report, they match as near their condition as may be: although it proves very much inferior, yet it is not to be counted a dishonorable marriage. Master Fox in the story of Queen Mary's persecution reports of a worthy religious Duchess of Norfolk, which married to a godly gentleman, one Master Berty, (far under a duke's state) with whom she fled the land, and in that most wearisome flight (as it proved) found him a most faithful and loyal husband to the death. So then, if there is a general proportion of aptness so that the disparity lies only in a degree, not in kind, it must not be censured: all cannot lie under the equator, under the same line and latitude; some may admit many degrees off. The truth is, in this confusion of all things, it is not to be expected that marriage should keep quarter with exactness more than other circumstances of life: in some cases we must abate and yield of rigor, lest we split all. Men are grown to enhance their degree to a higher pitch than formerly; and it will be hard to convince high stomachs of means or inequality; their ambition has too high a pitch. Those persons are fitter to observe this rule, who are mean in their own eyes, and equal themselves to those of lower degree. To leave them therefore with their great hearts and hopes, let me yet yoke them with Paul's counsel: whatsoever is pure, honest, just, and of good report that ensue; abhor that which is base, uncomely, and absurd. But if it appears to the judicious that your carnal, covetous reaches and aspiring spirits have exercised themselves in things too high, for ambition, state, or worldly ends; let the issue be what it may (as commonly it is repenting) I pronounce such matches to fall under this second rule's censure; they are unapt, therefore dishonorable.

Phil. 4.8

Psal. 131.1

Use 1.
Instruction.
No curiosity to
marry aptly.

I come to the uses of the point. If the honor of marriages stands partly in aptness of it, then hence it appears that it is no curiosity for any to regard aptness. Men count this direction to be frivolous; imagining that marriage has a gift of itself, either to find equals, or to make such (as the old proverb speaks of friends) and to wash off at once all eyesores; furthermore, it will be hard for such to fray away sorrow, and so shall you say when you have tried. One would have thought Pharaoh might easily have kept out frogs from his privy-chamber,

Exod. 8.3

but it would not be. I dare promise none of the most equal marriages that they shall be free; but as for humors, rashness, base and by-respects, they never did so find it. Those that catch up wives all at once suddenly must repent them at leisure. Be instructed then to think no care sufficient in this

Judg. 21.23

kind; stay not till mistress Experience convinces you of your folly, in condemning others, but falling into the pit yourselves. So much for this first.

Use 2.
Admonition against
thinking too
highly of our
own strength,
in unapt marriage.

Secondly, be admonished not to think too highly of your own strength, as thinking it sufficient to bind bears (as the proverb is) and to defray any unaptness whatsoever without trouble. Oh, says one, let but my turn be satisfied, and fear not me; if I have once pitched my affection, I am not so soon unsettled again. Alas, you judge yourselves by your present pangs, which overbear inferior dislikes; but who are weaker to digest inequality than such as think themselves wisest and strongest? Many have said as you say, If I may have state sufficient, no bodily blemish shall trouble me. Another, If I can get a religious wife, one hundred pounds will content me as well as three. If I may marry one whom I love, I care not for portion, etc. But alas poor green heads, before a few years are over your heads, when you have scummed off and licked up the upper sweet of your marriages then your thoughts will go to work, I have deserved portion, and religion, and beauty too; and what not. Then will your wandering eye fasten upon others, whom you see to exceed you in portion, birth, sweetness of nature, feature, and the like; then your carnal part will lower and vex at your lot, and then you will say, Oh, I might have been wiser; and so you must either bite in all as ashamed of your choice, or else utter your discontent, to make your lives uncomfortable. When you behold your parents to wax estranged, your kindred aloof, your means decaying, charge increasing, and the Devil throwing in baits of such and such men and women, so personable, rich, and brought up then will it appear upon wise terms, you have rejected the counsel of apt marriage: and yet many fools (who are appointed to it) cannot beware the second time, but rush themselves into as unmeet matches as before, if not worse. Therefore acknowledge your weakness, hearken no more to such spokesmen as are apt to prompt you with wives of their own fancying: (which is the ruin of many ridiculous men, to take wives upon other men's trust) ascribe not too much to your own wisdom; rather think yourselves of all others, most likely to be deceived by your eye or affections. Say thus, A man I am, and but a man, and nothing of a man is strange to me. I am as like to snare myself, and as unable to endure a snare as another, therefore I will prevent it early. I embrace God's allowance, as well to please myself with aptness, as with religion: God is the God of order, as well as goodness. Nothing hinders why other accomplishments may not be sought with grace, (so that is chief) and it had need please well, which must please ever, or be an eyesore forever. Surely, if God gives me my liberty, I dare not snare myself. And I see that as there are many wives, who for want of religion are a snare; so there are also many religious, who for want of other accommodations make every vein in their husband's hearts to ache before they die. You are not made of brass, but of flesh, as others are, and have affections equally disposed to the like distempers: it is your wisdom to know yourself.

And surely, he who would but weigh the odious fruits of unequal marriages might easily be drawn from them. What an imputation is it for a minister, young in years, to match himself with some old woman for what she has? How meanly is his discretion esteemed; and how basely does his covetousness hear always after? How should such a man persuade others to trust God, when all men see the bastard of his own unbelief carried at his back? What vile affections are bred in secret in many such, desire of the death of their companions being grown decrepit; irksomeness of spirit, in tedious bearing the sickliness, unhelpfulness, and unsociableness of each other's bodies? How many have we known, who being discontent with their lot, seek to other younger ones, and defile

Terror to affecters of unequal matches.

them: some within their own dwellings, polluting themselves
with their servants? How many murders have unequal matches caused, of infants so begotten and born? Moreover, how
many have been the cursed attempts of poisoning each other,
to be rid of the loathed party, husband or wife? What one as-
size passes without such precedents? I do not know any one
thing in the conversation of man which causes more disasters
than unequal matches do, directly or indirectly. Some being
ashamed of their foolish choice care not what they attempt to
be eased of them. Others crossed of that lust, which (like the
belly) has no ears, and will not be curbed, will venter any joint
to satisfy it: and to say truth, no tongue of man can sufficiently
express the misery of spirit (which many, otherwise not of
the worst) do endure, through conflicting with their own ill
lots and corrupt spirits in this kind: and the wearisomeness
of inequality in one kind forces them to as bad in another.
Men's first wives being forty years elder than themselves, when
they have buried them, partly through eager desire of posterity, partly longing after the other extreme, marry a wife forty
years younger, and so are lashed with their own whip; and as
much loathed by the latter, as they loathed the former. Fools,
to shun one extreme, incur another.

<table>
<tr><td>

Use 3.
Reproof.

Branch 1.

Corruption al-
ways affects a
contrariety to
the ordinance.

Prov. 30.23

</td></tr>
</table>

Thirdly, let this be reproof to the unruly humors of
many persons, either in first or second matches, which always aim at that which is most contrary to their conditions. I
have noted that if there are any apparent defects in a man or
a woman, they are so far from humbleness under it, or giving
themselves content in such as are defective in the like, or other
kinds (which yet is equal) that rather they itch after and covet
such yokefellows as do exceed as much on the contrary, and
are of the best perfections. How ordinary is it for men to affect better than they deserve, to cover their own defects and
to satisfy their lusts? And how wearisome does it prove? For
as Solomon says: The earth cannot bear the burden of unequal
marriages, as of one that is heir to her mistress, that is, upstarts
become impotent and insolent, scorning to take it as they have
done. On the other side, he who takes an inferior party thinks
that she should pay for her preferment, and become so much
the more subject and dutiful. Now when both parties find it
otherwise, namely that the one waxes proud, and the other

thinks himself neglected, what a confusion grows hereby? Moreover, such poison I have noted to break out of some baser parties in marriage that because they are privy to themselves of inequality, therefore they are jealous of their husband's respect and love, think themselves despised, as not worthy to hold quarter with them, and when there is of all other least cause, yet then come they in with their irksome suspicions and they imagine their husbands to show more affection to strangers than themselves. Now equality would remove such misprisions. But to return, why should a country plain man, affect the neatness of a nice citizen, or a crooked person affect a person eminent for comeliness? Is not a country woman bred for a farm, more equal? Is it not better like went to like, that so neither might despise the other? Why should a low bred one affect a brave gallant or a poor one a wealthy? Why should a meek and gentle one defile himself with a shrewish spirit? Is it not the next way to sorrow? Does not unaptness cause a division at last? Therefore this is a fruit of old Adam, to covet most ardently that which is forbidden unto us, and against us. What folly and sin is out of measure sinful, if this is not? And who pities such as plunge themselves into misery, and need not? It is a kind of delight (in the obliquities of men, who no other can punish) to see fools to punish themselves, and lash themselves with their own rod, it satisfies indignation, (where charity abounds not) but deserves no compassion. Do not such sigh in secret (for their complaints are but rare to others because the error comes back upon themselves) and wish they had married as deformed, as poor and meanly bred as themselves. Do they not envy the easy and welfare that equal couples enjoy, such as make much of each other by the sympathy of each other's defectiveness or parity.

Another branch of reproof concerns them that despise the rule of equal matches. Now what comes of these unequals, that widows of estates must marry their horse-keepers, and gentlemen their cook-maids, but this, that to cover over their baseness, they must lay out their means to buy arms and titles of honor: or if not, yet enhance their farms, raise their rents, rake and scrape all they can get (whereas their predecessors lived nobly upon their means and kept good houses) and all to purchase estate, and purchase equality. What is this, save

Branch 2. Reproof. Contemners of equal marriages reproved.

to become the scorns of the country? Is it not due penance for violating the sacred condition of equality? I might here inveigh against the usual matches nowadays made between boys and girls, scarce yet out of their shells: but better occasion will offer itself afterward.

But to draw towards an end, let me exhort first such as are to enter into this estate; to whom I sing the former song, *Marry in the Lord*, still, but marry aptly, and lay the ground of honor in this entering with aptness. Be not led away with that error, which you set up as an idol in your conceits: bless not yourselves with your supposed happiness, as if you were by so much the more honorable than others of your rank by how much you have gotten a richer match than they; or because your marriage has perked you aloft, above your own condition, or theirs, or of whom you descend. No wise parents joy in their children's unequal marriages: let the model of such as are the most modest in your rank and order, be precedents for you. I am not so weak as to think that education, breed, learning, and gifts (although there is no great means) deserve not good marriages, religion concurring: but set not up your top-sails, and do not bear up yourselves above your worth, in this respect; but wait upon God, and be modest, lest he pull you down as fast. Dwell at home, affect not high things; if God has indeed a blessing for you in this kind (for else a great match may prove too hot and too heavy to manage) let God lay it in your lap, before you affect it, and let your goodness find you out, while you lie hid. And when it is offered you, yet swell not, say with David marrying Michal, *Seemeth it small? Had I not need to look well about me?* And with Abigail sent for to David, *Let me wash the feet of the servants of my Lord!* Go from the dignity to the burden, take thought how to live with such a one of greater breed and estate than yourselves: consider what affronts may meet with you (the best will save itself). Are you fit to drink of this bitter cup, if discontents should come into the place of peace and love, while the one is loath to stoop to the other's lowness, and the other fears offence if he should suffer it? Better it is to desist early than to bring a perpetual vexation upon yourselves too late: beg of God humble and wise demeanor, even all inequality by religious carriage, and self-denial lest your preferment prove a

Use 4. Exhortation. Affecters of unequal marriages learn to be wiser.

Rom. 12.16

1 Sam. 18.23
1 Sam. 25.41

Mat. 20.22

penalty rather than a privilege; otherwise, as he said of his diadem, he would not have it for the taking up (as being fuller of care than comfort) who knew the sorrow of it.

Secondly, to them who already live under this yoke of inequality, I advise the same which I did to them who are under an inequality of religion; look back to that section and read it. Only this let me add here; since your unsuitableness came from your own willfulness; do that now which you ought before to have done (somewhat out of season perhaps, but better late than never) humble yourselves under God's afflicting hand; remember it is unjust you should fret against providence, and your lot in that, which out of your own choice and free-will, you have brought upon yourselves. Keep to yourselves that straightness and pinching, which is only or chiefly known to yourselves. To live like malcontents, upbraiding each other, and quarreling with God is not only most sinful, but a disease worse than the remedy itself: seeing the time was, wherein you seemed to each other the most precious of all; it is reason that now you make the best of a bad bargain, and of each other. If then beauty, wealth, or the like objects so blurred your eyes that you forgot the rule of equality, remember you have sinned not only against your own souls, but even against them whom you have unequally married, who in another equal way, might perhaps have lived much better and more content than now they do; with companions of their own fashion: so that you should doubly wrong them by your discontents. Rather look up to God by faith and repentance for your error that it may be covered, and that God's anger being removed, you may find your yoke as tolerable as an unequal one may be. And as once a grave man said to one in this case, if God ever offers you a new choice, beware least you stumble at the stone which once foiled you. And so much of this second general also, and of the whole direction serving for the entrance into an honorable marriage; now we proceed to that which remains in the next chapter.

Branch 2. Counsel to such as are already unaptly married.

Jam. 4.10

CHAPTER IV

A digression touching consent of parents, and sundry
questions and objections answered.

Occasion of
this digres-
sion.
For handling
of consent of
parents, and a
contract.

Consent
of parents
necessary for
marriage, and
why.

I should now proceed to the second general head, whereof
I made an honorable marriage to consist: namely continuance therein in a holy manner. But I am occasioned to stop
my course a while, for the space of this, and the next chapter
because a hint of new matter being offered in the former discourse, touching consent of parents, and the contracting of
the couples: it will be looked for that somewhat is here said
about both before I wade any further in this argument. Of the
former thereof in this fourth, and of the latter (if God please)
in the fifth, and then we return. Touching this former, consent
of parents, if I should go about to make any set proofs of so
generally a confessed truth, which all ages, nations, histories,
laws both divine and human, common, civil, and even canon
too (though with exception) with one voice have affirmed: I
might seem not only to add light to the sun, but to weaken
that which I would strengthen: yet for order and form's sake,
a word or two may be premised for the necessity thereof, I
say necessity in a way of God, though not absolute: for this
business of marriage without parents' consent is one of them,
which ought not to have been done, yet being done, must
avail, for the avoiding of worse consequences. That is, consent
is not so essential to marriage as some other things are, that
the non-concurrence thereof should disannul it again. But
in a moral and meet way, it is necessary that marriage is attempted with consent of parents. And surely, if those heathen
laws seemed just which yielded unto parents power of life and
death over their children (supposing perhaps that love might
well enough be trusted) and thought it meet enough that they
who were the instruments of giving children their natural life,
might be permitted to be judges of the same children, in taking it away; or perhaps rather choosing that a parent might
kill a vicious child for some offences than the child kill the

heart of a parent by his dissoluteness: then surely much more may it be yielded to parents to have power to give life or to mar their marriages. I do not, by the way, justify the former law, but rather think it was a dangerous snare and betrayed the lives of many innocents into the hands of the unmerciful; and no doubt, if it were in force among us, it would provoke many profane and malicious persons to shed the blood of better children than themselves. But I plead the far greater equity of this law, that parents may claim a right in the choice of their children's marriages. Must parents have the worst of it, and be debarred from the best? Bear the burden of the whole day; the providing for their children, all means of support, education, either ingenuous or mechanical, help them to arts, stocks, and trades, which is but to be their drudges, if there is no more but so; and shall they leave them just at the point of marriage, and betake them to their own wisdom and counsel? Certainly not, it is good cause that they share in the honor, as well as the labor.

It is true, God makes matches, and parents cannot (as they desire) in such a world as this is (wherein all are for their own ends) provide for their children such contentful matches as they desire, but that is not their fault. God must help, or else they cannot, with the barn and winepress. But yet in such matches as are offered, parents must bear sway and stroke with their children: though it is not in their power to afford them such as they wish, yet this must not cause them to give up their authority to their children to marry as they desire, against rules mentioned. And that which I say of parents themselves, I say of father or mother-in-laws, guardians, and tutors, who by them, or by the law, are left to oversee and order the ways of children, not yet able to guide themselves; even though they are of such years and discretion as perhaps a parent, at least a step-father, might permit them to themselves. Yet it is the duty of such a child to take less rather than more upon himself, and to advise seriously with them (before he finishes the obligation) whether he has been well guided or not about marrying religiously, or aptly. Some parents, I grant, have exceedingly wasted their title and infringed their prerogative: for, such is their ignorance and injudiciousness in such affairs (having in truth never understood, in any degree, what their own mar-

Parents cannot do as they would in matching of their children.

Guardians and governors are to look to their orphans, as well as parents to children, in point of marriage.

riage meant, much less are fit to guide others). Also many are
so vicious and so debauched with sin that they have lost all
ability to advise, either in this, or in any other weighty business; but yet neither are these to be despised, but to be honorably handled, and especially if they shall desire to see and
judge with other men's eyes and brains; their children are to
yield thereto as well as to themselves. What special reports do
the Scriptures make of that care which holy and wise parents
had of their children's marriages? How did Abraham adjure
his servant to go to the house of his fathers, to choose a wife
for Isaac? How does the Holy Ghost brand Esau for matching
without the consent of Isaac and his mother Rebecca, to the
heartbreak of them? How does Isaac and Rebecca charge Jacob to meddle with none of the heathens? And, if any prerogative might have exempted any, then might Sampson, a judge
in Israel, have been exempt: who yet was not. For although it
came from God that he should marry that uncircumcised Phi-
listine; yet he would have his parents give their consent, Give
me her: and when they saw the way of God, they ceased. But
until then they argued as parents should do. What? Is there
no wife to be chosen for you out of any of the families of Israel,
but you must seek among the Philistines? Not so much as
Hagar that bond woman, but it is said that she took a wife for
Ishmael out of the land of Egypt: as if the Holy Ghost should
take it for granted that none of the church should question
it. If a son might not alienate his father's goods, without his
consent, there least of all himself.

I say, the Scripture testifies from the beginning that
this authority did reside in the parent, from God. God himself
the father of Adam, Luke. 3.38, brought Eve to him; he did not
seek her himself. A great and leading ground to the point.
And this prerogative God derived to parents (notwithstanding the fall and forfeit of Adam) forever. See Deut. 7.3. You
shall not take to your sons any wife of their daughters. Jerem.
29.6. Give your children wives. And Paul, He who gives his
virgin to marriage does well, etc. Neither is it sufficient which
Bellarmine, (the chief Papist of all who opposes this truth in
his 19. cap. of Matrimony, and that out of the Council of Trent,
Session 14. for most of other Papists do oppose him in it) re-
plies, that this text only implies, marriages ought not to be

See these texts:
Deut. 7.3
Jer. 29.6
Gen. 24.3,4
Exod. 22.17

Judg. 14.2

Verse 3,4

Gen. 21.21

Further proof
of the point.

made without the knowledge of parents: for God's charge does not only show what ought to be done, but that else the marriage is frustrate, as appears in Exod. 22.17. Where it is left to the parent to deny marriage in a case of uncleanness, which else urged marriage. Much more so then in a calm and undisturbed situation. See also Numb. 30.4. If a parent might frustrate a vow to God, much more a private civil act of his child to marry. Neither is this meant (as Bellarmine dreams) of a maid under years, but simply of one under covert: though of twenty years old: and so the Hebrew word *Nagnar* is taken Job. 1.19, and so another Jesuit upon this text confesses, a parent might frustrate any vow whatsoever. See Gal. 4. A son differs not from a servant, being under his father: he can dispose of nothing in the house, of his father's goods, without consent: how much less himself, who is the foundation of the family as the Hebrew word *Ban* notes? Another Papist, Espencaeus in his book of clandestine marriages professes the like against Bellarmine in the last chapter save one. Heathens have constantly been of this mind. Gen. 34. Shechem craves of Hamor to get him Dinah. Catullus, Plautus, Terence, Latin poets, Sophocles a Greek one, all both comedy and tragedy, who speak the customs of their times do intimate the same. One of them brings in the father distasting his son for a clandestine marriage thus, Call you me your father? Need you me for a father? Have you not found out a family, a wife, and children against my mind? The son answers. I yield up myself (father) to you, impose any task, command me what you will. Will you have me divorce the wife I have? Will you have me marry or not? I will bear it as I may. Justinian shows the meaning of the civil law, *lib. 1. Instit. Tit. de Nuptiis.* Then are marriages good, when made by consent of such, as whose power they are under. It is Beza's speech, in his Tract of Polygamy and Divorces: Civil laws about necessity of parents' consent are more known, more clear, more holy, than that any man can be ignorant of them, can darken, or can abolish them. Paulus the Civilian in his Title, touching the right of marriages says, Marriages cannot consist, except all in whose power the parties are, consent. Hottoman a famous civilian speaks the same in his book of chaste marriages, part. 4. The Counsel of Eliberis mentions the judicial law of Moses, confirming it. If a damsel has bound

Cornel, a Lap.

Terent. Andr. Scen.3.

herself by oath or promise in her father's house, and he gainsay it, it is frustrate. A Canon of Basil adds, marriages otherwise made, are counted but whoredoms. I conclude with Erasmus, no Scripture, no testimony of value can be alleged against this truth. If it is asked, whether upon the father's consenting, the mother dissent from the marriage: or contrariwise what is to be said? I answer. The mother's consent makes for the better being, but the father's for the being itself thereof: for he is the head of the wife and of the family.

Use 1.
Confutation.   This may be a sufficient confutation of Bellarmine and the Council of Trent (his idol, which its likeness he so adored that against Scripture and all laws he defends it) who does so strenuously maintain the lawfulness of marriages against parents' consent, that there needs be no more to confute him than the barrenness of his own defense, in which he always returns to his old song, that though nature teach parents' right, yet, not the disannulling of marriages upon non-consent. Touching which I answer, many reasons may enforce the continuance of a thing done (especially in so weighty a case as this) which yet argues not the well doing; that is the whole question. He urges the examples of Jacob and Tobijah. Whereas the one (although sixty years old at his marriage) yet did nothing without his father and mothers consent. Tobijah (if the text were canonical) had an angel with him to guide him extraordinarily. Indeed Esau's example he may plead for it (with an ill token of what is to come) who went against Isaac and Rebecca's charge. Much good do him with it. He alleges a Decree of Clement: A son is not compelled to follow his parents' choice. Who doubts it? But, does this follow, a parent may not compel his children to marry against their will, therefore a child may marry contrary to the parents? Certainly not. That which he adds out of Ambrose, she may choose her husband, ought she not to prefer God in her choice? comes to no more than this, that a virgin has power to choose (at least to refuse her husband) but yet with parents' consent. The argument he brings from the validity of the marriage of slaves against their master's consent, and that, upon the ground of the institution and ends of marriage, is doubly answered. First, that it is true, masters cannot bar their slaves of marriage, but yet they may limit the right of nature, by appointing them wives, for avoid-

ing wrong to their own estates. Secondly, the case between master-like power is not like to parental: for the power of the former is only civil, and therefore may be restrained by law; but the other is natural, and therefore need no restraint: since it is to be supposed that parents desire the posterity and marriages of their children much more than masters need do of servants. As touching that objection, that after copulation marriages are necessary; this proves not, that the power of parents is dissolved. For what absurdity is it for one to think that his second sin should favor and justify his former offence? But that, for diverse inevitable consequences upon the breach of a marriage already made, it is better for a parent not to use his right than to use it. It is the voice of the law, *Fieri non debuit, sed factum valuit.* So much for this.

Yet as there is no rule so general, but it admits exceptions, so does this. One is, the bar of God's law, in case of uncleanness committed by the parties before marriage: in which respect God forbade that they should by any means be parted: so that here parents' consent was, though not wholly, yet partly prevented, not in right, but in point of honesty by their lewd children, who forced a necessity of marriage upon themselves, being become as outcasts, not worthy of such care of parents to be cast upon them: besides it was to prevent beggary of the bastards, and the defiling of the land by fornication, if they had been permitted to discard such as they had defiled, and to marry chaste persons: for, it is better one house is troubled, than two, (since one must be) let them eat of the fruit of their own labors, and thank themselves. The law is mentioned by Moses: *If a man finding a maid, defile her, he shall surely marry her, because he has humbled her.* Another case is, the supine neglect of parents, when as they see offers made to their children: namely, when as they permit parties unknown, and pretending to be such as afterwards they prove not, but tainted with lewd qualities, and of no such estate as is made show of: I say, when as, through foolish credulity they believe all shows, or use not means to enquire thoroughly after their manners and deserts, but are cheated by their dissembling and hypocrisy: but all this while they harbor them, or seeing that their children are forward in their affections toward such, so that they are ensnared: and yet the parents suffer

Exceptions against this general rule. Exod. 22.16

matters to pass on, and hold their peace: then the rule of the Word ought to be observed, *That consent is implied by their silence*: and why? Because he, in whose power it is to stop evil, and yet does not, seems to command it. Not only if there appear no more cause of breaking it off than at first (for then it is only the headstrong will of the parent, unjustly discontent),

but although there should break out more hideous and odious crimes against the party. For it was the parents' duty to have used all diligence to have searched out the truth of things at first, and to have made all other matters clear, before such time as liberty is given to the parties themselves to ensnare themselves. For by this means it may so fall out that extreme danger may ensue, both to the party deserted, and to them that desert. Yet this I add that all means are wisely used to unstitch and dissolve that league by degrees, which has long been in knitting, rather than to do it rashly. Let parents present to both the parties their deep dissimulation, persuading them, between themselves, rather to break off than to incur a tolerable vexation by marriage; and live at perpetual feud with them, who seek their best welfare. But, if nothing will prevail, I say, as sad as the necessity is, yet the parent comes in too late

with alleging his prerogative. If (says the Holy Ghost) a virgin has vowed a vow (say it is a purpose to marry such a man), much more if such a likelihood be daily presented to his eye; and he forbid it, then he does no more than his authority may claim, for he is a parent, and may disannul it: but if he lets it pass, and does not gainsay it, he is supposed to resign up his right in refusing, and so to establish it.

Another case is in second marriages of children, men, or women. For although there is a difference of judgment in sexes, yet in this both are reputed to have equal liberty to match themselves, and to be discharged from the power of the parent. The first marriage made the parties one flesh, and divided them both from the parents' house and authority. So that in such a case the rule holds not. Paul does not extend the power of a parent over a widow, as to a virgin. In the latter, he always yields to a father his liberty: if he give his virgin to marry, or refuses to give her, he does well both ways: that is, foreseeing the danger of persecution, and with knowing the

strength of his virgin, that she is not necessitated to marry, he may refuse, or otherwise he may yield; he offends in neither. But after one marriage is expired, the widow is not so tied, because providence has settled her upon her own right. Howbeit, for the weaker sex, the case so falling out that she may stand in as much need of counsel at last as at first, indeed of more. This I say that it were the part of such widows to remember that they are children, and to ascribe a reverential and honorable esteem of their parents' counsel, out of wisdom and discretion, although a precise command of God does not absolutely urge it.

Lastly, parents must still look at the main point, that is, the condition and state of a child's both body and mind. For a parent understanding the case to be such, that a child cannot without deep discontent of spirit, and inconvenience of body, propending strongly to marriage, and shunning those continual and noisome vexations, which would attend the contrary; I say, cannot abstain: then, his authority not being allowed him, for the tyranny and hurt, but the good and welfare of his child, he ought not unseasonably and rigidly to dispute his right, or to hold it; but tenderly and wisely to release it, at the child's humble instance. And this I might also press in other cases as well as this. But because they will occur better upon objections brought against this point: I will stop two gaps with one bush, that is, both lay down the extent of this exception, and also answer a question, both in one.

Parents must observe the condition of their children.

For why? Here it is objected by sundry children (as I touched before) that, as near as they can, they observing the rules of God, in religious and apt choice, and being now to strike up the match, they say, the parents or guardians (at least of one side) willfully withdraw their consent. To whom I must answer with much caution, for the safeguarding of a parent's honor. First, you children beware lest you put any unjust affront upon your parents that may cause this rigor you complain of, and open their mouths against you. For if you do, their cause must be heard when you must stand by. Suppose that it falls out that your match is not faulty, after your trial of each other: howbeit you upon the presumption thereof have been your own carvers, and carried all with your own wits, leaving your parents to serve your turn after: and hereupon the parent being offended, looks not so much at the fit-

Children's objections against parents' carelessness in thier marriages, answered.

ness of the match, as at his own contempt. Who can in such a case justify you? In this case, especially if the parents are irreligious, and unable to value the price of a good husband or wife, I see not what course you should take, but to humble yourselves for your offence, considering in your own case, how unwilling you would have been to be so served. Parents, I grant, should not only hearken to, but run and ride to seek out good matches for their children, if any occasion is offered, and yet many of them are so stout, peevish, self-willed, and envious that of all other matches, they will cross them most which are the best. But yet, you children, cross not them, by forcing unequal conditions upon parents, in consenting to your marriages. Although you are granted to be religious, yet it becomes not you to think so well of yourselves, that being unequal in state and stock, or in other respects, you will force the marriage of one that has great means, under color of religion. For in this case a parent is not bound, but has his excuse. If God should move a parent in this case, considering how few are religious or thrifty, to match their children under-foot for the world in respect of grace, it is well and good: embrace their good will thankfully. But to obtrude your own worth upon their affections, you ought not: whether the parents are religious or not. The like I say, if the disproportion lies in any other kind. This by way of digression; that children be sure of it, that their matches are consonant and agreeable to the rule; for they may be godly, and yet not apt matches. But to answer the question, as it lies, if I say your matches are truly equal, yet your parents will not yield. Then, first, let such children count it the cross that they are fallen upon such parents; let them not domineer over them, and outshoot the Devil in his own bow, of resolution and stomach; but humbly submit to the parents, as parents in general, seeking by all means to win their love and respect, first or last, by your obedience and well pleasing. That they may see it and say: My child is as careful to give me contentment, as to serve his own turn. And (if need require) let such friends be used by way of mediation, as may best allay their opposite minds, showing them the ill consequents thereof. And lastly, set on the Lord also to encounter their intractable hearts, humbly supplicating that he would turn the hearts of fathers to the children, to melt them,

Counsel to such children.

and to give them the eyes of doves, instead of crocodiles. If all these prevail not, then (the discipline of the church being in force) course ought to be taken to make complaint of such wrong, namely that a parent abuses his or her authority to hurt, and therefore implore the aide both of the church and of the magistrate, to reduce parents into due order: for they themselves must know that they are under authority, and no further made the judges over the children, than as they can answer to God for their good carriage therein. And so also to require such a child's portion from them, as in such case is fit. But, if children cannot meet with such relief, I leave them under the cross which God has cast upon them, to take it up meekly and bear it, till God ease their chain. But, if the father consent and the mother only be obstinate, they may with good conscience notwithstanding proceed, yielding all due respect to her. So much for this.

Mal. 4.end

Parents obstinate in consent, to be curbed.

Mat. 8

Mat. 16.25

Another question here moved is this. Suppose that two parties have got the affections of each other, but the father on his deathbed, dissents and forbids the marriage: is the conscience of the child absolutely so tied by those irrevocable words that he or she may not dare to attempt marriage? I answer, that child which out of an honorable respect shall wholly forbear, for fear of after scruples; or shall piously incline to forbear, doubtless they betray a very awful heart to the counsel of their parent, especially if they are convinced of an over-ruling providence determining the business. But to affirm directly, that a child is always bound to obey in such a case, I dare not. Many circumstances must be observed, next to the rule: and therefore first I shall think it fit in this business, that the parties resign up themselves to the judgment of some wise and impartial men, who (without playing the vagabond) may judge whether such a marriage is according to God or not. If not, they ought so much the rather to dissolve it, as being not only contrary to parents' will, but God's rule also. And then there is no more to be said in it: for a pious child ought not to violate such a band as this, upon any affection to the other party, or like pretense. But if the marriage is found good and equal: then ought it not to be broken off, through the parent's refusal at his death. But the will of God being conceived to be for it, the parent's will must not contradict his.

Questions about parents' consent answered.

And hereto add, that it must indifferently be enquired, first whether the parent was a man truly judicious to pronounce such a sentence? Else sure it is a deadly snare. Again whether in his life he permitted the parties to consort in ordinary, till they had won each other's heart: for in that case, his denial is doubly unjust. Especially if he has actually given consent during life, and changed it without ground. Also, whether he was not alike various in his other conversation, easily drawn to or from by small persuasion. Likewise whether he has not in other of his children's matches, been hardly drawn to consent, no real cause of his dissent appearing. Whether refusal might not proceed from some other sinister cause and not the dislike of the match itself; as from privity to his weak estate, loath to disburse much, ashamed to come short of the world's expectation for discredit's sake, or the like. If probably these things do appear, I think the bare religion of the father's last sentence ought not to prevail against more forcible reasons to the contrary: and upon the weighing of these cases, the parties ought to think that they hear the voice of God, to bear down the parents. Although the dead parent cannot alter his words yet it may be supposed he would have altered it, if he had lived, because he ought. For this so much. If any more questions arise, I will handle them in some of the uses following, which now I hasten unto. And whereas they do concern both children in point of duty and parents in point of dignity, first of the first.

Use 1. Reproof. Terror to all rebellious children, who marry against their parents' consent.

And first here is bitter reproof, even terror, to all such refractory children, as have not only digressed from, but directly transgressed against this rule. If the duty of children is so manifest, how is it that so many children do at once break through this divine edict, as great flies through cobwebs, by the stronger laws of their own wills? Do you so degenerate (O you imps) from all modesty and obedience? That whereas you might marry, not only within the rank of your education, but also of religion, and the fear of God; now through your willful contempt of parents, not only do you choose unequal husbands among stablemen and scavengers, (for these are honest trades according to their places) but to graceless ones, and such as are deservedly by-words of reproach for their swearing, drunkenness, and all profaneness. Is this a parents' requital at your hands, that when there is no other trouble that should bring the gray hairs of your parents to their graves, than the treachery of those which came out of their loins and wombs should do it? For, as for the beggary you bring upon yourselves, who should pity them, who wrong themselves willingly, and choose themselves such a portion? Oh! But (say some of these) we did it in a sudden passion of love, and is not that to be pitied? I answer, considering what constant misery your short passion has procured you, you are likely to have the worst of it: it is well if others would learn to be wiser by pitying your folly. But, there is more in it than passion. For why? How many of such rebellious ones do we meet with daily, who contrary to all their parents' counsels, letters, running and riding after them, threats if they venture, promises if they obey, notwithstanding all the fears and jealousies, warnings and watch-words of their parents, yet with deep dissembling and lies, count it their chief happiness to keep off the suspicion of that from their notice, which yet all on the sudden they dare rush upon the most clandestine and desperate matches that may be! Indeed, after they have engaged themselves to their parents by vows and entreaties to the contrary that they thought they might rely upon them, Isa. 63. 10, as children that will not lie, yet then have they broken through all bands; I say, what is this, but the depth of subtlety and villainy? But still they object: the business was so suddenly brought to pass by persuasion, as we could not prevent it. Why? Do you wonder that your way should be so smooth, having such a factor of hell as you consult with, to promote it? Such proctors as for a ten shillings matter will license it, for half so much dispatch it, and send you packing to woe and misery. No, no, thieves shall never want receivers and concealers. But still you will say: it should not have been done, but now it is done and past. It is true, it is done strongly enough, I grant, for parents must digest that which they cannot vomit. But the necessity of the knot excuses not the knitting. And, you shall have many lookers-on upon such matches, who will speak much for them; the case being none of their own, who, if it were their own lot to have such children, would be ready to cast the first stone at them, and of all others, be most implacable with them. To whom I say, justify not sin in others; suspend your censure till

Cavils of such children answered, as will be loose in duty to their parents' consent: yet will have their parents tied to them in means and maintenance.

John 8.7

it is your own lot, as it is like to be the sooner, if you excuse it.

Oh! But for pity's sake, you must now help them with some means to maintain them in a hard world! Why? Will not love alone maintain you in calm condition, as well as it did in hot? What? Have you forsaken your parents in the main and come you now unto them for the by? Shall you have the pleasure and they the burden? Alas you divide badly! No, no, you must hold yourself to what you have chosen; parents have but small joy to maintain thieves and traitors with their means and estate, it cost them more the getting, than your easy matches cost you. But still they allege: Would you have God deal so hardly with you, when you repent? I answer, God forbid, but (if there is any sound repentance wrought in you) you should be as freely pardoned as we ourselves desire to be forgiven of God! But if you think to tie God to your sleeves so far to follow you with grace and repentance as fast as you sin, or to accept of that for sound, which you say is so, you much mistake it: he knows well if he should thus easily be baffled by one, he should have enough of your custom forever. But still you insist: Let us be accepted to favor as before. I answer: It is a greater matter than so. If we could as easily purge your hearts, as pardon you, we would imitate God, who does both at once. But since we cannot, we must deal with you as David dealt with Absalom, though upon a show of submission, he forgave him the punishment, yet (by your leave) he commanded him to his house, and received him not to favor. And as David wisely abstained from that in discretion, for fear of nourishing up the rest of his children to the like treachery: so parents had need rather to set up such children as beacons to the rest of their fry, to scare them from the like attempts, than (as many fools do) by over hasty reconciliation, under hope of their repentance, to encourage them to tread in the like steps. There will be time enough for that when they have bitten longer upon the bridle, and had leisure to repent that in coolness which in their heat they committed. And so much for this first branch.

It also confutes the practice of such children, as, although they will seem to rely upon the consent of parents, and cannot be condemned by men in the business, yet it is not out of any honor or obsequiousness to parents, from con-

Parents may be shy to disobedient children, and why?

2 Sam. 14.24

Branch 2. Dissembled and forced consent of parents by children is sinful.

science of the duty, or beholding God's authority in them: but from policy and necessity, because they know the parent is the purse-bearer: and as the proverb says: be it better or worse, we must be ruled by him that bears the purse. These may say of themselves as he once did, I swear with my mouth, but I carry an unsworn heart within me; so, in fact I yield, but my heart is disloyal. So that (they say) they must be well advised, for fear of overthrowing all. If their parents should take displeasure at their neglect, they might lose a future friend, and forfeit the hopes of their own good estate: and how then should they do? This is the pad in straw. This forces the eye of many children to be upon their parents, and to make them a grand mark or object of their duty. I say to you, as in another sense Paul speaks, let every man have the cause of his own comfort within himself, and not without: let not the duty of a child be resident upon the father's ability to benefit him, or to cross him: so that a parent may thank his wealth for his child's service, and say, if it had not been silvered or gilded over, it would never have proved. But, let it proceed from sincerity. Some will say, it is well that it comes any way. I answer: half a loaf is better than no bread. For by this means order is kept in conversation, and many absurdities held off, though there is no thanks to them for their obedience. For, surely if such children could draw from their parents what they wanted to fish from them, as that prodigal did, with a word speaking, they would soon bid duty adieu, and cut out the cloth in their own fashion, marrying as they desire: wherefore yield this honor to your parents entirely, as their due. Be humbled if it has not been so; make your peace with God for this, as well as for any offence else whatsoever; else God may exercise you by some unwelcome buffeting, to your cost, and perhaps make you to behold that sin which you were blinded in, in the glass of like disobedience of your child to you, even such a child, as (of all others) you presumed would be most faithful to you. Do as you would be done unto; measure out to others as you would have them to measure back unto you. So much for this second.

Gal. 6.4

Rom. 12.9

Luke 15.12

Mat. 7.2

Thirdly, this taxes other children also, who will perhaps suffer their parents to carry some stroke with them in their matches, but themselves will have the chief hand in it,

Branch 3.

Half consent of parents, or consent after their contract, is faulty.

and it must come in after the matter concluded between themselves. And then, at last, lest they should incur the reproach of refractory ones, they temporize and flatter their parents, causing them first to think well of, and then to ratify their marriages; rather indeed to salve their own credit, and for necessity's sake, than because they are willing. These counterfeit actors and forces of consent (as if it were voluntary) sin against the rule of consent of parents. Shall a child bind the parent to the good behavior in this kind, and then by his consent, countenance and shroud his own act, in itself unwarrantable? Consent is the parents' due: but while you do urge it unjustly, you make it your own work. You either do persuade your parent really to think well of your doing, and that is to deceive him: or else only to make show of it, and that is to make him equivocate like yourself.

Use 2. Exhortation to marry with consent of parents.

Shortly therefore, I exhort all couples that intend marriage, to lay away all covers of shame, to remove all colors, shifts, subornation of parents, and go to work plainly, deserve, sue, seek for the consent of parents. Leave is light and sweet: liberty against rule is pleasant in the taste, but bitterness is in the end of it. Remember, that is the best marriage, whose sweetness is best in the bottom: a natural motion is swiftest in the end: now commonly matches of your own making are best at first, and worst after. Aim at so peaceable a marriage as may be so in a sad strait and affliction, and may not pursue and accuse a man when he is wounded and sore: such a one as will not upbraid the soul, and say, this day I remember my sin and I feel this rod was of my own making. That which Paul speaks of the magistrate, obey him not for compulsion, but for conscience sake, for he bears not the sword in vain. So here, for the parent represents not God in vain, and his voice is the voice of heaven. Better err with a parent than do well without him. It shall be as health to your navel, and marrow to your bones: it shall procure blessing from your parent, whose curse is worse than a Pope's with book, bell, and candle. Obey them who are set over you, for good, for their sorrow will not be your joy: you provide ill in grieving them. Esau and his race were lord dukes for many ages: but his profane contemning and vexing of Rebecca with his wives, lost him his birthright, and at the last cost him ruin. Honor your father

and mother therefore, that your days may be long in the land
which the Lord has given you. Say you deny yourself a little
in this. Say you must conflict with a crabbed, intractable parent, yet behold God in a parent, when you cannot in a good
one win him by humility, contest not, a father's spirit will not
endure it. Duty may overcome and break his heart, but willful opposition will mar all. And I speak not this only in case
of young couples, living under their parents' roof, but in what
distance soever they live. Nor, only in a case that the parent
is wise, solid, judicious, and holy: for such a one claims it by
many respects: but, even when silly, when unwise, irreligious,
and obstinate. The good parent may pray for your success, as
well as endow and enrich you. But the bad and preposterous
cannot forfeit his right to his child, though he may disable it.
He must have the honor of your consent, though you cannot
enjoy the good of it. Above all, let religious children beware
of prevarication in this kind; calling in question their sincerity
this way: even though they meet with many rubs in their way:
yet let them by their good conversation, prevail with parents,
and seek God to break and mollify their parents' spirits, rather
than to exasperate. Indeed, let mothers have this honor as well
as fathers: perhaps they can better advise you. Howsoever,
they have merited this honor as well as fathers. Truly let all
such as are set in place of such by marriage of own parents,
all tutors, guardians, and governors share in this kind. Think
not that your youth and wit can see further in this kind than
theirs. Children will say that old folk dote, and are fools: but
old ones know that children are so. God has given them as
props, therefore despise them not. And to end, I say unto you
as Abigail to David, It shall not grieve you one day, but much 1 Sam. 25
comfort you, that you have not made sad a loving parent. You
shall never have cause to repent you. The way of the Lord (says
Solomon) is strength to them that walk uprightly. The word of Prov. 10.29
God (says Micah) is good to him that is upright. Though there Micah 2.7
were no reward for it, yet there is reward enough, even in this,
I have denied myself and obeyed. So much for this former
branch, the duty of children to parents herein.

The second branch concerns the dignity of parents. Branch 2.
They must conceive that even in their privilege there lies a duty Dignity of
too, to God, to the child. They must say as the centurion did, parents.

Use of reproof
to them that
neglect the
care of their
children.

I myself am under authority. Therefore here is sad reproof to
parents, for a world of abuses. Truly most parents may thank
themselves for their children's disrespect in this kind: they
never sought to nurture them up in God's fear: to inform and
teach them in the trade of God's way, or their own. But either
out of a foolish affection and pity, will never see nothing amiss
in them, as Adonijah and Absalom were to David: (and the
fruit was suitable) or a great and false opinion they have of
their children's dexterity and sufficiency in this kind, which
is the highway to their ruin: or else they offend in a base and
degenerate softness, which hinders them from maintaining
their authority in their children's hearts. Too much familiarity begets contempt: and if a servant overly coddled, will look
to be as a child, then will a child look to be overly familiar
with a parent. There is a mediocrity between excess of rigor in
many parents, whereby they are so dark and aloof from their
children, as if they were some other men's children, and their
slaves; (which breeds bad thoughts of them, base qualities of
servility and hollowness in children, and exasperates their
spirits against them). It causes children to think themselves
slighted, and as in other points, so in marriage, as if parents
were too high to take thought for it. Difference (I say) there is
between austerity and the contrary extreme, of foolish familiarity. For by this, children grow so saucy and effeminate that
they think it almost ridiculous to question it, whether their
parents will consent to their choices because they have been
accustomed to be soothed in all, by them, and never crossed.
Paul says well to young Timothy, see that no man despise you.
So I say to old parents. Do nothing which might forfeit your
authority into the hand of your boy or girl. Of all such I say,
as old Jacob to Reuben: Your dignity is gone. Lay the foundation, O parent, of that privilege, which you would preserve to
yourself in the wise managing of your child's spirit while he is
young and tender; for that is the season of leavening him with
such principles, as must work after.

Parents must
go in a middle
way between
austerity and
folly towards
their children.

Base shifts and
respects of
parents in dis-
regard of their
children.

Other parents so love their ease and vacation from
care and solicitude that, rather than they would take the pains,
they choose to commit all to wind and weather, leave all to
the will of the children, hit they, or miss they, they care not.
Do we know (say they) what will fit and content our children,

what woman they would fancy, or distaste? If we should ne-
gotiate in this work, our children perhaps, would curse us, for
ever after, and never love us more. We for our parts have given
ourselves contentment in our wives and matches, and we have
done well (God be thanked) and so (we hope) may they also.
Surely you teach your children good divinity. They see small
religion serves your turn, and you are better without it, than
with it: and they see that if they should marry any better than
the parents, the goodness of a wife would be but a superfluous
object to them, if not a continual eyesore, and therefore they
tread in their steps like a child strives to give contentment to
like parent.

1.

Other parents are also so inconstant in their humors
and aims at their children's matches that they can never come
to a point with themselves about them. Their hearts are carnal, and therefore never satisfied. For, either on the one side,
they are so wedded to the penny that (although they very
well might) they are loath to part with anything, for the present, to procure competent portions for the children. Or else,
they seeing their estate too narrow for their proud hearts, and
scorning that they should match their children no better than
they can, forbear altogether to yield consent to any: though
the years and desires of the poor children crave it. Or else they
aim at such portions for their heirs, for the helping forward
of their daughters' matches, or else look at such concurrences
of birth and parts that scarce any can please them. Others
are accessory to their children's bad matches, by their lack of
prevention and dalliance: (as before has been spoken) and
permitting their children unseasonable commerce and long
acquaintance with such, as they know to be suitable companions, cannot break them off after, when they would, because
they are snared. Others are too meddling and busy about
their children's matches, for they being led by no grounds nor
sound reasons, but fancy, do persuade their children to such
matches, as become most snaring and uncomfortable to them
for ever after, selling them to sorrow.

2.

Neither are parents guilty only about the match itself,
but also the consequences thereof. For why? Through their indiscreet love to their welfares, and their ambitious desires for
their children's enhancements, they grant greater jointures to

A contrary
extreme of
parents in
overmuch love
to children.

their eldest than their estates will permit, and so injure the rest of their better deserving children, and either must run themselves into endless debts by borrowing for them, or else be at their courtesy for the releasing of that, which they might have kept still in their own hands. By this folly they do a double mischief. For first, they set the elder on float to be some great person, and raise up their spirits above their estates, drawing them to great expense, company, and at last to ruin: and then for the making of the eldest a gentleman, they must leave the rest to beggary: either basely to depend upon their brother for means (which commonly falls short, and comes to nothing) or else to take debauched courses, to steal, to take deceitfully for their living. Thus the folly of parents (upon the sequel of their children's first matching) fills the world with bare younger brethren, with dependents, and idle ones, snaring them with perpetual discord and quarrels, and at last bringing them to most dishonorable ends. No, no: you parents, be wise, God has made you your children's carvers. Set your house in order, and do not make confusion among your posterity, to please the humor of one child: let all have children's parts. Do not rush yourselves into such debts, as your heirs must be fain to take all, and pay all, and so fleece the rest. Let the eldest (carrying himself well) have a double portion (education being considered, which the eldest are surest of) and the rest, a competent allowance; for perhaps they may do as much good in their places after, as the elder, if not more, for grace does not always go with birthright.

The 1. degree.

The 2. degree.

But, above all follies in this kind, that is most eminent, when parents, to make their children great, thrust themselves out of all, that their children might succeed them in their places, holding the candle to them, while they do all, and act their parts upon the stage. And by this means, both father and mother, who have lived in good sort all their time, come in their old days to depend wholly upon their children's courtesy. That part of their life, which of all others, requires best attendance and maintenance must now become most shiftless and desolate. They must come out of the hall into the kitchen, sit at table's end or in the chimney corner with a poor pittance sent them, and at last die in discontent, and repenting themselves of their folly. But, if they may be at good terms, upon condition of being their servants both without doors and within, as mean laborers and drudges, they may deem themselves well pleased. For when all strength and ability is gone, then are they no longer set by, but cast up for hawk's meat, despised, counted as burdens, wherefore to be eased would be no small joy to their children. And it is worse with some parents because they live to see all spent and consumed before they die, one and other, stock and branches, all withered and come to nothing. Be wise, you parents, yield not yourselves captives and prisoners to your children: no prison can be more irksome to a parent than a son or daughter's house. Trust neither of them in this case, for in truth, you make the snare, and your children put it on you: you wrong your children in putting that into their hands, which God has denied them. Love must descend, not ascend: it is not natural (says Paul) for children to provide for parents, but for parents to provide for them, therefore invert not providence. Look to your consent, and look to those consequences following upon your consent; be sure to hold stroke sufficient in your hand for the securing of love and duty from your children. You will say, all children are not alike in this case: it is true; but the best will bite, and the ordinance of God must be attended unto, as the first rule in such cases as these. Sure bind, sure find: if you must come down, rather choose to fall into the hands of God, than your children.

Neither must I pass by guardians and governors of orphans in this point: many of whom being left as managers of the stocks and portions of children, being now secure of any eye to see or judge them, do most treacherously betray poor children to misery, both before, and in their marriages. They make the children's money, payments of their debts, enhancing of their own states, and housekeeping: bringing up the children at mean terms, binding them to base masters and exposing them to the hardest conditions, for back, belly, and conscience. When their time of payments come they bring in great bills of expenses, under color, and pretend great debts and charges lying upon them for the execution of the wills of the deceased. As for their matches, they put them off to inferior persons, such as very mean portions may content and satisfy, diverting the rest to their own ends: and by one cun-

Abuses of guardians and governors of orphans in this kind of neglect sundry ways.

1.

ning slight or other, eluding the allegations and complaints of their orphans, and leaving them to stand to their lot, or else to sink in their sorrows. Our days are full of these examples: and as full of the just hand of God upon such privy thieves

2.

and traitors as those. Another sort of guardians authorized by the law to be so (although of late God be thanked, better order is taken that parents or next of kin may be the undertakers for the children if they will go to the price), do make a mere market of their orphans, and sell them as sheep and swine for money. Quite overthrowing the purpose of the law, which is to be faithful for the good of the orphan. Instead of offering, even providing, meet wives for them, such as might be every way suitable to their place, birth, and worth, what do they? Surely, they turn to the spoil, and offer them such as they know will be unwelcome, and so thereby purchase a great fine unto themselves, and leave them to their own choice and fortunes. Others, more dishonestly, force base and inconvenient matches upon them; either matching them to their own children and so raising their own estates thereby or else selling them for money to others; (and which is worst of all) lest the orphan should suspect and shun the offer propounded; what do they? They marry them in their childhood at ten, twelve, or thirteen years of age, long before the time of meet cohabitation, sending the one to travail, till he has fulfilled his young wife's years: who when they return, come to them with

Woeful fruit hereof.

a forced affection, and that breeds disdain where there should be greatest affection. And hereby grows such distaste between the parties that they abandon each other's fellowship, bed, and board, expose each other to most desperate snares and to promiscuous lusts, and if there is any reconciliation wrought, it is but violent, and the cursed fruits of the separation do so distemper their hearts that they fall at new jars for their unchastity and disloyalty of bodies. They renounce some of the children as none of their own, and so do but pass on a most uncomfortable time of marriage, more dismal than to live in a wilderness, because the necessity of an unwelcome chain makes it doubly wearisome. And as themselves, so they who were the authors of such matches, do live together at deadly feud, at continual suits, the one striving to revenge himself upon the other, till both their estates are ruined. I do not hereby exclude guardians from that due respect which the law affords when their care and respect to their orphan's welfare is suitable to the calling of a governor. But, whatsoever the law allots, the conscience of one that fears God should be so tender that themselves being no losers, in respect of the charge which they have been at, they should deal with the orphan mercifully in all other respect of advantage, which a man of no conscience would encroach upon. Such as look at their own peace and the honor of their profession, will be wary in such undertakings to make their retreat sure, that nothing may after be cast upon them, which might soil their name or religion, or give occasion to others, either to stumble at the practice or to make it at a precedent for the like impiety.

To conclude, I say this to all parents, who will be ruled by the Word, boast not of your honor and privilege, to do hurt with. Shun all those base distempers of which I have treated at large, as the infamies and reproaches of bad parents or governors. Sin not on either hand, either on the right or left, neither by base sluggish neglect and contempt of this charge, nor yet by any abusing of your liberty to the prejudice of your children. But walk in the clear way of duty. To which end, consider, your prerogative is allotted you by God, no otherwise, than that you might undertake the duty more cheerfully. Be circumspect, painful, wise, and helpful to your children (so far as your means will admit), with a free, bestowing heart. God tries your love and integrity by this occasion. Times are now grown such that the best parents cannot improve their love and affection to their well-deserving children, as it is wished: the world is at such a high rate that they whose estates are not very great can hardly light upon a comely suitable match, especially for daughters: there are none so mean nowadays, but look for as good portions, as in our predecessors' time, would have been thought a very good portion for men thrice above their fashion. And it is the disease as well of the children of God, as of men, to slight good matches, where excess of portion attends not. Indeed, I am persuaded, it is the cause why God's hand is so manifest in the ill success of most matches, because God was never so little looked at in marriages as now. But as for these things, let both good parents and children count it their affliction: bear it meekly, and leave it to God.

Use of exhortation of parents to attend their children in this great work.

Let your love be nevertheless to do them the good you can. It is not in your power to do all you would: God will have somewhat left to himself. Smaller matches with God's presence and blessing, (for all I see) may in short time, equal far greater, in success. Do that for your children, in your education, means, counsel, prayers, and providence, which is in your power to do, and as for the rest, remember, marriages are made in heaven, and from there must expect their happiness: you can do no more than you can. And, for this whole argument, namely consent of parents, thus much.

CHAPTER V

Touching a contract. What it means. The substance of it.
Answer to some questions about it.

Concerning this argument, the first inquiry will be about the word (contract) how and in what sense we here use it. Then touching the necessity or indifference thereof. Thirdly, concerning the performance and act of contracting. Fourthly, touching such reasons or respects as whereupon it may seem to be reasonably practiced. And then we shall answer such questions, as are or may be made against it, or about it. Lastly we will conclude with some use of the point. For the former of these we here make a contract, a relative word importing an antecedent act between two parties who intend marriage. That is to say, a private, mutual, free, and unconditional promise having past between these two persons to marry each other, and no other. But here this contract is not meant; but a more solemn and open binding expression of this former promise made, that it may be ratified and strengthened, as becomes a business of so great consequence. So that before we come to any other consideration we must premise a little touching marriage promises made in private between the single parties, it being presupposed that they are not within degrees prohibited, and further that they are without all exception, of inconvenience, or ill report and scandal (as in the case of first cousins is manifest) and the nature thereof. For we must know, that although an explicit or expressed contract has in it the greater force external before men, to tie the parties to marriage; yet the mutual promises of them both jointly made, either at the first, or afterwards, do as deeply bind them both before God, and in court of conscience, as the other does. And indeed the difference between them is not formal, but accidental: and both are true real contracts, or covenants, the one as the other: and if there is somewhat in the expressed contract which is not in the other, in respect of outward obligation: then may there be truly said to be somewhat in the

Second digression to the point of contract.

Contract in what sense here used.

Promises of marriage, the root of a contract.

To be very
cautiously
made, and
their proper-
ties.

former, which is not in that, in respect of essence. For the
being of the expressed contract rests in the former, namely
in the deliberate, voluntary, mutual, and honest resolutions of
the parties among themselves: which being past, give the essence to marriage before the other came, and is the foundation
and ground of the latter. For else it might be said that any passage of expression between two before witness, falling from
parties, though in rashness, or in sport, or upon a question
demanded, might carry the force of a contract, which no man
of any sense can imagine: namely, because the expressed contract before witness implies a former mutual consent between
them, not now to be questioned: but yet for special causes, to
be more solemnly and publicly testified for avoiding of great
inconvenience. And this appears plainly by the effect which a
contract or promise produces: and that is a great alteration in
the parties, who before such promise, were their own and had
the stroke in their own hand to dispose of themselves as they
please: but, after their mutual promise, they cease to be their
own, and pass over themselves (not their money, or corn, or
goods, but themselves), each under God to the other, so that
now each has power over other, and only one over the other.
In so much that whatsoever other promise should possibly be
made, by both of them, or either of them to any other, besides
themselves, if confessed, does disannul itself, and is *ipso facto*
void by virtue of the pre-contract or fore-promise so made.
But although it is denied, yet it nevertheless binds them before God so that they shall be forever culpable before him, of
treachery and spouse-breach, without repentance. If this were
considered, doubtless it would awe the spirits of many hot and
unsettled young ones from such attempts. But of that after.
Here only I say, that seeing the true nature of self-renouncing
and self-resigning resides as really in a private promise as in a
witnessed contract, therefore they are not two things, but the
same with diverse circumstances for special reasons, annexed.
So much for the acceptation of the word.

Real contracts
as good as
verbal.

To this I may add, that in some cases, reals may coun-
tervail verbals: when as a thing done implies as much (in the
judgment of a discreet man) as a promise made in words. As
if a person formerly intermitting a purpose to marry another
yet hearing that she is attempted by a new lover, shall repair to

the party and say, so it is that you know there is love between
you and me of a long time depending, so deep that I dare not
in conscience yield my right in you to any other; wherefore
I pray you, if any such thing is offered, accept it not: this in
conscience ties the party to marry her, and is equivalent in
promise, and if there is a witness, it concludes against him,
that shall desert her. Why? Because he defrauds her of a possibility of equal weight to his own marriage. So again, a man
has desisted to prosecute an offer of marriage with a woman,
virgin, or widow (all is one) and the woman addresses herself
to a far off dwelling, perhaps thousands of miles out of the
kingdom. The man hearing of her situation, comes to her and
tells her that whereas there has been some intermission of love
and marriage-suit a long time, yet now he cannot permit her
to go that long voyage, his love is so deep towards her, and
therefore dissuades her journey.

  Here I say, that although the woman (if free before) is
at her own hand to go, or not to go, yet if she consents to stay,
the motion made is equivalent to a promise of marriage: and
cannot in conscience nor righteousness be broken off by the
man. Many like instances might be used, but these are sufficient.

  The use, etc. This being thus, what should the punishment be of such counterfeits and impudent knaves, who dare
falsify the matter of a promise, that is, impudently aver and
beat down a party that there has been a covenant and promise
of marriage between them, when as yet never any such thing
was in the world? I say such persons ought to have the uttermost penalty inflicted that the law can impose: as being an
extreme impeachment of the credit and estate of the innocent
party, and a mark of intolerable audaciousness in abusing so
solemn a thing to any counterfeit ends of base wretches, not
meet to live in a commonwealth. An example whereof we
have lately had in our corner, by so much the more odious,
because so insolent.

  Before I pass from this point of promise, it may be
asked, what promise does realize marriage before God? I
answer. First, it must be mutual; secondly, voluntary or free;
thirdly, without error; I mean such as does overthrow and contradict itself. First, it must be mutual and equal, not of one to

What promise
for marriage
does bind.
1.
A mutual one.

the other only, but of that other to him. For if such a promise
is a putting off one's self into the power of another: then, as no
man can put himself into another's power without an act of his
own resignation of the liberty he had in himself, so neither can
each of the two parties give up their liberties without mutual
consent to each other. For in marriage, the yielding up of the
right of one receives a right in another: and therefore it must
be mutual and reciprocal. If one shall pretend the promise of
the other, and yet suspend his own, as thinking hereby to tie
that party to his own time and leisure, himself being free, he is
deceived. For marriage consent must be mutual; and the party withdrawing consent, does in that respect extinguish and
make frustrate the other's promise from snaring the promiser:
except afterward the other party also shall as freely come in as
the other did, and so make the promise mutual and equal. I
have heard of a sad accident in this kind that befell a suitor to a
maid, being a gentleman of good personage, he seeing himself
to have won the affections of the maid and thinking himself
sure enough of her, without any deep obliging himself unto
her, pleased himself in his conquest and there rested: so long
till the gentlewoman perceiving herself slighted, fell to as deep
a disdain of him as he had been indifferent to her: in so much
as another match being offered her, she embraced it. But the
report thereof coming to the gentleman as he was playing very
solemnly upon his lute, he suddenly starts up, and breaking
his lute all to pieces, instantly went out of his wits. A notable
item to all that they play not fast and loose in matter of mu-

2.
A free or vol-
untary one.

tual promise, and speedy dispatch of marriage. Secondly, it
must be free and voluntary, not drawn forth by circumvention
and subtle tricks or policies, either of the parties themselves,
nor yet their agents and spokesmen: nor extorted by fear and
threats, either of parents (when they are desirous to put off
their children for their ease, and are set to dispatch the matter) or by the parties themselves (as when the man menacing
the woman, and attempting to ravish her, except she consents,
or to do other violence to her, do hereby force a promise from
her), or any other who are active in the business. And this I
would have noted that although parents do not use any com-
pulsory and terrifying courses to draw their children to inconvenient matches; yet if they do carry themselves sternly

to their children in an indirect way, and refuse to hear them who are third parties, using weighty reasons to dissuade; or if the parents do not rather in meekness convince the child by reasons invincible out of the Word, or other respects of good reason and discretion, that it is a meet match, yielding still to the child's objections (who must abide by the sorrow, when the parent goes free), then I say that the overmuch reverential awe of the parent, smiting into the child a loathness to offend, and taking deliberation away from it, that so it is led in a cord of necessity to do that which else it would not do. I say this ought to be counted as a compulsion, and such a child to be pitied and freed from the contract. Or, if marriage proceeds and ill consequences follow they must be all fastened upon the parent, not upon the child, and the child may claim the best amends. I say then, such promises bind not in conscience because the principle of willingness is absent: and the party would never have consented, if such fear and compulsion had not been used. I add this, except afterward the party being freed from such fear, and returning to herself, shall express another consent free and ingenuous: then the former impediment cannot frustrate this latter promise.

Thirdly, it must also be without deceit or false opinion: and that in such a kind as opposes marriage essentially. Hence those heathenish precedents of marriages are frustrate, when one sex marries the same (Nero was a horrible example), when a eunuch marries a woman, or a woman marries a hermaphrodite (one of the epicene gender), when a man is deceived in the person, as Jacob in Leah, put into his bed instead of Rachel (notwithstanding the act of copulation): but especially when the party supposed to be pure and a virgin, proves defiled and corrupted: in such a case, if it breaks out before the marriage is consummated, it does justly infringe the promise, and makes it of none effect. This is said touching a binding promise. But touching this last of error, understand it of no other errors accidental, which do not of themselves cross marriage. For, though they may be such as gave occasion to the party to consent, and had the error been foreknown, the party would not have yielded: yet because they disannul not the real knot of marriage, that is, peculiarity of person, by defilement, therefore they are presumed no other than in some

3.
A plain one without deceit.

What that is.

cases would have been admitted: and therefore the party must stick to his or to her promise, nevertheless; and therefore let them either bear it as their desert for lack of inquisition, or if they did their endeavor to be informed but were deceived, let them take it as the trial which God has put upon them; the promise binds still, except the other party releases it. And so much for this question.

Use 1.
Admonition
to all parties
to beware of
their marriage
promises.
Some use would do well before I leave it, because the point is but occasional, and shall be no more returned unto. And I would urge these two uses following, the one of admonition, the other of reproof. The admonition is, that single persons be well advised of their promises, before they make them. And indeed few words might serve if the former item were well regarded: namely that the speaking of a few words at once, may forever dispossess them of their liberty, never to be recovered: fools once, and slaves perpetually. So that it is no matter of slightness and merriment, no play, no trifle, no sport, except you will call that a sport which may cost a poor wretch both body and soul. Abner indeed called murder a sport, but bitterness was in the end of it. Be advised therefore: and let this point, seasonably as a hammer knock home to the head the former exhortation of marrying in the Lord, and wisely to look well about you, before you venture. I pray tell me, would you willingly make another man master and owner of any commodity you have for nothing? Say it was but your horse or cow, even if it was but a dog, which you set by? I think not, how much less of yourself? Are you so silly as to resign up the right of yourself, and to make yourself a prisoner, a captive in the prison of marriage, from where there is no escape? Certainly not, except you are mad and hate your own flesh. You would not do that with a breath, which all your worth cannot revoke and undo. As Solomon says, beware how you become surety for a stranger: quit yourself speedily, and deliver yourself as a roe, and as a bird from the net of the pursuer. Man or woman, youth or maid, look to your promises. I think resignation of a man's or woman's self to another, had not need to be to everyone that comes, to every unknown stranger, to each unchaste, irreligious, and indiscreet companion, which might make your life irksome forever. In the promise is the foundation of marriage: whether it is well done or ill, it can be

done but once, therefore let it be deliberately, wisely, and well done. Oh! Let it be a solemn thought with you, my promise gives away myself and takes unto myself another, my liberty is gone. If a woman is urged to give up her right only in a little copyhold she will shrug at it, and think well of it before hand. And yet she may possibly recover a better piece of land, for a small matter. But this free hold of your person, and your liberty, once resigned up and forgone, can never be recovered again. Therefore I say, be well advised before you forfeit it.

The second use is terror and reproof to all who have disguised themselves in these kinds of inconsiderate, rash promises. You shall have leisure enough to repent, if anguish will suffer you. Also of all violent parents, who to be rid of their children, force them upon unsuitable marriages, which their children had rather parted with their lives, as venture upon: and so bring upon them a lasting monument of misery. If, says the parent, you refuse this match, I will never own you for my child, I will dispossess you of all. Moreover, what say you to parents who first deflower virgins, and then force their children to marry the harlots, for a cover of their own villainy? Is not this cursed love, and cruel command of an innocent child? But to be short, especially it rebukes the baseness of many, who cast arrows and deadly things, and say am not I in sport? That is, who twist themselves with strong persuasions and arguments into the hearts of such as they sue unto, and having so done, break off all again, and wipe off every crumb off their mouths as if they had eaten no bread. Oh, you uncontrolled persons. What? Are solemn promises but cobwebs, which great flies can break through? Make you no bones of them? Do you snap these bands in two as Samson did his cords and green withes? There is one who is stronger than you, who will not be mocked, but bind you for bursting in chains too strong for you. But perhaps you will say, if it were my lightness and giddiness, it was very sinful indeed, and I deserved never to be trusted more. Yes, perhaps your word shall be taken, but it shall be by such a one, as shall make you do penance against your will, all your life for the breach of that promise which you willingly made. But you have since that heard sad reports of the party: for instance's sake. That the woman is no housewife, or is a melancholy person, not fit for

Use 2.
Rash and inconsiderate promises of marriage very foolish and sinful.

your temper, nor yet (in a second marriage) for your children, or she has some of her own, or some such blemish now you have found out: well either these are true or else false. Are they false? How basely minded are you, whom the prattling tongue of some false sycophant, jangler, or gossip (loving neither her nor yourself unfeignedly) should shake that affection of yours, which being well grounded once (as you supposed) drew from you promises of marriage? But say they are true in part, or wholly. What then? They come in out of season, the steed is stolen, it is too late now to shut the stable door: affections are snared, you may not desert her. Were you not in your own power before? Has any man forced you to resign it, save your free self? You are snared: and I say, if she should release you, it is her meekness and discretion, but it is your rashness: if you were fined as he was, who defiled a virgin, for the satisfaction of her discontented spirit and questioned name, you were well served. No other satisfaction can duly be made her, than your return again to her with so much the more affection, by how much your deserting of her has been long and irksome. Let the falling out of friends be the renewing of love. You departed once that you might return forever. And thus much for this occasional point of promises.

Now I come to the second general: having showed therefore of what contract I am here to speak, namely of a witnessed and professed contract, it may be demanded whether it is essential or not, to marriage? To which I say, that the essence of marriage consists in the former promise made mutually to each other. Therefore, there is no essential necessity of the witnessing and professing thereof before others, but marriage may stand as real and firm, in point of substance without it as with it. Howbeit, I conceive it to be of very special expediency and use for the advantage and good of the parties, as I shall after manifest. All sorts of people, even very heathens have always esteemed espousals, betrothals, assurances, contracts, and affirmances (for they are all one) to be very solemn matters, as the words they use, and the ceremonies then performed, do testify. So sacred and reverend it has appeared to all sorts that there seems to be a finger of God pointing out the usefulness thereof. Witness the assembling of the friends of the parties on both sides to be spectators thereof that so the

Question. Whether a contract is essential to marriage?

Answer.

Contracts very ancient, and of general use.

blessing of it might be more effectual. Witness that instance of Boaz and Ruth who were (as it were) affianced in the gate of their city, before many solemn witnesses: who being called forth to testify the contract, did assent thereto, and by their acclamations and thanksgivings and prayers to God for them, graced and honored the same. So that it is no wonder if the church of both Old and New Testament did practice it. And it is particularly specified in the generation of Christ, that when Joseph and Mary had been espoused together, before they came together, she was found with child, of the Holy Ghost. The Hebrew writers tell us of the forms and tenor of words used among the Jews, namely, that by diverse real ceremonies they strengthened the promise which had passed between the parties, and that in a set meeting of the family. Sometimes they did it by tickets of paper, written by each of their hands, and delivered by each other mutually. Sometimes by very solemn words of obligation passing between them: sometimes by a piece of coin given and received, which by the change of possession, argued the possession and assignment which one made and surrendered to the other. All to show that they accounted this business no trifle or toy to be wantonly used for the pleasing of carnal humors, but a divine ordinance requiring firm and strong assurance of each other. The forms were these, behold, you are betrothed unto me, or, be you betrothed unto me, or the like. If it was without witnesses, it was frustrate. The solemnity hereof was acted under a tent, canopy, or tabernacle, set up for the occasion, to show inwardness and secrecy of marriage affection and benevolence. This was distinct from the act of marriage itself, which followed sometime after, and was done with great festivity and with many songs and epithalamiums of the boys and girls of the bride chamber, alluded unto by our Savior, Luke 5. After the contract followed the dowry bill, which was from the man to the woman: though the woman brought a portion to the man also, as appears in Caleb's bestowing his daughter Achsah upon Othniel, yet usually it was the man's act to endow the wife only, and to purchase her unto himself. To these may be added (which I add lest any should accuse me of singularity) the joint consent and practice of the church of God among ourselves, especially such as fear God, (though we condemn not those who do

Jewish contracts what?

Josh. 15.16

not) and there are extant in print sundry books published by authority, and by name one of M. R. G. wherein the practice of that reverend servant of God is at large expressed, when he contracted couples. So that I hope, touching this second branch, little more need be added.

Action and performance of the contract, how to be done.

Touching the third, which is the action or performance of the contract. And that stands in three personal acts. The first is of him that leads the contract, or guides the two parties to express their former consent. Who ought to be a meet person for gravity and experience, able to teach them (if need require) the duties of that condition, and to answer such scruples as might arise in their minds about it. In a word, such a one, as by his presence might cast some awe and authority upon the minds of the parties, and assist the action with some correspondence. One that may be wise to discern of the frame of the parties, and therefore by questions may sift out the truth, to prevent danger, as by demanding whether they formerly have engaged themselves to any other man or woman, person or persons, showing them the dangerous sinfulness of such dalliance. Also, whether they have freely and without fear, and with the mutual consent of parents, testified, by presence, or by their hand (if doubt is made) consented mutually in heart, to this contract. The second person is the parties contracted: who ought to follow him that leads them in the contract, thus, or in like form of words; first the man, then the woman: I Thomas, John, etc. do take you Joan, Mary, etc. for my espoused husband, or wife, and I promise to marry you shortly without fail, if God will. And so with some short counsel and prayer to God to dismiss them, as true man and wife before God. The third person is the witnesses produced: who being moved thereto, answer and say, we are witnesses of this contract, by which these parties are betrothed to each other, and will testify it, being required.

Rational respects in which a contract may be used.

The fourth general is the rational respects in which such a contract seems very meet to be used. And they may be reduced to these three following. As first, the suitableness of the contract to the witnesses of the attempt. It is meet that such things are done orderly, leisurely, and by degrees, not rashly, suddenly: and therefore, although a promise has passed between the parties, yet as the matter grows riper be-

The 1.

tween them, so it is comely that it is no longer kept secret, but
manifested, that thereby they may be awed with the more fear
and jealousy of themselves, from uncomely and audacious enterprises one against the other's chastity. Secondly, to prevent
inconstancy. The nature of flesh is vain and all men are liars.
And it is seen as much in this subject, as in any other. As hot
as youth is in her vehemence and passion, yet the best of their
gold proves brass oftentimes, when they weigh things in cold
blood. Add hereto, that this base world is full of curiosity and
jangling, talebearers and flatterers, who fill the ears of couples
with idle and ungrounded surmises: whereunto they whose
ears as credulous, do lie open, and hereby their affections are
unjustly alienated, against each other. Thus fools love lightly,
and leave as lightly, others of themselves, not knowing their
one spirit, take a toy in their heads, and without all reason,
run into humors of fear, jealousy, melancholy, and conceited-
ness against each other, and so withdraw themselves suddenly
from each other, and change their minds. They do not (as
they say) affect so well as at first, they observe some lightness
in each other, some ungoverned tongue and passions, or they
distaste the kindred carriage, or training, and upon these eyesores, either so, or seeming so, they repent them, and fall off.
And yet perhaps some of these have had time long before to
consider themselves. But who can make a coat for the moon?
By this means, as God is dishonored, so the innocent party,
wiser and of more solid affections, is deluded, indeed sometimes driven to desperateness. And had not here need to be
a cord to tie a Proteus in a knot from slipping? Yes surely,
witnesses had need be solemnly used to witness to the contract, that if they will still be so fickle, they may be compelled
to faithfulness, or else handled as their treachery deserves. I
have heard of some who have gone to the doors of the church
to be married, and yet shrunk back. And whereas it is objected, may not things appear in time worse which before lay
hid? I answer yes, but you should have thought so before, and
suspended your promises: except you made no other promises
than you indented together to keep or break, and that each
should consent to the other's resolution, either to proceed or
desist, which I think is a fulsome course, and makes a promise
needless and frustrate.

Suitableness to
the weight of
the thing.

The 2.
To prevent
inconstancy.

The 3.
The benefit
of the parties
contracted.

Thirdly, this may serve for the benefit of the parties contracted. For, as it was an ancient custom among the Jews when two parties were contracted, to pray to God for them, and to bless them solemnly: and (no doubt) the parents or such as supplied their rooms, did annex some word of exhortation to them, from the experience they had, both how great a work they entered upon, and how raw and green they were to digest it, so I say I think it not amiss, that some grave person did the like now. The contract ought not to be a bare surrender of each other; but an instilling of some discreet watchwords and charges from their elders, touching the mutual duties of both, jointly and severally, and so prayer for a blessing to be added. Solemn things should be handled accordingly even in the outward fashion of it: for men are sensible and sensual creatures, and are led by outward objects to inward apprehensions. Still I say, I do not affirm this course to be of the essence of the contract, but yet a very suitable addition, if it may be had: and much making for the better dispatch thereof. And, what season is so apt as this? When the ewes of Laban were to conceive, Jacob (warranted by God) set rods pilled and straked before them, that the fancy of the creature being heated in the act of generation, might the easier carry in the multicolored species. So here, the sight of so solemn a work as this is, of contracting two, and making them one flesh, will more easily and thoroughly stir the imagination, and the sense being moved, does the more familiarly convey the instruction to the understanding and heart. A pity therefore it is, that the molds being so ready to fashion it, that the melted metal of instruction should be wanting unto them, they being so capable. And this I think is the cause, why there are sermons made at baptism, the supper, at funerals, and such occasions, to let in the doctrines of the things into men (whereunto in general most are so averse), because, as there is a season for all things (which is like apples of gold and pictures of silver) so also for this: and that is, when by the novelty and strangeness of the thing never done before, the mind is provoked to an expectation, and so sets the wheels on work to receive and apply things according to their worth and use. This for the third. Only one word more I add: if any should ask, what form of instruction was meet to be used at such a time, to the parties contracted? I answer, I prescribed none: this whole treatise following shows their duties; two or three sentences culled out of each branch may serve at such a time, if wisely applied, as the several uses of the parties may seem to require. So much for this fourth.

Now I proceed to the fifth general, touching the questions arising out of this contract. The first may be, what is to be thought touching the publication of the contract in the assembly, and touching the minister's act in marrying. For the former, I say, it is a very discreet and necessary act of the church: for as much as the procuring of the safety and good report of the married, is a point of religion. Now the private contract of two in secret, or with a few, reaches not the end of publication because it is more likely that the body of a congregation may sooner give notice of any precontract between the parties than a few witnesses can do: and as for the parties themselves if they are guilty, it is much less to be expected that they should accuse themselves. So that, for prevention of such a confusion, as to marry precontracted persons, what course can be too safe and sufficient? True it is, when all is done, it may prove but little to purpose, through the subtlety of the offending party: but when that is done which can be, the church is free: the mischief ought justly to light upon the wicked delinquent. Well therefore is it in this case, if liberty is denied to parties (at least in so common a way of a fee, without difference, or special inquiry about the fitness of the dispensation), from thwarting so wise and orderly a device: which being done, people would not itch as they do after private marrying, to oppose publication, and that upon humor, and vanity. For through such a base custom, it comes to pass that one learns of another, and now he is thought but a peasant who declines not this lawful provision of the church. Rather those who are of fashion and wealth, should think it their honor to submit to this practice that they might give the better example to others, and so approve the justness of their marriage: and stop the gap of privacy and of clandestine matches, without consent of parents, a world of suits upon pretended precontracts, and as much sorrow to parents who by this disorder are robbed of their children, and cannot understand of their marriage, till it is past revoking.

5. General. Touching questions.

Question 1. Whether publication of the contract is necessary?

Question 2.
What is to be
thought of the
marrying by a
minister?

Answer.

The second question is, what is to be thought of the marrying by a minister? The question arises from the difference of other country's fashions in this kind. In the Scriptures, we see it was civilly carried, and dispatched by the elders in the gate: and now in some of the Reformed churches, we see it is performed in like sort, officers being appointed to take their names, to book them in a record, and so with a short ceremony to dismiss them. But in my judgment, the practice of our church to do it by the minister is every way most convenient. For by this means, the publicness of the action makes the matter more solemn, awes the parties much more, both before marriage to carry themselves so, as they may not be ashamed to show their faces in public, to justify what they had done. And if there were liberty given to parties in this kind to marry upon their private contracts, what a world of sin might ensue, as in some to live in a course of defilement, and to abuse each other's bodies at their pleasures: in others to leave each other, even after the knowledge of each other, besides making of that vulgar, which cannot be preserved too warily. I deny not, but that possibly some persons so marrying, might do it without direct sin against God: but what is that to the scandal which is occasioned thereby? We must so look at that we do lawfully in itself, as not forgetting our rule, that we procure things honest before men. Whatsoever is pure, and of good report, that we must ensue, and so the peace of God attends us, not else. Many acts may be good in the doer's conscience, which yet are subject to the suspicion and ill construction of others. In such cases, a man must ask this of himself, if all should take such liberty to himself, what would ensue of it? And this would check his proceeding. The Jews (as the writers tell us) had a strange way of contracting couples: namely, for the better securing of the match, they permitted the use of copulation for once to the parties, and no more till marriage, upon a great penalty. But finding great inconvenience to grow hereupon (as no wonder it did), they forbade any such course of contract: and who so attempted it, if it were proved, he was scourged with rods openly, for reproach's sake. So much for this second.

Now a third question arises upon this, that in our former discourse I have spoken of a lawful contract that is lawfully

entered upon, between such as are within degrees permitted. Whether first cousins may marry, answered.
So that, it is asked here, whether first cousins may marry? To
which, this I say, that I observe of late time many more divines
to incline to the affirmative than formerly have done; and some
of them, godly as well as learned: and not only so, but (which
I wonder at, seeing such novel and forbidden things are too
soon run upon) that they do write for it, and have determined
the marriages of some in this way, contrary to the affections of
some of the parties, bearing them down by the judgment, and
giving occasion (probably) of snaring their conscience after,
when the crusted sore shall break out again. But to the point.
First, for my part, I should much rest in the generality of that
charge, Levit. 18.6. *None of you shall approach to any that is
near of kin to him, to uncover their nakedness, I am the Lord.* I
demand what is meant here by kin? Is not it to be meant both
of such as are near in blood, and also affinity? And, is there
not very great nearness in blood between the uncle's son and
the uncle's daughter? Tremellius, as learned a Jew as most of
our later Jewish writers, in his Diagram upon Levit. 18, at the
end, is so bold as to take it for granted, that as it is unlawful
to marry the uncle or the aunt, so the he and she first cousins
(*cognatum and cogratam*, says he) and yet alleges no text for it:
as if he would have the matter taken for granted. And in the
annotation upon the sixth verse, he says thus, *Of thy kin*, that
is, of those who are specified hereafter, or which by analogy of
comparison with them are understood. And who are they? In
the end of the chapter he tells us, in his first corollary, the marriages of collaterals (either by affinity or consanguinity) are
forbidden to the fourth generation. Is not this plain enough?
And he adds, there was no use of it that the Holy Ghost should
name them, the case is so clear. I suppose the testimony of
one such Jewish textman as he, should overweigh the opinion
of many novel writers. But (say these men) if the Holy Ghost
had been against it, might he not have named it? I answer,
yes, if he had thought good, but an argument from negatives
prevails not. Rather, the not naming it strongly argues the
thing out of question. The text mentions not the nakedness
of the daughter-in-law's daughter, among the forbidden particulars: what then? May a father-in-law marry such a one? I
think not. The second degree is included in the first: namely

not uncovering the daughter-in-law's nakedness. Yet here is nothing but affinity by marriage of the mother: and is it not as rational that although the uncle or aunt's son and daughter are not named, far nearer of blood (though not in the descending line, but collateral) than they, yet their nakedness must not be uncovered, because the uncle's and aunt's may not? Tell me, if the wife's brother or husband's sister had not been named expressly, had it been a thing lawful to meddle with them? I think not. If the uncle is directly forbidden to marry his niece, or the aunt the nephew, shall not their children be forbidden to marry also, being but one degree lower? As touching the argument from negatives, it is so weak, that it is gone into a proverb: and might not a thousand absurdities be as well proved by negation? Dare these men argue thus against a Sabbath of the eighth day, because it is nowhere translated expressly from the seventh to be the Christian Sabbath? Again, what is more common through the Scripture than for particulars not named, yet to be included in their generals? It was not expressed in the fourth commandment that a man might not gather sticks on the Sabbath day: yet because in general God had charged that no dressing of meat, or bodily labor should be then done, but all be dressed and provided before, therefore the Lord commanded him to be stoned by virtue of the general commandment. And, are not these weak bottoms for men to warrant their own, or other men's marriages, because the contrary is not forbidden, when as that is forbidden, which is, if not further off, yet full as far? It is objected that many of the patriarchs did thus marry, and are no whit impeached for it. I answer, if that is a reason, then let us marry our half-sister, as Abraham did Sarah; for so he justifies himself to that Abimelech, yet indeed she is my sister, for she is the daughter of my father by my mother-in-law.

Do we not know how Terah's family after it came to Mesopotamia, and subsisted there, was far divided from the other families of Shem and therefore straitened much in their choice? Cursed Ham's family they were expressly forbidden to marry in, as being the nation which God would root out, and give it the posterity of Abraham: where then should they marry, but within their own narrow family? And we may well think they did as well as then could be done, and made such a shift as they did: for even those they married were idolaters, which was forbidden, if it could have been shunned: but one necessity pardoned another: better idolaters under no curse, than accursed Canaanites. If they had had larger breadth, had they so ventured? But they much press the example of Caleb's giving of Achsah his daughter to Othniel her first cousin. To which I answer, if it had been as they say, yet it was not in cold blood, but upon a condition made in general to any: but falling out as it did, it might have been an exemption by an extraordinary occasion. But the thing was nothing so, for Othniel is called the son of Kenaz, by the same liberty of speech which calls Christ's kinsmen his brethren. He was not the son of Kenaz, Caleb's brother, but the son of his son's son: so Tremellius upon the place. Brother (says he) that is, one descending from his brother, two or three generations removed. Each grandchild and each nephew or son of nephew, is called a son by the phrase of the Holy Ghost. But I incline not here to take off every objection. I return. Suppose I should grant them their desire that because first cousins are not named, therefore they are allowed, yet I think there is abundance of things which prudentially might move men to forbear these marriages. First, notwithstanding the long time that this tenet has possessed the spirits of some men, yet we see, the blemish and crock of it is yet unwashed out, indeed it cleaves still and abides upon it. The minds of men cannot yet put it on, as a garment fit for their back: still it is a generally questioned thing among the most, and even by such as are with much ado urged to it by such as think they see further than all men, yet scarce is the doubt exempt of out them, but they stagger. I make not this an absolute reason, but a suspicion and prejudice against it. And why should any man choose rather endlessly to beat his brain to evince a thing of so doubtful truth, than yield to the contrary practice, which no man can doubt of? Is it not wisdom to do that which is safest? Can faith and doubting stand together? And can that be done without sin which is not done in faith, but wavering? Surely the plaster which men study to make for this sore is far too narrow to cover it. Again, the scruple being not removed, what a tumult does it cause among God's people, especially what jealousy, estrangement, and dislikes among the kindred? We should aim at all com-

I make no quarrel, but only show my opinion, leaving others to themselves.

munion, not alienation. Besides, when God has vouchsafed so great breadth and liberty, who should strengthen himself by mixture of blood, and (as Nicodemus says) going into his mother's womb, to be born again? Not to speak of that observation, that God has not blessed it with such increase, or integrity of affection. And it is not (to conclude) among those things that are pure, and of good report.

And surely, if this is a great reason of the unlawfulness of marriage between degrees forbidden, because thereby that natural honor and awful esteem of parents, and consequently of such as are near of kin unto them is embezzled and violated (for what is more repugnant to respect and honor, than the familiarity of carnal admixture) then I am sure the reason holds as well between first cousins as others of kin: for nature has put as due and chaste a respect of honor between them, as between those who are namely forbidden in Leviticus. But the former is avowed by many writers, one whereof I produce, Augustine's speech *de Civit. Dei, book 13. cap. 16.* I know not how it comes to pass that there is a kind of natural instinct in the modesty of man (and that praiseworthy) that to whomsoever he owes any modest and chaste honor, for kindred's sake, from the same person he restrains any marriage affection, which even the chastity of marriage blushes to violate.

Question 4. Wherein differs a contract from marriage? Answer.

But to proceed, here is another question, wherein does a contract differ from marriage, since that the substance of matrimonial union stands in the contract, what is there more in marriage itself? Or what reasons are there for the dissolution of the one which are not for the other? I answer. There is great difference between the strength of a contract and the strength of complete marriage. For the strength of the former stands forcible by the private consent of the parties. I mean this, that although God is in a contract, yet so, as the parties which consented, may also dissent, when they find that consent did hinder the private good of their married estate. And so, when it appears that the one party is unqualified for the other through many evils that break by after intelligence, then they that made it may break it. But marriage has a strength by public consent of the law, and the custom of men, and therefore it is above all strength of private promises: and admits no dissolution by private consents. The union of contracted ones

God is in a contract for good, and not evil: but in marriage whether good or evil.

is a union of imagination, or of affection, so long as it is within such bounds. But the union of marriage is a union of state and condition, standing in right, and law, above all private affection. If private contracts are broken off (as they ought not without consent), there is private satisfaction given to the parties: but if marriage is broken off, there is public scandal given beyond all satisfaction. The regard whereof ties the hands of married ones behind them from all liberty of consent to dissolve the knot: because as it concerns the body of the state to see sin punished, so to see good established, when it may be so. For in the time of Moses, the hardness of men's hearts was so great, that they would be curbed by no law, each man's will was his law. But now law having got the upper hand, men's wills must submit: because better it is that one couple suffer, than the law, which is the bond of public peace and welfare. So that this authority looks not at men's private contents or discontents, but makes a voluntary consent, which might have been broken, to become necessary and irrevocable. And whereas it is instanced (as before) in the point of comparison of incontinency committed before marriage, (not known till after) with that in marriage. I say, I deny not but formerly and really both ought to dissolve it by the word, yet (as before I noted) the wisdom of the church, putting difference, is to be regarded: neither is the sin (in every degree) so extensive. In this case therefore that speech avails: Better admit a mischief, than an inconvenience. Better pull down a smoking chimney than admit a continual smoke in the eyes: so, better endure a bad marriage (which is the lesser) than a breach of law and right, which is the bond of the whole body. Besides, before marriage, the deserting of the one party, infers a liberty to desert another: the forfeit of the time allotted to marriage, by the error of the one party, may forfeit marriage itself, in the will of the other. Such a portion promised by parents in fraud, and after withdrawn injuriously dissolves the marriage because it is such a fault as opposes the condition of the first consent. The same I may say of any similar violations, which yet, after marriage itself hold not.

But let me not be mistaken in what I have said. I would not be thought to make promises of no value, because I make marriage of greatest strength and virtue. For although

One is better spoiled than unity.

we have a rule, that is, in the same power to break a law, that first made it: yet it holds not in contracts, without special warrant. Not each pretended sudden impotency of body, not each suborned infamous slander of the parties, or either of them, not every devised flim-flam of a giddy brain must be accepted to make a spouse breach. For what is this, but to open a wide door to all baseness, and to expose the laws of God and man to open contempt and mockery? But such cases as I have mentioned, if they can be sufficiently approved to those who are the witnesses of the contract, so that all doubt of treachery and falsehood is taken away, then it is free for the contracted parties to desist if they will. Howbeit, not without mutual consent. For suppose that one of the parties pretend debility of body, yet the other party knowing herself to be in a way of God, and to be bound to trust God in his way, either for the recovery of strength to the weak party, or for strength to wait upon God in the way of disappointment: shall refuse to release the other: then I affirm that other party is tied still by virtue of the contract, to marry. God's weakness is stronger than man's strength as the apostle speaks. And whereas (commonly) rationality and wisdom of the flesh does step in here (for self ever crosses God) and shall either out of disdain, self-love, fear, or other sinister respects, say: if he will needs break off, let him: if she will needs break, let her. As good to do so as to proceed with discontent. And it shall be well seen, I scorn him as much as he scorns me. I answer. No, these are base tricks to shake off God's way: let that prevail. But if the unruly party will depart, the innocent is discharged to marry another.

Question. Why a space is allotted between contract and marriage? Answer. I go on. Another question may be: why is there a space or distance usually appointed between the contract and the marriage? I answer. It is fit to be so, for this end among others, that the parties might seriously and solidly, both apart and together, weigh and consider, what the business is, which they are entering upon. For being now contracted, and settled in their affections, from starting from each other, what remains but that both conspire to this end, that their knot may be as truly virtuous as it is necessary: and that the necessity of it may not prove tedious for lack of virtue and religion. If grace knit the knot, then they shall be as unwilling to be broken off as the band of marriage makes them knit so, as they cannot:

when the strength of the band strives with the sweetness, how delightful is it? And that it may be so, both the parties should endeavor, as in the last use I shall press more fully. The space allotted them is not to prepare for fine clothes, to bid guests, to provide good cheer, nor (I speak to the meaner sort) to set themselves to seek the best advantage of money at their offerings, to hire for themselves a hole to thrust their heads in: or a farm to occupy. All these things (in a moderate way) are useful; but God is the God of sea and land, and all abundance and store is in his hand. His are farms and dwellings, and sheep and cattle, and the treasures of the earth; he can give to whom he will: and as Job says, although your beginnings are but small, yet he can make your increase great in due time. Make you no more haste than good speed. Seek the kingdom of God and the righteousness of the same, and make it not your solemn care to plod upon great matters, or to enter upon marriage with a fear of poverty, that you and yours shall prove beggars. Plod both of you how this solemn estate may find you well prepared; and for other things cast your care upon him who cares for you; and in well doing, and means using, commit yourselves into the hands of a faithful Creator. This work would be done even in the threshold of marriage.

But a question here still arises, what space is most convenient for contracted ones to abide so until marriage? I answer. Neither so large and long a space as might exceed and shatter those affections which have been settled, so that the parties should now stagger in their steadfastness towards each other, and wax weary through the prolonging of time. Nor yet (on the other side) so short as should hinder their serious addressing towards marriage. Both extremes are to be avoided. For the first, we know in reason and experience that when a contract loses her ends through overlong protraction of time, it taxes the doers for their hasty attempting of that which might have been better delayed. Occasions are given thereby to take offence at each other, that they should seem formerly to make sure of that which afterward they seem but indifferent unto. From this may grow secret bitterness and surmises of heart, tending to breach and division; and so worse may follow, that the one waxing looser towards the other than he to them, there may seem to be wrong received;

Question. What space is the most convenient? Answer.

and so the wronged party hearkening to bad counsel, and consorting with company of ill note, may grow to some new league, not only out of an unclean, but even a revenging disposition, thereby procuring estrangement of heart and irreconcilable difference. Now what a base and absurd abuse of the ordinance is here? How easily might wisdom have prevented all, in removing an occasion of danger? On the other side, when the time is too short, marriage rushing rudely upon the contract in an instant, it defaces the characters of instruction, which should have taken deeper impression, and so crosses the end of a contract as much (in another kind) as the former: taxing also the discretion of the party so hastening, in that he either did no sooner move a contract, or in that he moved it at all. For if there is no difference between a present promise and a promise shortly to be performed, to what end is contract when only marriage would serve? So that a middle space is best: the Jews at the first aimed in their contract at the striking up and securing themselves of the marriages; and after, took large liberty of a year, or half a year, for the consummation. But after, they found they lost as much in the hundred as they got in the shire, and that hereby they endured great inconveniences, many more things falling out between, when the cup and lip are so far asunder: and so, amending their error, they grew to pitch a shorter time. So that it must be the discretion of a man which must herein moderate it: I would think a matter of a week or ten days a complete space; but because occasions may so fall out by absence and travel, that there is more present use of the contract, than of the marriage, and that for settling of minds: and sometimes when speed is intended, yet delays fall out, therefore the due ends of contract and marriage being observed, and good considerations agreed upon by parties (who best know what should hinder them, and what should further them) it is to be left to providence what space is most agreeable. So much for this.

Question. What if either party defiles itself before marriage? Answer.

Another question by occasion hereof, may be moved: what if either of the parties defile themselves by incontinency before marriage? I answer. There need no doubt be made what in such a case ought to be done: for no doubt the contract ought to be broken off. By the law of God, it was death both to the defiler and defiled. This is not a place to determine

whether that law is positive or perpetual, but I should count
him a greater fool than that Levite, who in such a case should
not break off his marriage, as we see in Joseph's case of error
about Mary, before he knew the truth. But if it is demanded,
What if this treachery is not known before the marriage is per-
fected? I answer. I know the judgment of canonists and Popish casuists is one, and divines another. As touching the practice of our church, it is no doubt grounded upon better and
wiser principles: not only because marriage came between the
act and the accusation, and so seems to disannul it (for who
knows not, that the root of it was error?). But to make the
ordinance of marriage more solemn, and to teach people not
easily to admit of separations, which I think is the cause why
divorces being once admitted, the guiltless party is prohibited
the remedy of a second marriage; which being allowed by the
Scripture, would not else be forbidden now, were it not for the
honor of marriage, and the opposition to Jewish abuse (who
used divorces frequently) lest every loose, idle person, having
the liberty of a second marriage, should rush upon the pikes
of divorce. And so (in charity) it is to be judged in the case
of uncleanness committed between a contract and marriage
that separation is cut off, not as if it were not according to the
desert of the offender (for it must have been so among the
Jews, as Moses expressly speaks in that case, when the marks
of virginity could not be produced) but for the safeguarding,
and solemn esteem of marriage, which oftentimes ought not
to have been, but being done, prevails; the honor of an ordinance, being esteemed above the content of this or that married person. This I thought good to say of his question. As for
more, it is not now my purpose: and, as for divorces, I hope
I shall easily be pardoned, if I say not anything. It is already
sufficiently treated of: and, I being here only to speak of an
honorable marriage, it would be as death in the pot, if I should
here come in with that, which of all other things is the most
absolute opposite and dishonor unto it.

I choose rather to end all with some short use. And
first, if contracts are so useful: this is reproof to all such as
deride and vilify this so ancient, so useful an ordinance or
practice of the church: and think it scrupulous, and superfluous. Tush, say they, what a waste is here of words? Must we

Use 1.
Of reproof of
all disdainers
of contracts.

first marry in the Lord, then aptly, and then be taught at our
contract, and then consider of the weight thereof? Here is
preciseness indeed; do not others as well without it? I warrant you, if once married, you will be sure enough without
this ado! Somewhat like Christ's disciples, if this is the case
between husband and wife, it is better not to meddle at all.
So say these, I had rather live single, than make such a stir!
But I answer these two ways: first, as Christ answered them,
no, says he: it is not better not to marry at all: if any man can
abstain upon the gift of chastity, let him: but all cannot. So say
I, if it is so easy to take up a single life, you may: it is best, no
doubt; provided that you mean a single one, and a chaste one
also: for otherwise if you mean (as Papists tell their priests,
better a life of uncleanness than marriage) it is more desirable
to live an unchaste, single life than to make such ado before
you marry, I should greatly pity, but rather sharply tax you for
your labor. For (to come to my second answer) tell me I pray
you, what think you of marriage? Is it a life of looseness and
of the flesh? Else why are you so loath to be well fitted before
you enter it? Surely, you must know that marriage is rather a
curb to the flesh, and a bridle serving to restrain the looseness
thereof. And, do you affect carnal liberty in a condition of
restraint thereof? No, no: rather, if by any means, you might
compass a cheerful and contentful marriage, you should be
glad to take the pains for it, and roll every stone under which
such happiness might lie, and well too: what is a little pains
for a perpetual good, and to shun a constant misery? As Naa-
man's servants told him, if so be the prophet had enjoined you
some great thing, would you not have done it, much more to
wash and be clean? So I say, if the service were far greater,
would you not admit that when the scope is marry and be
happy? Oh, but is it enough (say these) that we are precise in
worship, religion, and in our conscience to God, but we must
be so strict in marriage? So strict: how strict? Would you not
take as much pains for a purchase, even for a good horse or a
good hawk? Would you presume both were good enough if
price enough was set upon their heads? Certainly not, but the
rather you would look to your bargain. So do here: think not
a wife unquestionable because of her price: enquire of her true
value; when you are married, and are stung with his or her un-

quietness, unfaithfulness, and uncleanness. Oh then! What injunction should be put upon you, which you would not yield unto, to be eased of such a burden, in a right way? But I cannot promise you that you shall prevail then so well as you may prevent it now. Do as some gentlewomen do, they will take no maids to train, they will have them trained to their hand, or else none. What will a fool not do out of season to shun sorrow when he has smarted, but in season, that he might not smart he will not stir a joint, nor wet his finger? To verify that of Solomon: To the fool God gives toil and vexation for his portion because he will not be wise for his own ease. But I have before purposely handled this point, I will trench no more upon it. So much for this use of reproof.

A second use then (to finish all), is exhortation to contracted couples to prize their contract for the use of it. I shall not need to joy them of it, that now they have their desires accomplished (that will come alone), but let it be their care to sanctify themselves and their marriage, for time to come. It was the custom of the church of the Old Testament to offer sacrifices to God upon solemn occasions, as upon solemn meetings of the family: when wars were attempted, upon any special service of God to be performed, as fasting, thanksgiving, Sabbaths, circumcision of the children, recoveries from sickness, enjoying of any blessing, Hezekiah and Jonah delivered, offered sacrifices, made songs and vows. Marriage therefore, being a special change of estate, such as befalls once in the life, should have no less solemn preparation for entrance into it. The entry of young ones into this condition, cannot but amass the thoughts and possess the spirits and powers of the soul, more than ordinarily; striking jealousy into them, lest their success should not answer their expectation, and they should not be happy in each other. So that upon whom should all this care and burden be cast, save Jehovah: who has said to married persons as well as others, In nothing take thought, but in all things commending yourselves to God by prayer, and cast your care upon him for he cares for you. Let this be your care, even the promise of God. Indeed, in the verse immediately following this text of marriage, the apostle meets with this corruption in couples, let not your conversation be in covetousness, for he has said, I will not fail you, nor

Marginal notes:
Exhortation. Contracted couples, prize your contract.

1 Sam. 13.12

Job

Heb. 13.5

forsake you. It is no easy thing to stir up a dead heart, to reflect meditations of our future estate: take this time therefore,
now the thoughts and passions of the soul are up in arms, now
the iron is hot, strike some impression of God, faith in his all
sufficiency and providence, into yourselves. And as the lord
of the manor, at each alienation, comes in for his heriot, so
now, at this your change, pay God his fine, the best jewel of all
you have, devote yourselves, give up your souls to him with

Zech. 12.end
1 Cor. 7

mutual consent: rest not in the prayers of others, but set close
yourselves to the Lord in your own supplications both apart
and together without separation. Astronomers call the twelve
days of the nativity critical, for the twelve months of the whole
year; the days of your entry upon marriage should be even
such; for look how the constitution and frame of them is, so
may you expect the time of your marriage will be either for
God's use and the honor of your marriage, or for your own
ends. Unblessed entrances have naughty successes.

Recognize with yourselves, what the solemn opinion
and hope is, which the Lord, his church, and yourselves have
conceived of you. Tremble to think how woeful a defeat it is
to frustrate them and yourselves. Acknowledge God to be the

Deut. 33.end
Luke 22
Gal. 6

ordainer of this estate, look what rules he has directed you
unto for a happy life in this kind, muse of them, set your hearts
unto them, and let them sink deeply into your hearts; take the
Lord as a solemn witness of your intents and purposes to walk
by rule, as you look for peace. And by strong resolutions bind
your fickle hearts as with cords to the altar, and pray God to
set his seal to them that they may prove as good silver in the
performing as they seemed in the promising.

Counsels
especially for
such.

And more particularly, these two things I advise you
unto: first, look what especially base distempers and lusts
you have found to sway in you, either formerly, or since your
purpose of marriage, labor to purge them out that you may
not carry defiled bodies or spirits into the married estate. As
physicians at the end of a disease give their patient a cleansing potion, to expel all scurf of bad humors remaining; so do
you: you are entering into a pure and honorable estate: honor
it before, by burying all your idols, and cashiering your base
lusts, that they crowd not in with you into the wicket of marriage: lest if you shall dare to carry an unclean, froward, covet-

ous, discontented, and unsavory heart with you into that estate, the Lord shall accurse you, and make them as Judas's sop
unto you, to defile you forever after. To the pure all things are
pure, but to the impure everything, even the very mind and
conscience, are defiled. Secondly, look what feeble seeds of
knowledge and grace were sown before marriage, you ply and
attend them carefully for time to come. Promise, even secure
the Lord beforehand, that no contentment of flesh, no humor-
ing of each other, no reaching at commodity, shall so forestall
you, that this work of God should be forgotten by you; rather
lay all sacrifices by the altar, and renew your covenant, both
God's with you, and yours with him; tell the Lord thus: When
my husband, my wife first met me, I was very busy in grounding myself in the principles of knowledge, the sight of sin to
humble me, the truth of the promise to cast me out of myself,
upon the arms of mercy. I was occupied about the doctrine
and use of regeneration, union, and the new creature; now, let
not this marriage of mine deface these fair beginnings; it is appointed for good, let us therefore meet for the better, not the
worse. Take me on further (Lord) as the child takes forth his
lesson, let the sun of my light and grace not go back, but forward, ten degrees: in all my hearings, sacraments, public and
private use of ordinances, growing in the truth, as it is in Jesus,
that together with judgment, sweet affections, and again with
tender affections, sound judgment may grow and increase in
me.

And thus I have finished this point also of a contract,
being the second piece of my digression from the point intended, namely, the honor of marriage, both in the entrance
of it, whereof I have spoken in the first three chapters; and the
continuance of it, whereof in the chapter following shall be
treated.

CHAPTER VI

*Return to the first argument. The honor of marriage in the
preserving of it, during the marriage life.*

The second
general
preservation
of the honor
of marriage in
the conversa-
tion of it.

To return then from where we digressed: now it follows
that we come to the second part of the honor of marriage:
standing in the careful improving thereof in the marriage conversation. It is the nature of honor to love attendance; and
they who have found an honorable marriage, must wait upon
it, and keep it so. And it is a true speech, that it is no less a virtue to keep a man's wealth, name, or honor than to purchase
them. Job tells us that God has denied wisdom to the ostrich
to look to her eggs, to hatch them when she has laid them.
She forgets the work of laying, and leaves them in the sand for
the feet of wild beasts to destroy them. The apostle John wills

2 John 8

that lady and her children not to lose the good things they
have received, but to get a full reward. It had been better that
some had married with far less shows of goodness, and hope
of thrift, except they had kept it better; for there is nothing
so miserable as to have been happy. The praise of that good

Prov. 31

woman in the Proverbs is not that she was virtuous before entrance; no, it was her proof and practice which made her honored, and her husband in her. Many great captains have got
a sudden crown upon their heads: but they have died with a
bare title, and lost it with more shame than the glory came to
which they got it by. It is not said, that Zechariah and Elizabeth were worthy couples in their entrance; but both in their
married course, walked with God. Paul does not only teach
married ones to be married in the Lord, and no more; but how
to live together and maintain conjugal affection, and to keep
that knot by subjection, compassion, tenderness, and faithfulness. Rest not in this (as some scholars do) that their names
are up, and then fall to idleness, and prove dunces. So many
couples are like the image made of gold in the head, silver in
the breast, but worse and worse downward. They would have
their marriage bear up itself, whereas that is, as she is used: if

she is not cautiously observed, she will take a vice, depart, and carry her honor away. Some husbands and wives, through the slighting of religion, as thinking it needless to acquaint themselves with God (as Job says) in all their complaints, wants, and distempers; others by looseness of heart in company, whereof they make but small choice; others pampering themselves with ease and wantonness, lying open and naked to an unsuspected enemy: soon blast that honor of their marriage, which at the first they seemed not dishonorable to enter upon. And others have done the like, by improvidence, by needless meetings, gaming, or the like idle courses, others little observing each other's temper, and so preventing many discontents. Others also by presuming to find at the hands of another more respect and affection: or expecting greater wealth and estate than they found, grow to distastes and debates; then to seek stolen waters, as weary of their own cisterns: and thereupon grows a decay in their estates, discredit among such as esteemed well of them, poverty, imprisonment, and separation from each other. And, what is all this, save to cast their crown into the dirt, and to profane it willfully? Whereas, had they resigned up themselves and the success of all their hopes to God, walking faithfully and keeping covenant both with him and themselves, humbled themselves and submitted painfully to their callings of magistracy, ministry, or private life without ambitious reaching at matters above them, they might have kept their crown and garland fresh and green. Surely, had they set themselves to embrace those graces of God in each party to win love and amity between them, bearing with infirmities, and covering them with tenderness: how flourishing had their head and honor continued without fading, even to this day? But it shall be enough in this place to touch only in the general, upon the equal necessity and coherence of this second duty with the former, for all such as would preserve their honor inviolable. That which I shall further say hereof may more seasonably come into the use of that discourse which shall ensue, after we have cleared the point itself; which because it is large, and will cost consideration, let us enter upon it.

It may then be demanded, wherein this art and skill consists, of saving this honor of marriage so unstained? The answer is, it stands in two sorts of duties; whereof the former

Honor of marriage to be preserved, partly by the joint acts of both, and partly by the several acts of each party.

sort concerns both husband and wife jointly and undividedly
to practice. The latter concerns each of them in several, the
husband apart, and the wife apart. Let us then begin with the
former.

Four joint acts of the married. Those duties which concern both equally are four.
First, unity in religion; mutual love; similar loyal chastity: and
suitable consent. Touching the first of religion: my meaning
is, that as they are entered already with a religious spirit, into
their marriage, so they must continue: not only to be religious still, but to cleave mutually together in the practice of
all such means of worship, and duties of both tables, as concern them; I say, in the parts of religious conversation to God.
More plainly, first, that they are united in the worship of God
publicly, both ordinarily upon the Sabbath (and occasionally
at other times and seasons) as also extraordinary. The Word
must be heard by both jointly, sacraments mutually received,
prayers frequented, and all the worship attended. Secondly,
family duties, concerning both themselves and their children
and servants, as reading of the Scriptures, conferring of them,
prayer, and thanksgiving: exercising those, whom God has
committed to their care, in the principles of Godliness and the
Jointness in worship a main preservative of honorable marriage. several duties of inferiors. The husband being the voice of
God when they are both together; touching which, more shall
be said in the several offices belonging to the husband. If he
is absent, and there is no man of better sufficiency to present,
whom both of them allow of, then ought the wife to discharge
the duty, as hereafter shall appear. Thirdly, and more especially those several duties of worship, which in private and apart
from the other family do concern them: which although they
ought to perform alone also, yet not always, but jointly and
mutually: as to confer, read, pray, confess, and give thanks.
Fourthly, they must be united in the duties of charity to the
poor, hospitality to strangers, relief of other both public causes
and private persons, whom by occasion, God offers to their
regard. Fifthly, that mutual harmony in all religious relations,
both towards themselves, as instruction, reproof, advice, admonition, or encouragement; or else others, in the communion of saints (of which read more at large in my Catechism,
Part 2. Artic. 4), or else in their general and exemplary conversation in the sight of the world, which, when it is mutual, is

resembled in the glass of each other's practice, but if not, then loses her beauty as we see in the opposition which the Holy Ghost makes between Abigail and Nabal in that point.

1 Sam. 25

Before I answer any questions about this, I must ground and prove it by reasons and Scripture. For the latter, it needs not many proofs. That, of these two worthies, Luke 1.6, may be sufficient, of Zechariah and Elizabeth, that both were upright before God, in all the commandments and ordinances of the Lord, without reproof. In which sentence most of those five particulars named before, are touched. That of the apostle may be added, that they defraud not each other except in the case of fasting, lest (says he) your prayers be hindered: that is, your joint communion in religious worship. Now, if there must be such an intercourse in extraordinary duties, how much more in ordinary? But it is objected that Zechariah chapter twelve bids them in their deep humiliations, to be apart; this seems to contradict jointness. I answer. The phrase is not to be exclusively taken, that they should always be apart; for the prophet's scope in the words is that there be singular uprightness in their humiliations, for which cause he enjoins secrecy, because he mourns truly who mourns without witness, but this excludes not jointness in other times and cases, because fervency being as well required in them as sincerity which is more stirred up by mutuality, it is meet they should be mutual in that respect, as apart in the other. So that these two (as occasion differs) exclude not each other.

And there is special reason of this duty. For first, God is not now the God of them apart, as before, but jointly, as married: of them I say, and of their seed: and therefore now, God must be sought jointly by them both, not only in several, as in their former estate.

Reasons of joint religion of couples. Reason 1. God is their mutual God.

Secondly, the good things which they receive from God though they pertain to their several happiness, as their faith, hope, and knowledge, yet they reach to the furtherance of each other's grace; if they are bound then to trade with the whole body of communion for the increase of grace, how much more one with another?

2. Because the grace of each furthers both.

Thirdly, whatsoever they enjoy, good or evil, in a manner they enjoy it in common. Their sins are common (God may punish the one in the other): their gifts and graces

3. They enjoy all things both good and bad in common.

are common (both blessed for the other's sake), their infirmities are common (each being a fellow feeler of the other), their blessings, as health, wealth, and success, are common: their calling and business common, tending to the common good of them and theirs: their crosses common, even their punishments, their posterity, their dwelling, and their friends are common. Should their God then be several? Shall their religion and worship be disjointed? Certainly not: mutual wants and needs must unite and reconcile them to one God with common consent.

4.
Religion is the cement of all fellowship.

Fourthly, religion is the golden cement of all fellowships and unions, both to knit, and to sanctify the same more firmly and closely together. That union, which is not thus fastened, is but as the union of those foxes, backward, by firebrands in their tails, soon dissolved, and very hurtful. The Jews have a pretty observation upon the Hebrew name of the woman, the first and last letters whereof make up the name Jah, God: which if they are taken from the middle letters, leave all in a combustion, for they signify fire. If God enclose not marriage both before and after, and is not in the midst of it, by this band of religious fear; marriage is nothing save a fire: a contentious and an unpeaceable condition. But this consent of both in the Lord is the most firm and blessed of all. Those terms are ever strongest and best agreed, which agree in the best third, or couple. Now the Lord is the best, and the safest band. What a sweet glass is it for husband and wife to see each other's face, even heart in, to be acquainted with each other's graces, or wants, to be assured of each other's love and loyal affection, then to look how they stand affected to the band of their union, I mean fellowship in religion, faith, hope, and the fruits.

5.
From one instance, namely their necessity of joint trust in God.

Fifthly, let us examine this truth, but only in one prime and chief act of religion, and that is faith in the all sufficiency of providence: and that will teach us the rest. What is the married estate, save a very stage of worldly care to act her part? Single persons never come to understand what care means, till marriage comes. That is the black ox which treads hard upon them. How shall this tread be borne except faith in the promise act another part, of holy carelessness (I mean in point of carking)? Surely, as the fashion of some countries is to hang up a care-cloth in the bridechamber, to cool the heat of other affections in the married, and to put them in mind what an estate they are entering upon; so, well may this cloth of care ever hang in their chamber, except faith take it down and fasten their care upon him that cares for them, cutting off all superfluous carking. Now this grace belongs jointly to both of them: not only to the husband, who follows the world hard to please his wife; but also to the wife, who (as the apostle says) is as ready to please him. What a gulf of care do both plunge themselves into, except the Lord vouchsafe them his antidote? What craft, tricks, cozenages, and deceits will they not find out, to scrape and rake together, all being fish that come into their net? What clamors, discontents, and brawls will arise if defeated of their wills? What baseness will utter itself upon any other expenses than expected? But let the Lord be their portion, rock, and defense, and what can distract them? How sweetly will both draw in this yoke, if, as they have made God the God of the hills, so they can make him of the valleys, I mean, the God of their bodies as well as their souls? Now, if this one joint gift does so run through all their life, what will joint consent in all graces do, as hope of salvation, fitness to die, mercy, compassion, love, fear, meekness, and the rest? All which in their kind, under faith, serve to furnish the married condition with contentment and welfare.

Sixthly and lastly, what can so assuredly bring in blessing to the bodies, souls, posterity, families, and attempts of each other, as jointness of religion? When both are agreed of their verdict and one builds up as fast as the other? When no sooner the one enterprises anything, but the other joins in a commending it to God for blessing. They are not daring to go to work in an unblessed way, without God. That no sooner they spy an infirmity, much more a corruption in each other, but they reserve it for matter of humiliation, against next time. No sooner they meet with a mercy, but they make it matter of thanks, keeping the altar ever burning with this fuel and sacrifice. What a sweet derivation is this to both, of pardon and blessing? What a warrant is it unto them both that each shall share in all good, when as both do equally need it, so each seek it of God? When God is made both of court and counsel, privy to all doubts, fears, and wants of both, what can so as-

6.
Nothing has such a blessing annexed to it.

sure them of a happy condition when censuring, condemning, or quarreling with each other is turned into a mutual melting in God's bosom, for the grief and complaints of one another: when in Christ their advocate they sanctify all to themselves and make all things pure to them, bed, board, love, crosses, and mercies, which else to others are unclean and defiled. This for Reasons.

Question. What if the one party will not join with the other? Answer.

A question here offers itself, if the grace of the married must be joint, what is to be said when the husband will not concur with the wife, or she with him, in such duties of piety or mercy, as do mutually concern them? Must she then desist, for lack of jointness? I answer. The question is much harder if it is made of such a husband, as not only does not concur actually with the wife, but is contrarily minded unto her. I will therefore frame the answer to both cases. I say then that the wife may supply the defect of his non-concurrence with her, in these acts of religion, or charity. For why? His defect of joining, although it may hinder the grace of the duty, yet it must not hinder the essence of performance: better is it, that God is served in prayer, in teaching the family, training the children; that the poor are relieved, and good done, as it may be, than not at all. Not only because the defect may possibly proceed in the man rather from impotency and weakness: in which respect, the wife making supply (especially being eminently better fitted than other women are) does as it were, obtain acceptance of both, as if both could join, and the husband could be the mouth of the woman to God. This being provided, that her gifts consist in a humble modesty, as in other sufficiency. But besides also, though the husband is opposite to good himself, yet if he connives at good in her, she must not under any pretext, detract the duty from God, by his lewdness, and incur double wrath from God. I add further, although he is actually opposite, that is forbid it to be done, yet as the case may require, through necessity of present miseries, she is bound to step out from her ordinary course, as Abigail did in Nabal's desperate abandoning of David's servants. But I wish the reader to suspend his thoughts awhile, till I shall find fitter occasion to treat of this answer: which will be afterward, partly in the duty of the husband's understanding, partly of the wife's subjection. Here therefore, I do but touch it.

I proceed to the use, as I began. And that is, first reproof of a foolish contrariety of couples in this kind. They
will be religious in marriage, but how? Indeed as they were
before: they will go apart by themselves, and severally; but,
this jointness of worship, they abhor, as too strict and needless. They will grant that they must read, pray, and confer, but
it must be as formerly, either apart, or with other company;
but as for imparting themselves to each other, they are loath
to utter their ignorance, barrenness, and ungroundedness in
the principles, or their spiritual forgetfulness, unthankfulness,
and lukewarmness, especially the defect in marriage duties to
each other. These they are ashamed to make each other privy
to. God only is (they think) meet to be acquainted with them.
Why? Are you such strangers? Were you not as able before
marriage, as now, to do this? Are you now in no deeper relations than before? Then you could not, but now you may do
otherwise, and will you not do it? I cannot better describe
the folly hereof than by the fondness of such wives, as when
they speak to their husbands, they call them by their names,
or place, master such a one, or John, Richard, etc. so, as any
other might call them, as well as they, or as they might call
them, before marriage. Surely the name of your relation, husband or wife, I think, is fitter for them than common names.
The like I say here, such a religion (I believe) is fitter for you,
as might best agree with your near union; and not such as
any unmarried person may enjoy. Woe to him that is alone
says Ecclesiastes, for if he falls who shall help him? And, to
one, how should there be heat (he means of generation)? But
two are better than one: how does this agree with the course
of such? They are alone even when they are two: and they
are two (divided) when they should be as one. Surely if they
should claim power in several over their own bodies, or power
to have a several purse, or a stock going apart, it is less sinful
than thus to nourish a worship of God, wholly apart from each
other. May any so fitly join in mutual confession or thanks
as they, who have but one God, and can (as one soul in two
bodies) fellow-feel, and compassionate each other's case as his
own? Is there any rent so bad as in a seamless coat? What can
this division savor of, but pride, singularity, and self-love? Or
how would the Devil desire to rule, rather than by this sepa-

Use 1.
Reproof.
Severalness of
religion in the
married sinful,
if affected.

ration? I ask, do you hold the body, or the body you? And, who hurts you herein, save your own body and soul, by refusing such a succor? Would you not think it an unkindness in the heart and liver, if it would keep in all spirits and blood within themselves, and transmit none to the parts? Must it not threaten (as he said once) putrefaction and obstruction to themselves, and ruin to the whole? So much for this first.

Branch 2. Hinderers of each other in such joint religion, to be taxed.

Secondly, this reproves all such couples as are rather hindrances to each other in the matters of God than helpers either in ordinances or duties. Such as, when family duties are called for, either by husbands or wives, then they lay logs in each other's way, then of all other times, their business sticks to their fingers, then they have most irons in the fire to attend, errands abroad, or children within, to run upon, to dress. If private duties are occasioned, much more awkward and untoward they are. If any duty of compassion and mercy offers itself, visiting the sick, counseling of the distressed, helping of the needy, comes in their way, they vex and cross it, dismay each other from it. Furthermore, and yet professed to be religious nevertheless. Oh woeful ones! Is this your consent? Do you thus honor your marriage? Did you enter it with some opinion of religion, and do you thus promote it? Is it not a sweet flower bouquet for you to smell to, to hear your husband's allegations, this duty, Sabbath, sacrament, fast, had been done, sanctified, enjoyed, had not you hindered? Take heed, God will not be mocked! If this is done by the religious, what shall the irreligious do? If this is done in the green tree, what shall be done in the dry?

Branch 3. Such as do rest in each other's religion, taxed.

Thirdly, it reproves all such as basely rest in the religion of each other, though themselves look after none. Many women good for nothing but for drudgery, yet have a conceit husband's prayers, their zeal and holiness shall serve their turn, and under that rotten rag, they shroud themselves. No, no, this plaster is too narrow for the sore. If each party will fare the better for other, both must combine, both must pray, fast, sanctify their blessings and crosses, wives must not plod for their children's backs and bellies, leaving the care of their souls and good government to their husbands. What is this, but to be a true slave, but an unfaithful wife? Rather say this, husband, I have a part in them as well as you, sure I am, they have received as much of old Adam from me, as you. Oh, that I had as careful a spirit to train them up as you. So in other parts of duty, rest not either of you in other's religion, being barren yourselves, for each tub shall stand on his own bottom. The goodness of one shall not be imputed to other; but the soul that sins shall die. Take heed lest it be verified, two shall be in one bed, the one taken and the other refused! As God has made you for marriage to be one flesh, so see that by grace you are one spirit.

Fourthly, to these may be added the preposterousness of such couples, as are then safest, when as they forsaking their bosom fellowship, run into the company of strangers, to converse with: to them they impart their marriage discontents, crave counsel, advice from them, betraying (by their practice) their husbands to base report; all, and more than all their grief they pour into strange bosoms, refusing their own, who are much better than themselves, and then it is best done when most privily, and furthest from their husband's notice. But they may never hear of anything from them, except with upbraiding and discontent. They must either hear of it from strangers, or not at all. Oh, how many of these housewives have deceived minister, friends, and husbands by their subtlety? Until afterward their sin betrays them, what mettle and stamp they are of! The truth is, their love is unfound, their hearts turbulent, their tongues querulous and clamorous. But, if their husbands are taken from them, and their eyesores removed, then religious persons and the minister shall no more hear of them; their hearts are upon new liberties, all their groanings are vanished, and the next husband (though less religious than the former) pleases them better. Oh woeful hypocrites, thus to color over a rotten heart with religious complaints! God shall meet with you, in your kind, and make yourselves at last your own judges when his plagues seize upon you! Repent beforehand, and prevent them, if you are wise. Your sin is hereby worse than others, who perhaps of mere ignorance neglect this duty, being otherwise honest. To whom I give this caveat, let your sin this day come to your remembrance, amend it, and the good Lord regard not, but pass by your former errors upon your repentance.

As for those couples who are both agreed in their

Branch 4. Married persons who forsake their own fellowship and run to strangers, faulty.

Use 2.

graceless contempt of this duty, as they also are in all ordinary worship of God, they belong not to this place; I have before spoken to such in the point of unequal matches. They (of all others) are furthest off, let them prepare to make answer to their judge, who being commanded to honor their marriage with mutual religion, dare mock God this way. Indeed in one sense it may be said, they are equally religious, for the one has as much as the other, neither barrel better leading, for both are profane, and as they entered so they continue. Well, God could have promoted you to some honor: but you have chosen shame, he has poured contempt upon you, thank yourselves.

Use 3. Cause of the unhappy and unprosperous state of many couples is want of mutual religion.

Thirdly, this teaches us the true cause, why so many couples lead a sad, comfortless life: some cry out, they can have no peace with one another. Others, that they thrive not, cannot be well reported of, or their children disquiet them. God is against them, nothing prospers. Alas! What wonder! God is the last end of your thought; he is not set up in your married estate! He is thrust out into the back room; who yet should be all in all, chief in your souls, prayers, family, and worship. He is nothing at all, and is it strange nothing goes forward? How should it? Surely if it should (as perhaps some as bad as you thrive) I should think he meant to destroy you! But now, since he sends this bailiff to arrest you, and fills you with adversity, I hope it is to bring you to a parley (as Absalom in burning Joab's barley) to provoke and stir you up to lay hold upon him, in due season! Consider yourselves, set him up better, honor him and he will honor you, but if you dishonor him, he will (as Samuel told Eli) lightly esteem of you. Prevent it in time, before he comes upon you worse; he has hitherto been only as a moth, and destroyed your beauty, but he can tear you in pieces as a lion, if you look not to it! Pick out the secret canker out of this apple, else it will consume all. And this I add, although you should swim in all welfare, and prolong your days, if this is all your mourning, for corn and oil, it shall be given you as a curse: if you see not God's meaning, and honor not your marriage, by resigning up your crown, and casting it at God's feet, depending upon him for blessing; you shall die dishonorably, and live without comfort: it is not all the wealth you have that shall help you to joy, but rather as quails shall all come out at your nostrils, and leave you desolate.

Fourthly, let this be exhortation to all good couples who fear God, to be united in their religion together. And here give me leave to speak a word or two of some particular duties: and then of your general conversation. Touching the former, I would touch these two, the one touching family worship, outward, the other touching that grace mentioned in the fourth reason before, I mean faith in God's providence, which is inward. I begin therefore with this. Consider both of you, there is but need of it, in this your course of worldly dealing: most couples have met to increase carking and distrust, as much rain to make a torrent. The Devil will so stuff and fill them with carking and covetousness, their own base hearts set upon the creature will so inflame them, the error of the wicked will so pollute them through lust, by their cursed example that many who meet together in hope of becoming saints, after they have met, prove little better than disguised heathen. Well might the apostle join the caveat of marriage here with that of covetousness in the next verse: and mark his phrase, let not your conversation be in covetousness: the words are, roll not (as the door upon her hinges) in the love of silver: his meaning is this, marriage is a rolling up and down from one carnal business to another: the calling, the looking to children, buying in, paying out, stocking the grounds, raising of commodity thereupon, going out and in, and walking in a round of the world: nothing but scuffling and shuffling to get and scrape: except there is this gift of faith to season the heart in all this orb and round: to settle it in the center of providence, to sweeten it with affiance in God. Alas, else all the questions will be, how shall these chargeable servants be fed? How shall all these debts be paid? What losses are here in our cattle? How poor are our takings in our shops? Our trades are mean, our children are many, what shall we eat, wherewith shall we be clothed? Alas, little thought I at first entrance, that marriage had been of this dye, I thought all had been white and fair: now I see corn, cattle, husbandry, and housewifery, all lies at the courtesy of mercy, the stock is out, and except God bless it, may never come in again, except God give success, good seasons of weather, crops will fail, rents will be unpaid, and we may die beggars. What? Did you think marriage was but a song, a sport, a honeymoon, of one day's

Use 4. Exhortation to all good couples to be joint in their religion.

Both inward, as in faith, and the like.

jollity? Did you not consider that it is a perpetual exercise of faith, for yourselves, for your children, for your servants, and business? If you did not, then learn wisdom now: God has set you in it, to try you, what mettle you are made of: whether it will make you disguised heathens, or gracious believers, who commend yourselves and all to God, shutting up yourselves in his ark that the floods of great waters overflow not. I tell you marriage is a stage for faith to act upon, to cast and venture all upon him, who will care for you, and promises to do all your works for you. Be therefore both of you just before God, walk in this command of faith, as well as any, indeed this before any. Take no carking thought how children should be maintained, educated, portioned, and married. Do not as one lately did: having one son born, he vowed he would have no more, whatsoever came of it, for he meant to leave that child all his estate (judge by the way into what noisome snares a base heart brought him into), and he would have no more, to be beggars. Would it be thought, this Devil of unbelief was so rank? Why, marriage will make covetousness a venial sin (worse than the Pope makes it), without faith.

Faith is the principal prop of the married.

Be resolved of it, faith must be your only help, to stop you from drowning in this gulf. Else no farm or occupying will be great enough: you would think all your life but a moment, for the satisfying of an insatiable spirit. So many irons at once in the fire, till one mar another, and overthrow all. Else, you will pick quarrels with your trades, and be ready to forsake them as fast as you embrace them, and so weary yourselves with losses, till ruined. Else you will be so sordid, so pinching and base in your housekeeping, so subtle, false in your selling, you will grow defrauders, oppressors, usurers, and cheaters in your traffic and trades, so eager in your toil, so impatient of a defeat, so injurious and unmerciful not only to your beasts, but even to your wives, selves, children, and servants: so base in your works of charity that both God and men loathe and are weary of you. What patterns of such married ones does almost every town afford? And when God frowns upon them then they gnaw their tongues for vexation and wax as profane in the first table, scorners of worship and Sabbaths, as before unjust in the second. Therefore, live by faith both husband without, and wife within, this is a joint work of both

Infinite miseries of the married through the distrust of God's providence.

(of your several duties I shall speak after). Does gain come in and wealth abound? Set not your heart upon it: be not giddy, wanton, or sensual: faith abhors such behavior and settles the soul in a sober frame of thankfulness. Does God cross you? Distrust him not, deject not your hearts, God is able to supply it. How else was David supported when not only city and wealth, but also wives were carried captives? Surely by faith he comforted himself in God, and recovered all. Am I in debts? God will pay them. I came not into them by my sin, but God brought me in by providence: he therefore shall bring me out. Have I losses? God will restore them as to Job. Am I sick in body, diseased, husband and wife each lying upon other's hand, threatened by creditors to go to prison, fallen into the hand of a merciless landlord? Faith will cast you upon a merciful God: and although the common proverb is, faith will never buy corn or clothes: yet do but improve it, and you shall find, it will be like Solomon's silver and answer all things, buy all markets. She serves a master who can mollify the hearts of the cruelest enemy, who will sooner suffer the lions to be hunger-bit than his poor shiftless lambs to want. All the fish in the sea are his; his are all the sheep on a thousand hills, all the mines of red and white earth, all the money in all men's purses. All things are Christ's, you being his all things are yours, and shall be cast in as a surplus unto you. You need not say, husband, wife, we shall be destroyed one day by this poverty; therefore we must fall to indirect courses, as others, to bring in the penny. No, let atheists say this, they who have a God to trust to, let them never dishonor him by such doings: thereby making him their enemy, lest they are compelled to speak for somewhat. He that clothes the grass of the field and the lilies, which neither labor nor spin, much more will do for them that trust him. You serve no hard master, nor one that needs your sin to serve his providence. This faith must be *Domina fac totum*, she must do all and suffer all, and carry all, she must be the stirring housewife (or else in vain do others stir) who can do more with sitting still than all others, though each finger were a thumb. By her therefore and her daughter patience possess your souls, and commend yourselves to him, who will effect your desire. This for the former particular, for faith in the promise.

Family duties
and private
worship are
necessary for
good couples
to join in
closely.

The other particular is outward, which is the joint serving of God in the family. Though both of you pray not, yet the one hold it up in the other's absence, and set up God with both hands in your house. Let prayer, reading, and other worship be first in your dwelling and sanctify it, at your first entrance, and afterward season and sweeten it, and all, both persons and things that belong to that. Let all go under the banner and protection of God by it. It must be as the temple morning and evening sacrifice, what else soever you add thereto, you may, but this must be constant. The Holy Ghost loves to honor this sacrifice through the Scripture. Daniel would pray at the season of it, Elijah would offer his sacrifice at that time, and so the rest. And this sacrifice made all the rest welcome and blessed. Therefore be joint in it; begin not zealously at first and end in the flesh, which is the custom of most couples. Look not awry with an evil eye upon it, to cast your businesses so unhappily as to trench upon the season thereof: as if your hearts secretly grudged at God in it, and could scarce bestow it. Both of you be just before God in it: striving who should go before the other in it: be no snare to each other not only by your backwardness and murmuring at it, not so much as in your indifference of spirit toward it: lest you defile each other by it, and so you grow mannerly to put it off at first, and then by degrees by any trifling occasion to outwear it. Know it, that by the defacing of this, you outwear all blessing, and go in the row of them of whom it is said: pour out your wrath upon the families which call not upon your name. Be very serious to task yourselves to it, to press each other not only to a performing of it in general, to say a few prayers, but to be instant, fervent, and constant in it. The seasoning of your children, the awe and government of your servants depends upon it: and where it is wanting, both proves ruinous and brutish, besides the misery of the whole family condition. Use all wisdom you man, all prevention and early care, you woman, both without and within, that all business and occasions may be set at a stay and dispatched that this weighty affair stands not abandoned for them. Be sure that your heart smites you often in the day, when shrewd turns befall your children, your house is in danger by casualty of fire, your husband and you quarrel, or any other sad accident happens; to say, these are because we sought not God this day: therefore is this mischance befallen me in my cattle, or in my travail, or by a fall off my horse, or ill success in my business, or the like. Let not the coming in of friends, strangers, break it off: sit not loose to it, lest each toy unsettle it. Awe the family to it, both join in the drawing of your inferiors to reverence it, lest if form and commons once break in, the next news is weariness, and so breaking it off. And with prayer, let solemn calling of the children and servants to account be practiced. If you can possibly let the morning rather than noon be your appointed season, lest necessary occasions deprive some, whom it concerns. Choose it before meals if it is possible. If the greatness of household hinders that then take heed that drowsiness, slumber, and the Devil set not in their foot to mar all, which for the most part is the canker of most family duties: which through custom is made nothing of, till it has cast out duty itself upon the dunghill. I shall speak more of the man's duty in special afterward: this now I thought good to premise in general. And this of these two particulars, of the joint duty of couples is said. Now I come to the general exhortation, and so finish the chapter. *Needful to use private worship.*

      Let it be therefore exhortation to all good couples to be mutual in all religious duties, ordinances, and service of God. This will strengthen the wheel of marriage life as the strong spokes in the cart wheel strengthen it from cracking and splitting. Live not like strangers to God: for so shall you never be inward with each other: your life will wax common and fulsome, past and spent out in a shadow and vanity, even vexation of spirit: and at your death, you shall say, Alas we never knew one another truly. I dare not snare you for setting of canonical hours, or for frequency of duty. I leave that to your own experience, who should best know each other's wants, or at least your own to draw you to it. It is not meet that families are made privy to the privacy of their governors. It is the next way to make them despised. It is best referring them to your own seasons, except yourselves are the whole family, for then the difference is taken away. I say, there may be secret cases wherein even each party may choose secrecy; in such, be wise and pour out your hearts to God apart, as it is like Rebecca did in the strife of her twins. There is a season for all things, and marriage secrets are sacredly to be kept. Therefore *Causes why it should be so.*

I say let this be the chief pearl of the marriage crown; search out all your corruptions. Make a register of all favors of God, which God has granted to you and to your wife in common; such as at the time of receiving, seemed most precious, and might ill have been spared. Mark how the Lord has gone before you and ordered your conversation. Consider together how happily, and yet perhaps hardly you met in marriage: what sound love and covenant the Lord bred at first in you: how they have since held firm; and although many things have come in to weaken them, yet they have not prevailed. Consider how your hearts are drawn daily to each other: calming your unquiet spirits (which otherwise would not keep compass) so that you look not upon each other with the eyes of serpents, but of doves. Observe how Sabbaths and sacraments are blessed, how your faith and peace grows, your fears decay, how your corruptions are purged; what dangers in body, state, and children you avoid; and what sorrows, which encumber others, you are free from. Also what success in your children's tractableness and towardness: what faithfulness and subjection in your servants (for is it not God who makes many stout stomachs of both sexes, subject to weak governors? as David says), how your fellowship with the good increases, what new blessings are fallen upon you, in persons, names, trades, and posterity. Mark also well where Satan most insults, and where the hedge is lowest with you: what corruptions (as old sores) break out in their seasons, which yet seemed to be quashed before; what lusts of the heart, lust of the eye, or pride of life bubbles up from within. Look not each into himself or herself, but each into other as having interest deeply planted; yet do it not with curiosity but simplicity. By this means both abundant matter and manner, as oil to the lamp, will offer themselves to nourish this ordinance; all lust of sloth, all rust of ease, weariness will be filed off. And a free heart to make God the umpire of your differences (if any be, as how can it be avoided, but a root of bitterness within, will less or more break out), the composer of your hearts, the granter of your requests, and the gracer of your marriages will be obtained. And fear not lest this course should in time weary you, or alienation from each other should grow to distaste this duty; for the Lord who has founded it, will own it and can bless it, and keep out disorder;

Great benefit of private joint worship.

Counsels about it.

and the sweet fruit of this service will so both prevent, attend, and follow you in all your ways that you shall feel yourselves to walk before each other, and both before God, less loosely, more soundly and safely. For why? How can it otherwise be when both of you remember whom you used to go to (as to the oath and covenant), both in your confessions, on which you shame yourselves for your failings, and in your requests, craving pardon and purging, and where you have done well, to praise him for support, and to be thankful for that administration and protection of his, under which (as his beloved) you have been all the day long.

I conclude therefore, go to God more jointly than ever; hold, and pull more hard and close together, so often as you go to the throne of grace; especially, when as with that good Jacob, you are resolved not to cease wrestling till you are blessed. Compel him to send you away with your request, else you cannot be answered. Go by a promise in your Advocate and say, Now Lord, this new state of ours requires new manners, new self-denial, new faith, new life, a double portion of grace; beg it therefore as Elisha did; all that belongs to you, requires a new part in you: and, who is sufficient for these? Make yourselves nothing: and God all in all, who can satisfy you. Separate not yourselves in these duties as others do in congregations, or others in board and bed, but say, Come, let us pray together, confess, give thanks, I am as you are, my people as yours, my horses as yours, my thoughts, affections, members, as yours. By this means, love shall so grow that it shall outgrow all distempers. You shall say of each other, I never thought my wife had the tithe of that grace in her heart, or that my husband had half that humbleness, compassion, and faith, which now I perceive. Those evils, those infirmities, which would forever have estranged some and caused distaste, I see in him, in her, breed so much the more love to my soul, sympathy, and mercy. This from this wellspring of joint worship shall flow streams of honey and butter (as Job speaks) into all the life. Especially when crosses and straights shall befall you, then shall God be nearest of all unto you, and be afflicted with you in all; because you have made him the God of your mountains, he will be the God of your valleys also, whereas others, who never thus traded with him, shall be sent

Exhortation to private intercourse with God.

to their idols and to shift for themselves. And as touching the
first duties of mutualness, namely of these four jointnesses of
religion and worship, thus much.

CHAPTER VII

The second mutual duty of the married, namely,
conjugal love handled.

I now proceed to the second main and joint duty of the married which is conjugal love. For the better handling whereof it will not be amiss first to premise somewhat, touching the nature of it: and then to show some reasons why it should be jointly preserved, adding some means whereby it may be done, and so, concluding with use.

The second joint office of the married, conjugal love.

That infinitely and only wise God who both upholds by his providence all his creatures in their kinds and subsisting, and has by one soul of harmony and consent accorded each with other for their mutual aid and support. Much more has his hand in the accord of reasonable creatures, their fellowship and league together, as without which they could not well continue in their welfare and prosperity. And therefore, for the more sweet reconciling and uniting of the affections of one to another in every kind of league and fellowship, both the more general and common, standing in outward commerce, and the more near and close, as in friendship and marriage; he has accordingly planted in every nature, sex, and person more or less sympathy that the one not possibly being able to subsist without the other, might by this tie love each other and be knit to the other in union and affection. This appears even in the most remote contracts of buying and selling, borrowing and lending: wherein although the league stands rather in things than in persons yet even there is seen a general kind of love, each man choosing to trade and traffic with them whose spirit and frame is most suitable to their own. When God meant to enrich the Israelites by the bounty of the Egyptians, he darted in for the time such a sympathy into their hearts that they found favor in their eyes; so that nothing was then too dear for them, jewels and gold and silver, till they had impoverished themselves. And in those combinations of men which are grounded in law and civil order in commonwealths

Love ought to be jointly preserved for the honor of marriage.

Not only bred by peculiar instinct.

and corporations, although there is a necessary bond to keep all sorts within order and government: yet there is to be observed between those members a more peculiar bond between some than others, through a suitableness of disposition that is in them, whereby for special causes, the one does more tenderly affect someone or other, than the common body can affect itself. This yet does much more appear in the league of friendship, wherein we see God does so order it, that by a secret instinct of love and sympathy, causing the heart of the one to incline to the other, two friends have been knit so close to the other that they have been as one spirit in two bodies, as not only we see in Jonathan and David, but in heathens which have striven to lay down their lives for the safeguard of each other. And that the finger of God is here appears by this, that oftentimes a reason cannot be given by either party why they should be so tender to each other. It being caused not by any profitable or pleasurable means, but by mere sympathy, which is far the more pure and noble cement of union than what else soever. Moreover, in the very senseless creatures is to be seen this amity and nearness that as some have an antipathy to each other, as the shadow of the walnut is noxious to other plants; so the elm and the vine do naturally so entwine and embrace each the other that it is called the friendly elm; who can tell why? Much more then in reasonable creatures, it must be so. And hence those heathens (that could go no further) make the very constellations of heaven, under which two are born, to be the cause and influence of their accord. I know not what star (says one) has tempered my nature so fitly to yours that we should be so united. And another, scoffing at one he distasted, tells him, I love you not certainly, and yet I cannot tell why (for you never hurt me), but this I am sure of, that I love you not. What wonder then, if God for the preserving of that band which is nearest of all, most durable of all, and the most fundamental of all: has much more caused a secret sympathy of hearts to live in the breasts and bosoms of some men and some women that are to live in the married estate (whereof no reason can be given, save the finger of God), whereby I say their hearts and affections do consent together, of two to become one flesh, the most inward union of all. Why is it, that (all others set aside, sometimes more amiable in themselves, richer, better bred, and the like) yet through this instinct of sympathy (a hidden and unknown cause), two consent together to become husband and wife? Surely by this it appears that by how much less reason can be given of this temperament, so much the more God is in it, as purposing by a more precious and uniting band than ordinary to knit them together, whom he purposes to maintain in such a league, as must endure and cannot be dissolved, when once it is made. So that we see marriage love is often a secret work of God, pitching the heart of one party upon another for no known cause; and therefore where this strong lodestone attracts each to other, no further question needs to be made, but such a man and such a woman's match was made in heaven, and God has brought them together.

But, because the finger of God is not so manifest in all matches as by a secret inspiration to unite them, and because man being a reasonable creature is led in affections, not to live by sensual appetite, as a beast, but by rational motives and inducements: therefore providence discovers itself herein also: even framing the matter so that oftentimes where this natural inclination fails, and where in likelihood some antipathy and contrariety of spirits would appear; yet, by some accidental endowments of religion, of education, of eminent natural parts, of sweet disposition, even that party pleases best, who yet was as likely to displease as much as any in the general. I say this is a providence more general than the former: so ordering things, that where mere sympathy fails, yet another band may prove (to some persons) as pleasing and lasting, when as they see that one defect is recompensed with another eminency and perfection. Who but God has so accorded it that many a woman of exquisite beauty and person, like to attract love enough (in a mutual way of man) should yet come short of inward wit, wisdom, and abilities? Surely he, who does all so well that nothing can be found out after him better than he has made it, has thus appointed it, lest if all perfections should concur in one impotent subject, the heart would be too big for the bosom, and swell into an excess of pride and self-love. And on the other side, who has so ordered it that oftentimes where beauty fails, where their person is ordinary, there yet, these uncomely parts should be clothed with greater honor, of

But oftentimes by outward occasions and motives.

virtue, understanding, industry, providence, and other qualities of worth: and all for this universal end, that there might be an equality? So that whereas the person in some regards might be an object of disdain, yet in others might be to a rational and wise man, a meet object of esteem, her gifts drowning her defects, and so sustaining the poor creature from contempt and scorn. This God does by his wisdom so order contraries, that being brought by his own skillful hand to a due temperature, they might cause a most pleasing harmony: so that oftentimes a nimble wit joined with a more slow, a phlegmatic temper with a sanguine, a melancholic with a merry, a choleric with a mild and patient temper, might behold the workmanship of God herein with such admiration that the frame of spirit which in the general might seem most repugnant, yet in respect of the necessary usefulness and commodity thereof, might find most favor. And why? Surely because similitude of distempers might breed confusion in the married estate, whereas the one quality allaying the other might reduce the body to a sweet harmony and correspondence. So that still we see God has a hand in this union of hearts in the married and although some unite through a secret sympathy: others from some confessed good and amiable object in the party loved; yet God is in them both, that by a strong matrimonial knot the married couples might eke out that love and affection towards each other, which else neither the need of each other, no nor religion itself could alone maintain and preserve. And so much for this second branch.

Conjugal love is a mixed affection.   By all I have said it may be perceived that by conjugal love, here, I mean not only Christian love, a grace of God's Spirit (for marriage borders much upon nature and flesh): nor yet a carnal and sudden flash of affection, corruptly enflamed by concupiscence (rather brutish than human): but a sweet compound of both religion and nature. The latter being as the material, the former as the formal cause thereof, properly called marriage love. And this love is not a humor raised suddenly in a pang of affection, ebbing and flowing. Sometimes when the parties are set upon the stage abroad, among company and strangers, where they would act a part for their credit (for family and place where they live ought to be their true stage of action); but a habited and settled love planted in them by God, whereby in a constant, equal, and cheerful consent of spirit they carry themselves to each other: each hollow companion will exceed, at an odd time, and put down true lovers: And how? who if they were tried by their uniform love would be tried as jades and betray themselves to be counterfeits. Whatsoever is according to God is equal, though but weak. So is this, of the love of couples. No union of imagination, mixture, nor yet bare affection, but an effect of divine institution, between two (for polygamy is the corruption of marriage), not to be dissolved until death, except uncleanness divorced it. This love is (as the echo to the voice) the vital spirit and heart blood of this ordinance causing a voluntary and practical union of two, without which union alone by virtue of God's institution is but a forced necessity. For then has this ordinance her perfection when this solder of love being added thereto makes that union, which cannot be broken, to become such a willing one as (to choose) would not be broken. Else friendship is a better one-ship than marriage, because that may be dissolved when it waxes a burden, whereas this holds, be it ever so wearisome. But then is it happy when the lover and the loved enjoy each other: else the fellowship of those married ones, whose love has degenerated into bitter hatred, is as good as the best: for the worst, marriage is such that (till one ceases to be) it cannot cease to be a knitting of two in one; no time, no distance of place, no sin (except adultery) breaking it off: but how miserable a necessity is that which has no law, no remedy? Hence God has allowed so many respects and liberties in the choice of husbands and wives, because he would straighten none, but that they might live lovingly, except the fault is their own. So that as he who marries for other ends, religion being neglected, offends chiefly, so does he also who shall marry one religious, without due caution of other things which might strengthen love, even he shall sin against the comfort of his own life. And it is certain that the longer the love compounded of the forenamed causes does last, marriage is but a carcass void of life. And the stronger the tie is the more irksome is the marriage, being frustrate of that precious thing for which it should love groundedly.

Let me add some reasons why this so joint a bond Reason of it. should be carefully preserved. First, nothing is so precious among men in worldly respects as that for which the husband loves and desires the wife; and she him; no union so strong as this; no joy in any outward union so content as this; nor able to wish well to the thing loved as this. For though I must love my neighbor as myself, yet I am bound to love my wife otherwise for both kind and measure than my neighbor; truly and in some sense, better than myself. And it is truly observed that this rule of loving our neighbor is rather to be expounded privatively or negatively than positively: forbidding rather to do any hurt to my neighbor, which I would not do to myself, than commanding to do him so much good as to myself. Since by this means I should be bound to feed and clothe him as myself, which is abused. But my wife I am bound to love as myself in both respects as myself; both in the negative and affirmative sense. Hence is that of the apostle, no man ever hated his own flesh, but nourished and cherished it, even so ought a man to love his wife as himself: not only in distress, for so am I bound to love my enemy, if your enemy hunger, feed him, etc. but constantly and at all times. Hence is the general rule urged mutually upon both, husband, love your wives as Christ loved his church and gave himself for it, to purge and wash it that it might be without spot: and the like he professes upon the wife to him; wives love your husbands, etc. noting it to be a reciprocal duty.

But yet this I must add, that this so mutual a duty is yet required of both in a different manner. For the more clear understanding whereof, observe, that as the love wherewith Christ loves his church is a more abundant and bountiful love than that whereby she loves him again; truly, her love is as her other graces, fetched from his fullness, which he communicates unto her by his Spirit, so is the woman's love in the carriage thereof to the man's. And as the dim light of the moon borrowed from that principle of light the sun; so by proportion, the love of the wife is as borrowed from the love of the husband. He is the fountain of the relation, she follows as the correlative, and her love is the stream issuing from his spring. Love must descend from him as the oil of Aaron's head descended down to his beard and his clothing. So that the manner of this imparting love must be orderly: the husband is to offer, to bestow, and communicate himself first to his wife; in a

Eph. 5.29

Rom. 12.20

Eph. 5.25

Tit. 2.4,5

Conjugal love, though a joint duty, to be carried in a several way.

Psal. 133.2

free, bountiful, full love; she is not so much bound to vie upon his love, or to love bountifully and actively as to reflect and return upon himself his own love, and that in a reverent, amiable, and modest manner. Thence is it, that as often as Paul uses the charge of husbands loving their wives (which is very frequent), yet he very seldom, and but once urges the woman to love her husband (but as if he would have them, their love, and all to be drowned in their subjection): he presses them to be subject to their husbands; wives submit yourselves: and, let the wife reverence her husband. Noting, that although the married estate is an equal estate, yet the carriage of both must not be the same, but the love of the one must be conveyed with royalness without tyranny, the other in loyal sweet subjection, without slavery. So then, as the head and other inferior members are equally parts of one body, yet the head in a different and more singular manner than the rest: so ought the case to be between husband and wife. And hence it is that according to the custom of all nations the husband seeks the wife, the wife loves after she is loved: except it is here and there in some odd person, noted for folly or immodesty. The man's authority mixed with the woman's mildness, his activeness with her passiveness and acceptance makes the sweet compound. As the sun exhaling vapors out of the earth draws them up into the air, and having altered their grosser quality, sends them down again with more abundance and fatness to refresh the earth as with her own store; so, the lovely disposition of a virtuous wife, drawing love from her husband into her own heart sweetens the vapor and returns his own upon him again with a double pleasing grace and comeliness. And as we see that the meat, which the stomach receives, except it is cold or hot, scarcely admits kindly digestion; because being lukewarm it cannot work upon that meat which is like its own temper; so, if you take away this temper of natures, love is loathsome in one manner and fulsome. For, what is more loathed by a discreet man than a woman with mannish qualities? And, what is more irksome to a loving woman than a man effeminate? Therefore, let the man keep his liberty in loving; avoiding all base uxoriousness, softness, and wanton affection of his wife, and let the woman shun all uncomely boldness; and taking upon her with authority in the carriage of her love towards

Tit. 2.4

Eph. 5.22-24

What that way is.

him: it becomes him to play the captain and lead this service of love, and it beseems her to tread the same steps and follow. This is the wisest contention, whether one shall love the other with the most cordial affection, in a true way.

Use 1.
Reproof.
Branch 1.

I come to some use of the point. And first it much condemns the course of such as bear any stroke in the marriages of others, who are so eager and peremptory in striking through the match that they omit the tying of the knot sure (which is the main point), and so become the occasions of

Forced and loveless matches dangerous.

forced matches, empty of love. Alas! You little consider of time to come and what a sad entrance you make into an estate of life, which needs the mutual improvement of a stock, which you never care to procure them at the first. And even so are couples themselves herein exceedingly to blame; in that they set the cart before the horse, dragging (in a sort, as he those oxen he had stolen into his den by the tails) the wives which by head and shoulders they have gotten into their bosoms, the contrary way. Sympathy of heart or amiable qualities which should attract love towards their persons and cover any such defect as a carnal, curious eye would stumble at, these they set not in the first rank, but as the kite upon the prey so fall they eagerly upon something in the woman, neither praiseworthy nor amiable (for as the philosopher says who praises any for wealth, or that which is without) but either profitable or sensually pleasing: these they think will carry love after it. But by that time they have tried at leisure and found that love is not compelled, but a thing which must be persuaded and extracted by some deservingness of the qualities in the party loved. Then finding no such thing in the party married, they perceive how preposterous they have been, and would amend

And in what respects.

their choice (if possible) with the forfeit of much other commodity. But it is too late, for what shall a man give for the recompense of love if absent? Or what shall it profit a man to have won a wife, with all other advantage, in whom is no true amiable thing to win affection? What a sad bondage is it to be tied forever to one you cannot love; an object of disdain, of hatred, of loathsomeness, and of odiousness? A thing wherein there is not a drop of that which is desirable? How woeful a burden would it be to have a dead carcass bound with cords to your back, to go with you everywhere? Who your heart tells you, you know no one woman or man of a hundred whom you cannot as well find in your heart to love as her? So that in all the companies wherein you come and dare utter your thoughts, this must be the first complaint: you were compelled to marry her or him whom in your heart you never could set your love upon: so that you were driven into the net and taken as a bird in a snare. Oh, if love is one of those joint duties which the married should continually nourish, what shall become of them who never joined together before marriage to compass it at all? What is this, but to prepare for themselves perpetual vexation, should I call it, or desolation?

And secondly, how does this reprove such, as although first entered not without some affection to each other yet, through a vain, empty, and base spirit neglect the careful keeping of such a jewel as love is? Tush, they think that it will keep itself, although they live at random, and hang it upon every hedge. If love (say they) is the matter you talk of, let us alone, I warrant you, we love each other as much as anybody, there is no love lost between us, we have one another's heart as it were in a box. Hear me I pray, what kind of love is that you mean? Is it a mere carnal and brutish appetite, or a virtuous and religious love which I have spoken of? Perhaps (for the present) you suppose yourself enamored with some external thing which you see in her, not yet comparing that one with ten other most odious qualities which in time will wear out the humorous contentment and doting delight you have in that one. As years come on, sickness and crosses, alas, that insufficient one object being blasted, and no other object coming in the room to hold you satisfied, how must your affection quail and starve in your bosom, you should first have laid the ground of your love in such a desired object of virtue, modesty, and worth as might have held water, and not shrunk in the wetting. The most resolute loves vanish in a short time, where the fuel of love fails. But to go back, suppose you had grounds of first love to your companion: what then? Do you think that this edge will hold without daily whetting? When you foolishly slight the due attendance of this love, do think it a toil to nourish it, and moreover dare cast water upon this sparkle as never fearing it will be quenched. Do you wonder if this, your darling, is lost on the sudden for lack of looking to? No,

Reproof. Branch 2. Love will not nourish itself, but must be nourished daily between couples.

By what means love may be nourished.

no: you must fix your eyes upon those first objects which won
your love to your companion: not run up and down into all
places with unsavory complaints of husbands and wives! Not
looking at the parts of others, to estrange your heart at home.
Love is a bird with wings, soon gone out of the cage of your
bosom if it is carelessly set open. You say you have it in a box,
but what if you lose box and all? Therefore, shun those complaints which fools make! Oh! If my husband had the qualities of such a man, were he of such understanding, religion,
parts of speech and memory, tenderness and amiableness that
such and such a one is, how could I love him? Then comes in
he with the like, If my wife had the properties of such a woman, so chaste, so kind, so wise, so able to keep her tongue, and
observe the laws of silence or of speech; so zealous, provident,
and the like, as other women have, how worthy would she be
of love. Dare you thus dally in so weighty a business? Dare
you like the gnat fondly fly about the candle as secure of burning? Oh unworthy of love, each from other! Should you look
out abroad upon objects which belong not unto you, hurtful,
not helpful? To increase emulation and envy, not affection,
what are you the nearer? Pour upon your own husband and
his parts, let him be the veil of your eyes, as Abimelech told
Sarah, and look no further. Let her be your furthest object;
think of no virtues in any beyond hers: those that are but
small, yet make them great by often contemplation: those that
are greater, esteem and value at their due rate, that you may
know them to the full weight, having weighed them in the
balance. This putting your sickle in your neighbor's corn will
prove too hot and heavy; it will cause your own to shale and
perish the while. It is a better work of the two for you to think
you see wonder in your own companions, though there is little
in either; than to be quick sighted in seeing the gifts of others,
be they ever so excellent; at least it is the far safer error of the
two. It must be the mutual reflex and exchange of gracious
and sweet virtues in and from each other, rebounding as the
sunbeams from the wall that only can hold you in an invincible league of amity! The marking of each other's goodness,
compassion, fidelity, and chastity, which must continue that
first love, which at the first they caused. You need not quench
love: it is enough that you withdraw this fuel, and look upon

Gen. 20.16

the infirmities of each other (the only damp and choke pear of affection), these alone will kill it. And when other fuel fails (as I said before), let religion step in and make it up: this will keep harmony in other discord. Read over that divine Song of Solomon. Setting out the blessed union between Christ and his spouse the church; wherein is most lively expressed what inward content and feeling of joy each partakes in the other through the sight of each other's perfections. She in her head, because in him she beholds all fullness of wisdom and grace; and he in her, because of the reboundings of those ornaments and graces of the Spirit wherewith he has furnished her. So much for this second.

Thirdly, this must be a serious caveat to all married couples to nourish their love, and to preserve it entire, which will the more easily be obtained if they shall consider those sad effects which come from the decay of it in the lives of couples. As Solomon speaking of drunkenness says, whence are red eyes, whence are wounds and quarrels? Are they not from the red wine? And James, whence are wars and contentions among you? Are they not from your lusts that fight in your members? You seek and enjoy not, but miscarry in all your attempts, and see not whence your misery comes? So say I, whence are those endless debates, differences between the married, that they are always seeking for blessing and longing after a happy life, but still it goes further and further from them? Alas! Because they dream still the fault is without doors, in this and that, bad servants, ill success, improvidence: and sometimes in each other: but never set the saddle upon the right horse: the disease is within their bosoms, they have lost their first love to each other, they are waxen sapless and unsavory in their spirit and affection one to another. While that lasted, all went forward in a sweet manner, cart went well upon wheels: for the spirit of mutual love made it slick and trim, the oil of love set it forward: but since this was exhausted and dried up, all went to havoc, the sinews of society, the band of peace and perfection, of thrift and welfare being broken, there is a dissolution of the frame, and a shattering of all. Children have no edge to do their duties, servants have no joy to do their work, and loveless couples are lifeless and unfortunate. Indeed the salt having lost her flavor is good for

Use 3. Admonition to the joint practice of conjugal love. Prov. 23.29,30

Jam. 4.1

Danger of
breach of
conjugal love
is sad.
nothing, save to be trodden under the feet of contempt and
scorn. Whence are those mock-divorces so frequent in the
world, whereby couples separate from each other; some from
bed, from board, from house, and so far that one shire will
not hold them; being barred of a real, they please themselves
in a local contentment, which yet lasts not, the names of each
other, much more the companies being odious. Hence come
those hideous precedents of conspiracies one against the life of
another; adulteries, villainies, even murders practiced against
husband and wife. He who despises his own life is soon master of another's, and how can a man choose but despise his life
2 Kings 7.4 when he feels it wearisome. As those four lepers said, let us be
desperate and rush upon the Camp of Aram, for what is our
life worth, we are but dead men, we cannot be worse: so may
loveless couples say, whatsoever we do, we suffer, we cannot be
worse (though we are not) than we are. A dead dog is as good
as such a living lion. Hence again come those manifold suits
and pursuits abroad, exclaiming jealousies at home: the trea-
Judg. 18.23,24 sure is stolen, love is gone. As he said of his idols so I of this
love, you have stolen my gods, and do you ask me, what ails
you? The fence is broken, the sluice is pulled up, and all goes
to wreck and confusion. There is as much use of a bone out
of joint, even of a man out of his wits, as of such a couple. Fidelity, modesty, and housewifery in a woman degenerate into
carelessness of body, of soul, of state, and of name, into mere
vanity. A woman not loving her husband will not delay to pull
out one eye of her own, to pull out both of her husband's eyes,
as the fable tells: rob and spoil herself of goods and good name
that she might spoil him. Even many have devoted themselves
to a defilement of their bodies, to be revenged of each other:
mere hatred and spite has drawn them to such sin as lust alone
would not have done. This taste may be sufficient to warn all,
who are not forlorn, to look to themselves to beware how they
embezzle that sacred stock, which God has inspired all such
married ones therewith, whom he means to sustain in this
state with integrity and honor. Marriage is honorable, keep
then the pledge of it entire which is love. It is like that image
in the capital, called the Paladium, which if it ever came to be
seen and profaned, threatened ruin to their commonwealth,
therefore they kept it in a most affected secrecy and safety.

God has bestowed it to make the difficulties of the married life tolerable (which else, the multitude of them would make irksome); and shall a man having but one string to his bow cut it in two? Or a city having but one engine to defend themselves cast it away? Let it be a warning to all sorts therefore.

Lastly, this point must be exhortation to couples to practice and discharge faithfully this joint duty of marriage love, each to other. Wheresoever you are, whithersoever you go, whatsoever you do, remember you carry about you a precious pearl, look to it, prize it and preserve it as your life. There are sundry motives to press this upon willing couples, as hammers to drive this nail home to the head: and indeed I may say of it, as he once said of one, an honest man need not, a dishonest man will not be warned. The general motive to both husband and wife is God's charge to them: live and love. Both of you think thus, he bids it who better knows the use of it, the danger of the contrary, than such silly ones as we. Commands of God are solemn things, especially such as serve for a trench, for a fortress, and a fence to hedge in an ordinance. He that dares violate it shall pay for it sweetly. Therefore, set your heart to obey this rule, and say it is life or death. It is the crutch of your lame limbs, if that fails, you must fall; if the shores break, the house ruins. Obey God out of love: discern his sovereignty in this charge; love him and love one another. If you love me feed my sheep: says Christ to Peter: If you love me keep my commands, says he to them all. And, if you love me, love each other (says the same voice to couples). Do not dally with such edge tools. Say not oh man! What, shall I lose my liberty, and tie myself to a woman? Nor she, Shall I forgo my will and tie myself to a husband? Is not the world broad and large? Yes, but as full of sorrow and woe as it is wide and broad, without this preservative. It is a good hard theme, I grant, to handle. I will therefore reach out one or two motives in particular to each party: and because arguments for time past, as former covenants made, great affections in the first heat of youth, like May bees fly away and are soon forgotten. I will mention such as afford themselves daily to couples in the course of their life. To the man, I say, your wife is bone of your bone and flesh of your flesh. She is another self, woman made of man, taken out of you, a glass to behold yourself in. When

Exhortation to couples to love jointly.

John 21.15
John 14.15
John 15.12

Gen. 2.23

the Lord brought this model of Adam's self unto him, consider how natural, how precious, and how welcome she was. What? Is not your wife as natural an object to you?

Motives to the husband to love his wife.

Secondly, your wife, so often as you look upon her is a deserving object of love and compassion: she has done that for your sake, which you would not have done for her: for she has not only equaled you in forsaking her father and mother and family, that she might be one flesh with yours, but she has forgone her name and put all her state and livelihood into your hand. If you stick to her, she is well, if you forsake her, she has put herself out of all her other succors. Her subsisting is imperfect in herself, it is wholly substantive and real (under God) in you. As the Lord Jesus speaks of the eye that all the sight of the body is within it, if therefore that is dark how great is that darkness? So, if you desert your poor, shiftless wife and leave her mends in her own hands, how great is that desertion? Thirdly, consider how much labor is put upon a weak vessel, daily, in diligence, in stirring up the commodities of the house, in attendance upon children and family, and such providence as is required of her. Her trouble is great in the peculiar acts of marriage, great are her pains in conception, in her bearing, in her travail and bringing forth, in her nursery and bringing up, till they are out of hand at least: and some women exceed others in this kind: for some shift off this work carelessly, and commit their babes to strangers as if they were too good to nurse them, when yet their breasts are full and their bodies strong: whereas others put forth themselves to the uttermost and therefore deserve double affection. Consider oh man, if not the drudgery of your wife in this kind (if there were not a command and promise to make it sweet) then that finger of God and providence, disposing so, that a weak one should do that with patience and cheerfulness (as a work of her place), which all your strength is not able to turn your hand unto. Love her for that impression of divine wisdom, which you see stamped upon her: what man is able to endure that clamor, annoyance, and clutter which she goes through without complaint among poor nursing infants, clothing, feeding, dressing and undressing, picking and cleansing them; what is it save the instinct of love which enables her hereto? Who has taught the poor bird, even a silly wren to make her so curious a nest as exceeds all art of man to effect? Is it not the natural instinct which love has put in her? So ought you to nourish that love in your wife which puts her forth to all her marriage service. If God was not in her spirit she would cast it oftentimes, or she would go through grief with it as she does. It is the best requital which can be given her from man, to help digest so many sour morsels, sad businesses; and all too little. For it must be the Lord who must tell her, that although she bear her punishment in her childbearing, yet it shall be sweetened by mercy, for she shall be saved thereby and obtain more glory thereby, through faith and patience, than she who bears not. But above all the grace of God in so frail a creature: the wisdom of the spirit shining in her words, counsels, actions, and examples should be most admirable of all, and the chief lodestone to draw affection from the husband, as in David's esteem of Abigail in that kind, may appear.

1 Tim. 2.15

1 Sam. 25.39

The same may be said of the man, to draw respect and honor from the woman (if she is not degenerate), and to love her husband. For why? In him may she behold yet more manifest steps of God's image than in herself. They say, there is in some kinds as much of the Creator in the ant as in the lion: in the former, excellent skillfulness, in the other, power and majesty: so here. In the man shines out more authority, government, forecast, and sovereignty than in the woman. By the man, as she at first received her being; so, still she enjoys from him countenance, protection, direction, and honor: in a word (under God) light and defense. To these add, they entered their league solemnly, but they shall part sadly. A time there is to embrace, but there shall be a time far from embracing. Improve it well therefore, love, live, and leave. Bitter else will the review be of a life past, representing the fruits of a loveless marriage, a tedious pilgrimage, whereas the memory of a loving husband or wife shall allay the bitterness of death to the survivor. And indeed if that indenture which couples first make solemnly to God, to keep this sacred knot inviolable and unstained, was well kept: this darling would grow up in the house as that poor man's only lamb did, whereof Nathan tells David, which ate with him at the table, slept with him in his bosom, and was to him as one of his children (so Bathsheba and Uriah are described): so dare I say, should this pledge

Motives to the wife to love him.

2 Sam. 12.3

be to them both, and through it they to each other; strongly fenced beforehand against all occasions of the contrary (for that which preserves itself always destroys the contrary), and so providing that this twine may live and die with them together. Some dream that old folks are past love: and foolishly impropriate it to the heat of youth: but alas, the anciently married (if right) may as ill want it as the young; surely worst of all when old age has proved it to be sound; then may the married cease to love when they cease to live. Therefore roll each stone to find this grace: buy it whatsoever it cost, fell it not, whatsoever you may have for it: lest you be as he who sold his birthright: which once gone could be no more recovered, though sought with ever so many tears. And truly for the most part, it is noted that when it once gets a fall, it proves almost impossible to solder it again; being as the native heat and moisture of the body, which once spent (they say) is irrecoverable. And so much of this second joint duty of the married, conjugal love.

CHAPTER VIII

Treating of the third joint duty of the married,
namely, chastity.

The third mutual service of the married follows to be spoken of, namely chastity. A dignity, held by a duty, both the virtue of preserving it, and they who are the preservers of it, are honorable and, while we are discoursing about this, we seem to be in the center, in the chief of the honor of marriage. Other honors are excellent additions and ornaments, but this is the being of it: marriage delights in being quiet, peaceable, rich, and in credit, but, provided always the main is entire, else they lose their value. As it is with the rich, their pleasures, feasts, companies, and liberties please them well, but how? They still presupposing the root to be sound, their stock and state to be unquestionable. Every accidental of marriage is pleasant, because chastity which makes it so is taken for granted. It is the fairest flower, the richest jewel in the garland, the crown of marriage. And well it may be so styled: for as a crown is blasted if it has a peer, and a competitor to amate it, so is this, if the chastity thereof is impaired. The want of other happiness may, in a sort, be supplied in this: the wife is sheepish, or shrewish, or the like; but the comfort is, she is chaste. Whereas if she is unchaste there is no comfort in it, that she is fair, rich, personable, or well bred. The peculiarity of marriage stands in chastity. I am desirous that my money, my land, and my friend are my peculiar ones, and that no man may have a right in them save myself. Yet rather than I should lack them, I had rather have them in a community than want them altogether. But chastity is such a peculiarity of marriage that I rather choose infinitely to have no husband, no wife at all, than one that is unchaste. Many endowments so honor marriage when they are presen,t as that yet being absent, they disannul her not: they make it a sad, an unhappy one, but undo it not. Chastity is so real, so essential an attribute that the absence thereof quite destroys the being thereof.

Third mutual duty of the married, chastity.

Chastity is the main joint duty of the married.

The institution of Christ is sufficient to approve this duty. They two shall be one flesh: not two, not three, not joined to this harlot, that adulterer. Malachi tells us, he who had spirit enough in him to have devised and bestowed further elbowroom in this kind, yet foresaw that closeness and entireness of spirit, such as the married couples ought to embrace, cannot subsist in multitude. The first number, two, are enough to grow into one flesh: and love would vanish into lust, baseness, and brutish commonness, if the bridle were let loose into manifold copulation. Sin not therefore (says the prophet) against the husband and wife of your flesh: moreover sin not against him that made them one flesh, and only them: for that were to tax his Spirit and ordinance. And wherein do rational creatures differ from sensual, save in this honorable peculiarity and propriety? Which, not the Scriptures have revealed, but the very law of nature has dictated and engraved in the minds of the very heathens: who have censured promiscuous lust with as severe laws as the Word itself; many of them I say, especially in the case of adultery. As for that looseness of the first times, wherein men took the liberty, both of many wives and of those frequent divorces whereby they stained their bodies with unbridled pollutions: although the former was permitted in the first times of the church, the number whereof was scant (being cooped within the narrow bounds of one family), and the latter winked at by the Lord and his government, for the unavoidable hardness and rebellion of that Jewish nation: yet neither was allowed of, but abhorred, and as the times grew more enlightened, so such commonness and vagrancy of lust grew to be restrained till it was quite out of practice. Hence that of the apostle, having dissuaded marriage in times of danger and persecution: Nevertheless (says he) to avoid fornication, let every man have his own wife, and woman her husband. And in the rules given to ministers, the same apostle foreseeing what a sad precedent the common sort would snatch to themselves from the practice of the minister; precisely charges him, that if he marry (which he forbids not) yet he should be the husband of one wife. Noting doubtless that all chastity is not seen in abstinence from strange flesh: but in the restraint of corruption from coloring over uncleanness, with a marrying of many; which is a double sin, not only mock-adultery, but a defiling of an ordinance with that pollution which it abhors, and sin (as it were) by privilege. And let every man (says Paul) learn how to preserve the vessel of his own body, in holiness and honor: mark how the one goes with the other! Why does he press it? Because it is the temple of the Holy Ghost; and he who defiles the temple of God, him will God destroy. We need go no further to prove this duty of chastity to be the crown of marriage than that text (keep your vessels in honor): we know a like phrase of the Old Testament when a man shall lie with a maid, he having humbled her: what is that? Surely he has taken her honor of chastity away: her credit is gone. And fitly in this text, the apostle proves marriage to be honorable by the undefiledness of the bed. God (says he) has put honor upon it (as carnal a thing as it seems) pour not any contempt upon it by unchasteness. So Jacob says in his dying words to Reuben: Although you are my strength and crown by being the first born, yet because you went up to your father's bed, you are unstable as water, your dignity is gone. And the child (we know) begotten thus is called a base; a mark of dishonor to father and itself. Solomon tells us that such a one gets himself a blur, which never will get out. Jephthah a valiant man, yet a bastard, was scorned and cast out from among his brethren, had no child's portion; and Sampson by his wild lust became of an honorable judge, a fool in Israel.

> 1 Thess. 4.4
> 1 Cor. 3.16,17
> Deut. 21.14
> Gen. 49.4
> Prov. 6.33
> Judg. 11.1,2
> Judg. 16.21

Chastity then (you see) is a general duty for all them who seek to maintain their honor unstained, nothing does cleave so deeply to marriage as this. I have noted before some accidental stains by inequality, when ladies and their horse-keepers, young girls and old men match together, when a prince marries a beggar, a bad with a good, a Christian with a heathen or heretic, or if marriage proves contentious and unpleasant, who sees not a reproach? But these are such stains as may be washed out in time either by repentance, or (in a sort) by second better marriages. Only the stain of unchasteness is like an iron mole, which nothing can fetch out; it is like the leprosy which fretted into the walls; no scraping the stones could cleanse it, but it must be demolished. Death may end the parties, but not the memory of the shame. David's repentance took away the guilt, but not the reproach that abides to

> Amplification of this truth.
> Lev. 14.44,45

this day. So then, I have begun with the duty of love, which must be the first and inward cement of couples (for what is crystal worth if it is broken?). I say, as love is the inward band of preserving, because the outward action follows the affection: so now, I proceed with chastity, which is the main charter of love and the patent thereof; evidencing that the heart loves entirely because the bodies are kept pure from pollution. I deny not, but there are thousands of none of the most loving ones, nor religious ones, who yet loathe adultery and filthiness in this kind: but yet there are many also, not the worst for repute, whose marriages are spotted with this stain: and all to show that where the root is lacking, ten to one, if the branches do not wither. The restraint of providence is such by a common light that many are kept perforce from this dishonor. And yet this proves not, but that the inclinations and temptations of others are such that they lie open to this snare as much as to any. We must not neglect the urging of the duty because some are innocent: for some are so in same who are not in deed, and some in deed who are not in spirit, and some in spirit and yet no thanks to them: let the point fasten as it may and find out the guilty (the guiltless are out of the compass of it). But the age is generally debauched, and iniquity carries all as a flood before it. Although the second part of this treatise, treating of the denunciation against this sin, may perhaps more fully discover this disease with the cure of it: yet here (by so fit occasion) I shall press the jointness and honor of the duty by a few reasons, exhortation, and motives.

Reason 1.
Chastity is the main support of union.

Touching reasons: this may be one; chastity is the main support of union, as the contrary is the chief dissolver of it. No other fault (if once the marriage is lawfully consummated) does infer just separation (by authority of the Word) save this of uncleanness. Therefore must that which maintains union be the greatest pillar and prop of marriage. Prostitution of the body profanes the honor of it and casts it into the mire: and therefore the cardinal virtue that must bear it up must be this chastity. If so, then ought it by joint consent to be maintained by both parties.

Reason 2.

Secondly, it must be jointly done because, although the honor of pure marriage requires both to conspire in mutual chastity, yet the defilement of either party is sufficient to

overthrow the honor of it. As we say of a virtuous action, all
points must concur to make it good, but any one defect in
those will serve to make it vicious, so here. Marriage dishonor
does not need the consent of both party's dishonesty: if one is
disloyal, it is as good as both. Not before God in point of guilt:
but men in point of honor: for to manward, guilt and reproach
(in a sort, especially here), lose their difference: the innocent
party being pitied with as much dishonor as the guilty is reproached. Therefore this joint duty of chastity must be supported most carefully by the joint care and pureness of both
parties. Add hereto that defect of this joint closeness may
bring a shame upon marriage (though perhaps not so great
yet as true) as well as a greater crime committed. As the philosopher says, glory is not in the glorified, he is but the object;
the agent is the glorifier. Therefore fame and report is well
called by some, the married one's saint. For by fame they either stand or sink. Now, how easily may fame snatch the least
neglect of the married in this kind, to raise suspicions? How
closely curious had they need be of their course and pureness,
who cannot keep their own honor in their own power sometimes, do what they can? Is it not the misery of many to be
defamed without cause? Neither smoke nor fire appearing,
but perhaps some mistake, error, or advantage of a foul mouth
being the spark that kindles the fire: and yet it sometimes little
avails (for the point itself of honor) whether a man is guilty or
is taken so. How great had that caution need to be that should
preserve the honor of chastity?

The third may be this (as I noted before), God's setting his print and mark of honor upon marriage in appointing
one to one. How serious and solemn ought the meditation
of this charge be, being not human, but divine? And (to repeat nothing) if the violation of this sacred band had such a
blemish cast upon it by the Lord, when yet it was covered over
with a mantle of connivance, and the practice of so many holy
patriarchs and saints who were guilty of it: what shall be said
now of that uncleanness which proclaims itself like Sodom?
If polygamy was a state of uncleanness in God's esteem, and
seldom went without a scare from God's stroke (as in Jacob
and David and Elbana's cases appears, especially in that exor-
bitance of Solomon) what shall be said of that which carries

The defilement of each party is enough to defile the whole state of marriage.

Reason 3. God has ordained one for one.

the bastard at the back, and wants the least rag of any veil to color or excuse it? Attend this reason and shun this sin.

Reason 4.
It covers all
other defects.

Fourthly, that must be looked unto jointly by both the couples, which has such a covering faculty in it, and sets the varnish and luster upon each other's endowment of it.

But itself can
be covered by
no endow-
ments.

My wife has defects, but she is loyal: by unavoidable errors she may offend, but by voluntary she will not. From her the honor of my marriage comes even when both of us are dead and gone, in our lawful posterity, the crown of parents. She is beautiful (says one), personable, well descended, rich (says another); indeed but she is chaste, says a third, this crowns all. What else was her beauty, but her bane; her devotion but profaneness? She that thought no crumb clave to her lips because she had paid her vows, yet escapes not her eternal reproach because she was a disloyal harlot. Tell me, were you married to a chaste wife, blind of an eye, lame of a hand, a leg, whether you would change her for one sound in all, being unchaste? I think not. That which then covers all wants is worth the due improving and careful attendance.

Reason 5.
It is the
cornerstone
which holds
in the whole
building.

Fifthly, this chastity is the cornerstone that holds in all the parts of the building. A chaste wife has her eyes open, ears watching, and heart attending upon the welfare of the family, husband, children, and servants. She thinks that all concerns her; estate, content, posterity: this rivets her into the house: makes her husband trust to her, commit all to her, heart and all. But the unchaste, having lost his or her heart, is loosened from the whole body, thinks nothing pertaining to her: is ready to part the children, leaving the lawfully, and choosing the misbegotten for her portion, that so she may go to her paramour.

1 Sam. 18.28

That which Saul (through mistake) thought Michal would prove to David, that does an unchaste one (without doubt) prove to her husband, a very snare. That which I said before of love may be said of her sister chastity, she is painful, close, does all things, hopes, believes, and endures all things without grudging. The frost is nothing by night, the heat by day, toil in both, because he loves her, she him, each are faithful and loyal to each other. Who should not nourish that tree, which has such branches?

Whereupon some think the English and Latin words (chaste) do come from a Greek word signifying to adorn, noting that chastity is one of the chief ornaments of the married: and so of all in either sex, one says. As the face of a statue or fair picture razed, or the head rent off: so is the most beautiful, rich, and honorable person if chastity is gone. It is (as that father speaks) the ornament of the noble, the exaltation of the low, the beauty of the abject, the solace of the sorrowful, the increase of beauty, the glory of religion, and the friend of the Creator.

Lastly, chastity preserves marriage in honor and ought to be jointly again preserved, because it preserves that joint blessing of God, which makes it honorable: and that in sundry respects, the first being the fruitfulness of the womb. Many think a fruitful posterity rather a cross than a blessing, but the godly are of his mind who said, she shall be as the fruitful vine by the side of your house, and your children as olive plants round about your table. The adulterer and adulteress are cursed with barren wombs, fruitless bodies. There is not now such a cursed water to try the unclean by rotting the womb and bowels of the harlot; nor to become a water of blessing to the chaste. But instead thereof, there is a curse of God upon the one, and a blessing upon the other. Even the adulterine mixtures of beasts (as the mule coming from the ass and the mare) have a brand of barrenness, nature stopping all infiniteness and confusion as most contrary to herself; how much more the bodies of adulterous husbands and wives? And whereas it is objected that some harlots are fruitful, and some chaste wives are barren; the answer is, still the curse holds upon the bastard fruit of the one, and the blessing upon the soul of the other. As the prophet encourages those holy eunuchs that kept God's Sabbaths that it should go better with them than if they had sons and daughters; even a place should be given them in the house of God, and an everlasting name, that never should be cut off. So does he here to all chaste ones when he cuts off the cursed race of the unclean, then he continues to the godly (though barren) a better name than posterity could attain unto. Secondly, to the chaste belongs the blessing of legitimation; but to the unclean, the curse of illegitimate ones; to bring bastards into the family as lawful heirs, how execrable, and how unnatural is it? The children of Gilead cast out Jephthah because he was the stranger's issue.

Reason 6.
Because in some respects it makes marriage honorable.
Psal. 128.3
1 Respect. Fruitfulness of womb.
Num. 5.21

Objection.

Answer.

Isa. 56.4

2 Respect. Blessing of legitimation.

Gen. 21.10 Sarah said well of Ishmael: the son of this stranger (though of her own gift) shall not inherit with my son Isaac. But the curse of the adulterous is to leave their wealth to bastards. As the Lord cursed the garment made of mixed linen and wool: the field sown with sundry kinds of grain together: so much more, the illegitimate posterity of defiled persons. As eagle's feathers consume the feathers of other fouls; so, the unlawful brood of the unclean devours the lawful, till at last that fire consumes them and all, which is threatened the children of the whore and the adulterer, for it was unlawful fire that begat them, and

3 Respect. the same shall kindle and burn till it has destroyed them. And
The curse of thirdly, to the chaste, even a curse is turned to a blessing. The
sin is turned sorrows of conception and birth turn to the salvation of the
to blessing by pure and chaste (being faithful) whereas the blessing of mar-
chastity. riage turns to a curse to the other. As all things are impure to
Lev. 14.40 the impure, as the ceremony also made the things and vessel to be defiled, whether wood or stone, which the leper touched. But especially to the impure in bodies, truly, their very consciences are as impure as their flesh, and thereby, whatsoever they do touch, use, partake, or possess is made filthy because

Tit. 1.15 their nasty consciences tell them so. Even so, to the pure all things become pure; as our Savior says of alms. Give alms to the poor of that you have, and all the whole lump of your estate

Luke 11.41 shall be clean unto you. So here, if couples keep themselves pure, in body and spirit, pure are their prayers, readings, conferences, Sabbaths, sacraments, and service of God. Indeed in Christ all things are pure unto them, their health, estate, eating and drinking, duties, fellowship and benevolence, bed and board, and all they take in hand. Now (to finish the reason) if it is under such a threefold blessing, then so happy a virtue as chastity, ought to be jointly preserved by both the married

Question. persons.
How chastity   But here it will be demanded, how should chastity in
may be pre- marriage be preserved? And in how many things it stands? I
served. answer. In these four. First, in the chastity of the spirit. Sec-
Answer. ondly, of prevention. Thirdly, of the bed. Lastly, of the body.
Four ways. For the first, the center of chastity is the mind and spirit. If
1. The spirit that is pure, there need be no keepers (as he once said of those
2. Prevention Romans, the richer sort of whom kept their wives' chastity by
3. Bed eunuchs) if that is unclean, no keepers will serve the turn, un-
4. Body

bridled lust (like the wild fig) will soon mount over the wall. The first care then must be to keep that clean from whence (as our Savior says) all filth proceeds, I mean the heart. Get the Lord Jesus to come in with his Spirit to cleanse your husband, your wife; to wash them and make them undefiled to himself as his own spouse, without spot or wrinkle of willful baseness. Get him to cleanse that Augean stable, that thoroughfare of base thoughts (the master wheel of your soul, the will and affections), the thief that betrays all: and then, the root being pure, so shall the branches be. Solomon aims at this; my son give me your heart, and let your eyes delight in my ways. And why? He adds, for a whore is a deep ditch, and a strange woman is a narrow pit. If your heart is pure, your eyes and senses, your body and members shall follow and not delight in the false appearance of a harlot. Who is he whom God loves? Surely him who is upright in spirit, such a one and only such shall be kept from her, but the sinner shall be caught in her snares. If the thoughts are impure they will betray the body to the eyes, ears, and company of the unclean, and Satan will play the proctor, soon bringing one unclean person to another. There is a contemplative filthiness of the fancy and senses (which the Lord reckons the adultery of the spirit), by baseness of spirit within, nourishing disloyal conceits, inward dalliances, capering thoughts and fancies of uncleanness, both sleeping and waking: and so set the door open to outward actual defilement, which although providence restrains, yet are odious to God, and will break out in time. Yet I would here speak with caution. I know in the best (unmarried or married) there is naturally planted this imaginary and ideal uncleanness, steaming up from the furnace of concupiscence, a natural principle, not always subject to the law of grace: it is a law of the members, in a double sense, a dye in grain; but yet so long as it is abhorred, opposed, and quenched by all possible diligence it shall not be imputed: provided that the means to subdue it are not slighted. But I speak of a heart permitted to itself, without control and bridle. For when the door stands loose upon the latch, how soon may it be opened? Cracked glasses, we know, last not long: they wait but for the next knock and then are gone. Alas! What thanks is it for a man not to be unclean for lack of opportunity, or because

Mat. 12.34

Prov. 23.26-27
The first. Chastity of spirit must be kept against contemplative uncleanness.

Why it is so needful.

he was overruled for a time? The religion of these times is come to this. Suspect by men what you will, so you can prove nothing, what care they for giving occasions of ever so much suspicion? Is this your honesty, that because you can weary them in the court who accuse you, therefore you are chaste? Moreover, because you dare purge yourself by oath (like a foresworn wretch), therefore you have wiped every crumb of your lips. Is not your conscience as a thousand witnesses nevertheless? I tell you, you have your brand in heaven already and perhaps upon earth too, or else are next door to it. And what difference is there between these two, not to be approved for chaste, or to be thought unclean? It is hard to say whether many men and women have lost their credit or their chastity sooner. Lust if once it kindled, as the sparkle will kindle to a great fire, will soon snare us and bring forth fruit unto death. But, if there is pureness in the bent of the spirit, and the sway of the soul tends to chastity, the streams will easily become pure. So much for the first.

The second. Chastity of prevention is necessary.

Secondly, there must be chastity of prevention also. That is a narrow survey of the cinque-ports of the soul, by which traitors to chastity arrive at the shore. Preserve the inlets of your soul, I mean the outward senses, ears, eyes, inward fancy, and ideas of evil, closely and firmly, and then the body will follow. Still we must proceed by degrees. The spirit lets in sin to the body by these conduits and channels. David sweetly prays, set a door before my lips O Lord! So, set a watch before my senses that there come in no vanity! Lord not only lead me not yourself into temptation, but forestall all other tempters that I be not led: for you preserve the souls of your saints, and he whom you love escapes them all, which another at one time or other shall assuredly fall into. It was David's misery to cast his eye from the roof of his house in an unwatchful manner, and there wanted not one to further the occasion. So Samson. Those who loathe the act, will also abhor the fomenters thereof, all extravagances of senses and sensuality: all setting themselves to sale, haunting of markets, fairs, night-meetings, wakes, dancing, and common festivals, which with all the like occasions, alehouse hauntings or frequenting of forbidden and noted houses, as give aim to the flesh to play her part; all needless travels and journeys, with-

What it is.

2 Sam. 11.2

out warrant, among multitudes of all sorts; all Dina-like rov- Gen. 34.1
ing and gadding about without due cause: all loose carrying
about the eyes through the air of the world; all gestures, becks,
and aims of an unchaste heart soon appear to such as are of
like temper: birds of a feather will flock together. Intemperate
diet, excess of gaming, delights, pampering the flesh; amorous
books, sonnets, stage-plays, effeminate disguising, and array-
ing of one sex in the other's attire, a thing censured by all writers both moral and divine; jesting, and unsavory rotten com-
munications, allusions, similitudes and discourses: what are
they, but as bawds and panders to uncleanness? Drinking of
hot inflaming wines or waters in a usual distempered custom
(no infirmity of nature requiring), what are they (in bodies hot
and lustful of themselves) save inflaming of lust and spurring
of a running horse? I say especially in such persons as neither make use of the ordinance nor yet abstain from excess of
provocation. Must not (of necessity) such sinful excess have a
like vent? And where there is no chastity of prevention, making men abstinent from promiscuous occasions, is it like there
will be chastity of body, like occasion being offered of the one
as the other? No doubt, a body desirous to be chaste will also
be very cautious of meat, drink, fashions, softness, delicacy,
and pleasures, which will be as oil to the flame: and he who is
not chaste in the suburbs is not to be trusted in the city. Dives
in all his riot and luxuriousness must escape hard if he is not
incontinent.

 This argument (I know) is common: I need not insist: Why this is
save only for the custom of these days, which will needs sepa- here urged.
rate means from ends, and be seen going onward to the den
and not seen to come back, and yet maintain it that they kept
out! This is to divide the things, which God has not separated.
I give to all who would shun this plague, the counsel belonging to it, soon, far, and slowly. Get from such occasions, as
soon: go from them as far; and return to them as slowly as
possible you can. If your eye, your right hand or foot cause
you to offend, pluck them out and cut them off (not as Ori-
gen did carnally) and cast them from you; but make yourself a
spiritual eunuch for the kingdom of God, and for chastity, use
all contrary means of holding under your flesh and boxing it
till it is black and blue (to use Paul's word) if you will preserve 2 Cor. 12.7

your vessel in honor: indeed, count all too little. If this counsel is meet for the married themselves who are under the remedy, what shall be said to the unmarried? Surely I say, touch not pitch lest you be defiled. Make covenants with your eyes with Job; remember our Savior's divinity, beyond the Pharisees: anticipate all your steps and passages; put your knife to your throats if you are given to your appetite, and venture not upon forbidden dainties, to try if they will surfeit you. But, if after all means, both of prevention and preservation of body and spirit from this taint, yet you feel your natures to recoil, and concupiscence to want ears, then hear that voice behind you saying, marry and burn not. But yet, take this counsel with you, still carry this rule of prevention with you into that estate, lest you marry and burn too, and so the disease will, if not be worse for the remedy, yet may prove never the better for it.

The third is the chastity of the bed. The apostle tells us here, the bed is undefiled. Surely, as he told his children at his death, they should find their kingdom, so I may say of this, it is as it is used and kept. For it is the great wisdom of God, which has so concealed our infirmity, and covered it with honor, that the bed should be honorable. But it imports us so to keep it then: and that against a double infirmity; the one of snaring and the other of defiling us. By snaring I mean defrauding each other, by any means, under any colors: as when by discord and difference of minds the body is disabled: when the one party denies due benevolence to the other; by pretended excuses to satisfy a base heart. When religion and conscience, or infirmity are falsely alleged to cross the ordinance; in this case let the apostle overrule. Let the husband and wife yield to each other, etc. Refuse not the lawful and sober use of the remedy (except when both in private consent in some extraordinary duty for some little season before), some add the preparation of the Sabbath, rather I suppose from a pious heart than the warrant of the Word, although I wholly yield to the equity of that abstinence, so there is no snare of a rule: for he that generally follows this light must not be snared by any rule (except he has vowed it voluntarily, and then it binds in another kind). But I leave the decision of that to the wisdom of such as can discern between expediency and inexpediency, lest Sa-

Job 31.1

1 Cor. 7.9

The third.
Chastity of the bed.

Two extremes here.

The first.

1 Cor. 7.3

tan prevent us: for we know his devices, how he seeks to snare
them that are weak against their intentions, and under color
of a better pureness, he seeks to breed a weariness and disdain
of the ordinance. He is an unclean spirit and cannot tolerate
that which holiness has invented to prevent sin. Let such as
are privy to this rebellion humble themselves and repent, remembering that marriage takes off the propriety which each
had before in himself, and gives away the power of the body of
each to other without contradiction. And there is more in this
than most will take notice of. And some openly profess that
they abhor this judgment, being yet expressly grounded upon
the letter of Scripture.

The second extreme is on the left hand, when men The second.
abuse marriage to a defiling of themselves, and under pretense
of general lawfulness, run into excess. This is as odious as the
former. It is not the wisdom of a Christian to choose the uttermost brink of the river to walk upon because it threatens
slipping in: nor of his liberty because it is allowed. Our greatest offences are commonly about things lawful, when as we
dare not attempt the unlawful: whereas religion is much more
tried in the use of liberties allowed us. And it is strange under
what sorry and thin covers the conscience of one will shroud
itself when as once it has cast off the love of closeness: half a
loaf is better to a Libertine than no bread. Whereas a sound
spirit should think thus, in this God tries me, what mettle I
am made of, whether to be tender of a command, when I have
the bridle laid upon my own neck, or to run away with my uttermost liberty when I have some granted to me. Doubtless
he who will take all that he can, in liberties, shows he is but
kept in by violence, in commands, and but for shame, would
desire God's cords were more slack and suited to his lusts. I
speak, because it might scarcely be believed what baseness,
immoderateness, and licentiousness grows in many even by
the occasion of the former point, of benevolence. They will
stretch it beyond the bounds of modesty and bring themselves
into such a bad custom that a bear robbed of her whelps may
be met with and stopped as easily as they crossed of their lascivious and luxurious appetite. Some brutishly imagining that Lev. 20.18
the very law of God forbidding carnal knowledge (during the
term forbidden) was but a ceremony, not grounded upon the

perpetual natural absurdity of the action: wherein they betray themselves by their swinish appetites to have drowned the true dictation of nature in themselves, which most heathens themselves acknowledged.

Others are wholly ignorant of all pureness and chastity, in the demeanor of themselves to each other: for though Isaac and Rebecca sported themselves, yet doubtless in no base or uncomely manner. Many philosophers and politicians in their laws made for the good of commonwealths, led by no Scripture or religion, yet for the preservation of health, vigor, and strength of body, for the shunning of diseases occasioned by this, as well as unclean mixtures, have set down their judgments touching the modesty and mediocrity of marriage converse, forbidding frequency and licentious use of it. I had rather express myself so, under their person, than in mine own words, knowing to what language he exposes himself of scorners and profane people, who do but glance this way. I say not as they say (Plato and others) once weekly or thrice monthly might be a model of convenience in this kind for the greater part of number of men's bodies: because I know, there can be no set rule for all persons, seasons of marriage, and varieties of bodies because variety of subjects causes variety of rule. But this I affirm, that if heathens could rove at such a mark, in the dimness of their light, and all for the restraint of excess: I should think it rather meet that Christians, especially in years (who by their place should teach the younger to be sober), should rather aim at being under the line than above it. But as it is not youth (where there is a chaste spirit) that can provoke to excess in this kind: so neither is it age (in any profession) if it is once tainted with defiledness, which will persuade men to moderateness: but as brute beasts their will is their law, and even in those things they know, yet they corrupt themselves to the grief and sad woe of their companions, who know not how to redress it. Loath I am to speak that in this argument with many sentences, even in two words, if one might serve; and heartily wish, which yet never will be obtained that (at least) the religious might be laws to themselves in such kinds. But the experience of the contrary may plead some pardon for that little I have said. Some must speak, and where more aptly than in a treatise for the nonce.

Gen. 26.8

Heathens shame us Christians in this.

But how shall we know when this due measure is observed? Surely then when snaring concupiscence is prevented, and fitness of body and mind thereby purchased, freely to walk with God, and to discharge duties of calling without distraction or annoyance. And so doing, much freedom may be enjoyed (both the former extremities being avoided) and God's wrath prevented: which I cannot say whether it more hangs over the heads of superstitious Papists for vowing a forced chastity, contrary to the express rule of the Word, or upon married persons for abuses in either of the two kinds. Concerning the former, we know both into what odious enormity of lust the Lord has suffered them to be plunged, both unnatural and unlawful; making them the execration of the world for their lust. Touching the latter, I leave it to the experience of the wise to consider; both what vexation the neglect of this ordinance has caused to many, who under pretexts of their own have refused the mutual due to each other; who afterwards seeing what woeful snares they have brought themselves into, as seeking the company of harlots and adulterers, have been deeply terrified, wishing too late, with sorrow, that they had denied themselves and subjected them to the ordinance. And so for the other extremity, when due regard of chastity has been neglected, what weakness, diseases, and inability of body and mind to calling and duty has ensued! Moreover, when presumptuous lust has broken bounds of womanly modesty, reckoning all seasons alike, what marks has God set upon their own bodies for their incontinency, and so upon the bodies of their children, surely and upon their minds and whole constitution, the one by disguisement of countenance, the other by defiledness with the like sin (for what was bred in bone, will not easily out in flesh), when as I say, men have met with these penalties then they have justly confessed wrath to seize upon them. And indeed, although there was no religion, yet if men were but philosophers, to understand the natural mischief and poison of such ways, they could not but loathe them. Therefore, let a wise mediocrity be observed: sanctifying our fellowship and fruit of bodies by earnest prayer that both may be clean to us. Make not that help, which God has given as water to quench, as oil to enflame. There is a white Devil as well to corrupt, as a black to abhor the remedy. But such debauched

Marks to know the moderation of the bed.

Popish forced chastity.

And affected abstinence from the benefit of the bed compared.

Inconvenience of both unjust abstinence and excess of liberty compared.

filthy persons the looseness of our age is come to, in all kind of lust that I verily think if those chaste Platos and lawgivers of old times were now living, although heathens, yet would be scorned by many Epicures and Libertines in the church: who think it a curb to their will not to live as they desire, worse than beasts and savages. Therefore we are they, who stand to God's bar, a rule to ourselves, following the steps and practice of such, as in our own degree and rank go for the most moderate in either sex. As he said of the endless questions arising about moral actions, let it be, as a wise man would judge, so I say of this: for questions of this nature are so impossible to be decided punctually, as other the like are of fashions and liberties of our common life, that except they are put to a compromise, there will be no end made. So much for this third.

The fourth and last head of the mutual duty is the chastity of body.

The fourth and last chastity is that of the body. This I make one duty by itself. For although it is true that if the three former were kept this would follow alone; yet I say, when all is done the body is not to be trusted too far. This sin of uncleanness is a running sore in our flesh, hardly cured. Even many (otherwise good) persons, though kept from the act, yet by all their strife have scarce felt themselves free, through a bodily propensity to this evil. And Satan is ready to do in this, so in other sins, even by how much the sin is loathed, by so much the more to exasperate this sin: not to speak of the falls of those worthies in Scripture. So that, except there is a special arming ourselves against snares objected and laid in our ways (which are innumerable in the lives of such men as have to meddle in the affairs of this life) and that with resolution, both before and upon the occasion, to preserve ourselves: all our former course taking to shun temptations by our senses and the like will do us no pleasure when they are brought home by the Devil to our door, and laid in our lap, presented in a lordly dish with secrecy, ease, and fair colors. Mere suddenness of affront (mark what I say) when nothing else could do it, has prevented some, that it has made them all their life, slaves and miserable. Take heed; bring not unclean bodies to the married estate and bed: lest being married, this dog is not easily rated from the carrion. There must as well be a fidelity of body as spirit, a holy strength to ward off blows, to cut off deadly temptations by the middle, by our well ordered members, as

not to call them in, by well-awed senses and carriage. Chaste
Joseph was not only resolved not to provoke himself to sin,
but when he was suddenly surprised by the offer of a harlot
unsought for, he abhorred the object as if he had been warned
beforehand. It is one thing for a man to have grace, another
thing to have such a presence of it that when our base hearts
are in a readiness to embrace, present grace is nearer the door
to thrust it away and abhor it. There is more danger in a prepared snare, made ready to our hand, than in the speculation
or foresight of that which may possibly befall us. So much for
this fourth: which I call chastity of the body, in a special sense,
to note, even how the whole man ought to be as well strengthened against the suddenness of a temptation, as beforehand
kept from the means leading thereto. And perhaps there are
some sorts of men whose sad experience will construe my
meaning herein better than others can.

Gen. 39.8,9

    I now conclude the whole chapter with use of exhor-
tation and with some short direction to set it home. First I say,
let all who desire to preserve the honor of their marriage look
to their chastity. Drink of the waters of your own well, but let
the cistern be your own. Seek not to strangers; give not your
strength to the harlot and your years to the cruel. Abhor all
sweetness of stolen waters. Let not your teeth water after forbidden dainties lest you find bitterness in the end. If meddling
with your neighbor's hedge, you may fear lest a serpent bite
you, how much more with his bed? Let your own wife delight
you, she is the woman whom you chose for the companion of
your youth: transgress not against her therefore. Let her love
satisfy you and her affections equal your embraces: let your
appetite be subject to him, and share the duty and the honor
of it between you both: and keep chaste till the coming of the
Lord Jesus. Know that this is an equal duty of both, God having bestowed the power of each over other, upon both. Think
not your husband tied to this rule, O woman; nor you your
wife tied, O husband, and the other free: the tie is equal.

*Exhortation
to the duty of
chastity.*

*Prov. 5.2-9 and
chapter 9*

    It is not jealousy of each other, which can preserve this
honor; no, it is the canker of marriage. Bathsheba describing
the condition of a good woman tells us, the husband of such
a woman rests in her, his heart settles upon her. Noting that a
wise man, observing virtuous qualities in his wife, judges her

*Against base
and unjust
jealousy; it is
most odious.
Prov. 31.11*

the same towards himself, which he is to her. A good man (such a one as Joseph was to Mary, a just man, one that had no worse thoughts of jealousy towards her than she had to him, loath to entertain the least suspicious thought against her) will always esteem her by himself. Why should I think that her conscience, chastity is not as tender to her as mine to myself? What can it come from, save a base heart inclined to treachery against my wife that I should imagine my wife should be false to me? Surely was it not a sin to do such a thing, or wish it done, it was but just that an unjustly jealous husband should meet with that he fears that so he might be jealous for somewhat. Many civilly chaste women, having been drawn to commit this folly by no greater motive than the vexation of jealousy: as not fearing God, and therefore thinking they were as good to commit it as to be always falsely charged with it. And mark it, it is commonly the sin of couples unequal in years, who having married younger husbands, wives than themselves, lie open to this temptation. Alas; I am too old to give him or her contentment, they seek such as are like themselves; when as yet the parties are as clear from such aspersions as the new born child. What? Have you offended once, and is there no remedy but you must solder it by a worse? I speak not as if I would make men panders and bawds to their wives, through their folly and careless confidence, exposing them to any temptations and winking between the fingers. For what is this save to give aim to a chaste woman to be lewd? No, but to shame that impotency and baseness of either sex, whereby each is prone, contrary to the good carriage and approved conversation of the other, yet to surmise in them falsehood and ill meaning. What can be such an incendiary, to set all on fire between couples, as this cursed mischief of jealousy, which is oftentimes (upon mere mistake of some word, guise, or action, nothing tending that way) rooted in the spirit of man, or woman, that neither all the assurances of truth between themselves, nor yet by mutual friends, can compound the matter so, but still there must be a pad in the straw, and their smoke must argue some fire? And yet when all is done it proves a mere idol of fancy, nothing in all the world.

The Lord indeed appointed a trial for the jealous man against his wife: but we must not conceive this was to breed or nourish causeless conceits. It was no doubt first brought to the judges in criminal causes to determine what the matter was, and (as our inquests do) to cut off all mere surmises: else what a bondage had it been for a wife to be so hurried and defamed? And although it is true that for the hardness of their hearts the Lord permitted more liberty to men at that time (being sturdy and rebellious), should that be any encouragement now to Christians to nourish such trash in themselves to make their spirits, their prayers, their whole life sad and miserable to themselves, and to be so embittered against each other that even when they would fain shake off their own conceits they should not be able? I say no more of this elf of causeless jealousies: but this for the party sinning, no man shall need to wish his greater torment than he has created to himself; let him thank himself that his own sin has eaten up the marrow of his bones. The greatest pity is to the party innocent and sinned against, who is to be advised, while there is any hope of recovery, to strive by all caution and exact circumspection of carriage to tender the weakness of the other, hoping that love rather than anger has bred it: but by no means disdain them, and to walk loosely under pretext of innocency. But if the disease is so rooted that it will not be healed; let them enjoy their uprightness (for the way of God, is strength to the upright, as Solomon says, Prov. 10.29) and not be dismayed but look up to God, who can clear their righteousness as the noonday, and plead their cause against their oppressor: joining prayer to God to quit them accordingly. This I have said of unjust jealousy: as for that which is just, I say as much against the guilty party, wishing the law was as strong now as it has formerly been against all violators of this sacred knot. And for this branch so much.

Remedy of the innocent party.

     I had here purposed to insert some other watchwords and directions, but I consider that in the latter part of this treatise more full occasion will be given of this argument. So much therefore shall serve for this chapter.

CHAPTER IX

Containing the description of the fourth and last
joint duty of the married, namely, consent.

The fourth
general and
joint duty of
the married,
consent.

The fourth and last duty equally concerning both parties married is consent and harmony of course each to another. Both the former of chastity and this do grow as springs from the stock of love: the former in the bodies, this latter in the lives of both. For this I would have the reader conceive, that the former of love and this of consent do not differ save as the root and the branch, the cause and the effect. Love being the noble groundwork, this the sweet building upon the former foundation: both making up marriage, to grow to a happy frame and building, which who so behold, can no other judge, but those parties are well met and dwell commodiously. It will better appear in particulars how the one differs from the other.

This then is the point, that both married persons ought studiously to maintain this grace of mutual consent, as a main piece of that which must maintain the honor of their marriage. Such a thing is this of consent. As may appear, both by the judgments of all those, who either (by woeful experience) could never attain it, though their eager desire after it may prove it to be the crown of marriage, or the more happy experience of such as have attained it, according to their desire, and found it to be no less than I have spoken. For the former of these, who needs to question it, but that must be most honorable, for the lack thereof, the estate and contentment, even the whole welfare of thousands has perished? Who covets that with earnestness, which has not some rare felicity in it? And when a man has with all his skill sought that, which yet (when all is done) he cannot achieve, even is further off from, what remedy, but such a one must lie down in sorrow? If the deferring of the soul's desire is the fainting of it, what is the utter defeating of it? Whereas, not for the present only, but for ado (for ought appears) a man foresees his own misery, and must of necessity survive the funeral of his own happi-

Reason 1.
Branch 1.
Experience of
such as want
it.

Prov. 13.12

ness.

For the latter, who doubts of the honor and price of that commodity, unto which, they who have enjoyed it, do esteem all as mere dross and dung? Even all their wealth, beauty, and birth, which yet do much confer to a comfortable life. What shall it profit a man to win all these, and to lose his own contentment, in a sweet amiableness of conversation? Or what shall a man give for a recompense of it, if it should be in hazard? Thus will everyone speak of this blessing, except he is a fool, to whom the sunshine is wearisome, for the continual shining of it (and yet this fair weather may do hurt, so cannot consent) or such as to whom nothing will seem precious save by the want of it. As for all wise men, they will affirm it. That then, which in both the confessions both of desirers and enjoyers, makes so much for the honor of marriage, justly deserves the joint consent of both parties to ensue and maintain.

Secondly, the very nature of this jewel, the nobility, the praise and price of it in general is a sign of the worth, and how it deserves the joint care of couples to maintain it. It may challenge equality with the things of greatest price and excellency! Oh sweet amiableness and concord, what may not be said of you? You are the offspring of God, the fruit of redemption, the breath of the spirit. You are the compound of contraries, the harmony of discords, the order of creation, the soul of the world: without which, the vast body thereof would soon dissolve itself by her own burden as wearisome to itself, and fall in sunder by piecemeal from each other. By you, oh sweet peace and concord, the heavens are combined to the earth by their sweet influence; by you, the earth confines the unlimited waters within bounds, both earth and waters nourish those inferior vegetables; by you, those same creatures nourish the sensible; by you, those sensible again return their food to the most noble members of the world, the reasonable; that so the spiritual part, which is above the rest, I mean the inner man and new creature might by them, for them, and in them all honor his Creator. Oh divine consent, the sweet temperature of bodily complexions, the blessed union of soul and body, the law of government to commonwealths and societies, the band of perfection in the church, the reconcilement of God with man, the recollection and confederating of all things in one,

Branch 2. The experience of such as enjoy it show it to be worth the preserving jointly.

Reason 2. The price of this jewel in her nature deserves the careful improving of it.

The praise of consent.

both in heaven and earth, the life of the family, the daughter of love, sister of peace, and mother of blessing. Can you then, who are the life of all things, choose but be the honor of marriage? Shall all other creatures know no other marriage band, and shall the truly married be without it? Is it so sweet and good a thing to see brethren to dwell together in affection, although they cannot always in place and habitation, and must it not be more sweet to them, who are both in affection and habitation inseparable? If in distance of bodies by necessity, yet if it is so sweet, what is it in the necessity of each other's presence? All this considered, what a joint care ought there to be in couples to nourish it? How stupid do they declare themselves to be, who do not feel it? The beasts, the birds, the plants are sensible of it, and strive to put forth themselves to all mutual offices of service to each other for the improving of it, as loath to forge such a jewel, and shall married Christians be senseless and careless of it?

Reason 3. Consent has a divine instinct in it.

Thirdly, that which is honorable both in the coherence and consequence of it deserves mutual care in couples to preserve it between themselves. But such is this consent. For mark, when love has once combined and incorporated two to one, what an instinct does it breed, and what influence does it instill into each party for the useful services belonging to their place? Each bee flies abroad to work and carry home to her hive, being once appropriated to it. Even so here. Readiness and willingness in each party to his and her office, the man to toil without in weary labor and travail, and the woman within doors, both without complaint; these flow from the genial consent of each other. Hence nothing is thought too much, benevolence, providence, forbearance, patience, fidelity, and secrecy; all virtuous offices. The husband complains not that the burden lies all upon his shoulders; the wife (as weak as she is) mutters not that her sick husband lies upon her hand, and spends all from her, like to leave her in want. Both cheerfully go on, acted by providence to look upon a promise, and all because a secret accord of spirit puts them forward to the work. The reason comes to this issue: that which is as useful and gainful, as it is pleasant and contentful is as the dew of

Psal. 133.2,3 Hermon, and the oil upon the head of Aaron, in both so much grace, marriage deserves that the married should enshrine it in their bosoms and nourish it with joint endeavor.

Lastly, this grace of consent is that which brings the Reason 4. Lord himself to rule and reign in the family over the married Consent themselves and all that pertain to them, then well does it de- brings God serve the care of all married persons to join themselves in the into the mar- promoting thereof. It is an honor to a house to be frequented ried. by the great and honorable: how much more when the Lord of heaven and earth shall condescend to dwell in our houses, to come in, to sit, and sup with us? Whom should he sooner do so unto than to the peaceable and consenting? We know that old maxim of Machiavelli, if you will reign, divide: and our Mat. 12.26 Savior affirms it: If Satan cast out Satan, how shall his kingdom endure? Certainly not. Satan must cast out unity and amity, if he means to reign, that he may bring in hellish discord and confusion. Even so, if God will reign he must cast out Satan that he may bring in union and consent between couples. There is no agreement between Christ and Belial, light and 2 Cor. 6.15 darkness. Then (and never till then) shall religion, prayer, Sabbath duties, holy exercises, and love to the saints be entertained when consent has taken up the room of each other's heart. So much may serve for reasons.

But wherein (may some say) stands this consent? I A question answer. By these few heads it may be conceived (for the par- answered, ticulars of consent they are infinite as the occasions of life are). wherein con- First, in consent of spirit, of mind (I mean) and affection. Sec- sent stands. ondly, consent of speech, or the tongue. Thirdly, consent of Answer. practice and endeavors. For the first of these the principle of In 3 things. marriage consent must be rooted in the heart; that each think 1. and affect the same things. As in Ezekiel it is said of the beasts In consent of and the wheels that when the one went forward the other did heart as chief. so, and when the beasts were lifted up, the wheels were lifted Ezek. 1.19 up, for the spirits of the beasts were in the wheels. So ought it to be between couples, one judgment, one mind, one heart, one soul in two bodies; the spirit of the wife in the husband, and his in the Lord. That which the flatterer says in the comedy (the hatred of the name being removed), that should the wife say to the husband. Say you a thing? So say I. Do you deny it? I deny it too. And in a word; I am prepared for the nonce to agree with you in all things, good and honest. What is more beautiful to behold in marriage than that whereof it is a resemblance, I mean, the harmony between the Lord Jesus the head and the members, namely his church? Read the Song of Solomon. See how the church echoes her husband's voice in all he speaks; see how she pleases herself in his comely proportion, attire, and gestures! And he again in hers; how she depends wholly upon his beck and countenance, joys in his presence, mourns in his absence, reposes herself in his bosom, being asleep, watches his awaking, follows after him, hangs upon him in his departing, longs for his return, and having lost him runs after him as one distracted, and betrays her life to be bound up in his, as Jacob's in Benjamin's. This inward complacence, well-pleasing, and well-apaidness of couples in each other is the very quintessence of marriage peace and contentment. As in the mystical body of Christ, we see what an instinct is in them to maintain their own being in the welfare of each other. All envy, wrath, suspicion, jealousy, unkindness, pride, censure, and whatsoever else savoring of self-love and separation, being odious to them. Each doing his own service, content with his own portion, mourning with any that is ill at ease, and glad of their welfare.

2.
Consent in speech, necessary for the married.
2 Kings 3.7
Prov. 27.19

Secondly, this consent must be in the speech and language of them both. It is true generally, but in this point especially, that speech is the discoverer of the mind. Look what the abundance of the heart is that will vent itself at the mouth. So the husband and wife should answer to each other, as Jehoshaphat to Jehoram, I am as you are; my people are as yours, my horses as yours. Truly, the speech of each to other should be (without flattery) as the glass to behold each other in. As face answers to face in the water so does a man accommodate himself to his friend (says Solomon) how much more the husband and wife to each other? They should even resemble each other's frame and temper (in the Lord) with all ingenuity. As the beams do represent the sun in her heat and light, so should the sweet carriage of the wife, argue the body which gives her influence, even her husband's virtues.

3.
Consent in common life and occasions of it.

And lastly, there ought not only to be this harmony in presence only, but in absence also, even in the way of their conversation: abroad in company, in duties of Sabbath, of Christian communion, whether together or asunder, such should be the reflection of a wife's carriage that all that see her may see the wisdom, thoughts, and affections of the husband in her: not a carriage of her own, as of one severed from his way, slighting his as if she were wiser; but humbly submitting judgment, will, and spirit to his in the Lord: and where there is any difference, so it is grounded, keeping it secret, and acquainting God with it, as she did when she felt strife in her womb, that he might reconcile it and settle it aright in time. For in such a case, discreet concealment will far sooner reduce them together than open expression of their differences. The actions of the one should be the shadow of the other's, indeed a model thereof. As it was once between David and his new subjects, whatsoever liked David that was presently pleasing to all his people; they agreed at a hair's breadth. This threefold cord of heart, mouth, and work is not easily broken.

2 Sam. 3.36

I shall make these three appear better in uses of the point, to which I hasten. First then, what bitter reproof is this to most, even of such as seem to stand to God's bar and trial? I pass by the ruder sort of barbarous people, rustic and profane (who never yet came into the garden where this grace grew), such as pass their days either in brutish and Nabalish churlishness, brawling, fighting, and quarrelling together; or else consent only in evil, serving each other's turn according to those vices they are inclined unto, as the world, to take together portions for their children by hook or crook, or pleasures and liberties, or pride of life and fashions, or envious pursuit of their enemies, slander, or the like sins of the tongue. I say, to leave such; who would look for such differences of spirit and temper among such as pretend great zeal in profession? A man would think, when he looks narrowly into them, that they are set as marks of opposition to each other, rather than resemblers of their affections, joys, and desires. Verily I have often seen it (to the shame of such I speak it) that among some ignorant couples, whom only natural likeness of manners or civil education has handsomed, there is found more love and accord than among some such as daily keep on foot the worship of God in their families. Shall I praise them in this? Certainly not. I know, the sorrow which hereby you procure to yourselves is punishment sufficient for your folly; but you must not escape so: but shame you for such contrariety of spirit. Many men and women are so cross to each

Use 1.
Reproof.
Vulgar guise
of married
ones, rude and
rustical.

The dissentions of religious couples, the shame of profession.

other that they think this consent rather a weak and silly fruit
of a pusillanimous spirit, truly a shame rather than an honor
to their marriages! And that then they have quit themselves
best when they can whet their misery upon one another, jarring and jangling, and pleasing their froward and ill pleased
spirits in displeasures and differences. And can you, or dare
you nevertheless, board, converse, and bed together, and go to
the house of God, and there hear and partake the sacrament
of communion as if there was nothing amiss? *Can two walk*
together, except they be agreed? Or do you cast arrows and
darts, and say, you are in sport! What villainous hypocrisy
is this, thus to habit yourselves in sin that the custom of it
should make you senseless of it, and cause a falling sickness
of discord, that you know not the way of getting in again? All
day war and deadly feud, and yet lie down at night and wipe
off each crumb from the lips. Moreover, what do such, except
make the ordinances of God covers of their shame and wickedness! I doubt whether such of these, or they whose debates
break out into separation so that neither town nor country
can hold them, are the worse of the two! I say in point of
presumption, though their sin is not so exemplary. What a
pageant is this for the Devil to laugh at? How out of measure
sinful is your sin? Tigers and bears have their agreement, and
shall such distempers reign in the marriages of the religious?
Shall fraud and oppression be found in the seat of justice, or
a froward, waspish spirit in the proper element of peace and
consent? Where shall peace be looked for if you disagree in
marriage? If you war and contend, who should agree? Or,
who should go about the families of religious ones, to seek
out matches, when as such as these hatch up a brood by their
lives and examples, more fit for the Devil to govern in than the
Spirit of God which is peaceable? Shall such as should one day
judge the world (if they are as they seem), yet are fain to refer
the desperate quarrels of wife and husband to the arbitrement
of friends? By which occasion, matters growing to be ripped
up between you, perhaps the coals of juniper are blown to a
greater heat than before by these bellows, and the hope of accord set further off than it was. Surely, as the corruption of the
finest bodies is most loathsome, so are the contentions of such
as should be most quiet, commonly most tedious: for sin loves

Amos 3.3
Prov. 26.19

to be out of measure sinful. So much of this first.

Secondly, this should be abasement, and deep hum-Use 2.
bling to all such couples (out of whose breasts this sin has not Humiliation
chased away all remorse and tenderness). Oh man! Remem-to all faulty
ber, the Lord has created you in his image, made you as God couples.
to your wife, a man of more solid mold and frame, able to bear
impressions and occasions of discontent. It is the honor of a
man to pass by an offence: the Lord abhors that you should Prov. 20.3
weaken yourself by a willful opposition of a weaker sex. What
a poor victory is that, when you have matched a silly woman!
No, your honor stands rather in passing by her folly and weakness: not in a currish blockishness, not in a surly stoutness
and pride of stomach, not in a controlling, imperious carriage,
and thwarting tongue. This is to betray your own strength,
and to outshoot the Devil in his own bow. This is to smite all
due honor out of your wife's heart; and (as oil to the flame) to
enflame and provoke her spirit to be sevenfold worse. Rather
do in such a case, as workmen in coalpits used to do when the
candle burns blue, they suspect the damp to be coming, which
would stifle them, and therefore they strive to get out, who can
get first, and when the damp is over, then to work again. So,
give place to this damp and distemper of discord and contention, and when it is over then return to your wonted course.
And, in conclusion, look to find small fruit of violent striving. For, as Latimer said, he that gets the victory here, gains
sorrow, and he that loses, loses peace. The gains which you
get you must put in your eye, and see never the worse. You
shall repent yourself at leisure that you did not redeem your
peace upon harder terms than the curbing of a base appetite.
You shall lose your sweet words in your bitterness; your liberty with God to lift up pure hands without wrath or doubting shall degenerate into fear, barrenness, and bondage. Your
prayers shall be choked in your throat, and perish in the uttering, which you were once wont to pour out purely, confidently, and cheerfully. Therefore obey this charge of God and
prosper. If the Lord bless not your endeavor, yet, it is better for
you to deny yourself and to wait the issue with patience than
bootless to strive against the stream. The like I say to you oh
woman, is this a life pleasing to you, always to live like a sala-
mander in the fire? Is this an element so welcome to you?

The duty
urged.

Consider (poor wretch) how you degenerated from your creation. You were molded by the hand of a wise work-man, to be a tender and yielding nature, the weaker vessel; and do you delight in a spirit of contradiction? Will you resist your maker and your head, both at once? Should you think it an honor, to you, to carry in your bosom a proud wrathful and shrewish heart, and in your head a stinging tongue? Oh, it is more agreeing to you to be melting, mild, and overcome evil with good! If this ought to be done to an enemy abroad, that if he need, you should clothe him, feed him: if to him who

Luke 6.27-29

reviles you, you should return good language; if to him who would take your cloak, you should cast your coat also (to show how meek you are) that so you might be like to your father, who does good to the evil: what then shall you do to your hus-band, that you might resemble the Lord Jesus' tenderness to his church, whereof your marriage is a shadow? As you would that Christ should handle you, so do you oh man, handle your wife, and you oh wife, your husband! Go together (as once a couple did, being convinced by their minister's reproof) and break heart each in other's bosom, confess how far you are off from your first frame, what dishonor to the gospel you have been, and woeful joint enemies to that joint and mutual peace which both of you should have hatched and nourished between yourselves. Beseech the Lord to shed his love and spirit into your bosoms, his peaceable, amiable, quiet spirit, which can turn your swords into mattocks and spears into plowshares: who can make the ox and the lion, the bear and the lamb to feed together, that is, take out your fellness and put into yourself a heart of amity and consent. Then shall you be another while for the honor of that ordinance with equal endeavors, which all this while you have so reproached.

Use 3.
Admonition.

Caveat 1.
Be not too
confident of
yourselves in
an attempt of
marriage.

And thirdly, let it be admonition unto both parties; and first, let me say this, enter not into marriage in a con-fidence of your own strength. When couples first meet to-gether, youth, strength, and carnal confidence upon their own means, with fleshly contentment in each other, makes them dream of a dry summer and think I shall not be moved. It will always be a honeymoon with me: as if the bitterness of an unquiet heart were passed away. But poor souls! You know no more your own spirits, than Hazael did, when hearing the prophet telling what a cruel wretch he should prove, he asked: Am I a dog to do such things? You daub with untempered mortar, which will fall off in frosty weather; but, when experience has schooled you, and showed you the discontents of marriage, and with what bitter ingredients sin has poisoned your hoped successes; when husband proves an unthrift, wife an ill housewife, business in the world cross and left-handed, when also cares, fears, losses, charge of children, sorrows of the womb and nursery, bad children, debts, and straits come upon you at once (none whereof you have grace to prevent). Oh then you see that your first merry meeting will not bear off all assaults! And yet, what should I speak of such things? When a base heart in the midst of all contrary mercies, pampered with the creature, but wickedly proud and unthankful, can and often does cause this woe to couples, more than all adversity! Oh, this canker grows out of blessing more often than affliction! Wherefore, enter this estate with self-denial! Humble yourselves, be as Ephraim, who was as a heifer unused to the yoke, but after, he repented and smote upon his thigh. Do so yourself beforehand, and beg armor of God for the hardest: boast not of the best before you put off your harness: the best will always save itself.

2 Kings 8.13

Jer. 31.18,19

Secondly, know this, that although the Lord should free you from such disasters, yet marriage of itself (without special grace) will try of what mettle you are made. Even mere continuance of time, custom, and usual society will (by corruption) procure a fulsomeness and satiety, certainly a weariness of each other. Acknowledge therefore that this frame of your marriage will not stand alone; it needs daily props to keep off an impatient spirit! For why? The mere spirit that is in you lusts to envy; inclines to crossness, elfishness, and self-willedness of spirit, when as yet there is no vexation without to cause it. What need is there then to ply the Lord with prayer, for the sweet uniting of your spirits and calming of your hearts? That the peace of God passing understanding may fence or (as the word is) beleaguer and hem in your souls (or as a garrison keeps a town safe), may preserve them with the knowledge of God, and possess them in patience. Alas! Let all your whetting and provoking each other be reflected back upon your own selves, fret with indignation against the root

Caveat 2.
Pray for this
sweet gift of
calmness and
amiableness.

Phil. 4.7

Luke 19.22

within, purge out that leaven; and then your hard hearts shall melt into tears for each other; spend your time of jarring, in prayer and earnest request to God for mercy and pardon. That he would take off your rough edge, and make you polished and squared stones to couch in the wall of this building: which before could lie no way. Oh! The Lord (for all you know) may make you blessed means of each other's conversion, that you may bless him that ever you met, who so often has cursed your own eyes for seeing each other. Let the fruit be as God will: sure I am the cross of an uncomfortable yoke should persuade you rather to spend all your life in prayer than in rebellion. For it is better (if it must be so) that God delay your desires, while you are praying, than while you are sinning, and stopping the course of prayer.

Caveat 3.
Put on the
Lord Jesus, his
meekness.

Thirdly, put on the Lord Jesus, and he shall so furnish you that you shall not need to take anymore thought of how to fulfill your base lusts anymore. Put him on, in his long suffering, meekness, and bowels of compassion, as the apostle speaks: which will not only prevent those evils of an unquiet and unsavory spirit, through a well-satisfied heart: but also

Rom. 12.end
Col. 3

will teach you to bear and lie under your cross, and to be as God will have you to be. Fight not against God, but put on the armor of peace, as a breastplate, to bear off all the darts of distempers. If the Lord will not be entreated one way, ply him another. Remember a heart armed with holy resolution in this kind is shot-free, and able to conquer a city. The patient in spirit is better than the hasty, and the end of a thing is better than the beginning. Patience carries with it half a release; it is (as it were) boot in beam. If then, your wife and your husband cannot be won to consent, yet, if you can possess your own spirit, you shall conquer hers. The best victories are by yielding in this kind. Strange is the nature of a quiet spirit: it must prevail at last because it will wait until it has no refusal. But especially, it has this power in it, to quench any fiery dart far better than any resistance and wrath. If cannon shot falls upon the wool-pack, it loses its force: but if upon a stone wall, it batters it to pieces; and a soft answer puts away wrath.

Mark 4.39
1 Sam. 4.5

Bring Jesus into this ship he will allay all the waves: bring this ark into the camp of debate, and it will make all whist and quiet. When the whirlwind arises suddenly from the heart of

an unquiet man or woman, and like to that tempest of Job 1, Job 1.19
assaults every corner of the house to ruin it, yet if this spirit of
a soft voice encounters it, all will be soft and calm on the sudden. The cause why the house of Job's children fell down was
because it was such a wind as beset on every side. So it will
fare with you: if when one wind is arisen in the house, then
by and by another is up in the other corner to resist it, woe to
that house. Then is the season of your calm O husband, when
your wife's heart is up in heat: and then of your quiet heart (O
wife) when your husband fumes and storms. But if both are
up at once, be you (O man) the wiser, and say, it is now out
of season for me to meddle. Else you will throw down your
house, and destroy your own peace. The second blow makes
the fray: therefore while the cloud is as a man's hand, little in
the entry, give over quickly before it covers the whole sky and 1 Kings 18.44
causes such a tempest, as clouds when they follow rain, which
is a continual dropping: and make sick weather for ado.

Fourthly, if the Lord exercises you with this following Caveat 4.
cross, beware lest you forsake his way, and through tedious Renounce not
discontent, consult with flesh and blood to use carnal shifts. God to use
carnal shifts.
It is not your violence to go to work by strong hand, to bear
down your wife's stream by a stronger one of your own; by
either threats or much less blows (a base remedy, and which I
wonder should either come into any wise man's thoughts and
pen to advise, or heart and hand to practice), or any other
policy of shame and dissuasion, which God has blessed to effect it. If he had, it had surely more prevailed than it has. No,
it is the only victory of heaven and grace; whatsoever fleshly
wisdom, and rashness or device of man, has or may practice in
this kind, I speak not: extremities may plead excuse from the
greatness, but not the realness of the sin. Nor yet do I deny but
that a carnal way (for the present) may help against the present occasion. As I heard lately that a man put to his wit's end,
agreed with his friends in London that dwelt near, it seems,
that when they heard the drum sound from his house, they
should all make haste to take his wife in her scolding vein,
and so shame her. So they might cut off a finger, but who shall
mortify the spirit? Surely the drum comes short of that cure,
and a woman will scorn to yield up her weapons at the sound
of such a charm. No, alas! As the Pope's blessing makes no

armor of proof: so neither is any medicine of man's devising, shrew or scold proof: for a sudden they may please by their violence, but at time of year, the malady will have his course. To this, I might add a contrary extreme of carnal wit: that husbands thus matched will seek to flatter and demerit their base wives, serving their own wills, be they ever so wasteful and proud: suffering them to be all in all, to carry all the stream, and to throw house out at windows, and all to win them to some indifference, slavishly subjecting themselves to their usurping and domineering spirit. They (in truth) must buy, sell, let, hire, take all, and pay all, staving off their husbands from intermeddling, except at their own courtesy, what they shall wear, spend, or carry in their purse. Others, will redeem their peace by casting all the tackling into sea; let their wives jolly and ruffle it out in what manner, measure, or companies they themselves please to spend at their pleasure, keeping their husbands at a beck. Indeed, suffer them to keep and harbor varlets under their noses to defile their beds and family with filth and bastardy: and all that they may be rid of unquietness. And when upon these terms they have bought repentance too dear then they must either die in sorrow, or live with baseness and dishonor. In general, I like your patience (for some yielding does well) if limited: but your cowardly, base heart, distrusting God's ways and method, except you relieve yourselves by sinning, that I abhor, and affirm the remedy to be far worse than the disease.

Caveat 5.
Keep each
party the
bounds of his
place.

       Fifthly, I warn all couples that they run not beyond the bounds set them by providence, to intermeddle with the affairs concerning each other. It is the folly and boldness of many women to be so curiously prying and pragmatic about their husband's matters (which concern them not to busy themselves about, but to rest upon their fidelity, except they see just exception), to be so inquisitive into their actions, companies, and occasions, so jealous of them (unjustly) that, although I allow not of the effect, yet I say, it is a just provocation to the spirit of a wise and innocent man, to differ from his wife. And again, many foppish husbands do so intermeddle in the element, and about the peculiar employments of the women, taking upon them the managing of their cookeries, their dairies, and housewifery, as if they must have an oar in each boat. What wise woman would not break into a mixed passion of fulsome indignation and contempt? What husband would not be carried to extreme discontent? God has appointed their station to them both, the one without, the other within: lest by idleness and sloth, they wanting their several works, they should wax unsavory, and lie open to foreign vice: but this is to turn the ordinance topsy-turvy, and instead of not doing, to overdo, and cause discord at home. Therefore keep your station: provoke not each other, which gives occasion (oftentimes) of that mutual curiosity. Mutual consent will not consist with mutual meddling in this kind. To this I might add another caveat against the darkness and closeness of carriage of couples, to each other, which does breed this evil spoken of. For, though each party is to be trusted in his or her own sphere, to act and deal: yet neither must forget the other, to bear an equal share in the common welfare; and therefore, to conceal themselves and walk aloof as in the clouds, one from the knowledge of the other; as never to impart their mutual affairs, never to communicate together, or consult with each other, what is it, but a despising of that equipage and equality which marriage claims? What is it, save provoking of each other to turn a mutual spirit into a private one; to turn equanimity of love (that thinks no evil, but construes all in the better sense) into jealous suspicion? What imports it, save that their ways are unthrifty and unhappy, so that they are loath to discover them till all is too late? And then at last, endless broils grow upon such affected secrecy, and a necessity of violent sparing, lest all should perish: both extremities, to be shunned by all wise couples.

Sixthly, as the proverb says, take not counsel in the combat: for then there is no season for counsel, then the spirit is in the power of passion, and temptation present, as a bowl running down the hill is in the power of the descent. Take counsel therefore before, and use your skill in preventing that which is hardly endured. Observe your husband's frame oh wife, and your wife's oh husband. Study each other's natures, and count it your wisdom and vantage, by that you shall easily guess, both what may provoke and also prevent it; and, what may both content and so procure it. But they who let all go at six and seven, suffer the upper millstone to run upon the neth-

*Caveat 6.
Be prepared
for the hardest,
before.*

er, they may be sure the Devil will see there shall want no corn, and then there will be grinding. Studious shunning of occasions, with wisdom and pious caution, has in time, wrought many an unquiet heart to some calmness; except there is so cursed and churlish a nature, as delights in distemper, even to choose, and would rather die fighting with its own shadow than be at peace. I say, when a Nabal sees an Abigail, watch her opportunity, loath to provoke him in his madness, willing to hold off whatsoever might disquiet, and further, what might please and satisfy: how can he, but at last break his heart in her bosom, and say, come my dear wife: you are more righteous than I: for I have sought your grief, but you have overcome me with your wisdom and meekness; you have heaped hot coals upon the head of a froward husband, and made me ashamed to behold the ugly hue of my passion, in the glass of your meekness and discretion. And this for admonition.

1 Sam. 25

The last use briefly shall be exhortation. Strive, all you husbands and wives, who seek to live in godliness and honor, to establish mutual amity in your spirits, and consent in your conversation. Alas! Husbands and wives should be as two sweet friends, bred under one constellation, tempered by an influence from heaven, whereof neither can give any great reason, save that mercy and providence first made them so, and then made their match; saying, See, God has determined us, out of this vast world, for each other; perhaps many may deserve as well, but yet to me, and for my turn, you excel them all, and God has made me to think so (not for formality's sake to say) but because it is so. When I consider that we are not meet only, but meet as we should do, not as many mismatched ones are, more meet for some other man and woman than for each other; so that we can say as he in his motto, what we are, we would be, and would be no other than we are; the only meet ones, for one another. Oh then! How it raises up my spirit to admire and magnify God's dispensation! Oh, if it were thus, how sweet is it to see married ones to live together! As the ark carried by the power of God, above the highest mountain in the world, fifteen cubits, so should mercy carry them above all contentions and turmoil, that they should know no such. As they say the tops of some high hills are above the middle region, and so above all those vapors of frost and snow and

Use 4.
Exhortation
to the married
to use cordial
consent.

winds which inferior grounds are infested with: so, so should
these be above far worse: and behold others beneath, molested
with such things, even with wondering at their happy escape.
And as all the hills and valleys, which make the parts of that
earth where they are, unequal: but cannot hinder the roundness of it, because the circular figure of the whole, swallows up
all particular unevenness into itself: so should those passages
of inequality between couples, here and there passionate heats
and dissenting from each other, be drowned in this consent
so that they should vanish as clouds without rain and storm,
though not without some darkness and lowering.

And, if all did befall otherwise than meetly, how
should each outstrip the other afterward, in humiliation and
repentance! Oh base wretch (should you say) should I be
weary of welfare! Should I return to nourish secret poison in
my heart, to hazard my precious peace and should I venture
all upon a cast, to try whether mine be my own or not? Shall
one dead fly defile a whole box of precious ointment? No, far
be it from me to forsake my fatness and sweetness, by which I
have cherished the heart of God and man, of wife, of husband,
(like that bramble exalting itself above the trees) to bear up
myself above, against each other, by confusion and discord?
No: far be it from us to suffer the noise of hammers, saws, or
axes to be heard in our temples hereafter! We were squared
in God's mount by his workmanship, not needing now any
such edge tools! Rather let us be like him, who was typified
hereby, whose voice was not lifted up or heard in the streets,
who never trod upon a bug or worm to kill it, broke not the
bruised reed, nor quenched the smoking flax. As he, the head
of his church is to his church, so will I be to my spouse and
beloved, amiable and consenting. Enough to marriage is the
necessary unavoidable grief of it, such as must be in it by God's
allowance, for trial. I will not seek to add needless to necessary, but pull away as much as I can: and when the needless is
taken off then shall the necessary be the better born. Offences
must come; occasions will arise. Pharaoh's own privy chamber cannot be free from frogs, as well as other common men's:
and the sweetest May-month may have frosty mornings and
cold evenings, surely there will be sad days and sorrowful affronts at one time or other; able to affront the most peaceable:

Marginal notes: What is to be done by both after a differ-ence, even to repent and be humbled. Judg. 9.9-15. 1 Kings 6.7. Isa. 42.3,4. Mat. 18.7. Exod. 8.3.

Phil. 4.7
but the peace of God and marriage, which pass understanding, the peace of conscience and family, running in a stream together, will keep the hearts of the good so firm and stable that they will lose their wills and humors ten times rather than this jewel. And if, when all is done, there must some dreg of old Adam cleave still, it shall not be for hurt, all shall turn for best to the peaceable, to search all which is in their hearts, to keep them humble, to exercise self-denial, and to teach them that the best marriages upon earth must have their eyesores, lest we should say it is good being here, for the best and purest peace will be in heaven, where there shall be no such relations as these, but all fulfilled in our eternal conjunction with our head the Lord Jesus. Also it must teach them, even when the weather is most contrary, yet to imitate the skill of the mariner who will not strive against the winds, but rather coast, and fetch a compass, to gain ground and further his travail.

Conclusion of this main duty. And so I finish this last of these mutual duties of the married, which is consent. Ensue peace with all, especially with yourselves. Ground it in that peace with God, to pardon and accept you: and this will be as the rush growing in the mire, a peace always maintained by a better, never failing. Walk according to this rule, and the peace of God shall be with you. Try no carnal conclusions, tempt not God, and be not weary of welfare. Though it should turn from you, yet follow, and take it by the lap of the garment; hold it fast; it is the free-simple of good couples. Let it rule and overrule, to forgo anything rather than it. They, who angle with golden hooks, had need look to it, lest if they lose their hook, all their catch equal not their loss. And so doing, consent shall make your marriage honorable; till it brings you to enjoy that peace and blessed consent of saints in glory, which shall be a perfect sweet without any bitter, a life without end. And so much also for this chapter: and for these four duties mutually concerning marriage, for the preserving of the integrity and comfort thereof.

CHAPTER X

*Return to the personal offices of each party. And
first the husband. His first duty handled,
to be a man of understanding.*

Having handled the joint duties of both, we come to lay down the several duties of either party in marriage. And what great difficulty will there be in this latter, when the former is once settled. As in a fagot, each stick is kept straight and whole, while the band holds: so, let the married parties once be united in the former duties which stand in equality: it will be no difficulty to maintain these which are peculiar. When as once the retreat of the army of soldiers is made sure, each soldier fights merrily in his rank. So here the main work being dispatched, and mutual security being given and taken from each other, of religion to God, of love to each other's person, of chastity to bodies, of consent in the life and whole course, what hardness can there be in the residue, for particular offices of each other? The nave of the wheel being strong, the staves well fastened: how easily will the wheel and orb of it run, and what a sweet current will there be in the same? Touching the particulars then, first of the man, then of the woman (for both must manage this common stock of honor by their personal industry). The man's first duty is to walk as a man of understanding with and before his wife: that is, so to behave himself that he may sweetly strike into his wife's spirit a due reverential love and esteem of his person and headship, for the virtues of a husband: such as may satisfy her to be a meet guide of her life, by his gravity, stayedness, and prudence of carriage. That her heart may tell her in secret, my husband is indeed a man of understanding. A husband, who would save the stake of his own honor, should set down that for his maxim, let not your wife despise you: for if once the woman's heart despises her husband, the whole frame of marriage is loosed. This is Peter's counsel to husbands. Likewise husbands, dwell with them according to knowledge or understanding. He seems to contract

Coherence of the points.

First peculiar duty of the husband is to be a man of understanding.

What this is?

1 Pet. 3.7

all the work into this comprehensive rule, in a general sense; as if any branch might fitly be derived from it: but here I take it for the first special gift of the husband, as a head. He that has a good head-piece is a man of good understanding and judgment (that is the peculiar virtue of the head): for as it is the highest of the members, so it is to lead and guide the inferior powers of the soul and the members. In the head is the eye, which outwardly leads the latter, as the brain and wisdom are within, which guides the former. In that semblance is this gift of understanding, the most peculiar to the head, the husband: the wife must follow, as the will and affections and members do follow the judgment. There need be no more proofs of the point, reason convinces it sufficiently.

Particulars wherein it consists.

The greater question is, wherein this duty of understanding consists. For the answer whereof, I think (as he once being to teach the art of memory first would teach the art of forgetfulness) it is best to show what it is to walk as a man of no understanding, and then the positive. First then, to walk understandingly is not to walk aloft in the pride and vain conceit of yourself, saying to the wife as he is walking in his palace, am not I great Nebuchadnezzar? So, do you not know (wife) that I am the head and set above, made to rule? That you are made of my rib and for my use, and not I for yours but for my own ends? Yes, I will have you to know it too, that I am a man by myself, and am able to manage a woman better than she. No, first learn to understand yourself before you prove a man of understanding to your wife. A man of understanding is (as Solomon speaks) of a cool spirit, not a proud, insulting, and domineering spirit. He that is such a one has need of such a woman as to his cost, may teach him to understand himself better. First learn to rule yourself, if your will is too strong for your wit, and you are hurried by your lust, against your knowledge. As the apostle says of another, he that cannot rule his own family is much less able to rule the church of God. So, he who has not understanding enough to rule himself is very unfit to rule a woman. That husband, who stands upon it, that he will lord it and be all in all, bears sway over his wife, as his underling, and who shall control him? He may perhaps, when Mistress Experience has well awed and tawed him, repent of his lording it, and wish his understanding had laid another

First in what it consists not.
Dan. 4.30
1.
Not in a high spirit.

Prov. 17.27

1 Tim. 3.5

way. Add to these, such as will be ruled by no other man's counsel, save their own, and yet have little of their own neither (a true mark of a fool) but rashly rush upon their dealing and affairs, saying: What I do, I will do, what I have written (as he said) I have written: my will shall stand for my law. Prove it for better or for worse, I am resolved to do as I want and what is a man's liberty, but license to live, to speak, and go to work as he desires without control, as they, Psal. 12. Is it not lawful to do with my own, as I desire? If I give all I have away, who shall gainsay me?

So again, this is no understanding, for a head to get some shreds of religion by the end, or to be able perhaps to speak of a sermon, or to pray, or read a chapter (which yet many such do not) or keep some show of a Sabbath; but, to neglect all the practice of his knowledge in his life, to expose himself to all looseness of carriage, baseness of example, living within doors currishly, spitefully, without doors shiftily, cunningly, deceitfully, and offensively. Moreover neither is this to be a man of understanding, to seem to give way to good counsel, to hearken and nod to good advice, to give fair words; you say well indeed good sir, and speak to very good purpose to show no verbal resistance. For of this sort there are many, who yet have no power at all to amend: but having praised the man, yet turn their backs and do as they did before, not stirring an inch. They move upon their center as the windmill round about, but stir not one hair from it. Oh (says one) a very facile man, and easy to be handled. True, but hard to be changed: he has a trick for you, worth ten of a rebellious refusal: for he will say as you say, but do as he desires. To end, neither is it any mark of an understanding man to be able to give counsel to others, either in God's matters or the world, or to make others to say: Oh! This man is of great parts and deep understanding, see what wisdom and experience he has gotten! Whereas all this while this wise man, whose head is aloft in his counsel to others, falls into the ditch for lack of taking counsel himself. He cannot guide his own way, nor order his own conversation aright. In generals he is very free and full, because he is carried only to the object of truth and judgment, till you come to particulars, and then occasions of his own profits, will, pleasure, or ease and ends do so hamper and ensnarl his spirit, that

2.
Not in a rash self-willedness.

John 19.22

Psal. 12.4

3.
To know but not to practice.

4.
Not to give way to good counsel, but not follow it.

5.
Not to give counsel to others, and not to himself.

this man with his great understanding becomes a very fool for lack of a special wise heart to apply knowledge to his own occasions: as Sampson was able to judge Israel, but his lusts and passions cast him out of the rule of himself. These then, and the like argue no man of understanding.

Secondly therefore, he is a true husband, and a man of understanding, who first has denied his own wisdom, and is abased before God in the privity of his own wants and inability to manage this great affair of marriage, or to walk before his wife as a man of understanding. To say of this, as Solomon did of his government, who am I Lord that I should walk before this great people? To say as holy Agur did: Doubtless I am a fool, and the understanding of a man is not in me: every day I have not half the wisdom that a man of my condition has need of. I say it is one step to a husband's understanding to be convinced of the defect and disproportion of his abilities to guide the way of marriage. To think of it neither so highly as if it were above his possibility to attain, nor so low, as if he had enough and to spare for it. David being nominated to be Saul's son-in-law did not vaunt himself in his abilities as Absalom after did, but said thus: Think you it so easy a thing to stand in this relation? And Abigail a woman affirmed by a judicious man to be of great counsel and understanding, yet thought not herself so: but being sent for to be David's wife, answered: Alas! I am more fit to be a handmaid to wash the feet of the servants of my Lord! I say this holy, humble diffidence in ourselves is a surer mark of an understanding man than the former. Especially when the sense of a man's nakedness carries him to God to pray (as he did), Oh Lord, I beseech you, give to your servant an understanding heart! This pleased the Lord well, that he asked this only, not other matters for his own ends, long life, riches, or honor: so, if you sue to God for such a headpiece of wisdom, as might guide your marriage course aright more than for welfare and jollity in the world, it is a sign that the chief thing is more prized than the inferior. So secondly, to be a man of understanding is to be a subject to God himself before you undertake mastery over others. To say with that centurion, I myself am under authority, I come to the bar myself, and give account of my headship; I am fellow servant with my wife, and I have a master in heaven myself:

Second branch. What is to be a man of understanding? 1 Kings 3.7-9

1. To renounce our own understanding. Prov. 30.2

1 Sam. 18.18

1 Sam. 25.41

2. To be first subject to God, and so to govern others. Mat. 8.9

it behooves me to use my headship sparingly, not to lord it, lest I become scorned myself for taking upon me in that office which has more service than worship tied to it: my rule over my wife is not imperious, but royal and princely, not over an underling, but copartner with an equal: so that, if with all my understanding I can bow my wife's will by a mild persuasion, not by austerity, I have quitted myself well.

Thirdly, to be of understanding is to be more sensible of the burden and work of marriage than the honor of it. I say, to apprehend what cost and care belongs to my wife's soul, how to mold it unto true lowliness and meekness for God (which is of great price with him); to instill the principles of Christ and self-denial into her (or to nourish them if already instilled), to cause her to see into that scope and view of religion, which is the change and subduing of her will to God. Oh, what a work is this, and who is sufficient for it? Was it but to manage her outward man and carriage towards myself, towards her children, in her family, and before others, in point of subjection, love, and wisdom, oh it exceeds my understanding! It exercises me with more thought than all her portion contents me! Oh! I must carry her to God, and commit her to him to be trained to this great business! Lastly, to be a man of understanding is yet a point of further extent; for such a one is of an excellent spirit throughout, a man framed by God within and without, with a spirit for marriage, a spirit of cheerfulness, discerning, diligence, dexterity to devise and dispatch, also humbleness, courage, and patient enduring. By these, such a one first orders his own personal way of religion, conscience before God, conversation in tongue, dealings, and example before men. Then, next he walks before his wife as a wise man ought, and he attempts not to rule others before he has got the upper hand of himself. But, having begun (as physicians do sometimes) to try conclusions upon himself, then he prescribes to others. I say that these and the like graces concur to qualify a man of understanding in point of marriage; as (God willing) in the sequel shall more fully appear.

For which purpose, let this further be enquired into, in what main things consists this virtue of a husband, walking as a man of understanding toward his wife? I answer. In these two, first in matters of God, then in such as concern the

3. To be more sensible of a burden than an honor.

4. To be qualified with a spirit of all sorts, as occasion requires.

Particulars of this general, two.

1.
It appears in matters of God.

married relation. Both these will procure and maintain the honor of marriage on the husband's part: and the contrary will prove dishonorable. For the former, I will here touch it only so far as the purpose of the point requires. And first, it is requisite for the husband to handsel his understanding with the matters of God. That he count it his crown, first, to seek the kingdom of God, and that for itself; and from the savor thereof, as one well grounded in the Scriptures, to be able to express his knowledge to his wife until she conceives the like. And, having so done, that he set himself to walk accordingly towards his wife, both in the general, to instruct, admonish, comfort, resolve, support her, and especially in all private or family duties, to be her mouth to God, and to present to him the wants and petitions of all that depend upon him. Both indeed ought to know, they have several souls to save, and not to wrap up themselves in one another's grace. Both ought to be a spiritual body of Christ, anointed with his prophecy and priesthood: yet, as the man is the image of God especially, and her head, so ought the consecration of God to rest upon him, in more abundance than upon her: that she and all the rest may be replenished therewith. So that he (for his part) must be as her priest, and his lips must preserve knowledge for her:

Instances wherein.

to give some two or three instances of this point. First, for the discharge of family duties (whereof I have spoken before) he must purchase for himself a horn of oil, not only (as one says) for his vessel to be savory, but for his lamp to shine. My meaning is not to force such knowledge upon him as is ministerial, exact for degree (God requires no service beyond the ability and talent received, be it one or three). It is not required that he should be an interpreter of the Scriptures; that he gather punctual doctrines, to clear doubts and objections, or to make distinctions and applications beyond his calling and object. This would be but to make the family duties a stall to vend himself upon, and to pride himself in his parts and endowments (as many have done so long) while at last thinking themselves too fledge for their own nest, they have boldly leapt out of their shops and trades, into the pulpit, thinking themselves as meet to preach as the most able ministers; no, in no sort (I know there is difference in men for their skill and understanding in matters of God, and for sobriety and humbleness of spirit, whom I much honor, and desire not to trench upon, or discourage any governors in this kind, especially in such a profane world that runs a contrary stream). But impartially I desire to utter the truth by so just an occasion: and this I say, it is enough for a private person to insist upon such points of doctrine, and especially of catechism, as he has by his careful attention, heard in the ordinary course of the public ministry handled; to cull out such, and to impart them to his wife and family, in a familiar manner, upon confessed grounds, and upon easy texts: whose sense and scope is plain and undoubted; thereupon, fastening such exhortation, admonition, and watchwords as best befit him to utter who should be best acquainted with the state of such as are under his roof: rebuking sin, pressing duty; but otherwise as for texts of darker nature, abstaining from them, and leaving them to a public gift of interpreting: which is abler to rectify judgment, answer doubts, and settle the conscience.

Secondly, he is to apply himself to his wife, as a man of understanding, in the private way of her soul, helping her out of her fears, answering her doubts and questions according to the light he has received abroad, to reconcile her timorous and scrupulous spirit to God, by the promise, so often as she staggers, and to enlarge her with those comforts, to acquaint her with such directions for her walking with God, as himself has had experience of in his afflicted conditions, to fellow-feel her, to be afflicted with her, to confer with her about her growths or decays, her slips and recoveries, and so about the fruit of her both public and private worship and service of God: to satisfy her in any such difficulties and dangers as she meets with, and so to help her as well in the extraordinary duties of humiliation and thanks, as occasion requires: of which I said enough in the joint worship of God before. And so thirdly (to conclude this point), he is also to be a man of ability, to encourage, hearten, and quicken his wife in respect of any outward burdens she undergoes, to condole with her in them, to underlay her as the beloved in the Song of Solomon does his spouse, that so two may bear that which one cannot, and the toil may be the more cheerfully undergone, when she sees that her head steps into his uttermost to bear the brunt, and discharge her from the dint of trouble! Alas! How far are most husbands from

Song of Sol. 8.3

The backward-
ness of most
husbands in
this kind.

this course? Where are they whose understanding, humbleness, and love seeks the good of their wives herein? How seldom do they apply themselves to such public ordinances on
the Sabbath or weekday to enable them in knowledge or seek
the help of minister or other to guide them? Or suppose some
hear or note sermons (which now is grown each man's case,
and not amiss except they find that the gain of writing, mar
the power of the truth in their affections) yet they shut up all
presently in their notebooks, without meditation or aiming
at the purchase of a lively stock, of understanding; nor thriv-
ing upon their hearings, by proof and experience of that they
know. Or if they have knowledge, yet how surly and conceited
do they grow, drawing their wives rather to errors and fancies,
and busying themselves rather about matters beyond their
reach, and of less consequence, before they are grounded in
the main. How sad are many women for their want this way,
that alas, when they ask their husbands at home, they are little
the better, if not much discouraged! Their husband either despising the light of knowledge, and so walking like blocks and
idiots in all matters of God: or else filling themselves so with
other trash, that knowledge runs over, and is spilt upon the
ground: or if they have light, yet resting in generalities, never
coming to the experience of the way of God, or life of faith.
And by this, they wax barren, and tell their wives, they are no
preachers, they must go to ministers if they will talk of such
matters, for it passes their skill to deal in them!

2.
Understanding
in matters out-
ward, requisite
for the man.

Now secondly, touching the man's understanding in
the matter of the world, or marriage affairs. He must be as the
guide of her youth, going in and out before her: able to direct
her way and course with wisdom; not only in point of obedience to God, but also in circumstances and matters indifferent: for her company, for her solitariness, for silence or speech,
showing her what her person and place will admit and bear,
that she does not either over or under set up, or cast down her
sails, but live within the bounds of her place, for her company,
attire, household furniture, expenses of children, what is pure,
modest, sober, of good report, what not; who are safely to be
conversed with, and trusted in so bad a world as we live in,
who to be shunned: he must be her eye to see by, her hand to
work, her foot to walk with, to discern things and persons,

how they differ: and these things she must not only learn by the ear from his discourse but discover by marking his practice and example. Beholding in his glass an image of understanding, how wisely he can conceal things not to be uttered, how he warily prevents danger to life, name, and state: how he can avoid the snares which are laid for him; how he shuns ill company, removes offences from the bad, keeps peace upon good and safe terms with all men, handles business of weight both without equivocating and reservation of an ill conscience; and on the other side, without betraying himself, and exposing himself to hazard: and in both how he preserves innocency and uprightness. Besides these, she may behold in him, neither on the one side cowardice in a good cause, nor on the other, folly in the bad handling of it: how close and secret he is to them that are faithful friends to God and himself; how he is neither basely stingy, nor yet vainly lavish: that he is neither lightly credulous, nor yet sinfully distrustful: in his liberties, neither taking the uttermost, nor yet scrupling the moderate and lawful. Thus I say when she sees the image of God shining in his understanding and behavior, she shall be far from despising him, at least justly, for grace is honorable, and makes the face to shine, even before such as have little good in them; much more such as can observe it. Even more, she shall honor him, as her head, see cause of entirely loving him, devoting herself, first to God in thanks for such a blessing, and then to him in all loyal affection. No woman save a Michal can find any disdain in her heart of such a husband. And (which is the crown of all) she shall represent and act her husband's virtues upon the stage of her own practice and conversation. So much for this second.

If this is the duty, how much to blame are many husbands of all sorts, we ministers, you people; who in matters of God suffer their wives to live at random, because they see it requires some labor to manage the souls of their wives, by that near communion I have spoken of. Therefore they pluck off hand quite from board, and leave them wholly to themselves to sink or swim. The very ground of the sluggard does not so speak against his sloth, by the briars and thistles wherewith it is overgrown, as the souls of these men's wives, by their profaneness, and their lives, by their immodest and rude behav-

Use 1. Reproof. Husbands not walking as men of understanding to be blamed. Prov. 24.31

ior. So they can hold bodily welfare, farewell, sleep, and play, and lie down in a whole skin; what care they, what becomes of them? How many inclinations are there in some tender plants (at first marriage) which through the neglect of husbands, vanishes? How many sweet parts and graces which lie and rust, for the want of good improvement? How many blemishes and wants (which wise and seasonable counsel might redress) are suffered to grow remediless? How many husbands might say of their wives, as once a shrew said of her husband, she could have lived sweetly with him, if she would? Meaning it was not passion, but a spiteful heart which hindered it: so, it is not ignorance, but a base and lazy heart which does this. Had they been worth their ears (God seconding them) they might have improved them sweetly. And how gladly would such wives have blessed God for their counsel, if they might have been beholding to them for it? What honor had they received for their instrumental help to convert, support, and save them? If you do not this work how can you say you love her, or your heart is with her? Surely you shall pay the sad shot of her sin. If no place in your house, bed, board, closet, walk, can witness for you, if any common work steal away your heart or leisure from helping her: if she run into riot because you staid her not: how just is it that your life go for hers, wherewith God entrusted you?

Use 2. Terror. Husbands who cannot guide themselves worse.

Secondly, how great cause is there that some bad husbands should tremble to consider that they have been so far from guiding their wives with understanding, that alas, they lack all wisdom to guide themselves! So that, if their wives should be so unhappy, as to tread in their steps, they must of necessity fall with them into the ditch of all error and profaneness. Alas! How full is the world of women (not the worst for disposition and hope of good), who yet through ill planting (because they see that else they must live a dismal life), not only stumble at the threshold and go not one step forward, but ten degrees backward: being fain to comply with their husbands, and wax tenfold more the children of the devil than before? What is more easy than for a weak chameleon, a faint and weak creature, to resemble the color of each cloth it is laid in, when they see no fear of God, nor reverence of man, care of Sabbaths, conscience in dealings, savor in examples: to fall to the like; especially finding a sweetness and well-pleasing to the flesh, and nothing to gainsay it? How basely dare they speak of sincerity of the ministry, how vain, frothy, and fashionable grow they, their husbands reading them the lecture, and as Abimelech, saying, what you see me do, do likewise? How full is each corner of Lamech's desperate varlets, who act villainy, wrath, rage, envy, worldliness, pride, and scorn before their wives to cast them into the like mold of wickedness?

But, if it falls out that there is any more wisdom in women matched which such Nabals to observe and judge aright; how can they choose, but underprize them for want of understanding? Is it a wonder that a woman (except very humble) should extremely vilify such a head? Does the apostle justly reprove men for wearing shag hair (like women) and for shaming their head, or being ashamed of the glory of God (which they resemble by the uncovering of it), and shall not these dishonorers of their headship much more be condemned (as in this matter of walking like men of understanding before their wives)? Yes surely: it is no wonder that their complaints against such husbands are so frequent, and that they can nourish so little honor in their hearts towards them, who pour out so much contempt upon their own heads! I do not patronize such women as do so, but yet their disdain is in some sort venial, against them who do so violate the ordinance. What a clog is it to be matched to a man who instead of stayedness and due wisdom, is not so much as sensible, when he is told of his follies? So openly ridiculous that (as oil in the hand) it betrays itself to all men. So shallow-brained, fickly, easily led aside by any bad counselor to any loose, unclean, and wasteful course. Who makes as many promises, as he has fingers on both hands, and that daily, but breaks them before he goes to bed. What wise woman can endure it, to see him who should understand himself, to be so silly, credulous, and injudicious that each base cheating companion can cozen him of his wealth, rob him of his money, make him drunk and pick his pocket? Such a fool, as will lend every man he meets with, that would borrow, not shillings, but pounds, without any band save a bare word, as good never a whit as never the better, to such as are not worth that they borrow. What indignation would it move in a woman to be compelled to follow her wise

Use 3. Instruction. Many wives justly stumble at the folly of their husbands. 1 Cor. 11.14

Passages of folly in husbands. 1. Instance.

husband to the alehouse, to gaster him thence from drinking and reveling, spending of his time, thrift, and honesty, making herself a by-word, to pull him from the pipe and pot, to avoid worse dishonor? Moreover and yet to avail little also, but even to see herself sinking and perishing by piecemeal, while she beholds in him the cause; when he follows him that leads him to the stocks.

2.
Instance.

Or what wise woman could endure a fool within doors, so full of passion, so talkative, so contentious with children and servants, so weak in government and in his pangs, so over friendly with his servants, fond and apish with his maids, ready to traduce his wife in the hearing of strangers and the family, as if he put no difference between times, persons, or occasions? If a foolish woman by her tongue and unseasonableness is such a shame, indeed a rottenness of bones to a wise head: what is he (who should be the head, to her) when his carriage is so burdensome? I have seen an evil (says Solomon) oppression occupying the place of justice. As if he had said, for a poor man to steal a stick off the hedge is sin, but for a judge to oppress in the place of judgment is notorious: so, for the husband to play the fool instead of a man of understanding, how disordered? How shall the wife sustain her repute or esteem in the family when he that should honor her, by his reproaches, withdraws her own children, servants, and neighbors from their allegiance and duty?

3.
Instance.

What a vexation is it likewise for a woman to be matched to a husband, who is so idle and so unfit, to set himself on work about the service of his place, so ready to fleece from her all that she has, so helpless in his place, so giddy and gadding up and down from place to place after his companions, pleasures, and vanities, that it is hard to say whether she were better without his company to rule his servants, or have his room to avoid noisomeness?

4.
Instance.

Or again, how can a sober nature endure a husband, who is never in his element, save when he is in his jigs and jests, unsavory scoffs and scorns, at every one, wife not excepted, that comes in his way? And in his humorous extremities so contrary that either he cannot be pulled out of his melancholy and mopishness, being discontent; or being humored, cannot be driven out of his froth and lightness. Like those fiddlers whom the poet describes, who either cannot be gotten for any need to play, or if they fall to it, can never be done!

Who can digest such an inconstant and uncertain humor, as perhaps, for a week or ten days in a fervor will put on the habit of the most diligent and provident husband, to follow his business: but on the sudden (as one that forgets himself) rushes again into his vein of good fellowship, soaking himself in his pots, as if he would take revenge of himself for his former abstinence, and make even with himself by spending twice so much by day after day, as he saved by his diligence? What is so irksome to a woman, in company, where she becomes, as to see her husband (whose honor should be her crown) to be the jest and laughing stock of fools, an object of May-game to each one, who will make himself sport with his baseness? I might be endless; but in a word, she that is yoked to a foolish head, what a spectacle is she of a woman miserable by necessity?

5.
Instance.

I conclude therefore this first branch of the husband's duty. Let every wise one abhor this idea of folly: endeavoring himself to the uttermost of his power (according to the gift of God), to walk with his wife as an understanding husband: both in matters of God, and the way of common life: that so he may draw from her (as the weaker) due acknowledgment of him in his place, as set over her for a guide and director. In whom (under God) she may repose confidence, applying both absent and present, without fear or suspicion: returning that reverence, which his worth has deserved: and bearing willingly with infirmities because her lot is fallen into a good ground. As for the husband, although his wife should not perceive his worth (for some good wives cannot), yet seeing it is his chief understanding to see none of his own virtues, but to conceal all, let him choose rather to be a man of knowledge, though his wife should not behold it, than to be magnified of a flattering woman (as some are) deserving contempt.

Use 4.
Conclusion
with exhor-
tation to
husbands to be
men of under-
standing.

And now I should have passed to the next point, had not this come in my mind, that the apostle in this charge includes cohabitation: for he who must dwell with his wife, as a man of knowledge; at least must then dwell with her: else the subject is taken away. Where else (I pray) save in his house should his understanding appear? Or where should he shine else, save in his own sphere? This is that which the apostle

Cohabitation
of the man
with the wife
necessary.
1 Cor. 7.10

charges them, who were yoked with infidels (themselves being converted), that they depart not in dwelling from the unbelieving party: if he or she would depart, so it was, but let not them, if the other will abide. I wish that the woeful age we live in urged this my admonition: which I have glanced at by passage before; but here as the duty of this place. Persons of great rank and quality, think themselves lawless in this kind. Even a base thing they deem it, to dwell with their wives. Not only not one bed, board, roof, town, and shire, but scarce one kingdom can (long) hold some of them. And some are so noted for this trick, that it was good at last, they would note themselves. Each distaste and discontent to their unjust, unreasonable humors is enough to cause a settled, habitual separation between them and their wives, not for days (which in cases is allowable) but for months, quarters, years, many years together. Who doubtless, if they might have Jewish liberty would much more gladly be divorced; and what gain they by their separation? They gain dishonor to themselves, sorrow to their wives, I might say snares to them both: distemper to family, ruin to their estate, wrong to their country; ill example to inferiors, and scandal to the irreligious. Besides, both occasion to themselves abroad, clandestine societies and leagues with those that are luxurious, wanton, defiled women: and lay offences and snares in the way of their wives at home (except they make the more conscience) to forsake their covenant and to expose themselves to like uncleanness. For why? Their husband is gone a far journey, and you know what follows. Surely your amends is justly in your hands, who provokes it! Husbands should say to their wives as Ruth to Naomi: As the Lord lives, nothing save death shall part us. Your house, your children, your church, your God, and no other shall be mine, till death separate. It is not the way for you, for the obtaining your base ends of your wife to depart from her (pity it should): but rather to exasperate her. It is cohabitation, which is blessed to solder breaches in time, not separation. The practice of the greater sort is so rife nowadays that it grows common among the inferior sort, and will be a sore incurable. A deserted lady, or gentlewoman, has become a common notion. As one said, now the dogs bark at the masters of family when they return, as if they were absolute strangers: forgetting them as they did

Use 5. Humiliation to all that refuse to cohabitate.

Reproach of separators.

Ruth 1.16

their wives. Oh shame! Let kings that are wise keep near their crowns, and husbands that would be happy near their wives: not turning Jew and Samaritan, who intermeddle not. Such husbands as care not themselves to become whoremongers; or to make their wives as good as themselves, let them depart, but let all others dwell together with them as men of understanding, bringing in honor to their marriage by this personal duty. So much for this chapter and first office of the man, is spoken.

CHAPTER XI

Proceeds to the second personal duty of
the man: providence.

Second several
duty of the
husband,
providence. I proceed according to my order to the second several duty of the husband, and that is in one word, providence. As he is the husband in name, so must he be in deed: he must play the good husband. Neither has he his name for naught: for the husband is as the house-band, which (as the corner-stone to the sides of the building) holds in all the parts of the house: which would soon dissolve and crack if (under God) his providence did not support it. He is the steward both for his wife and himself: especially without doors. He is not to put his wife to it, as one insufficient himself to manage it, but (considering she has her hands full at home) he is to under-take the whole burden abroad: as being the party to whom (by divine dispensation) the credit of the well improving it does belong: and therefore upon whom the shame of the contrary must lie. God has put into him a spirit of deeper insight, fore-cast, prudence, and prevention than the woman, to this very end. And to say the truth; the Lord has imposed this burden upon him in Adam, instantly upon his fall, as the penalty for his base yielding up his authority to his wife, and enslaving his spirit to hers when yet his free will abode entire. True it is Adam was to till the garden before his fall, even during his innocency: but that was a labor most sweet and content-

Eccles. 2.26 ful unto him. To the sinner does God give toil and sorrow (says Solomon) and so, since his sin, labor has waxed a toil and vexation to him, and is, so that now in the sweat of his brows, he must get his living. He that shakes off this yoke, is a double rebel, both against the first charge in innocency, of not disobeying, and secondly against the penalty of subjecting himself to travail. In respect hereof, Job says: Man is as natu-

Job 5.7 rally born to labor, as the sparks to fly upward: as naturally deputed by God to the one as subject by his own sin to the other; as the Hebrew word [gnaval] imports, which includes sin and toil in one. The woman brings all her state and stock, putting it into his hands, resigning it up to him as her agent, and the more able party to improve it: if he fails her, he betrays both his trust to treachery, and her state to embezzling. There are two sorts of infidels taxed by the Holy Ghost: the one in our Savior's words: Take ye no thought what ye shall put on, or eat; for your father knows what is meet for you. And why? The infidels do but so. And the other by Paul: He that provides not for his family, has forsaken the faith, and is worse than an infidel. Excess of providence, as well as defects of it, both are taxed by the name of heathenism. Therefore, so far as good conscience will permit, the man is bound to the law of providence. He must oversee the affairs of his own household, as Solomon speaks, he must look to the flocks of sheep, and herds of cattle, laying in provision for them: by this one, urging the whole bailiwick of providence requisite for the support of the family. And that which the apostle speaks is to the same purpose: That the husband looks in his way, after the things of the world, that he may please his wife: he speaks not of it, as of their blemish (so they add no excess and sin to the act) but as a necessity imposed by God's command.

Mat. 6.25,26

1 Tim. 5.8

Prov. 27.23

1 Cor. 7.33

Now as touching that point that the husband in several must close with this special duty of providence, appears by the honor which hereby he procures to the married condition. And this I suppose no man will question. For why? Wherein stands the prince's honor, save in the wealth of his subjects? And wherein is the honor of a state save in both? What peace can subsist, what war can be supported without wealth? Even so here. The husband is the prince of the family, if he is base and beggarly, what is more ridiculous? What is so pitiful to behold, as a poor king, a titular prince, that has nothing to support his state, save a bare right being the while most forlorn and forsaken? So, how shall things belonging to the diet, attire, and welfare of the family be provided if the treasure fails? And how can that choose but fail if providence, the channel of this fountain, fails? If the pilot of the ship is idle or asleep, what shall become of the ship? Must it not run on ground, and be swallowed up in the quicksand? And, what a dishonor is it for him who should count it a more blessed thing to give than to receive, who should reach out alms to six

Reason of it in general, he honors his marriage by it, and how?

and seven, and do much good; himself and his family to become burdensome to others by his penury? Especially when, not the hand of God (which can overthrow the best providence), but the improvidence of the idle or ill occupied husband has procured it. Again, when the husband honors marriage by this providence, those who fare well by it, honor him back again with the rendition of his own. The weak woman and the shiftless children, seeing what a prop and father of a family the Lord has set over them, acknowledge his care, with honor to God, and reverence him as the instrument of their welfare, next under God. He resembles after a sort, God himself, whom Paul calls the Father upon whom all the families of the earth depend, and are called by his name: whose honor it is to fill all with his blessing, to provide for all creatures their due food in season, as they need it, with clothing and other things both for need and comfort: even so, the eyes of all the family mediately look up to the master thereof, looking that by him as a steward, the Lord should furnish them with necessaries; surely, to end this, how honorable is such a husband, even in the eyes of them among whom he lives? How are church, commonwealth, and town beholding to such, as are provident, for the upholding of peace, the gospel, and the poor? If all were careless husbands what must become of all these? Some I grant shall ever be poor, but these subsist in all these respects, by the aid of the provident, when as spendthrifts do nothing but pull down the house with their hands. The conclusion is, if the personal diligence of the husband does so much honor his marriage, he has good cause to put to his best care, to be provident.

Eph. 3.15

But here is the question, wherein this providence of his consists? For answer whereto: I conceive that this point might tempt me to enter into a commonplace of providence; but I will waive that in this place, attending the point as here it stands, cutting off whatsoever does not peculiarly touch this relation. I say then, this gift stands in sundry points. First and principally, it stands in learning perfectly the trade of his way, even while he is young. If there must be teachers, *Teach a child etc.*, then there must be learners. This is the seminary of providence in husbands that they have learned their way, in youth. There must then be a foresight of things to come, in

Question. In what it consists? Answer. First, in the thorough skill in the trade of his way. Prov. 6.6

youth; and a willing subjection of themselves to such wisdom
and painfulness, as may enable them, with skill sufficient in
their trade of life (what sort soever it is of) to be provident.
The very ant is taught by instinct: but it is not so here, man
must be trained with much ado and discipline to be provident. First, by wisdom, he is to shun all unlawful, scandalous, **1.**
and base ways or trades of life; and apply himself to that way Shunning un-
which is most warrantable, and best agreeable to his nature lawful trades.
(whether ingenuous or mechanical) and that by the direction
of his wisest governors and friends. Mock trades savoring half
of idleness, half of work, base trades which import a shifting,
indirect, and ill reported way of support, and profane godless
trades of life must be abhorred such as to be a serving man
for inheritance, to keep an alehouse or bowling alley, to be a
stage player, dancer, or the like. Secondly, he must compass **2.**
for himself through God's blessing, by learning the mastery of He must get
this or that meet trade, ability, and experience to himself, to wisdom and
make him a provident husband. He must have his eyes in his insight, not
head, to observe and mark the secret of his way, that he may scorning them
get insight and experience. He must not be so wise in his own that can direct.
way as to slight them who should teach him the right way,
which may maintain him afterward: but he must subject himself with teachableness to their direction, that a habit of skill
may accrue thereby. For, not only through the total lack of a
trade, but the half still in the trade, and inexpertness therein,
many of all sorts procure to themselves most uncomfortable
and shifting courses in marriage, whether bred to means or
wanting them.

To this add curiosity and giddiness of brain, in med- Curiosity in
dling with many trades, and fickle weariness in attending trades must be
upon one's own, carrying a busy heart and eye over the trades abhorred.
of others, having many irons in the fire at once so that some of
necessity must be marred: this error must be abhorred. And
there is none more common: and yet very dangerous, stealing away the heart from a settled applying of the mind to one
thing, distracting it to many: as we see how many curious
brains, prying into things beyond their skill, and trying conclusions, for the satisfying of their humorous spirit, have laid
all their estate and hopes in the dust.

Thirdly, a stock must follow skill, to help the improv-

3.
There must be
a stock, more
or less, to oc-
cupy.

Job 8.7

4.
Application
of himself to
his object with
diligence.

ing of skill. The best husband may sit still, if he lacks the wherewithal. Yet, we must know a little stock is a stock as well as a great one, all have not the like abilities, but all sorts must be occupied about their stocks, more or less. They who have but one talent, have suitable expenses, or contentment in less: they must not bury it, but employ it as far as a little will extend, looking at the promise. Though your beginning is but small, yet your latter end shall be full of increase. Although other trades outstrip them by their stocks, yet they go not so fast forward but providence and blessing may follow, and sometimes overtake them, if there is faith and patience to wait, and not be discouraged. Each man's stock is his own, or ought to be. Such as have not the patience to be doing with a little, but must hasten beyond rule, to borrow, and rake a stock together, or to follow their first credit out of breath, until they load themselves with more dealings than they can digest, are not likely to attain to much, but lay a foundation of bankrupts. For, a competent stock followed with moderate diligence, though it is sure of no great increase, yet usually frees the owner from excessive losses: which are much worse than slow gains.

Fourthly, skill and stock being gotten (though some trades consist more in manual work than stock, and others in the activity of the mind, not the body), there must be an applying of the one to the other; else providence fails. The upper millstone of skill must run upon the other, of stock. The hand and the saw are not enough to cut the log in two; there must be a hand of life to move and draw the one upon the other; and so, somewhat comes of it. This mortmain of sloth will spoil providence, what skill and stock soever there is besides: and therefore there must be all dexterity, cheerfulness, and painfulness exercised to keep life in a trade. A wise, seasonable taking in of wares, of commodities at the best hand, paying old scores before new are made warily: and a putting off in season, not overpassing our best market and opportunity; an accommodating, pliable, and acceptable spirit to traffic with others (a fine gift to be a chapman if it goes without baseness and flattery, and with truth and simplicity). To be as ready to put off or take in without either rashness in the one, or covetousness in the other, are all meet properties for a provident husband. The apostle, Rom. 12.11, has one sweet rule for this: *Not sloth-*

ful in business, but fervent in spirit, serving the Lord. So far as
God's work is not hindered by our own, it is a comely sight to
see a man active in his employment. The diligent hand (says
Solomon) makes rich: and, in all labor there is abundance, if   Prov. 10.4
it is wise. He said not amiss that said: I love when I eat my
meat to eat heartily, and when I am at work to follow it closely:
so to do each thing as if (for the present) I did nothing else.
It is a common saying: He that keeps his shop, his shop will
keep him. The speech is usual. It is not enough not to be
idle, except a man is well occupied too: early up and never the
nearer, is to small purpose. A wise, judicious head is as good a
tool for a trade as a nimble apprehension; lest cost without wit
proves waste. Here then observe some rules.

First, begin your action and workmanship with God: Rules for dili-
and the rather if your service is the work of study, of the mind   gent improve-
especially. Trust not your own wisdom, but commit your ways   ment.
to God. That so, as you have shunned a bad trade, so you must   Prov. 16.3
abhor all baseness in a good one, which easily creeps in, under   Rule 1.
color. It is in vain to build, except the Lord is the master build-   Begin with
er. Except the Lord watch the city, in vain are the watchmen: God.
in vain it is to eat brown bread and drink water, rising early,   Psal. 127.1
and lying down late; for, he gives rest to his beloved. Many
have miscarried in their thrift and prosperity; no man can tell
how or why save only that irreligion has bred a secret canker,
and shut God out of doors. I have noted it; some cannot keep
out the waters from flowing in, and wealth from increasing,
while they in a manner sit still: and others fray it away by their
eagerness. For the one counts it the honor of their faith to sit
still (your strength shall be to sit still) and make no haste: the   Isa. 30.7
other by their haste, fill themselves with snares. God will be
the chief mystery in all trades: not manufacturers and mer-
chandise only, but even sciences and ingenuous studies: even
scholars must place the Bible above all their books: and all
sorts of set prayer above and before all their work.

Yet so make God's providence chief, as not destroying   Rule 2.
your own. Beware of base cowardly sloth. Ease slays the fool,   Yet destroy not
both body and soul. It puts hand in bosom, but is loath to pull   your own.
it out. It is like Jacob, for frost and heat, and all weathers; it
frames lions in the way, if it should put forth itself, lusking in   Prov. 26.13
a bed of idleness, loathing action. Such should not eat. The   Prov. 18.9

idler is the companion of the waster; while he rolls upon his hinges, folds his hands and yearns after more sleep and sloth, he hastens poverty upon himself, as the necessity of an armed man. The thorns on his backside are his emblem. Yet abhor being ill occupied, as much as sloth. There is a golden measure in all things. Our proverb says, better sit for naught than stir for naught. Rash, headlong, willful, and indiscreet busying of a man's self may prove worse than lying in bed: as some eager ones keep wares (at a good price offered) till they prove trash. It is a question whether there are more husbands that become beggars by the pot and pipe than by overmuch nimbleness, and deepness in the world, and meddling too much.

Rule 3. Beware of picking quarrels with your calling.

Thirdly, a good husband must beware of loathing and wearisomeness in his calling; when gains come not in, according to your expectation and desert (for I speak still to all artists, both studious and manual). Look not at other trades of quicker return and dispatch, to bring you out of conceit with your own. Abide in the vocation wherein God has pitched you. Hold the trade of your youth till old age; leave it not, either because you thrive not fast enough, or because you have thrived enough already: still show that your trade is not your only object. I deny not, but some cases there may be where the trade may be altered: as when stock is wanting, without dangerous borrowing upon usury: when it is so sunk that it affords no competency for the family: when some other is offered wherein as much skill as in the former, or some mark of providence appears that the change is from God. But, to pick quarrels with our trades that we might turn to such as we conceit to be speedier for return and gain, that we might be rid of our own, threatens future misery under the speciousness of present commodity. To go through many trades is the highway to beggary.

Rule 4. Subjection to God in a calling.

Deut. 33.8-10
1 Tim. 2.15

Fourthly, subject yourself to your trade of life, not for gain's sake, but for conscience (whether you get or not), as that yoke which God has put upon your neck, to try you: to tame your sloth, pride, and other sin, that the penalty of Adam's curse may become to you (as Jacob's curse upon Levi, through his obedience to God, became to him) a blessing. The travail of the husband's hands and labor may possibly be made to him (as the travail of the womb is made to the believing

wife) a benefit and favor. Only the rebellion of an unsubject
heart to the obedience of God (in what kind soever) brings a
curse. The richest man, even the gentleman, must hold his
trade still; the poorest also must abide in it: both, as in their
vocation. The Lord tries thereby the faith, patience, meekness, bounty, thankfulness, self-denial, uprightness, and pains
of the husband. It is not given for men to fledge themselves
and nip their feathers by, but to avoid temptations and snares,
which if we avoid not, but incur nevertheless (as most do) we
turn God's remedy into an increaser of the disease: that is, an
occasion of eager worldliness surfeiting with cares and excess,
a cause of oppression, usury, and unrighteousness. Besides by
the calling, the Lord would teach a Christian husband to know
what that portion is which he purposes to allot him, and what
not: and does thereby serve his providence in the competent
support of us, and ours, without sin and sorrow. For, such is
the portion of the righteous.

Fifthly, beware of moiling and toiling in the world, **Rule 5.**
only to pocket up and hoard treasure and store, filling our bel- Aim not at
lies with God's hidden store (as David, Psal. 17, describing the hoarding up
or multiplying
ungodly, speaks) which one day will bring a wasting and con- your estate.
sumption as fast, either upon ourselves or ours. But abhor all
such aiming to enhance ourselves above others for the jollity
and pride of life. This is the cast of most men, if once become
great, to bestow all upon their pleasures, in hawking, gaming,
prodigality, and wantonness that they might have much the
more (as that heathen said) to satisfy their lust and appetite.
To set their wives, children, and selves on float in the bravery
of buildings, in curious fashions, or costly apparel and the like.
The Lord can pluck your plumes quickly, if we drink to be
drunk, or forget our beginning to be from the dunghill (as indeed none grow prouder than such base ones): keep we moderation then, and be sober. God tries us by prosperity, what
is in us; we may enjoy the travail of our hands, and the benefit
of our welfare, so that prodigality on the one side and base
miserliness on the other (which commonly in this self-loving
world concurs) is abhorred.

Sixthly (which perhaps to some may seem strange), **Rule 6.**
God will have you maintain your husbandry and providence Serve God
by serving him with the increase of your labor, and his bless- with your
increase.

ing. Look about you and see what objects God has planted for your bounty to be bestowed upon. Your wealth, if it is a standing pool, will stink and bane you. If it is a stream it will be sweet, and all the bulk shall be pure unto you. As in the manna, all had their due; the plenty of the gatherer of much, abounded to the supply of him that lacked. By the decays of others, God tries you. If when blessing comes in upon you, you welcome it with an evil eye, saying: this is little enough to pay debts, this will do well to increase my stock, this is for the clothing of my children, I will spend this upon costly apparel for my wife: and all that comes is only for your own use; and you shrink up the bowels of your compassion so much the more. Know, this will destroy all as a canker bred in a fair apple. No, say thus, This plenty will serve me and God too: part of this shall supply the defects of my faithful minister, poor decayed neighbor, such a poor widow, such poor orphans, poor students at university: have you such a heart to the poor members of Christ, that no complaints may be heard in your streets, that you and they may meet together and worship God with the more joyful hearts, that the gospel and religion of God may be supported, both in peace and especially in persecution? It is a sign that God means to make your horn full, and your winepress to burst with new wine: well continue, and do so still; try the Lord if he will not requite you. Your goodness cannot reach unto the Lord himself; let it extend to his saints and such as excel in virtue. Send your treasure to heaven before you, cast your bread upon the waters, trust God, and after many days, if you trust God, it shall return again. Many rich husbands profess religion, but all their serving of God is no other than the poorest Christian may perform: to pray, hear, and confer: but as for the duty they owe to God as rich men, they cast it behind their back. They think that their works should hinder their faith: and so hoard up hundreds, even thousands together, but do nothing until God by degrees wastes and consumes both them and their posterity, as a moth, and at last root them up quite out of the land of the living. Beware of this curse therefore.

Psal. 16.2,3

Eccles. 11.1

Rule 7.
Take losses as
well as gains
patiently and
contentedly.

Seventhly, if any affronts, losses, ill successes, or discontents befall you in your course of providence, by ill debtors, servants, or children; look up in your innocency with cheerfulness to the smiter; as well as in your gains. Both are alike from him, even to wean you from the sweet milk of those breasts, which you are loath to be weaned from, to knock you off from hence; and to prepare your spirit for better welfare. Be patient; trades are as the sun, which though it set overnight, yet returns in the morning. Job's latter days, after he had been tried, proved happier than the former; and, when both the miser and waster shall both be left to want, the Lord yet shall sustain you, and your faith (which yet the world thinks will buy no meat in the market) shall be such current pay in heaven that it shall purchase you abundance upon earth.

Job 42.10

To conclude, let all your providence determine in this full point. That hereby, your heart may rejoice, you and your wife enjoying the fruit of your travail, that you may not be like to them that roast not that they got in hunting. For what has a man of all that sore travail and labor, which as a poor son of Adam, he has taken here under the sun save that a man eat and drink, and cheer his heart in the goodness of the giver: and rejoice in the wife of your youth? Let her share with you. I mean not as Job says: that he kiss his own hand, and magnify the idol of his provident head, saying; all this has my hand gotten: nor that he soak himself in the creature, and set himself to look upon the sun in her brightness, and the moon in her increase, adoring the outward means, and denying the Almighty: this is idolatry and sacrilege. No, but quietly and thankfully praising God, and rejoicing (as those Israelites were charged to do when they brought their first fruits) in all which they put forth their hands unto. Taking with a loving right hand that which God reaches out, causing them to serve him with a glad heart, for all which the Lord has done for them. Better thus, than as many do, pursing and stopping up in holes and corners, in a rage, or in the ground: and perhaps here one debtor running away with a hundred, there another cheater with fifty; or perhaps, a thief digging through and stealing as much in another kind. To the wicked God gives toil and vexation of body of spirit, more discontentment than all their plenty can breed peace: whereas the rest of the righteous is sweet, be their portion more or less, through the good will of him that dwelt in the bush, added to their providence. See then, that it is so, that you play not the block under all mercies, so that neither a

Rule 8.
Be joyful in all your labor under the sun.

Prov. 5.18

Job 31.27

Deut. 26

good day should mend, nor a bad pare you. But first for your outward condition, proportion your expenses according to your revenues, as near as you can: keep down your heart, and then it is lawful for you to live according to your means. Cut your coat according to your cloth, rather living at an under than an over rate; as knowing it is easier to fall than to rise, and yet understanding what scantling God allows; yet better to be a cheerful dispenser than a base stingy grudger at the use of what God has given. As the good woman said, husband better spend it freely as God sends it, than knaves run away with all. Then for your spiritual course, let your heart be doubly and triply cheerful in the Lord, saying with her, my soul magnifies the Lord, and my flesh rejoices in his salvation. If I ought to make him my strength in the lowest adversity: although neither vine should bear grapes, nor the olive her fruit, although there were neither calf in the stall nor bullock in the flock: how much more then, when my paths are anointed with oil, and my streams run full of butter and honey? And so much (if not too much) for the answer of this question, wherein providence stands.

Luke 1.46,47

Heb. 3.17

Use 1.
Reproof.
Branch 1.
Careless de-
serters of their
wives, odious.

I conclude all with use: and first of reproof for this point is fruitful in unfruitfulness; first, how many husbands are there, who (contrary to the vows made to their wives in this behalf, at their entry upon marriage) cast off this burden from themselves, and lay it wholly upon the weak shoulders of their wives? In the meanwhile they bearing themselves upon the fidelity or the drudgery of the wife at home, go abroad, and open the sluice and floodgates of prodigality and wastefulness, that all the labor of the wife at home cannot dam up the waters. They spending and spoiling more abroad in an hour than the woman can patch up or redress at home in a week: and so outstrip her way, by their own, till all be brought to ruin! Oh! The misery of such wives that suffer, should I say, or rather husbands that procure it: but indeed both one and other. Others leave their houses at large, committing all to wind and weather, to sink or swim, while they follow their lusts, companies, and pleasures without control. Thus, woefully inverting the method of God, injuriously laying a double load upon the weaker party till her shoulders crack again: who yet undertakes it to shun utter debt, and yet at last falls into it nevertheless. To these add another sort of such as enter into marriage without any calling at all, having brought this snare upon themselves by neglecting to learn the trade of their youth, for vanity's sake, and serving their lusts, and so, although they repent them of their folly, yet still they are destitute of skill in their vocation, and so expose themselves to a vain and wearisome course of life, to many snares and temptations, as this for one, basely to live upon usury: and wanting skill to bargain, buy and sell, either they must live upon the stock till it is spent, and then run up and down shifting and hanging upon every man's sleeve, or else live upon the sweat of other men, while they live idly so that of all other members of the commonwealth, they are most useless to themselves and noisome to others. Thirdly, others who under color of religion and zeal, wax careless in matters of providence, and in a diligent watching to their calling, and lawful employments, thinking it a venial error, even a praise to them that having somewhat to take too, yet they are not worldly: to whom it may be replied. Neither are you provident husbands to maintain your families: for you know that faithful attendance to a calling is far from worldliness: that is, rather the honor of a Christian husband to be provident. Moreover, some will run out from their shops and trades (as men weary of work), from house to house, hither and thither; and all under color of religion, as to hear sermons ten or twenty miles off in the weekday (their wives and children being unprovided the whiles) and being poor men, and behind hand, abide by the three or four days in places, to confer, to repeat sermons, to utter some gift of their own, as their memory, or prayer, or broach some new point of their own devising, or lament the evils of others: things good, in their kind and within their compass, but as they handle them, most odious and unseasonable. And thus, they delude such as are simple minded Christians, rob them of their goods, under these colors, by their craving, complaining, or borrowing; whereas, children and wife at home famish, and themselves by such bad custom, more and more wax unfit and disabled for the work of providence: whereas, during this time, they might have gained more at home by labor than they can scrape up by their ill courses, besides the reproach to religion. These are inordinate livers.

Branch 2. Neglecters of learning their trade.

Livers upon their usury are odious.

Branch 3. Improvidence under color of religion is vicious.

Fourthly, others, not having been trained up early, in some lawful trade of life, are fain to take up base and dishonorable ways and shifts to live upon; as, to get licenses for alehouses, to set up houses for tippling, dicing, and pleasures; others, shrouding themselves under the wing of great personages, set up bowling alleys, to toll in the gentry to pastimes (which they are much more prone to than to works of charity), and so, they withdraw inhabitants from their trades, spoil their servants with idleness, and toll in poor men of the country to drink and spend their money, and when the rain hinders their sports, then to their cards and dice within: and such are the remedies of men, who having spent their youth in idle service, must live upon the sin of others, and the overthrow of the country. Others, through idleness play the vagabonds, and take their vagaries, seeking their fortunes within or beyond the seas, or play the parasites to gentlemen, serving all their turns for their advantage, and most sinfully betraying them to wickedness. Others spend their time in devising and living by their wits, cleaving to young heirs, dissolute spendthrifts, to fill their bellies. Furthermore, how many heirs themselves,

who might have subsisted comfortably, either in their parents' family, or upon their inheritances; and followed their callings with success and blessing: yet, falling upon lewd companions, and waxing loose and unbridled in their manners, either match themselves basely and contrary to their parents' aims, or if married better, abandon wife and children, give themselves wholly to whoring, gaming, rioting, and wasting of their substance till they have stripped themselves of means, wit, and honesty, to the unspeakable vexation of parents, if they live to be witnesses, and of the utter desolation of souls and bodies, wife and posterity? How is the country pestered with such vermin? How does the Devil by this means uphold his kingdom (for he has fit covers for such cups), and hereby gather kites to the carrion, fits them with shirkers and horseleeches, who by flattering and admiring them for their bounty, squeeze out all from them, and leave them as gulls! Oh you fools! How long will you delight in eating and devouring your own flesh? Will no persuasion enter until, as Sampson was from his Delilah, so you are compelled from your lusts, and like fools to the stocks: that is from taking of purses by the highway, and such cheats, you are pulled to prison, to the gallows, and to hell itself, without mercy to stop you! Oh! You parents, cease your raking and scraping up of goods for such spendthrifts, or, for you know not what ends, for the increasing (to be sure) of sorrow to yourselves, while you live, and of sin, when you are gone! Do good with that you have, lest God sting you in those children, and children's children for whom you as basely hoard, as they pour out sinfully! Soothe them up no longer in their sin, who are likely to bring your hoary hairs with sorrow to the grave!

Digression admonitory to parents.

Fifthly, how many husbands are there, who by their heady improvidence, either borrowing to stock themselves more than ever they can pay, or selling their wares underfoot to procure present money (by which a while they feed their creditors) do for a short time set up their top sails, a while, bearing it out with other men's wealth, and when they can hold no longer then they leave them in the lurch: many such wretches, ruining the whole families of many better husbands than themselves, with their wives and children. More fit (in truth) to be hanged up, than to pester a commonwealth: and some other maintain their state and pomp by such desperate courses, even under a color of religion, causing hundreds at once to make outcries against professors when they prove bankrupts. Add sixthly, to these such hotspurs as will not be idle, but run into another extreme of willfulness, rushing upon matters beyond their skill and reach: affecting plots and inventions of gain, either by adventures, or by new manufactures, resolved either to win the spurs or to lose all. And so, they have lost all indeed, and withal drawn many with them (who were as greedy of gain) into deep expenses and forfeits of their states, and indeed they are both well enough served to teach them (as Paul speaks) to follow their own affairs with quietness. Others weary of their slow-paced trades, desirous to hasten them, how do they enlarge their providence (rather their greediness) as hell, thrusting as many irons at once into the fire as they can come by: adding house to house, and farm to farm, borrowing upon eight, gaining scarcely four in the hundred, yet dreaming of golden mountains. Until at last (the mistress of fools teaching them too late), they perceive their haste to have brought forth blind whelps, and wish they had

Branch 5. Indiscreet borrowings, overstockings, undersellings, bad husbandry.

Branch 6. Rushing beyond their skill and reach.

Branch 7. Ingrossing many farms at once.

Branch 8. Changing of callings.

made no more haste than good speed. Eighthly, how ordinary a course nowadays is it with men (as I touched before), to wrangle with their callings that they might change them, and seek others, till (as the dog catching at the shadow) they lose the flesh, and forfeit that they have: which is to cast their present real estate upon the casual and uncertain hope of things to come.

In what respects a man may change or divert from his calling.

Yet since this occasion is offered, I speak not as if all deserting of a calling, or diversion from it for a time is unwarranted. For sometimes it so falls out by providence that a man deserts country and all, and departs to such a place as will not admit a possibility of the exercise of his calling: so that in the one, he must necessarily yield the other. Again, sometimes the outward members, senses, and the inward abilities of a man desert him, and disable him from his calling: when as yet some slighter employment may perhaps befit him well enough. Necessity of banishment caused many holy men to make buttons and points for their living, who before had studied and written books. So also the trade may be so grown out of request, either by multitude of traders, or by deadness of the wares, that they cannot support the workmen: or they may be so low, and require so much work to be done for money, that a trader cannot live on them. Shall then the maintenance of the family hang upon the strict point of no change of a calling? No, in no sort. But in these or any the like cases (whereof are many), the end must rule the means, and any other lawful course, which lies nearest to the skill or sleight of the workman, is allowed for the support of the family. Only let men beware, lest out of a fickle, ungrounded, lazy, wearisome, covetous, reaching, and aspiring spirit they desert not their callings: and, if they must, yet let them choose to divert rather from them for a time, and return to them after, when providence yields opportunity for it, than show that they willingly and slightly were moved to abandon them at the first. But this by the way.

Branch 9. Insubjection to the rule of providence.

Endless it were, to mention all abuses in this kind: but to finish, how many have we, who through their rebellion will not be subject to the duty of providence? Others, who spoil all by improvidence, and having sold all, even their wives' clothes off their back, make a mock of it, saying: if any can make more of their wives than they have done let them take them! How many others, who having gotten a fair estate by their providence, yet waste it as fast by their jollity and lavishness, making their houses thoroughfares for epicures, and boon companions, disquieting their poor wives from their settled family business to wait upon such base companions, contrary both to her spirit and conscience! Or, if not, yet far from honoring God with their increase, or their marriage, with wise dispensing of their estate. These excesses have (as you may see good reader) caused me to lengthen out this argument as if I had not only treated about marriage providence, but providence in the general, and the contrary thereto. But I hope that some may light upon what I have said, and amend. Thus much for the use of reproof.

The latter use is exhortation. Let all good husbands honor their marriage and the Lord by a faithful improvement of this duty of providence. Let them avoid all extremities, both on the right hand and left: and in welldoing commend themselves to God as to a faithful keeper, and God all sufficient. Let them neither go to work carkingly, nor yet carelessly. Let them abhor idleness, and yet shun ill occupations. And by that I have said of the sin of improvidence, let them learn the contrary: and so shall they (as much as in them lies) build up the house, give good example to their wives to do the like within, serve God with cheerfulness, and enjoy the fruit of their travail with contentedness, when the slothful and prodigal shall perish and vanish. And for this second peculiar duty of the husband, namely providence, so much, and for this chapter.

Use 2.
Exhortation.

CHAPTER XII

Treating of the third and last personal office of
the man, honor of respectiveness
to his wife.

The third par-
ticular duty of
the husband,
respectiveness.
Gen. 2.23,24

The opening
of the point at
large.
Eph. 5.22-33

Now I proceed to the third and last duty of the husband towards his wife, which is honor, and due respect to his wife. The ground of which is the ordinance of God, by which, they are made one flesh. For so says Moses, when the Lord had brought the woman to Adam, he embraced her, saying: *This is bone of my bone, and flesh of my flesh. She shall be called woman; because she is taken out of man. For this cause shall a man forsake his father and mother, and cleave to his wife, and they two shall be one flesh.* Behold, with what honorable esteem he welcomes this, his blessed companion into the world. Now, it is true, the wife in this respect owes the same tie of tenderness towards him. But, we must know, this first lies upon the man; to her ward, because he is the root of the relation. We say that love descends from the father to the child because he is the foundation of the reference. Not, but that mutualness is required; but the original root must first impart himself. Now upon this root of union the apostle enforces this duty: No man ever hated his own flesh; but nourished and cherished it as himself. He then that hates his wife is an unnatural monster, and devours his own flesh. He that loves his wife loves himself. We know how it is in the body, union of parts causing sameness and uniform subsisting in one, procuring an exceeding tenderness, compassion, and sympathy between each member. So that although the foot stumbles and gives the body a fall, yet a man will not be so mad as to smite it because it is one with itself, and suffers the same fall with it. So here. The sameness of flesh, which the woman has with the man, makes him natural and sympathizing towards her: and not to hurt or hate her in her weakness and stumbling, but to bear with her, condole her, and count himself to suffer in her; his contentment, joy, and welfare not to stand in himself but in her, who is another self, and therefore to be as willing to wound himself, hurt and hate himself, as to hurt her.

By virtue of this union, and nearness it is, that there arises in the spirit of a husband (who is not degenerate), a marvelous, natural, and tender instinct of sympathy towards his wife in all her complaints and infirmities. She is one with him in all things, one in flesh, one in generation and posterity, one in blessings and welfare, copartner also in all crosses and wants. All these are common: the husband shares with the wife, and suffers in all her diseases, pains, and trials spiritual and bodily. Self does ill, and self-love is odious between neighbor and neighbor, even stranger and stranger: much more between father and child; brother and sister: but most of all in this superlative union of marriage, wherein two bodies may truly be said to be linked into one soul. Here then to affect a singularity, a privacy in so close a union, and for the husband to be a man by himself apart from her who is one and the same flesh with him, what a prodigious self-love it is? Union breeds love, and love, sympathy and compassion; but where self-love abides, union and love are absent. And from hence it is that in another place the apostle adds, giving honor to the woman, as to the weaker vessel: which giving of honor is nothing else save the peculiar office of the husband to his wife (and as I may term it, the way of his tenderness), when as he willingly resigns up his manly authority sometimes, and wisely abridges himself of that power to the uttermost, which else he might usurp over his weaker wife. And instead thereof, wisely considers, it is the honor of a man sometimes to be under himself, to forget his strength: there is a providence in the government of this vast world, and it stands in the overruling of some inferior creatures, that they may not know their strength over the superior, but be kept within compass (as it were) by a necessary and natural restraint. Even such a voluntary tie has the Lord put upon the more fierce and rough nature of the male to the female that there may not only be a consent, from hurting and offending each other (for so lions and wolves agree together); but further that there might be a virtuous and more generous forbearance of authority over the weak vessel: as acknowledging, the headship of the man is given him not to discourage or destroy: but to direct, benefit, and

Union is the root of this tenderness.

1 Pet. 3.7

build up the wife. That as God clothes the weaker members with the more honor; so, we should condescend and vouchsafe the same respect to the woman's weakness. Although a proud and base spirit would hold his own, leaping over the hedge where it is lowest; yet a wise and understanding head will of his own accord yield, and give honor and respect unto the woman as to the weaker vessel. Surely if a father is said to spare his own son who fears him: and the Lord will be master even over the parent, that he be not bitter to his children to tread them under feet, but count it his honor to pass by the corrigible errors of his children: then what should that sparing eye, that indulgent heart and hand, that honor and respectiveness be, whereby God sways the husband (being but her equal) towards his yielding and tender wife? And in a word, I say this giving of honor, is the more special way of the man than of the woman: for though she is so to him, yet in a diverse way, and in a more natural kind, as it were according to her frame: for who takes it not for granted that a thing naturally framed to tenderness should act her own property, and give honor as due desert to the husband? But in the man's giving honor to her there is a more virtuous and royal disposition, that is, an abatement of the right invested in man, lest excess of right might prove excess of injury and a yielding of that tenderness and sympathy, out of mercy and love, which else neither perhaps the merit of the wife would require, but to be sure the surliness and roughness of the man would not easily contribute.

Reason 1. Nothing gained by austerity.

And, of this, many reasons may be yielded. For why? Is there anything gained by austerity and roughness when the dint thereof returns upon ourselves? Is honor and respect lost upon the wife when it reflects back from her, upon her husband? Is it not well deserved on God's part when we not only behold what graces he has put into the wife, as treasure into a vessel of earth: but also how little is got by the contrary, when a rough husband too much yielding to that which is corrupt, does turn edge thereby in his wife, and force her to that which seems to be most disguised and against nature, that is, to be fierce against the husband? Again, as the apostle says: Do we not willingly bear with fools, ourselves being wise? And is it not as meet that we bear with the weak, we ourselves being

Reason 2. Wise folks willingly bear with fools.

strong? What a betraying, rather a forfeit of a masculine (not to speak of a religious) spirit and a betraying (not of a feminine, but) of a brutish and base folly, is it, when a woman shall be faint to bear with a husband's silliness and frailty, as the stronger with the weaker? What a dishonor is it to marriage? Besides what an obligation does a religious husband stand in to his yokefellow, for infinite many fruits of love and service to him in every kind? Not to speak of that command of God which is above all, tying the husband to his wife for conscience sake, though she should fall short of the duty as once a good husband said to an undeserving wife: Blessed be God yet who has given me a wife who will do this or that for me upon ever so unkind terms? But, much more, if she is deserving at his hands, for all her tenderness in sickness and health, is it much, if she receives due honor and respect from him? If you owe her your own self again for them, is it much, if you repay tender esteem and prizing of her? If you ought to lay down your life in some cases even for your Christian brother, rather than expose him by your unfaithfulness to danger, how much more should you expose yourself rather to the greatest hazard than betray her who is weak and unable to bear? Remember the precedent whom God sends you to, the Lord Jesus. As he loved his church, and gave himself for her to the death, that she might escape it, so ought you to redeem your wife in case of such a danger, when your bearing will laten the blow from her. When the Lord Jesus was taken by the soldiers: If you seek me (says he) let these my chickens depart. Take not the dame on the nest with her birds. Let these be free: let all the danger light upon myself. If then this tenderness must extend to life itself, surely then well may this tribute of an inferior rank be showed. But, I cease to discourse the point any further.

Reason 3. God's commandment.

Reason 4. We owe it to Christians.

   Well then (will some kind husband say) wherein stands this respect and honor which I owe to my wife? I should be loath to wrong her of nothing, which she might plead (through my ignorance), or which I (if I knew it) could bestow her. Well, in hope there shall be no love lost, and that your wife will requite it, when (in the next point) she shall come to the like trial: I will do her and you this favor, here to lay out her privilege and your duty. But first, it is not amiss

Wherein this honor and respectiveness consists.

again to recognize briefly that which I spoke of, the model and the canon of this duty, which the apostle lays down thus: As Christ loved his church. Before he had said, he that loves his wife, loves himself; but, knowing that self is sometimes an ill judge and crooked rule: he amends it by a better, even the golden rule of that honor and respect of Christ towards his church, which never fails or exceeds the mediocrity. What is then that indulgence and tenderness which you would either wish or look for from Christ your head? Teach yourself, thereby, your office to your wife (in the measure of your grace), and tender it to her. Do you desire always to be accepted of him, and find grace in his sight? Let your wife find the like from you. Would you have him do all your works in you and for you? Show you the like grace to her, do you likewise: require not the uttermost service from her, but let her do all in the comfort of your love and acceptance. Would you have him count all your deeds, not according to strict law and performance of full measure, but according to sincerity of endeavor? Do you also so esteem of hers, according to the will and affection from where they proceed, though they fail never so in degree. Would you have him to esteem you according to the better and not the worse part? So do you interpret her. Would you have him save you from sorrow? So protect you her, and let your love be her banner. Would you have him to feed you, and fight for you, to be your protector and champion? Should he stave off your enemies, and catch their wounds in his own side, which should else light on you? Would you have him to stop the mouth of each dog from barking or biting you, even to keep each cold wind from nipping and blasting you? Even so, stand between your wife and her harms, and cover her head in the storm and rain, not only with your cloak, but your best protection, against any annoyance. Would you have Christ afflicted with you in all your troubles, to pity you, suffer with, and sustain you by his patience, courage, and long suffering? So, let your blood run in her veins, and your marrow in her bones: sustain her likewise by your meekness and long-sufferance; she is also flesh of your flesh, and bone of your bone. Do you expect at last that he should at last redeem you out of all your troubles? Do you also (as far as lies in you) seek rest for her from all hers: let no enemy of hers encounter her

Eph. 5
The true model and rule of tenderness is the tenderness of Christ to his church.

alone, but know he has a double enemy to fight against, not easy to contest with. Yours are hers, hers are yours; rejoice to see her rid of all, if God see good, which way it seems best to himself to deliver her: meantime, be active, passive in all with her. In a word, whatsoever you would have Christ do for you, the same do for her, for this doubtless is to be conformed to your head, and to do the part of an honoring and respective husband to her.

These generals need to be branched out into some particulars: else perhaps, it will not be easy for everyone to conceive them. These therefore that follow may serve. First, let this respect begin at her soul: procure to that, the chief good that it may fare well. The tender love of Christ stands in this, that he gave himself for the church; why? Not to make her such as she herself would, not to give her the full swing and sway of her own will; but to wash her, to purge her, to sanctify her, as peculiar to himself, having neither spot nor wrinkle. So do you: begin with this, and this shall guide all the rest. Think not this to be your tenderness to your wife, to deal by her as David by Adonijah, whom his father would never from his youth, speak awry unto, that is, ask him, What do you? But rather in this is your tenderness, if by any ways of God, allurements, even mild and well-seasoned reproofs (if need be) you may be an instrument of her good. It is not tenderness, but exceeding and degenerate softness in a husband that, because his wife is well pleasing to him in some carriages, therefore he should rather suffer her to go on in deep ignorance of God and herself, and go the broad way to perdition, rather than he would grieve her, or speak one word amiss: especially, to be so base and remiss that, when he knows he might win her by his loving tenderness, he should rather neglect her by his carelessness. No, if you are tender truly, her soul will be your principal object, and you will present to her those tender mercies of Christ, those bowels of compassion in him to the church: never ceasing until Christ has by his blood washed her soul from the natural uncleanness of it, forgiven her, and taken away her guilt and blemishes. If her face were stained with some spots, how studious would he be to tell her of them that she might wash them off? How much more that Christ Jesus might call her his Hephzibah and Beulah: his

Particulars of the husband's tenderness.

Branch 1. Tenderness to the soul of the wife the first duty of the husband.

Isa. 62.4

dove, fair one, and preciously beloved, that he might behold
her washed and clean (as the sheep coming from the rivers
to shearing) from her scurf, accepted of God, and (as much
as flesh may be) without spot or wrinkle, either of guilt, or
apparent corruption: a vessel purged and prepared for every
good work? No work so honorable as this to make your wife a
vessel of honor to God first, and then for marriage. Thus Paul
describes that tenderness of Christ: and yet, that washing and
rinsing of her must cost some hardness, save that mercy and
love over sweetens it: and then it will seem pleasant. Nourish
and cherish and hate not your own flesh, in this first respect,
as Nathan's lamb, in the true bosom of the Lord Jesus, the most
tender husband that ever was.

2 Sam. 12.3

Branch 2.
Tenderness to
the person of
the wife neces-
sary.

     Secondly, your respect and tenderness must reach to
her person, and that in her safeguard and defense. Your wife
walks (under God) in the shadow of your wings and protection. You must be as a veil to her eye, to keep off the dint of
all lust and strange desires, as Abimelech told Sarah of Abraham. As the eyelid is made by nature a tender film and very
moveable, and watchful to the body of the eye, that no dust or
mote fall into it to offend it; so must the tender husband come
between the least aspersion of reproach and infamy cast upon
the name of his wife wrongfully. And when you are dead, let
her rest safe in the ark of God's protection, by the benefit of
your living prayers, before sent up for her, to the throne of
grace, that God would be a husband to the widow; that so even
when dead, yet you may speak. But, while you are living, you
must be as a wall of fire to her; let everyone that has ill will
to your wife (as many will have, even for that which deserves
honor) know that they malign yourself. Furthermore, herein
love her better than yourself that you will right some wrongs
done to her, which perhaps (if done to yourself) you would
pass by more strongly. Let her name and honor be as sweet
ointment unto you. The husband who shall content himself
in the general love of his wife, being yet supinely negligent of
her reputation, or enduring any, within doors or without to
disesteem her without sharp rebuke: or to be known himself
to see any of her weaknesses, with the least contempt, is not
worthy to have the comfort of her virtues, or the love of a religious companion. The same I say of her body, both in health

1.
In protection.

2.
In her repute.

3.
In her bodily
infirmities.

and sickness. Whatsoever diet, or warmth or shelter, either at home or abroad, by yourself or others, you see necessary for the preserving her in health and vigor from the least assault or impression, that neglect not: keep away weather, distemper, and disease for her: be as a physician according to the discretion you have, and the knowledge of her bodily frame and infirmities, in the absence of better help. Prevent all dangers from her which possibly might assault her; and whatsoever sorrow or sad news, ill and sudden accidents you deem, would disquiet her, turn them away if it is within your power, or keep them from her notice, lest they might overthrow her spirit or weaken her body. Even as our Lord Jesus did, so do you; if a danger must necessarily seize upon you, provide that it may not come to her knowledge, or as little amaze and affright her as may be. In her diseases, neglect no means, which your counsel, purse, or friends can help her to: advice for soul, physic for body, attendance and nursery to person. Grudge not that she lies upon your hand, but, as you would have (I say not her, but) Christ himself to tender you in yours, so do you her, in her defects. Let it appear to her clearly that her life is precious, and her loss would be uncomfortable. If the poor Shunammite, seeing her child dead, locked it up in the chamber, hastening to the prophet: preventing all agitation to her husband, all disquiet in the family, by taking it upon herself; how much more should the husband's wisdom and tenderness reach to the wife, that no sickness or sorrow might ever seize upon her more deeply than is necessary, if you can keep it off. *2 Kings 4.21*

Say not with unnatural Nabals, you took her not for sickness, but for health: for better not for worse: knowing that good wives in their health lay up desert enough to be tendered in their sickness. The wife is not for nothing said to be under her husband's covert. Do you as Boaz did to poor Ruth, upon the cold floor, and in the chill night spread the lap of your garment over your beloved. I charge you (says the husband in the Song of Solomon) O ye daughters of Jerusalem, watch by my spouse, sit by her and keep silence, wake her not until she please. Good reason she has more rest than you, let your waking be her security, gaster her not up too early: sluggish women will not, good ones should not be waked too soon. She is always in grief, and that for you and by your means; what *Unnatural husband's language.* *Ruth 3.9* *Song of Sol. 2.7* day, week, or month is she free through the year from breed-ing, bearing, nursing, watching her babes, both sick that they might be well, and well, lest they be sick. If she loses a child by the hand of God, or by casualty, her tender heart takes more thought for it in a day than your manly spirit can in a month: the sorrow of all lies upon her. She has need to be eased of all that is able to be eased because she cannot be eased of the rest. We read in the fable that the male sparrow once accused the female, for that she did not so much take pains in building of their nest as he did: but she replied, there was cause why she should plead exemption. She had all the trouble of laying the eggs, of sitting, of hatching and feeding them, and therefore some reason she should be spared in the building of the nest, let him do that, who did nothing else, and she prevailed. And shall not she, who alleges for herself, with more reason? Get her asleep if you can, but awake her not, till she please. And, tell me, shall not her ease be yours? Or can you have any if she wants? Little do you think of those gripes, checks, and pangs wherewith she walks, when as you go through stitch with your matters with a hardy courage. If all wives are not so, I speak not so much in their behalf: but the good wife is usu-ally so; yield her this fruit of tenderness, it is all the milk you give. Indeed, let your hollow cheeks, pale face, and sad heart be as a calendar in which others may read your wife's infir-mities, their number, their measure, and how long they have continued. I speak not rhetoric unto you, but divinity. As a husband must loathe uxoriousness, so, much more stoical in-sensibleness, remembering who it is who says: err in her love: let your soul know no other objects while she lives, let them be abhorred. And when she has breathed out her last, even when she lies by the walls, certainly in the molds, yet then is there another honor due to her memory, when she is not: even this, that your hand is upon your side for the loss of an-other rib, your sweet companion. Mourn not for her without hope, like a heathen (she is not lost, but sent before), but yet as Abraham, as Jacob, so mourn you, even till the days thereof are accomplished. Be not as the horse, as the fruit creature, without sense of her worth, your loss. Else some beasts will exceed you in tenderness: you are worse; a very block. And for this second particular so much.

Description of the husband's tenderness to the person of his wife.

Two extremes of tender-ness, namely roughness and uxoriousness.

Thirdly, show this respect in your ingenuity and Branch 3. openheartedness. It is an unkindness alone not to show love: Ingenuity and to walk over loosely, dismally, and darkly towards her. You openhearted- can do no more to a stranger. I say not that she is capable of ness. all secrets. There is a season for all things. And had Samson been as wise at last, as at first to conceal his secrets, he had done wisely. But there is a golden mean: conceal not yourself too far from her. Impart whatsoever is meet, let her know the difficulty of your business, if the knowing it may either afford her contentment or yourself advice. Let not strangers tell her of your follies, to cause her to suspect your respectiveness. She is but simple that may not speak a word in season. Rams'
Josh. 6.8
horns and empty pitchers have conquered cities, and armies: and the woman that called herself but a weak one, once de- 2 Sam. 20.18 livered Abel: and why may not your wives help you! It is no wrong to you for her to desire a voice in your affairs, who must be sure to smart in your bad success. There is (I say again) a discretion in ordering this business. Neither to impart those things wherein grief would overcome acceptance; nor to conceal such, as wherein by your imparting them, either her counsel might overweigh her grief, or at least prevent the suddenness of a disaster. It is a thing wherein the weak sex counts itself graced and satisfied, not to be made a stranger to those things, which love and ingenuity would and should impart. As for uttering anything, which is needless or might be a snare to her indiscretion and weakness, it is better kept away. But, darkness breeds ill blood of jealousy, hard thoughts, a striving for the like darkness of behavior, or to seek other bosoms to lay her complaints in, when you little think of it, and perhaps worse than all these. She is laid in your bosom by God that your bosom thoughts, hopes, fears, and desires, together with yourself, might lie in hers. So for this third.

Fourthly, comfort her in all her heaviness, and first Branch 4. for her soul and spirit. The anguish thereof and the wound of Comfort in conscience is of all others, most intolerable. Indeed, though it heaviness an- is only some outward grief, yet if it pierces the spirit with any other piece of more than common distemper, it exceeds any sickness and tenderness. impairment of the body. Show yourself more tender to her therein than in all common troubles. If your own wisdom, faith, or experience will not serve to heal it, seek out and enquire after an interpreter, one of a thousand, who may rightly and duly weigh her estate, both the causes and effects thereof. Upbraid her not with her zeal, which is to aggravate her disease. Fret not at her going to sermons; lay not the fault upon that, wishing you had never seen her eyes, quarrel not at your lot, accuse not providence because you see her in perplexities: perhaps God has begun with her that he might end with you. But however, cease not using all means till God has spoken a word in season to her very soul, saying: Deliver her, I have accepted a ransom: till her flesh comes again as a little child's, and she recovers peace. Happy are you if God shall so make you an instrument of her good that you also may be drawn nearer to God by affliction than prosperity could ever have brought you. And, suppose that the distemper seize only upon her natural spirit, as by melancholy, through passions of fear, and sorrowful objects working upon her mind, or through some hereditary proneness of constitution to mopishness and discontent; by all which God cuts her short of wonted liberties, calling, and service of marriage, and you from former contentments of life: be not in these disquiet and impatient. Nothing has befallen you which is not according to man: use the best means of restoring her spirit again, by physic, counsel, wise secrecy, custody, and tenderness of regard: and so wait with patience, till God restores her, or whatever is the issue, charge not God foolishly.

Job 33.24

Branch 5.
Spare her from
excess toil.

Fifthly, spare her weak body from all toil and labor of worldly employment exceeding her ability. Although she should be too much addicted thereto, and hardly held therefrom, yet dissuade her. She is your own flesh: you would think him unmerciful, who should break your back with too great a burden. So do you, and ease her. If nursery exceeds her strength, and yet her conscience will scarce permit her to lay aside and free herself of so natural, so religious a work, yet tell her, God loves mercy better then sacrifice. If God deny her ability or breasts, grudge not at God, at the charge of nursery abroad, to ease her at home. If she has not strength to be both wife and servant, let the latter yield to the former, redeem the comfort of a wife with the charge of a servant. Provide her that assistance and attendance, which is meet for one, who chooses to be, to do all in one for your sake, had not God denied her.

Strong shoulders are more meet for household business than decayed ones: and relieve her with seasonable tenderness, for there is a show of respect which appears all at once when the vitals are spent: a penny cost in due time will do more good to a sinking house than a pound, when it is ready to fall down. So she shall hold out the longer with cheerfulness in marriage duties. He that should do otherwise is not worthy to have a free horse, much less a willing wife.

Sixthly, yield her the indulgence of all decent and sober refreshings, and recreations of body and spirit, which may ease the tediousness of body and spirit, through the incessant and never-ceasing yoke of family businesses. Remember how often her faithful biding by it at home has enlarged you to travel abroad. Your ground and soil, if it lacks her alternative reviving and rests, cannot last long: whether by allowing her the converse of her friends for bodily, or of the ordinances (when she is straitened) both changes of air may do well, and help both body and spirit. At other times, some other releases of labor, such as occasion offers in many kinds, either nearer hand, or further off, quickly one, afterwards another, may cause her to return to that service with alacrity, which else she should attend with an unequal mind. *Branch 6. Indulgence in all lawful refreshings.*

Seventhly, connive and conceal with wisdom those invincible defects, ignorance, even though it is incapableness, which either the frailty of her sex or the special frame of her mind, or perhaps the inexperience of one untrained in some business, may produce. A camel cannot go through a needle's eye. According to her strength, so is she: look for no deed beyond power, nor wisdom above capacity. Oppose unto her invincible blemishes, her incomparable graces: which no art nor nature can attain; no flesh and blood can teach. Satisfy not, neither pardon yourself, till that honor which your heart can freely give her for that which is precious in her, makes you impotent to disparage her for her infirmities. Though perhaps others would note them, yet it is your best art to hide them. Remember this, perhaps even your wife's defects may make for your contentments. If she were a more complete woman, she would find more work to be humble; and in some of her abilities, might perhaps give you occasion of less patience. Here now is the trial of giving honor to the weaker sex; because God *Branch 7. Connivance at invincible infirmities.*

will have it so. Dissemble what you cannot amend. Oftentimes, her sudden filthiness or impatience comes not so much from herself as from oppression of mind, faintness of spirits, and much employment. Encounter her not with like passion, lest God show you your folly before you die, in another more unwelcome glass. Many a foolish husband has a froward wife because he will have one, has not the wit to have any other, any better. What an honor is it to your wisdom to bear with her confessed weakness? As going backward with Shem and Japheth to cover that from the eyes of others, which you yourself are sorry to see. Perhaps some other of her qualities have not a little graced you, cover therefore the rest with the mantle of your wisdom. And so perhaps, with that painter, by veiling a blemish in the face, which he was loath to express, you shall add to her beauty, to your own honor. When her passion shall be over, and her error past, she will more dislike herself through your concealing of her wants than you can dislike her for betraying your credit.

Branch 8. Commend her virtues.

Eighthly, commend her virtues, without foolish flattery: not as a man, who therefore marks them that he might praise them (which is baseness), but therefore commends them because tenderness will not suffer you to smother them. Grace can no more be covered than a blemish: both are as oil in the hand, inward gifts, outward parts and performances cannot but delight your mind and senses: let both in their season, for her encouragement, break out from you by a tender, loving acknowledgement. But as for upbraiding her before others or traducing her in the family by open reproofs, odious comparisons, and unsavory imputations; abhor it. Knowing that all your and her skill is little enough to keep her from contempt of inferiors: but if your contempt is added to the rest, it will make a breach, not to be repaired.

Branch 9. Supply of necessaries and comfortable supports.

Ninthly, allow her all needful, and some additional charges and supplies: let her have for comfort as well as necessity; considering how soon you would repine if God should straiten you with the only necessaries, but not the surplus of marriage comforts. It is not only thankfulness to her, but to God also, to rejoice in seeing your wife walk and demean herself cheerfully in the use of that liberal allowance, which your tender heart can bestow her. I do not here bid you to put the bridle out of your own hand, yielding to her the stroke of choosing to herself the fashions, attire, company, and expenses which she pleases, such as suit not with your place and sober contentment (for alas! what poor thanks should a woman give her husband for making her as proud as the worst): but I say, furnish her with such conveniences as your own judgment and respect thinks meet for her, and her sober mind and desires affect. Master Calvin, a man otherwise of somewhat a retired and austere disposition, yet being married, perceived that there are in women (as he prettily calls them) many tolerable follies and toyish vanities, which a tender husband should do better to oversee than deny her. He that will wring his nose too hard will draw forth blood, and there is a genial liberty to be permitted to a woman's liberties, companies, merriments, toys, and trinkets, which the gravity of a husband should shame itself in peering into. Many trifles they affect for their children (of that sex especially) many complements about themselves, some rearing to bestow upon the meetings and lawful merriments of their kind, which it is a poor thing for a husband curiously to enquire after: and his wisdom to trust her with, as knowing, she knows how to use them. Perhaps the French exceeded the English in these, but let this be the rule, better in such a case, wherein the spirit of a wife takes contentment, to be rather indulgent than too strict: so long as the main canon of modesty, thrift, and decency is not transgressed.

Lastly, since rules in such cases can hardly be given, therefore as the moral philosopher bids, do in this case, as tenderness and a respective heart would advise. That is ever the best counselor. Remember, you seek the honor of your marriage. Wherefore, whatsoever else is meet, loving, merciful, forbearing, and tender, as you expect praise, honor, or requital, ensue it: give no way to strict, stingy, and violent ways. He that handles a crystal or Venice glass harshly deserves to repent him for breaking that, which sleight and tenderness might have saved. Precedency in sitting is granted by a national custom to the sex of women: by which all other privileges of giving honor and contentment to the weaker vessel are intimated. A wise resigning up to her custody of things within, jewels, plate, and things of price, trusting her fidelity

Branch 10. Respectiveness must be the counselor.

and ascribing to her wisdom the overseeing and managing of domestic affairs incident to housewifery, without narrow, suspicious inquiry after the expense thereof, not distrusting skill or faithfulness: and so in like cases. And thus much is said in particular for the answer to this question, wherein this tenderness consists.

Use.
Terror to all base Nabals, and a description of such.

That which I have said in doctrine may serve for use and all: save that it is true which Solomon speaks: Bray a fool in a mortar, with a pestle, yet, will not his folly depart from him. So I say, a churlish, a froward, loutish, and ungenial husband will either see no error at all, in himself, by all that I have said, or hold his own nevertheless. I have seen an evil under the sun, Nabal married to an Abigail, a tender sweet companion, worthy of such a husband as her husband himself is unworthy to wait upon: yet so far is he from returning to her like for like, that rather the grace of the wife is a continual upbraiding to the husband's currishness; occasioning to his implacable spirit so much the more insolence, to insult over her, and to tread her under his feet. What sand is so weighty to the shoulders, as such a fool to a worthy wife? Well worthy after her death and loss to meet with lettuce fit for his lips, I mean with such a contentions Zipporah, as might outshoot such a Devil in his own bow. What one grace of a thousand does such a block behold in his virtuous wife? When did he ever feel himself burn if she was weak? What affliction of body or mind could he ever find in his heart to condole for his wife? What one kid gave he at any time to her out of his flock, or twelve pence out of his purse, to make merry with? What one lap of his garment did he ever spread over her! Or what, I say not blast of cold wind, but sad cross did he ever keep in tenderness from her, himself being both a nipping east wind to blast her hopes, and a perpetual dropping to dwell with? Many an infamy and blot has he suffered to light upon her head, though he needed not, himself being the upshot of all! Oh the snares which such unnatural wretches bring upon innocent women, but ease them of none! Oh the narrow eye they carry over them, watching them as the cat the mouse, from either good sermon hearing, loving friends, frequenting abroad, or Christian company at home! Stripping their bodies of good clothes, their purses of money, their hearts of delight, their souls of grace (as much as in them lies), if grace is not past their reach to rob them of! What one penny ever gave they them for good use? If they knew of any, who should endure the tempest of their violence, they will see their own turns served to the uttermost: but as for easing them of their burdens or being drawn to resign up their lusts and loose liberties, to join with their wives in the burden of house government: those Israelitish bondmen were as good to complain to Pharaoh, or those other subjects to Rehoboam, as they to their husbands, for their tale of brick should be but multiplied, and their fingers should prove heavier than their loins before. I might be endless: but I blame only the faulty, for I know (and God forbid else) all are not alike. Many, not only irreligious, but merely civil ignorant ones, have had tender, melting hearts to their wives; so unnatural wretches, are all unmerciful, respectless husbands in this kind, even bred upon the rocks and nursed up by tigers, truly fiends in the likeness of men. Let them alone: but O you woman that fears God, persist nevertheless in your uprightness! Serve God not man, and vile man for God's sake. Do not repent of your goodness, give your work to God, and still heap up hot coals upon the head of the barbarous, if they melt not they shall burn to hell, and bear awhile, he that comes will come, and not tarry, causing your light to break out as the morning and your righteousness as the noonday. He shall plead the cause of the despised wife, and quit her of her adversary: bringing his wickedness upon his own head. And of this third several duty of giving honor, and so of all the three, thus much is spoken.

Counsel to the wronged party.

CHAPTER XIII

Treats of the personal duties of the wife.
And first of her subjection to
her husband.

The special
duties of the
wife to the
husband,
three.

It is high time now, having dispatched the husband's duties, to proceed to the next branch in which the preserving of matrimonial honor consists, namely, the peculiar duties of the wife to the husband. Else I know husbands would tax me for partiality: and I confess, as I have no cause to conceal the privileges of the good wife from her husband, so neither must I withhold from her the knowledge of her offices and services towards him. The first and main whereof, comprehending all the rest, is subjection to her husband: the second is helpfulness: and the third gracefulness. By her subjection she answers his understanding. By her helpfulness she equals his providence, by her gracefulness she supplies his tender respectiveness: in a word, she answers him (as face to face in water) so she in marriage service with all correspondence. Else how shall the relation hold firm and entire? First then of the first. This duty then of subjection is the woman's great and chief commandment; and as James says, he that can rule his tongue is a perfect man, and can rule his whole conversation: so, she who has learned to be subject (for as Paul, Philip. 4, is not ashamed to say of that grace of contentment, that he had learned it, so may the woman say of this) is a perfect woman. That which was accustomed to be said of pronunciation in rhetoric, and of humility in divinity, that may be said of subjection in this business of the wife. Its breadth and length, it fills up all, truly, it is all in all, the whole duty of the woman: all others stick at this, grant this, and all others follow of themselves. Now then, this great duty of subjection (so much caviled at by the rebellious, and so much honored by the dutiful and loyal wife) must have a good foundation, both for the convincement of the bad, and for the encouragement of the good. The warrant then of this duty stands not in the opinion, choice, or will of man or flesh,

The first duty
of the wife,
subjection.

no nor of nations, because the world will have it so (for there is a world of women to gainsay as well as of men to allege it). But it is a firm law, from the will of the first ordainer; because God will have it so. That very strict imperial edict of Ahasuerus that every man should bear rule in his own house, proceeded in a sort from a discontent with Vashti, and a desire to be revenged for the dishonor offered Ahasuerus her husband, and for prevention of the like, for time to come: but if all this stream of authority had not met with another more strong one of divine ordinance, alas it had been no more terror to the sex of women than swords and spears to the whale's skin, even as stubble and rotten wood. No, no, it is an instinct put into the spirit of the woman, principling and convincing her understanding, will, and affections. The great God of heaven and earth will have it so.

  Whereof two reasons may be given: the one from the law of creation; the other from the law of penalty, following disobedience. For the first, The man (we know) was first created, as a perfect creature, and not the woman with him at the same instant, as we know both sexes of all other creatures were contemporary: not so here. But, after his constitution and frame ended then was she thought of. Secondly, she was not made of the same matter with the man equally; but she was made and framed of the man, by a rib taken from the man, and being formed by God into a woman, was brought unto the man. And thirdly, she was made for the man's use and benefit, as a meet helper, when no other creature besides her was able to do it. Three weighty reasons and grounds of the woman's subjection to the man: and that, from the purpose of the Creator; who else might have done otherwise, that is, yielded to the woman coequal beginning, sameness of generation, or relation of usefulness: for he might have made her without any such precedency of matter, without any dependency upon him, and equally for her good, as for his. All show a kind of ennobling the man's sex, and denying of her to him, as the head and more excellent: not that the man might upbraid her, but that she might in all these read her lesson of subjection. For otherwise, it is also true that neither the man without the woman, nor she without him, but both in the Lord. And doubtless as Malachi speaks, herein is wisdom,

Esther 1.20

Reason 1.
From the law
of creation.

1 Cor. 11.8,9

Mal. 2.15

for God was full of spirit; and has left nothing after him to be bettered by our invention.

Reason 2. From the penalty of disobedience.

The second warrant hereof is penal, and yet so much the stronger tying the woman, being now in a fallen condition. For this is sure, that (notwithstanding all I have said) yet the woman being so created by God in the integrity of nature had a most divine honor and partnership of his image, put upon her in her creation: truly such as (without prejudice of those three respects) might have held full and sweet correspondence with her husband. But, her sin still augmented her inequality, and brought her lower and lower in her prerogative. For, since she would take upon her as a woman without respect to the order, dependence, and use of her creation, to enterprise so sad a business, as to jangle and demure with the Devil about so weighty a point as her husband's freehold, and of her own brain to lay him and it under foot without the least parley and consent of his: obeying Satan before him, even God himself; so that, till she had put all beyond question, and past amendment, and eaten, she brought not the fruit to him to eat, and so, became a devil to tempt him to eat; therefore the Lord

Gen. 3.16

strips her of this robe of her honor, accursing her with this penalty, that her appetite should be to her husband. Which law is not as the law of the Medes and Persians (for that must alter), but a law which bred a law, an instinct of unequal inferiority, and smote into the heart of Eve, a falling from her station, and subjected her to her husband. This appetite here spoken of, not only meaning her weakness of desire for some special end, as benevolence, respect, or the like; but the total subduing of the bent of her spirit to him, not thinking her subsisting enough without him, but a confessed yielding up of her insufficient self (and that after a penal sort) to depend wholly upon him. A just hand of God upon her that she who would be paramount as a lady above him, in sinning: should be fetched down to a spirit of fear and subjection under him whom she had so basely dishonored.

Proofs. 1 Tim. 2.14

And from this root comes that of the apostle, that the woman sinned and not the man (meaning, not first), she was in the transgression: and what then? Therefore let her be sub-

1 Cor. 11.7

ject. Read the place. The man is the glory of God, but the woman of the man. Therefore she ought to have power on her head, in token of subjection and modesty. And again, I permit not the woman to usurp authority over the man, but to be in subjection. And Peter, Let the women be subject to their own husbands, lest the Word be evil spoken of. And to the Ephesians: Wives submit yourselves to your husbands, as to your head: for he is as Christ to the church, the savior of his body. So Peter adds: As those holy women formerly were in subjection to their husbands: Sarah by name to Abraham, calling him lord. By all these arguments these two apostles (not the one who was married, but the other unmarried) do conclude the woman under subjection; that without grudging, she might resign up herself (under God) to her husband. And doubtless, if it is asked, by what commandment this subjection of the wife stands in force, it is doubtless by the virtue of that fifth, which imposes obedience upon inferiors to their superiors (although in diverse degrees) with an implied penalty of disobedience. And questionless, if you look no further than the sin and curse itself, in the letter thereof, there is no less threatened to the woman than such a subjection to the man, as had pain and irking annexed unto it. Even as that other penalty also annexed unto it, of breeding and travail, extends to a mortal pain and pinch, as considered in itself. In itself I say: for notwithstanding all this, the Lord our merciful and indulgent Father, in and through the mediation of Christ, has in great favor assuaged and released the rigor and measure of these penalties, I have elsewhere treated hereof. If the common favor of Christ our redeemer had not eased whole mankind from the excess of all sorts of penalties, what is the life of man, but desolation and misery? But in mere pity to the accursed creature, weltering under her punishment, as a man wounded lies wallowing in his blood, the Lord Jesus has brought things to a reconcilement, both in heaven and earth. So that the heavens hear the earth, the earth the creatures, and they man: who else should subsist? If the ox, horse, ass, and other beasts, which by man's sin are of subjects, turned rebels against him, and bereft him of his lordship, were not again retracted to some useful subjection, who should come near them? But now their rebellion to us is moderated, and a shadow of our lordship over them restored, not to the godly only, but wholly to the nature of man: by whose industry, the wild-

1 Pet. 3.1

Eph. 5.22

1 Pet. 3.5,6

Catech. in part 1 and 3 article.

Col. 1.20

Hos. 2.21-23

He has re-
collected all
things both
in heaven
and earth by
Christ.
Col. 1.20

est are tamed. I say, by a common fruit of the superabounding merit of Christ. Such is the release of this penalty of women: for though for their abusing the end of their creation by hurting and destroying him, whose helpers they were created to be; the Lord abased them to a low degree of inferiority to the man, and that justly: yet through Christ, this extremity is dispensed with, and reduced to a tolerable mediocrity for the ease of womankind. So that God can make that a royal and honorable equality (after a sort) which sin made a yoke of tedious slavery. But to the elect it is far better; notwithstanding, through bearing of children, she shall be saved, if she continues in faith, holiness, and modesty: that is, her curse becomes a blessed occasion of salvation. So in this point of subjection: it becomes a wholesome mean to humble the soul under the mighty hand of God and the guilt of her nature, and so to drive her to Christ. And not so alone, but is a continual holder down of her soul under subjection to God in the course of her conversation. And both make her in this religious awe and subjection to her husband, so much the more precious in the eye of God, and all that know her. Behold a penalty made an ornament, very highly esteemed of God. And as for those women who fear not God, yet this indulgence of providence, if it is not a means to break their hearts, and to seek further to get a part in Christ's peculiar redemption of the elect: it shall be (doubtless) a double aggravating of their condemnation.

1 Pet. 3.4

Reason 3.
Hereby she
preserves the
honor of her
marriage.

Now for the third reason of the point, why the woman should for her part do to the uttermost to grace and improve the married condition, by being subject to her husband, appears by this, that by subjections she preserves the honor of her marriage in the integrity thereof. She is called the crown of her husband. The crown royal we know is a rich thing, and richly beset: all to honor a true king, when it is set upon his head in his coronation, before all the people. But a woman made of subjection is of a far more precious frame and metal than a crown, or anything which goes to it: and being set upon the head of her husband, honors him, not only in the day of his marriage, but all his life long, in the eyes of all that behold her. No crown gladdens the heart of a king, so as she makes glad the heart of her husband. He is her king and lord, though he should want this crown; for it is not a wife's rebellion, which can divest him of his authority and honor, in point of right: he may be a poor pitied king for lack of this crown, but in right, he is a king nevertheless: having his crown detained by violence from him, and woe to them that detain the crown from the natural prince: exposing the person of so sacred a one (whom God has made honorable) to reproach and dishonor; so here. God will revenge it, and make her that has kept it back, to rue it, and to pay full dearly for her presumption. But when this crown is added to the head of a lawful king, then is his honor made up to the full; and such honor is a wife subject to her husband. Not as a crown above but upon his head: her honor is not in being a crown aloft, but upon and for the husband. She is no crown of herself, but in respect of him whom she honors: receiving back as much honor from that head which she crowns, as she affords unto it. Neither is the honor of such a marriage between themselves alone (for honor is rather in the power of the honorer than the honored), but also it reaches to many others; we see it in Ruth married to Boaz. All the children of my people know you to be a virtuous woman, and him a happy husband in her, praying for them (as indeed it fell out) that they might do well in Ephratah, and be famous in Bethlehem. How can a marriage between an understanding head and a subject wife choose but be honorable? Who can smother the honor of such couples, or judge whether of the two is more successful in either, or who wishes not, it were his own case, or the case of any whom he loves, to be married to a wife so qualified? And well they may; for as it is rare to meet with such couples, so, the commodity which they procure to each other, exceeds all commendation. All this considered, a woman should be much to blame to desert her duty in this case, and to lay the honor of her marriage in the dust.

Ruth 3.11

What is then this subjection, and wherein stands it? For the former I say it is such a convincement of spirit in the woman touching the equity of God's ordinance (and her penalty in special) as causes both a falling down of heart in humility to God and her husband; and in her conversation to acknowledge and practice all such reverence as becomes her head. By this description it may appear in what particulars this subjection stands: to wit, chiefly in the spirit of the wife,

Subjection, what it is.

Subjection
twofold.
1 Pet. 3.4

1.
Of the spirit.

2 Sam. 6.20

Objection.

Answer.
Husbands
though but
meanly parted,
deserve sub-
jection by the
ordinance.

and next in her demeanor. The former is that same whereof Peter speaks of: The meekness of the hidden man of the heart, of an incorrupt and quiet spirit, which with God is much set by. He means an inward principle of subjection of the heart, which is first given up to God, purged of self and pride (the seed of insubjection), and then to the husband, for his sake. Although a woman has all outward accomplishments this way, yet, if her outward subjection begins before her inward (as many women's do) it will vanish at last, as a lamp for lack of oil. No framing of a woman by most exquisite education, outward forming of the body to delicate behavior, and semblance of subjection, can compass this anymore than an ape can attain the qualification of reason. No artificial respectiveness of the eye, the courtesy of body, the silence or composure of the tongue, or the like, can secure a husband of subjection, except all these are acted from a heart of subjection, through the conscience of the duty. But, if the principle is sound, and a heart fearing God, awed by a command issuing from Christ's love and a willing mind, not from necessity, credit, or restraint (which will go far and make a great show) then is this duty well planted, and will endure. What is all that Michal's bewitching love to David (which forced him to send for her long after her separation), to that one baseness, that she despised him in her heart? The woman then, must set up her husband there and shrine him in the secret of her heart; and then, all her external subjection will flow sweetly, fully, and constantly without grudging, and sit comely as a garment fit for the body.

But, it will be objected, there is no rule so general, but it admits exception. Women confess that, as the case may stand, and as the husband may deserve by his great learning, wisdom, gifts, grace, art, experience, or like abilities, some woman might be content to resign up herself to her husband and be subject to him, as to her head. But, as for ordinary husbands, whose deserts are small and their defects great (perhaps in some, or in most respects mentioned), it would prove a hard task for a woman so far to deny herself, as to be subject. To which I answer, God is not the God of confusion; he puts this burden of subjection upon no woman, who takes not the yoke of marriage upon herself; which the Lord does force upon none, but allows each woman to be her own refuser, and to choose for herself (if she can) such a man as she can yield subjection unto, for the excellency of God's image which she beholds in him. And there is no more than is necessary in this caution to prevent that base and carnal disdain, which else might arise in her heart against her husband, namely, when she shall meet with an object of dishonor, and find little to provoke due respect towards him: I say, the Lord, who knows that the spirit that is in man lusts after envy and scorn, would have this disease prevented to the uttermost, that so subjection might seem not to come from necessity, but from free will. But yet, still I say, if a woman will balk such a command, and, either out of a present humor, or out of a carnal conceit (at first) that she can lead and rule a simple man at her pleasure (which after she finds a harder theme than she knew) shall snare herself with such a husband as she cannot deem worthy of the honor of her heart. In this case, I will wonder that she would snare herself with such a one: but being married to her, I will press upon her the like duty of subjection, as if he were the most complete husband of a thousand: like (I say) for kind, although not for measure. For, tell me, poor woman, who thus cavils, what is it which God has aimed at in this ordinance? At your own ends, or his own and your husband's? Are you so simple as to imagine, when God has imposed a yoke upon you to tame your rebellion; that he will (at your instance) turn it to a contentment of your self-love? What singular thing do you in submitting yourself to excellencies and parts in a husband? Is it not for yourself! And who shall find out such a husband for you, whom you may not except against, as defective in some kind or other? Know then, that God has ordained subjection to a husband, as a husband, be he what he may (he is such a one as you have thought fit), and therefore, one whom God has thought fit to receive your subjection. If he has but indifferent parts and abilities, and not many men's gifts united in one, then consider, he has but the defects of one. And who are you, O woman, have you the perfections of many women? Therefore look upon your own defects, and your husband's will be overseen. Count your own parts but ordinary, and your husband's will be tolerable. Enlarge his a little, and diminish your own, and so you shall meet in the halfway, and make some equality. But howsoever God has set you in place of subjection, howsoever: either to a man of worth, for his desert, or to a man worthless, for conscience sake, and for the sake of him who has subjected you. If you obey for a command's sake, there is thanks, or if not, then for necessity's sake, and woe to you in both respects, if you are not subject. A Minister is commanded to preach and watch for conscience sake, not for living, or by-respects. A subject has not that name for that he obeys those laws of his prince which please him, but because his prince commands, except he will endure the penalties annexed. If then either a minister or subject will look at God, whether gain or no gain, whether good prince or unjust, and obey or else woe to both: then look also you woman at the bare command of God; dispense not where God does not. The same power that is in commanding all to obey their parents, forbidding all to worship idols, to commit sacrilege; that same I say charges all wives to be subject, and forbids them rebellion.

Exceptions in some cases against the woman's subjection.

1.

In case of unlawful commands.

Now yet I will not deny, but there is an exception to some kind of subjection. If your husband stretches his authority beyond God's bounds then and only then, you art permitted to restrain your subjection in that kind, with yielding a reason. It was not the sin of Vashti (as I take it), that she offered not her beauty and person to a vainglorious ostentation before the multitude; for, that might have been a snare to her as it was to others: but that she subjected not herself so far as was meet, to go to the king, and to acknowledge his sovereignty in all lawful, meet things, to give a modest reason of her refusal, promising to submit herself in all other. Even so here. Though the wife is tied, both in all direct charges of God, and in all other which repugn not, I mean in things pure, comely, and good report; yet if her husband will try her in the contrary, she must in all humble modesty refuse and say, Whether it is meet herein to obey God or you, judge yourself. So that, herein there must be wise caution used, that neither she straighten her husband's power, nor yet enlarge her husband's tyranny, of her obedience to it. For (to digress a little) not only the husband may press the subjection of a wife in things arbitrary, but even in the omission of some commands. An example of both will clear it. Two fashions of apparel are offered to a woman, equally decent and modest: she inclines to

the one, he to the other. It is his discretion herein to yield to
her the choice of her fashion: howbeit, if he will hearken to no
reason, but urge upon her his fashion, she must be obedient
and deny her own, for conscience sake. Again, suppose the
husband requires his wife at such a time to forbear the hearing
of a good sermon, and to hear another at another congregation; or to forfeit the hearing of the Word upon such a Sabbath
day, although in general he oppose neither hearing the Word,
nor keeping a Sabbath in the same kind and place; although
it is true that the charge of hearing and keeping of Sabbaths,
is God's: yet because these commands tie not to every time
and place, and may in some cases be omitted, therefore, let
the husband look to himself how safely he restrains her of her
liberty (lest God curse his usurpation) or otherwise; and stand
to his own adventures; but since such a restraint may possibly
be lawful (though he harshly conceals it from her), therefore
she must not contest nor hold chat with her husband, why he
requires it, but yield for the present, and afterwards return to
her liberty again. But if hereby he encroaches further to forbid her the ordinances, she must disobey. Only in a case of
particular abstinence, she must think thus, My husband sees
cause of such a charge, I will not descant, if he should offend,
yet I will not rebel, so long as any good construction may be
made of it, but meekly stoop and obey. I might be endless
in instances; I deny not, but many a good wife mismatched
and put upon sundry extremities is to be pitied and prayed
for: but not therefore to release herself from subjection and
break all cords in sunder, because unpleasing to the flesh. As
Peter tells them, they must strive for so blameless a conversa-   1 Pet. 3.1,2
tion, and subjection towards their husbands, though rude and
churlish, as may cause them to magnify the truth of God, and
justify their obedience, and wish themselves in like condition
with them in the day of their visitation. Look up therefore to
God and yield to many unwelcome services (if they are not
directly sinful, but abhorring to have the least fellowship with
them, as he said, Into their counsel, let not my soul come). If
you are pressed to any base thing, which conscience starts at,
as to keep loose company, to wear garish apparel, to traduce
the godly, or what else soever indecent and impure; forfeit
the pleasing of your husband on earth, and please a better in

heaven: who will bring forth his doves from the filthy pots, and that with honor, when they commit themselves to him in their innocency. Whereas flattering and temporizing women, who in show will hold with God, but yet keep quarter with ungodly husbands for their own ends; shall at last be detected for hypocrites and rewarded with reproach and dishonor.

Further qualification of the woman's subjection.

I shall insist in the next chapter in another exception, which allows a woman such a liberty in God's matters with her husband, as to prompt and occasion unto him Christian speech, good counsel, with modesty and in season: for the subjection we treat of is not slavish but equal and royal in a sort, as I have noted. But to go on: she is not so to be subject as if in all cases she ought alike to stand or fall at the bar and prerogative of her husband's will. Some cases fall out between them of greater difficulty, doubt, and danger than ordinary: such as extend to the hazard of estate, children, even liberty and life itself. In such cases (if they are but arbitrary), as removal from present dwelling upon great charge and loss, or, to places of ill health, ill neighbors, with loss of gospel; long voyages by sea, to remote plantations, or in the sudden change of trades, or venturing of a stock upon some new project, lending out, or borrowing of great sums, avoiding of debts, settling of estate, providing for children, costly buildings, great entertainments beyond ability, or such like instances, wherein the woman is like to share as deep in the sorrow, if not more than the husband; reason good she should share in the advice, and not be compelled to obey perforce. A husband perhaps in such cases may necessitate his wife to yield, but he does her the more wrong, for God in such cases leaves her to her freedom. Could a martyr in Queen Mary's days compel his wife to suffer in the same cause with himself, although both were of the same judgment? No: for her conscience was her own, and his measure might (haply) exceed hers many degrees in knowledge, faith, and courage. It has been by some very strangely determined that if a husband is resolved upon a remote plantation, the wife must follow by hand and by head. But, under correction it is neither so nor so: headship is not given the husband to destroy, but to help and edify. She has a judgment to inform as well as he, and must see her grounds clear as well as he: she must have leisure and time to deliberate

2.
In prompting the husband with religious counsel.

3.
In cases of difficulty and hazard.

of it as well as he, till she is resolved that she may do that in faith, which she does. Therefore (with modesty and discretion) it is allowed her to deliberate, to allege her reasons by herself, or by her friends, submitting them to the judgment of wiser than herself, and as she shall be cast and adjudged, so to deny herself and obey either way. And when God's will is made known, either he or she, are to rest, without further distemper with each other. Meanwhile, the husband is not to insult, threaten, and domineer over her as a lord, who had his wife's will captivated to his own: neither to desert and depart from her in a desperate way, but by all loving ways tenderly to draw her, and convince her by the strength of reason, and the bowels of compassion. God speaks not now by lively voice from heaven, in such doubtful cases, as once he pleased to do in times past. Sarah thereby knew God's will in her journey is to and fro, as well as Abraham, and had his promise of protection, as well as he. Therefore her subjection ties not women in like adventures, now, as then. But now doubtful cases must be scanned and determined, according to the nearest that Scripture or reason imports: that so her obedience may rather flow from consent than compulsion.

Thus, I have said more of the first branch than I had intended to do; not so properly, as necessarily, to spare myself a labor in another place: let me now sound retreat to my reader's thoughts: and come to the second branch of my division, that is, the subjection of the woman's practice. Which, although it is but a shadow without the other; yet that must not pass for the whole payment of the debt; for, who may not say, their heart is good this way, whereas their conversation shows it not? But a subject heart appears best when a woman says little of that which is within, but leaves to them to judge, who hear and see. And this practice of the woman's subjection must appear in these three particulars, in matters of God's worship, in matters of the world, and in her marriage converse. For the first, she is with an awful and single eye, and honoring heart to behold in her husband the gifts of God; as namely, that ability which God has given him to be in God's stead unto her, in all things pertaining unto her soul; as also to manage the services of God with her, either in the family or apart; as to read the word judiciously, to catechize and inform

Branch 2. Subjection of practice wherein three particulars.

The first. In matters of God.

in the grounds of religion distinctly; to admonish the family against the sins, and exhort inferiors to the duties of their order and condition, wife, children, sojourners, and servants. I say, she ought so to observe God's image in these gifts of her husband, as to feel no spirit in her to despise him, to gainsay, to compare, or censure them. Indeed though her own gifts are more than ordinary, yet to conceal and suppress them in this kind (except her husband shall at any time desire to be partaker thereof in private for his spiritual quickening, and then with all humble self-denial to impart herself with him), and enjoy them to herself in subjection. Note it, that the apostle when he is in the midst of his urging this duty to the wife, then does he touch this point, saying, let the woman learn in silence; and, I suffer not the woman to teach, or usurp authority over the man, but to be in silence. You must note that in this age, the Spirit of God was poured upon all flesh, so that women as well as men had great gifts of understanding and prophecy vouchsafed them: which (no doubt) might put them forward to express themselves before their husbands. Now, if such women, than how much more must ordinary women be subject in this kind to their husbands? She ought indeed to encourage her husband cordially, to proceed in such a course, showing it to be the joy of her heart, when she sees him to set up God in the family. She is to remove to the uttermost, all lets and stops which might offend; as unseasonable attendance upon business (which commonly offers itself most when it least should), also the complaints and trouble of children: with other occasions of the family, as that might by her wise prevention, be cast upon other times as well. I say, she is wisely to procure the opportunities of worship; but he is to manage and perform them: she being within doors, must take it her part to prepare and forlay the seasons for her husband's better ease and contentment in these duties: a wise housewife will be always beforehand in her business, that so the house may be empty, swept, and garnished for God to come in. She must abhor (as I said before) to jostle and shoulder out the solemn matters of God, or to cut them off by the middle and contract them, by the colorable pretenses of other matters. So tedious in her dressing and trimming that a pin must not be awry, so sluggish and lateward in her uprising, so curious about her chil-

1 Tim. 2.11,12

dren's speech, so tedious in her manifold proclamations and turnagains that it would irk any Christian husband to suspend God's work upon such fooleries, and yet either it must be so, or worse. No, no, account these things babbles in respect of the other; that one thing necessary: learn to outgrow all such old customs as base, in God's esteem. The Devil will never suffer a woman to want bones to throw in the way of duty if he spies a mind ready to admit them. If any part must lose, let the world's part be the loser. Subjection to the husband's will first begins with God: setting him up, and affording him his due. Nothing will more encourage a religious husband to be strict and careful in his way than when he sees his wife's zeal in this kind: nor more dismay and enfeeble him than the slackness and indifference of the wife, that she is so far from forgetting herself for God, that she will not afford him that regard which lies within her place to express.

But what then (will some say) is the wife then wholly cut off from the officiating of worship in her family? I answer, she has a great work of it, to seek God constantly by herself apart, at times meet: and, if her family consists of her own sex, she may like Esther with her own maids, in the absence of her husband pray with and teach her family and children, besides the private respect she owes them out of the act of worship. But (will some say) is she so straightened that in no respects she may perform these duties in the presence of the other sex in the family, or of her own husband, as the case may require? I answer, touching her servants the case is less difficult, being her inferiors as well as her husband's, and so she doing the duty of a governor to them, she is discharged, especially they are unable, ignorant, or unmeet to be so occupied, and ready to perk up and trample the authority of the woman under feet, by such occasions. But, touching the husband, although the case is more difficult, yet I doubt not but she may also before him, as well as the other, perform these duties, if these cautions are observed. For why? Serving of God in itself can hinder no subjection, but rather further it, in a lowly and humble spirit, privy to her own infirmities, only mark how? First, she may attempt it, in case of utter insufficiency of parts in her husband, I mean knowledge and understanding. Secondly, in case of invincible defects of expression and utterance in the

[margin notes:]

How far the wife may undertake the service of God in her family.

Answer. Yet with cautions.

Caution 1.

husband. Thirdly, and much more, when there is an utter
looseness and carelessness in him to look after it, much more
a vicious contempt, so that (as far as lies in him) the work is
like to be quite dismissed out of the family. Fourthly, if her
husband does allow her with all cheerfulness, or request her
to undertake it, for conscience, or if not, yet be content to give
way to it upon reasonable terms, of connivance: even though
not so equal terms, but with some lowering, and with break-
ings out now and then, or upbraiding of her; yet not forbidding and opposing, she must rather undergo some brunts for
God and her family, and bear them as meekly as she can, than
under such pretense to abandon the duty. But, if he is willing
and able, though perhaps unqualified for grace, she must not
encroach upon the office and discredit her husband: but by
all sweet means accepting that which is, and covering defects,
to draw him forward to that which is not, in token of a heart
truly subject. Fifthly, if she (besides her ability to perform
it) is also qualified with singular modesty and humility, awe,
and reverence, both of God and his angels, and her husband,
whose presence should always be solemn, and balance her
spirit to soberness and subjection.

Women denied this liberty must be patient.   If God deny her that interest and respect from her
husband which she deserves, so that he slights her parts, de-
spises her graces, and will by no means endure her service in
this kind; the effect is sad, to behold God cast out, and the
family deserted, and exposed to ruin: but her remedy is rather
to mourn in secret and by other wisdom to seek the relief of
this burden, than to break her bounds. On the other side, if
these respects are observed she may. For the Lord ties none
so strictly that either one must do it, namely, the master of
the family, or none. No, no: the Lord knows that oftentimes
he of all other parts of the household, least befits his place;
and besides, if the head of the family himself, even when he
is able, yet for reasons may resign up his liberty to another, a
stranger, who probably may honor God and profit the family
more than himself (in which case to stick to his privilege is a
sign of pride and singularity), much more may he (in the case
of usual worship, when the very substance of worship lies at
the stake) authorize the woman to perform it. For, although
he dishonor his headship; yet his penance is just for his sin.

Better it is that he is reproached and shamed for his sin (especially himself revenging it) than that God should be barred of his due; by both his and her withdrawing the duty, and the whole family wanting the ordinances. It was God's law that if the servant would willingly abase himself to slavery, his ear was to be bored: but his master was not to lose his advantage. And the wife is as well the mother, as the man, the father of the family. She is a part of the household's head, as the husband is the wife's head. Now if she is free from the dominion of her head, then is she the whole head of the family, and returns to her privilege: so that without check or control she may (being fitted) discharge the duty: but if being a widow (never used to it before) she finds this new task to be over tedious to her, then ought she to resign it to another, as (if she is of ability) to one maintained for that purpose, if not, yet to such a servant, as both for parts and humbleness may be meet to take it upon him, without offence: for else the remedy may prove worse than the disease, through his contempt. It being to contain a thing within bounds when it is out of his element. As touching the husband's absence (as I have said) she may doubtless more safely perform it with the servants than in his presence. If it should be alleged, there is in the family such as whom she may resign up the duty unto, both for dexterity and humility, I say little to that for the present, so long as her gifts are competent she is the governess, they inferiors, and the sad effects in bold servants of this course does not a little disaffect me: yet I will not deny a lawfulness altogether for her to resign it if she is advised to it by them that give counsel, as well as by herself. But, if such helps fail, what should hinder her from the cheerful and free undertaking of it? And so much for this.

Now secondly, she must also be subject to him in matters of his worldly estate. She is not to stand upon stiff terms and (as we say) upon her pantofles with her husband, touching her equality of right to his estate and goods, with himself: for here, the question is not so much of right, as employment. Now she must not distract the common stock from her husband's hand into her own, to occupy it at pleasure, to dispense the charges of the family as she desires, or pursing of the commodity as well as he: which is to seek a quartermastership with him; and to seek a double, not the single wealth of the family jointly. No, she must know God is the God of order, both in church and family: she must hold no quarter with her husband in this business. Two heads in a family confound all: her providence must be under his and be directed by his; running in the same stream with it, tending to one commonwealth, purse, and gain, not her own, but his and the family's. I say, while the husband is himself: for else, he being disabled either by age or infirmities, or some sudden distemper by God's hand, which suffer it not: she is to set to her shoulders to the uttermost rather than the state of the family be perverted. I add also, if he being a man carried by his inordinate lusts, and feeling himself to suffer his estate to decay, shall permit her to look into the affairs of the family (there being no child nor other to be trusted), she may lawfully undertake the charge rather than commit the ship to wind and weather. Moreover, I doubt not but the wife, so far as her skill reaches, being endued with a gift and skill in some mystery, which her husband is not, especially the husband being idle and slothful to improve his own stock, or perhaps having embezzled it already: may be occupied in that calling of hers: provided that she is accountable to her husband, whose stock she occupies: for, if she occupies a borrowed stock, she is praiseworthy for her industry but accountable only to her creditors: in such a case, if she share with him so far as to keep him from beggary, it is enough, for she aims at the support of her family. One thing more I add, if the husband shall allow his wife to undertrade with him, that is, for her own veils and contentment to use some petty stock for her own advantage: so there is no prejudice hereby done to her other housewifery in family, nor to her husband's stock, she may lawfully accept the kindness, provided that in the defect of her own skill, she is guided by his counsel to prevent damage, and improve her gains to the right ends, not the maintaining of sin in herself, or hers. But, setting these and the like limitations aside, she must be wholly in all her course for him and his ends; expecting from his wisdom and love, such recompense as is suitable for her honest support and maintenance. I am not ignorant that many husbands, some for sloth, others to avoid their wife's discontents, supposing to allay their fierceness of spirit by resigning their right, others, under other color of ministerial or burdensome service have,

Limitations of subjection in worldly things.

Prov. 31

and do, put the bridle of providence into their wife's hand (and that, whereas none of the former cautions do require it): but whether this swerving from the ordinance has not weakened their headship, animated the woman to an excess of spirits, causing that nature which of itself is too forward to wax more insolent; let experience judge. Inferiority is ready to despise authority, if occasioned: sin is out of measure unbridled: more easily held off from the occasion, than restrained under the occasion. Besides, that the husband's hand is cut off as it were by the wife's mortmain (for many wives perk up to meddle with the estate, suspecting that their husbands are more ready to do good than themselves) from that bounty, which both his place and will would admit.

But here likewise a question is made, whether it agrees with the wife's subjection to give to good and charitable uses of her own accord? That is, without the husband's consent. To which I answer that the seasons of well doing are to be distinguished. Such occasions there may be offered, and such necessities may lie upon the church, and upon the members of it by the rag of unreasonable enemies, oppressors, and persecutors, even such straights may beset the poor servants of God, as may discharge the wife from ordinary subjection in this case: as in the martyr's days (I doubt not) that many women borrowed leave from heaven to do good, who if they had stayed while they had leave on earth must have waited till their eyes in their head had fallen out, for anything their husbands would have yielded to. They dispensed therefore with their unwillingness in such a case and dispatched the duty. I leave the consideration of such necessities to be judged of by the wise, especially in these our sad times wherein the afflictions of God's church are little thought of by the most, who drink away and forget, eat and sleep, and stretch themselves upon their beds, not thinking of the affliction of Joseph: so they fare well what is it to them though the church perishes? But to return, for an ordinary course she may not put forth her hand to give of her husband's estate of her own head, except first she receives her husband's consent, which I speak because some women might have from their husbands if they would ask, but either distrust of their own loss, or scorn to give it, except they may give it with a high hand of their own, hinders them. A

Question. May the woman of herself give to charitable uses?

Answer. Ordinarily she may not, but in some cases she may.

1. In public miseries of the church.

foul shame for a Christian wife who should rejoice in God's way, and at the largeness of good doing, and honoring of God.

2. Secondly, except she has at the first made some reservation to her own stroke, of some such means, as might (without his notice) supply such uses, which being done, although he should seek to infringe that grant by after-exceptions, yet she ought not to yield to it in conscience, but with love and modesty hold herself to an agreement. But the truth is, many women, who have power enough to do good, do it not, yet blame their husband when the sin lies upon their own base hearts: as also many who have of their own to do it, will spare themselves and do it of their husband's, who indeed eat stolen bread and drink of the waters of a forbidden cistern. Now, I mean by reservation only this, that they have acknowledged no more estate to their husbands than they will yield upon marriage, desiring their jointer to be according.

3. Thirdly, except upon the yielding up of their whole estate to their husband's hands, they make such a mutual compact together that the wife shall enjoy such liberty without jealousy, ascribing to her discretion in that behalf, without jealousy or grudging.

4. Fourthly, except she has allowance by her husband to take to her own use the surplus of such money, as are granted for the expenses of the family (she faithfully providing for it without parsimony, and not defrauding any of their due), for that is to feed others upon rapine and stealth, in such case that which she spares is her own: and the like is the case of such veils as do by a kind of custom, issue undoubtedly to the woman, from her husband's trading.

5. Fifthly, except anything befall her by God's providence, gift, or special bequest of the deceased, wherein her husband does, and has cause to all other a portion, as being derived by her channel unto him.

6. Sixthly, if she does perceive by his behavior and love that when she does anything in that kind before his face, he gives allowance thereto as a gift mutually issuing from both their consents, though not named precisely, yet implied secretly.

7. Seventhly, and in a word, except she knows that such a practice of hers wisely ordered would no whit prejudge her in her husband's thoughts if he knew it, but be taken by him as an act of conscience, not to be opposed.

Decision of the doubt.   But to return, if none of these cases can be safely alleged, it is unlawful for the woman to put forth her hand to her husband's estate, under any color whatsoever. As, that their estate is (God be thanked) great enough to admit it: that they have small charge, and do little by consent, anyway: or, that her husband is extremely base, or that her dowry was more than ordinary; or, if she were again to compact with him, she would not do as she has done; or, because her housewifery is great, she deserves the liberty by her great gains or savings: or, her comparing her lot with other women less deserving than she: or that she is hardly handled, or she is to be pitied and pardoned if (the need of the poor so requiring) she exceeds the rule a little, for the greatness of the good which might so be done. I say not what God may in mercy do in point of covering the goodness of her meaning, if she does it ignorantly, but what right she has to do it, before God. Let such women as enjoy their liberty bless God, and beware lest they stumble at the stumbling block of their iniquity. As for the rest, let them mourn under their cross, but not ease themselves of subjection: knowing that their desires are accepted of God, for the deed, in greater inabilities than these, and therefore resting in their integrity, till God grants them greater liberty. The worst is, many women whine and ask questions while they live under covert of their husbands; who yet, when the Lord has set them free to try all that is in their hearts, have neither questions nor answers to make, but are bound with chains of their own from all good doing: showing that neither credit nor conscience was their motive. And doubtless where there is a sound heart to God, few women are so straited by their husbands, but they might by one means or another win them to some indifference. But for that which I spoke touching the necessity of times and danger of not affording of help to the distressed, and the like cases of extraordinary nature, it is sufficient that the church has been compelled to greater aberrations than this, as appears by Acts 1, and the act of Abigail to David, contrary to Nabal's resolution, may sufficiently evince. And so much for this second branch.

Thirdly, this subjection extends to the whole conversation of the wife in marriage whereof I say this, That she is to be generally attendant to this duty, and to have it in her eye daily, as if written upon her frontlets and fringes of garments, rising up, walking, and lying down with her continu-

The third. Her subjection in marriage converse manifold.

ally, whether God does bless or cross them in their goings out
and comings in: she must carry it written on her forehead,
subjection to my husband. In particular, take these. First, in
point of her attire, the common tenet of gallants and proud
dames is this, that whatsoever fashion is up, be it ever so costly, above her mean, troublesome, be it change, upon change,
have it she will. The fashion she holds is above her husband's
power, she must not be laughed at for her worn suit, because
she is not in the new cut. Peter could not speak of subjection,
but he must necessarily speak of this: as, for the sake whereof,
women otherwise subject, yet for their will's sake, will venture
a joint and forfeit subjection. In a case of meetness of fashion what husband so little delights in his wife as not to allow
her that which is indifferent? But hereupon to run before the
husband, even to that which is uncomely and excessive, either
for fashion or cost, I must tell women, it suits not with subjection. Not in gold (says he) embroidered attire, plaiting of the
hair; but in meekness of the spirit: as if subjection were much
a scene, and most forfeited in this case. I will not run into the
determining of fashions suitable to each degree. Let the so-
berest in every state determine it, and I had rather it should be
the husband should determine, than she. Love will be bountiful enough; and self-love may not be trusted. But oh! The
excess of this sex, both in married women and virgins (even
the wives of those who should be patterns to the world) is so
woeful in these days, and so hideous that it does not only help
to make a world of bankrupts, but to fill the world with curiosity and vanity! Wherefore let this be taken for a rule, never
was there curious, proud, and fashionable women, who could
stoop to be subject; by their ruffling, flinging, flaring, curling,
dresses, tirs, and forelocks, you shall know them. Custom (as
the world thinks) takes away offence: but by that rule nothing should be evil in itself, but in opinion. But a subject wife
puts little difference between such opinion and reality: for she
is known by her modesty, as abhorring to receive luster from
rags, but affording honor to her attire by her sober subjection,
be her attire costly or mean.

Secondly, her very eye, gesture, and speech ought also
to be reverential and mixed with modesty and blushing, arguing her submission and privity to her weakness. There must

1.
In attire.

1 Pet. 3.3

2.
In gesture and
composition
of body.

be a law, that is an authority of grace upon her lips, ordering her silence and speech with a sweet mediocrity, but even as a thread going through a cloth, so a gift passing through the whole man. That which is within, cannot lie hid: for grace will make the face to shine. Her very blush is ivy-bush sufficient, showing what is within. And on the other side lofty carriage, proud and disdainful garb, unsavory tongue, multitude of words, boldness of forehead, stoutness of stomach, loud cry (as Solomon terms it) betrays to all men what a plague her husband nourishes in his bosom. All the honor of such a husband, if it is not turned to contempt while he is present; yet is turned to pity when he is absent. Such a demeanor is more befitting some mannish Amazon or insulting courtesan than a woman of true subjection to her husband.

Thirdly, another piece of her modesty lies in her usual carriage at home, towards her husband's direct person. Familiarity and daily converse will breed no contempt in a subject wife: she is not so by compulsion, but by freedom, therefore she utters it equally and constantly. She fears not that imputation justly cast upon women, who abroad will seem very respective, good wife, let's have more of it at home! Sarah called her husband lord, meaning usually, it was not her holiday livery, but her workday phrase. Not he called her his lady (and yet it were well if such flattery could prevail with some Donnas), but she him lord. This reverence and subjection causes the wife to behold her duty in the countenance, projects, virtue, and way of the husband (as I noted before of consent). His service to God, government to children, and following of business is the glass which represents her: for either she sees all good, if she has skill to discern, or believes it in love, if she has none. But as for a controlling spirit before her head, she hates it as impious and degenerate. To take upon her to be the household oracle and idol, to overtop all, to be under none, is too hot and heavy for her handling, she loathes it as hell, to use Paul's word, for her heart, will, tongue, self, and all are not so much bound, as bind themselves to the peace: only the yoke is easy, and the burden light.

Fourthly, suitable must her subjection be before others, to that which is at home: as coming from one, not ashamed of that, which is her true honor. Many women are in their ex-

3.
Domestical converse must be subject.

Rom. 12

Mat. 11.30

4.
She must be subject abroad.

tremes. Some, although in private, they will not offend, yet, coming into company, think it a kind of slavery to profess the same honor and esteem of their husbands. And indeed, to flatter the husband is but a base office for the wife, whereso-ever, at home or abroad, arguing that a husband loves it. Such cup, such cover; but, wisdom keeps a mean, and abhors as much to smooth and gloss as to despise and neglect; that due reverence and subjection, which a good wife shows abroad, she shows at home, and contrarily: she is loath to have her hand out. Others are in another vein, and although at home, they make no bones to taunt and take up their husbands, yet abroad, are quite other women, so solemn and subject, as if the Anointed of the Lord were before her, as if she were the most subject, and he the happiest living. But as he said to the crab-fish, when she was stretched out in length being dead, but before crooked, so you should have lived; so to these: This should be always, and then safe. But this extreme as the other, a subject woman avoids without pain; for their inward prin-ciple levels all, saying, Whatsoever is according to God must be equal.

5.
In her tongue and company, subject.

Fifthly, her subjection also appears in company. A gadder, a gossip, one whose heels are over her neighbor's threshold, and, being there, is in her element, licentious and talkative, is no subject wife. Solomon calls her turbulent, that is self-willed and unsubject. And well he might: for surely no husband can affect a woman of such a trade, it is his bane, ex-cept he in his kind is a rover and wandering planet, out of his orb, and then better one house troubled with them than two. But whether he is so or not, whether he likes it or dislikes it, he must bear it. She will have her vagaries, her tongue is her own, and she upon her own bottom, and therefore not redeemed with a price, stands and falls to herself, and what lord shall control her? And sure as she cost little, so she is worth as little, and may go for naught. Alas, she is sick of home! There she sits, lowering and pouting, has no desire to say much: but lest you should think she has lost her tongue, she does but keep it, till place and time please her, and there she will be as much on the other side! She is like that fiddler, which was long a getting to pull out his fiddle, but when it was once out, there could be no putting it up anymore. Surely, as some women are fain to fetch their husbands from their ale-bench to shame them; so had some husbands need fetch their wives from their gossips, and yet, it is a question whether they were better to have left them where they were, lest they make a tragedy at home, of a comedy abroad. A modest wife is of another spirit. Home has her heart. She has work enough within doors, and dwells most within herself. She like the snail, carries her house always upon her back. She builds it with her hands, and bears it up by her shoulders; never going abroad, but then when it was an offence to keep at home. And, being abroad, the law of grace is upon her lips; her words are as the leaves of the tree of life, healing: and as the fruit thereof, life itself, and restorative. Out of the abundance of the heart, the tongue speaks: not so much, as well: not so long, as sweetly, seasonably; and when she holds her peace it is with her as with a beautiful face, wherein you know not whether the white or red is fairer, for both are beauty: so you cannot tell whether speech or silence does most commend her; but both do, for she knows both when to speak and when to hold her peace.

Lastly, subjection in a wife reaches to benevolence: for when the Lord set her appetite towards her husband, he planted subjection in her spirit; as also to nursery of her infants, except God deny her ability and strength. No sooner does the infant, which she has warmed in her womb and given life to in her womb, behold the light, but it whimpers and cries for the breast, as if it said, I am yours, nurse me. Look upon your breasts, whether dry or giving milk; if there is milk it is mine, and given you (my dear mother) to be a nurse, my nurse. The subject wife stops not her ear to this call. She seeks not breasts in her husband's purse, but in her own bosom; and, according to her power, takes her babe, embraces and nurses it. Ruth gave her son Obed the breasts, though Naomi dry-nursed it. When Pharaoh's daughter had found poor Moses crying, whom sent she for to nurse it, rather whom sent God to it? Oh the mother, to note God's verdict! No water, like your own: no nurse to the mother. As David of Goliath's sword, so here, it is best of all. None so tender, so chary, or so careful. Physicians for a fee will be suborned to be at the request of an unnatural mother, and to pronounce against the full breasts, and the milk thereof: to advise the husband, if you love your wife, your child, let

6.
In point of
nursery.

Ruth 4.16

her not nurse. Another physician advises the contrary, if you love your health, nurse your child: surely, if the scale hangs so even, if you please, let God cast it, there being no apparent let. A subject wife will bewray it this way, as soon as any: and the apostle joins it with subjection, in the place so often recited. She will do it, if not for her husband's sake who lies in her bosom, yet for that infant's sake which lays in her womb. Though she has not such wages as Moses' mother had for her pains, yet she has assurance of such pay from a better Master, who promises her she shall be saved, that she will do it for his sake, though for neither husband's, nor children's. That fee and wages, next to faith and love, will cause her to look upon her babe even in the worst pickle and hand that belongs to it, with so sweet and smiling a countenance that she would not for the pain of many nursings, forfeit it. Oh you coy woman, what are you? Are you richer than Sarah, weaker than Rachel, better than Rebecca, holier than Hannah, than all those matrons of old, who were honorable in this point of subjection? Whose daughter would you choose to be? Theirs who nurse not, or these? And by these six branches mentioned, judge oh you women of the rest. No one duty of many (I know) is less practiced. Consider what has been said and God give you understanding: love made Jacob count all weathers welcome for Rachel. Let her think all service sweet for him. Thus much for answer to the question, wherein subjection consists. Now to the uses briefly to finish with.

Use 1.
Admonition.
Shun rebellion.

And first let it be for admonition (if yet my words may reach unto and pierce any such) to all sad creatures, unsubject souls in this kind, to shun all rebellion against their husbands. If you will hearken to your corrupt will, it will tell you another tale, and quash all my former counsel. Oh, it will say, you may win the goal, and get the upper hand of your husband forever, if you are damish and imperious. It will make him to seek you, not you him. But subjection will say, that which I will get this way in the Hundred, I shall lose in the Shire. If I lose the better end of the staff with God, what get I by getting it of a poor husband? It is possible I may come short too, even of that; but sure I am, never was an unsubject woman powerful or prevailing with God. Therefore her voice is, A body you have given me, it is written in your book, I shall

do your will, oh God! Lo here I am, speak, for your servant
hears, and cavils not, and my soul answers, your face will I
seek, I will be subject. A Zipporah will throw the foreskin at   Exod. 4.25
her husband, the meekest man upon earth. Michal will say to
the holiest man living, even in the act of his zeal, what a fool
was my husband this day? But a subject one will say, I opened
not my mouth because you bid so: or if I have, once have I
spoken, but I will say no more, but will lay my hand upon my
mouth. If I have erred, teach me, pardon me! By crookedness of spirit, of tongue, I shall lose honor, gain reproach, even
hell too: but, by subjection, as I shall honor my head, so shall
he me! Indeed my yielding is the way to honor myself more
than all my recoiling, and to win that authority in his heart,
which no usurping can ever obtain. As is the shadow, such is
the husband's heart, and love: fall down upon it, and you must
overtake it, if you pursue it, it flees further off. So, if you contest and with strong hand resist your head, he will be as a lion,
and his courage will not stoop: but if you shall speak kindly to
him and win him by subjection, you have conquered him forever. God has appointed him to be over you: in seeking to be
above him, you provoke him to tyranny, and to challenge his
right, but cannot subdue him by rebellion. Remember, your
sex is crazy, ever since Eve sinned, sin is out of measure sinful, through the law, and Satan's incensing, loathes subjection
and affects impotency. But oh, you woman that fears God,
let that liberty with your husband, which your subjection has
purchased, satisfy your heart, seek no more, lest in catching
at the shadow, you lose the substance. Let your birth, your
education, estate, and endowments exceed his ever so much;
yet the ordinance of God has subjected you to your husband
with all your perfections. There is but one law for all wives,
both poor and rich, mean and great, wise and foolish, one and
other, that is to be subject. No Pope, nor prince, much less
the law of your own lust can exempt you: there were wives in
Paul's time, who because they believed, could have shaken off   1 Cor. 7.10
their husbands that were infidels. But Paul meets them ago-
ing, and turns them back with force upon their allegiance and
subjection: saying, except the separation begins from the unbelieving party, do not you who believe, desert the other. As
he said, set meat before them, and break their hearts, but smite

them not: so here, win them by all holy means, but oppose not. If subjection is due to heathens, much more to Christians.

Use 2. Exhortation of wives to subjection.

Lastly, this is exhortation to all wives who will stand to God's bar, be subject to your husbands. Let the spouse of Christ teach you, she is subject to her head: both in heart, she gives it to him; in eye, she delights in his ways, she is so to him in all matters, both of God and the world, she is so in her gesture and speech, abroad, at home, and in all. Be so, and prosper. Without this, none of your inward abilities, outward gifts, or even the graces of God will be a crown to your husband: except it is a crown of thorns. No, if you were ever so housewife-like, fruitful in children, rich in gold or jewels, except you add subjection, all will not amount to the making of a crown, except this makes it, nothing else will. All your jewels may be stolen out of your box, your money out of your purse, clothes out of your wardrobe, your back may be stripped of your costly attire, your beauty blasted with age, your body weakened with sickness, sorrow: your name sullied with infamy, your parts may decay: but your subjection no man shall rob you of, nor your husband of that crown. If you preserve that in your cabinet as your pearl, it shall supply and restore all those losses in the esteem of your husband. This will be the trench of your castle; all darts will fall short of it, as impregnable. Subjection is the true mother of love, sister of consent, root of all other matrimonial service, helpfulness in the next chapter, gracefulness in the next to that shall attend it, as precious handmaids. And she herself in the middle shall walk honorably, and honor marriage above all other virtues. Be it ever so meanly thought, spoken of by the damish and imperious women of the world, yet she will say, if this is to be vile, I will be more vile: truly, those that would disdain me yet shall be compelled to honor me, and say, many daughters have done well, but subjection has surmounted them all. And so much touching the first personal virtue of the woman, to wit, subjection, is spoken.

CHAPTER XIV

*Which proceeds on to the second peculiar
duty of the wife, that is
helpfulness.*

I now proceed to the second special duty of the wife, which is helpfulness. The former gift tells her that she must not be rebellious: this second tells her, what she should be, helpful and useful. It is not enough for her to be negatively good, not harsh, not rude: but she must be positively good, she must also be helpful. This comprises all her true useful service to her husband: and especially answers his providence. She must within doors, lay all her helpfulness to his providence without doors: that by both the whole frame without and within may be supported. She was made subject by sin: but helpful by creation, which yields a choice prerogative to this virtue, being of integrity, not from corruption. Of all the other creatures, says Moses, the Lord found not any one, which might be a meet match for Adam; wherefore he said, it is not meet the man should be alone, I will make him a meet helper: and so, he formed her of a rib out of his side, while he slept. In the former chapter then we treated of a peaceable, in this we must speak of a profitable, and in the next of an amiable companion.

But here in the very entry, a question is to be answered: in how many things stands this helpfulness? I answer, in three main things. First, and chiefly, in help to his soul: secondly, to his outward estate: thirdly, to the married condition: as for instance, to the honor of his name, the health of his body, the welfare of his children, the government of his family, the recovery out of any disaster, the averting of dangers, the advice about things weighty and difficult. I begin with the first of these. Touching which, although I have noted before, that she is to be subject to her husband in matters of God; yet this muzzles not the mouth of a good wife in helpful concurrence, but only in bold usurpation. She may (without hindrance to that) cast in her mites into God's treasury, and be a helpful

*The second
special duty
of the wife,
helpfulness.*

Gen. 2.18

*Question.
Wherein
stands this
virtue of help-
fulness.*

*Answer.
In three
branches.
1.
In God's mat-
ters.*

furtherer of his soul to all spiritual welfare and contentment in knowing, believing, and obeying, so it is done with humility and meekness. Although she is to ask her husband at home in respect of any usurpation, yet (as the case may require) she may, no, she must, in due season, being demanded, reflect back the fruit of that mercy which the Lord has showed, and the cost he has vouchsafed her for the good of her husband. And, as the Lord has gifted and graced many women above some men, especially with holy affections: so, I know not, why he should do it else (for he is wise, and is not superfluous in needless things), save that, as a pearl shining through a crystal glass, so her excellency shining through her weakness of sex, might show the glory of the workman. And how? In being only looked upon or wondered at, as a bird of fine colors? No: but, in reality communicating of that grace which she has, to her husband especially, as also to others in private communion of saints as occasion is offered.

Impudency of usurping women in matters of God, taxed.

One thing here comes to my mind; I would not be taken to patronage the pride and licentious impudence of women, who having shaken off the bridle of all subjection to their husbands, take upon them to expound the Scriptures in private assemblies, and to be the mouth of God to both sexes. Not blushing one bit to undertake by the four or five hours together, even whole days (if their vainglorious humor masked under the colors of humility may be suffered) to interpret the Word: applying it according to their way by reproof, comfort, admonition, and the like, as if women preachers were come abroad into the world. And yet these are such as dare oppose and confute the doctrine of faith and self-denial taught by the most able ministers of Christ: and tell their disciples that there is another way to be walled in, and that is the way of the Spirit which must give such a light to the soul and such an assurance of salvation, as may rid us at once of all doubting, fears, and unbelief, and translate us into a confident and secure persuasion of the love of Christ, without making question. As for any ways, means, trials, motives, and signs whereby the soul may come to be settled about the work of regeneration, these they abhor as savoring of the flesh, and not of the Spirit of light and inward evidence. In this kind they undertake most boldly to expound the Scriptures, and to resist all who are of another mind. Nor allow I others, who defending themselves by the practice of the primitive church, when the extraordinary gifts of prophecy flourished, whereby the moving of the Spirit, men to men, and women to women, did express and utter their thoughts and judgments concerning divine truths, which gift then was very necessary for the breeding up of ministers, doctors, and proctors, they wanting other helps of furniture and supply: but appertains not unto us, who both have ordinary ways of supply, and want that special presence of the Spirit which that first church had, to guide and govern the use of such gifts, orderly and peaceably to such ends as they belonged, without schism and confusion.

God indeed promised by Joel to the church of the gos-   Joel 2.28
pel, that he would pour out his Spirit without difference to all ages, sexes, and states of people: but not in such a disorder that a woman should dare in public, or in a private place after a public manner to declare truths of religion: usurping over men, and encroaching upon the laws of Christ. Such immodesties and insolencies of women, not able to contain themselves within bounds of silence and subjection, I am so far from warranting that I here openly defy them as ungrounded and ungodly: and I cannot but wonder that any should be itching after novelties, as being present in such assemblies, especially themselves being public persons, and such as ought to discern better between things that differ. To both I say, beware lest your pride of gifts, carrying you beyond the bounds of your private condition, and your curiosity in favoring and being led away with such disguised ostentation of graces, do not wrap you within in the sin of Nadab and Abihu, and Uzzah, and Uzziah who under pretext of holiness, adventured to profane hallowed things: moreover, of Korah and his accomplices, who murmured against Moses and Aaron opposing their calling and office. If when you are convinced by the Word, you will yet rebel, take heed lest you perish in his contradiction as Jude speaks, teaching others by their fearful example because they would take none themselves, if such as these had been from God the Devil would not have let them alone so long quiet in their attempts: but he knows distraction in opinions makes him reign in the world. And to these more impudent persons I add all such undertaking women,

Admonition
to all usurp-
ing women
in matters of
God.

who either in families, companies, or in the private converse with their husband, usurp authority, despising the graces of God in their husbands and others, and taking upon them all the speech at the table, to discourse of religion, to debate matters in question in the church, to decide things of difficulty, to spend all the time in hearing themselves talk of good things. These although they think they have learned many things, yet have not learned one great thing, namely, wisely to judge what their sex and state will admit. And therefore though haply what they speak is good, yet it is not comely for them, it is as a garment of good cloth but made into a garment very unfit for the body, for lack of taking measure beforehand. These are not helpers, but hurters by their unseasonableness.

But I digress not too far. No reason there is, why the impudence of the rebellious should prejudice the gifts of a humble wife, soberly improved. Neither does the Holy Ghost envie her the honor of her grace and helpfulness. But as Bathsheba says, Prov. 31.31, *Give her of the fruit of her hands, and let her works praise her in the gates.* Subjection and helpfulness interfere not one bit, both may agree well. Subjection caused the wife of Manoah, when the Angel appeared to her with a

Conditions of modest wives in acting of God's matters.

solemn message, to distrust herself, and to call her husband; when God prefers her, she modestly craves leave, and prefers her husband, and his judgment before her own: deriving her own honor upon him. Howbeit afterwards we see that (the case so requiring) whereas upon the Angel's departure from them, Manoah was left in a carnal fear, lest he should die, having seen God: his wife steps in with her helpfulness, between

Judg. 13.23

him and his fears, saying, if the Lord would have slain us, doubtless he would not have revealed himself unto us in this sort: to tell us we shall have a son, and yet to kill us. She saw further in this case than he, and therefore gives him advice what to settle himself upon. What could more aptly have been spoken? How is that of Solomon verified, a word in season is like apples of gold, and pictures of silver? And, how is Abigail

1 Sam. 25

honored for her wise counsel to a man, who for that her wisdom was so far from disrespecting of her, that he sent for her to be his wife shortly after. So that when David was in the way of heat and resolution to shed Nabal's and his family's blood, she encounters him saying, let not my lord do such a thing as this! It shall not grieve him, when he shall sit upon his throne, that he has not shed innocent blood. Oh! How comely a thing it is for Christian wives to come in thus with humble subjection, sometimes with a soft word to allay wrath, to stay the husband from prejudice against good persons and causes, to interpret all in the better part; to observe him when the Word kindles any affections in his soul, and presently to follow them home, not to suffer them to slip out and vanish: to provoke him to mercy and compassion, to draw him from a natural course to a moral, from a moral to a spiritual, to persuade him to equality and indifference towards such as are at controversy, to debate and decide things peaceably, to stay his hand from immoderate correction of children or servants when she sees passion prevail against judgment: truly, and sometimes with the same meekness and mildness to convince him of an evil quality or pang, as choler, discontent, worldliness, censuring of others, rashness, and the like, admonishing also to beware of the occasions which might lead thereto: wherewith she herself should receive the same from him. Sometimes to win his adverse heart to a more entire love to God's Sabbaths, to his Word preached, to his faithful ministers, and servants: to affect them, to associate them, and to renounce all his old company and fellowship in evil. To be always darting some savor of that which they have heard in public, and prompting him with it, that the world eat not up all. Oh! These things come sweetly as the latter rain, from a woman, who counts it her happiness to see her husband to be brought home to Christ, who mourns for his rebellion, and rejoices to see his heart broken. As Mordecai told Esther, so should a good wife tell herself, who knows whether you are come to your place for such a season, even to bring home one sheep to Christ's fold? Doubtless, if Satan were not a professed foe to such helpfulness, the work would proceed with more ease and success. So much for the first branch.

The next head of the wife's helpfulness is in matters of the world. Solomon as truly said of this as of any other virtue of the wife; that a wise woman builds her house. For though it is little (in comparison) which a poor woman can add to the estate of her husband, yet she must be all in all for the preserving thereof. So that an improvident woman is next

2.
Helpfulness in matters of estate described.

a waster in this respect only, and loses much: but if she is also a spendthrift and really wasteful, there is no end of her spoil till she has brought all to nothing, and overthrown both her husband's state and posterity. She is the moth, truly the canker of the marrow and beauty of his estate, and by insensible morsels, devours at length the whole substance. And because there are many queasy women (yet such as would be religious), that think it a piece of religion to be no housewives, let Bathsheba, a queen who might more stand upon her estate than the proudest dame may upon her dowry; in her instruction to Solomon speak. She describing a godly and helpful

Prov. 31

wife (and not only a thrifty one) as it appears from the twenty-fifth verse to the end of the chapter does couple her virtue and housewifery together. She opens her mouth with wisdom, and the law of grace is upon her lips (there is her grace): and she oversees the ways of her household, and eats not the bread of idleness (there is providence). And lest any should think this latter might be spared, it is to be noted that she spends the whole chapter in the description thereof, by diverse passages: whereas, the former she shuts up in the end of that chapter in a verse or two, although the more necessary: as taking it to be more out of question than the other; moreover, note how the Holy Ghost conveys that instruction by the counsel of a woman to all of her sex, to make the thing less subject to exception: pressing it strongly in an idea of such an exact helper: and that with pleasing rhetoric and variety. Why? Save because she saw it a virtue meet to be urged, as being that which many women will not acknowledge. Neither can the greatness and wealth of wives control this duty of providence, and that not for show either, or complement and praise, to let the world see what skill in spinning, in needlework, or in other matters they have, but for conscience sake. In Bathsheba's days gold and silver were common and as plentiful as the stones and fig trees: and therefore there was not need for queens or their maids to work so hard; and yet for the religion of the duty, she speaks so, as one who had experience of it in her own princely person, and had the oversight also of her maidens in the handling of the wheel and spindle, for flax and wool. And surely in great families both sexes had need to be yoked, and awed from the sins which come from sloth and idleness, although

I add, in a mediocrity, lest they trench upon the contrary of covetousness.

My meaning yet by all this is not to allow any woman the liberty of any such peculiar housewifery by herself, apart from the common stream and welfare of the husband and family, but in common with, for, and under him, though in a way of her own, best fitting her sex and education. For, I know there are housewives who excel in providing for themselves, and (like the steward in the gospel who to prevent beggary, when he should be turned out of service) can shift for themselves, who yet are but ill providers for the good of their husbands whom (to use that emperor's comparison) I may liken to the spleen in the body, which when it is fullest, makes the body emptiest, and so commonly, when the coffers of these housewives are fattest, their husband's treasure is leanest and lankest: whereas she should rather be a pipe to convey into his cistern than a sponge to suck from, or a channel to drain from his fountain. This yet is a common vice: not only of second wives prowling for their own broods or kindred: but of all sorts of women; and is caused by pride of birth, of dowry, education, or person: which to godless ones are occasions to withdraw them from the yoke of supposed bondage, though if a queen may judge of helpful and housewifely providence. In some others it is rather caused by old or late habits of luxuriousness, riotous, and lewd companionship: for now we have meetings of women-drinkers, tobacconists, and swaggerers, as well as men: lest Paul's prophecy of the latter time should be falsified, and (which is worst of all) secret and stolen liberties. These vices are like the daughters of the horseleech, crying, Give, give, but like hell and the grave, never satisfied. Instead of the licentious usurping over the husband's commodities, let women know that although they have a true property and interest in their husband's estates, yet when the use of the same comes into question, the Lord will have it, as well as other things, ordered by the husband. Neither may the bad qualities of the man, as his churlishness, covetousness, and enmity to virtue, authorize the woman to be her own carver; lest if this wicket should be set open to good wives, the bad ones throng in with them also, and usurp it to evil ends. God's law is one, and concerns all sorts indifferently. If women desire a

Wives must not have any peculiar wealth apart from their husbands, but in common.

1 Tim. 4.1,2

If they desire any stroke in dispensing the matters of the husband they must deserve it by good carriage.

stroke this way (as indeed some may more groundedly plead in than others in show), let them labor by their good deserts, to prevail with their husbands, and by their helpfulness and love to draw so good an opinion of themselves that they may with a willing mind, yield this favor to their wives, as to use their pleasure in a sober manner (provided that they spend it upon honest and religious objects). But, if God has laid another burden upon them (as I noted in the former chapter) of ill-natured and strait-handed husbands: let them take up and bear it as the cross which God has set apart for them, without discontentment or grudging. Especially second wives, having the charge of former brood depending upon them (further than by cheerful consent of their husbands, they are allowed), let them beware, lest herein they dishonor their profession, by yielding to the strong and tempting occasions of needy, unruly, and burdensome children, supplying their want by injurious pillage of the husband and his posterity. This by the way.

Three branches of woman's providence.

To conclude the point, these three especially concern the woman's providence; first getting, then storing, and lastly, dispensing those things which are committed to her charge. The first of these three is proper only to those women who sell their husband's commodities, or are allowed to be chapmen of their wares (which is the case of few), or such as by reason of some special skill in any crafts or manufactures, has some stock allotted them by their husbands, to trade and traffic with. In which way, they must use all good faithfulness, neither selling to their husband's loss, nor for their own secret gain, nor the hurt of the buyers, all which rules are in all trading, usually transgressed. Besides the housewifery of many tradesmen's wives, who learn their husband's skill, serve to the making of sundry wares, which serve to the upholding of the family and estate. In which case (as the other burden of family will admit) they are to show their best endeavor, both for the getting in of some part of the maintenance, and saving it from being spent about such household expenses as, by pains and thrift at home might be spared. And this is that which Bathsheba most insists upon. She labors cheerfully with her hands: she is like the ships of merchants. She brings home her food from afar. She arises while it is yet dark, her candle goes not out, she puts her hand to the wheel, and her hands

1.
Act of providence to bring somewhat in.

Prov. 31

to the spindle. She makes sheets and sells them: and gives girdles to the merchant. She considers a field and gets it; and with her hands she plants a vineyard. This is the image of the stirring housewife. It is well nowadays if women would abate of their superfluous ease and needless expenses (which they do the more easily lavish out, because they wholly rely upon their husband's purse) and instead of great merchandize and selling of wares abroad, apply themselves at home in private, about the supplying of the family wants, helping to clothe and lodge them by their diligence: for better and more enduring is that ware which is made than that which is bought: taking occasion thereby to busy their children in meet employments, and to prevent sloth, ease, gadding, stolen liberties, and vanities which the unbridled minds of maids, both of children and servants, are in these days pestered with, loathing labor and painfulness, and exposing themselves to the vices issuing from that time.

The second act of providence in the wife is the bestowing and safe storing up, preserving, and improving those commodities which her husband has brought to her hand. Which, as it is fit they should be put to her trust, so ought she (especially in her husband's absence) to be careful of them, that they decay not under hand, that they are not open and exposed to the stealth or spoil of servants, or violence of others. And herein, not only herself in person is to be provident, but also to be careful to oversee the ways of such servants or others, as are under her, as instruments to act that, which other business or infirmity hinders herself from performing. A wise housewife will contrive and dispose as well by sitting still and using her brain, as some other by bending the force both of soul and body. She cannot keep things from putrefaction, from rust, from fust and spoil, from moth eating and decays: cannot perhaps do each inferior work serving to keep all things neat and shining: but she may so oversee the ways of others, that they may prevent such losses, and procure such conveniences as are meet for the family. So that she may ease her husband from the inspection and care of such things as concern not his providence: to which task, if he is put, either for the things themselves or for the seasonable dispatch thereof, she should much discredit her providence and pru-

2.
Women must
be their husbands' storers
and treasurers.

dence, and burden her husband: whose work lies in a deeper and higher kind. Not, as if the husband should (as Laban of Jacob) exact each penny of the wife which miscarries, or be implacable for those losses which cannot be avoided (since his own wisdom cannot prevent many), but that she by her care must serve providence that no such complaints are heard of as might provoke him justly. As for losses which befall by the hand of God, both equally must patiently bear them. This is pithily alluded unto in that simile where Christ likens a good scribe or disciple taught to the kingdom of God unto the good housewife, which stores up both old and new, that is family provision of all sorts, which she brings out in their season, for meet use. Otherwise, what comfort should the man have in his bringing in supplies for family, household stuff, bedding, linen, apparel, and daily diet for the body if he might not trust to her fidelity at home to preserve them, to manage, to dress and proportion them to the use of the family? And surely, if she does her part wisely herein, neither on the one side being so loose in her storing that everyone may come by her commodities as freely and boldly as herself, to spend and spoil, to drink and embezzle at pleasure; nor on the other side abusing her authority and the power of the keys, so that she straiten the family of their due, and strangers of their hospitable welcome, for her own pinching and base ends: but go in a wise middle between both. I say, so doing, it may be said, there goes no less care and praise in upholding a house built than in building it from the ground: and she deserves, in her kind, equal commendation with her husband.

Mat. 13.52

3. In her dispensing.

The third therefore, is her dispensing and bringing forth the provision thus stored up, for the good of the family in due season, due manner, and due measure. For why? She is the man's steward and pensioner, and almoner in this kind, to divide the ration to the family and the poor of the place; and Bathsheba omits not this either in her idea of the good housewife: saying, she fears not the snow, for her family is all clad in scarlet: by snow meaning whatsoever want or affront may befall, and by scarlet, all defense or furniture for the family, and that which is not only for necessary, but sometimes also for honorable and comfortable allowance. And again, her husband is known in the gates, meaning by the livery which he disdains not to wear, because it is the work of her hands. And further, she gives a portion to her household and the ordinary to her maids. In these three stand the woman's thrift and providence: which they who want, must learn and count it worth a double dowry, as knowing that many a naked bare wife is better than some waster clothed in velvet, with her weight in silver. To this pertains the due observation of the seasons of the house: that inferior things prejudice not the better and more weighty matters of God, that all is done with foresight and forecast, that the members of the family want not that provision and due diet, attendance, and nursery which is meet for them, both in health and sickness: the younger children (under her care) are taught, trained, directed, and furnished, and the elder provided for according to their needs.

And such wives as have obtained and do improve this gift well, must beware of pride and self-conceit, that they take not occasion hereby to swell as if they were the props of the house: or else to cover themselves under it when they are reproved for other foul blemishes (for excellent parts in one kind are attended with sad corruptions). We read of Abner, the captain of Saul's army and protector of his house, that he was a great champion for Ishbosheth, a man of great courage and valor: but he was another way as lewd, unclean of body. Ishbosheth, being too young a novice to deal with such a politician chides him for it, Why have you (says he) gone in to my father's concubines? Abner, privy to his deserts, could not bear it, but flourishes against him, and upbraids him with his great exploits. Am I a dead dog, that you so speak to me about this woman? Is this the thanks I have for my great service to your father and his house? Must I be so taken up for halting? You shall know that I have been your patron! God do so to me, and more, if I give you not over and turn to your enemy David! Behold, how the Devil will so pride a man in any great gift that he will take scorn to be found fault with, looking that his merits should plead pardon for all his defects. So it is with many women (otherwise housewife-like and commendable) that they are waspish, froward, holding their husbands at stave's end, or otherwise tainted! But, will they endure to be told of it? By no means. Have I this (say they) for my providence and diligence? Furthermore (as Joab despitefully told

Provident wives' right hand must not know what their left does.

2 Sam. 3

David in his heaviness for Absalom, so they cast their husbands in teeth), I see now, if I had been wasteful and licentious, I should have been better accepted! Truly, a waster is not much worse than a shrew: thrifty or unthrifty you are little accepted, except subject and peaceable. Rather your one virtue should make you more studious of others, careful to shun other vices which should sully and darken them: but they run into another vein and ask their husbands, What if you had such a wife, so expensive and costly as this or that man has? Alas! What froth of a base heart is here! Who will deny, but a virtuous wife may sometimes come short of an exact housewife? Does that argue, that such a housewife may plead it, to defend all her grosser qualities? The town-clerk said well to the people of Ephesus, Diana is a great goddess indeed, who can deny it? But what is that to this confused mutiny and outcry? So here.

Acts 19.35

Therefore, O woman! If you are so worthy, let your right hand be ignorant of what your left hand does: let others praise you, not your own lips! Your bad qualities will sooner blemish your good than your good excuse them. For who, seeing a ring of gold in a swine's snout, wishes it not upon some fair finger rather than to be disgraced by the swine! It is true that a wasteful women is the bane of her husband in one kind, but so may the thrifty in another by her shrewishness; poison may kill, as well one, as kill many ways. And what avails it a man if he must die, that he rather is hanged than beheaded? They are but two ways to bring to one death. And what folly is it to turn off the accusation of a fault which admits no defense, by that virtue which is neither blamed nor aimed at! Join other good parts with providence, and then the lump shall be holy! But one sinner destroys much good; one dead fly mars a great deal of sweet ointment; as Solomon says of two duties, so apprehend the one, as you withdraw not your hand from the other. So I say to you, so lay hold on providence, that yet you renounce not your subjection! She that fears God shall come out of both extremes. There is no necessity that one is fallen upon by shunning the other! Ungodly improvidence is bad, and brutish drudgery is worse: the droil overloading herself with moiling and care, disables herself from goodness, and the improvident by her sloth, deprives

Admonition
to the wife
against this
evil.

Eccles. 7

herself of all opportunity, either of doing good or taking it.
The middle way is the golden way. Thus much of the second
branch of the wife's providence, in matters of the world.

The third and last follows and that is, in the service
of the married life, in the manifold passages of which, both
towards his person, his state, body, life, health, name, and posterity, she must be helpful. To this end she was made; of all
good couples that is verified, *two are better than one because
they have a good reward for their labor.* Eccles. 4.9. And if
one fall, the other will lift him up again. And if one prevails
against him, two shall withstand him: and a threefold cord is
not easily broken. Mark, the Lord has appointed marriage as
the union of two weak ones apart, to become a strong twist in
one cord, to make one strength. This is true of all combinations, two students, two partners, two travellers, two neighbors, and two friends, but above all, most true in the married
estate. In the absence of the one, the other is present; when
one is down and sick, the other (commonly) is up: in the ignorance, doubts, inexperience, and fears of the one, the other
is a helper at hand. Two see more than one: by my wife's ear,
foot, hand, and wisdom, I see, walk, work, contrive, and dispatch businesses which else I could not. No such vicegerent,
coadjutor as the wife, whether together or asunder. Though
the head has the leading part, yet the body has the attending
part, neither without other could effect anything. The acts of
marriage are reciprocal. As we see in them that handle the
long saw, there must be a pair of hands reciprocating the tool
through the timber, or else no sawing it into pieces. A helper
without a head is better than a helper alone. A little to insist
upon each particular.

First, the wife is to be a helper to her husband's person: even a bulwark, a fort (in distress) of safeguard and defense. She is but a little one, but oh, shall I not escape thither
and be safe (said Lot in that storm)? So is she a covert under
God against the storm and rain. She is so under covert that yet
she is a covert again. She is not terrible as banners, but she is
a safe buckler of defense against any impression of danger, of
enemy: either foreseeing and preventing, or meeting and re-
pelling it. Despise her not, there is a blessing in her. A woman
once delivered a city: another overcame an army, a third slew

Branch 3.
Of the
woman's
providence, in
the conjugal
life.

It stands in
sundry par-
ticulars.

1.
To his person.

a tyrant: yet there was another, a wife, Abigail, who objecting herself between her husband's side and David's blow, saved the one and the other from bloodshed. Such a prop was that poor Shunammite, who without any din or distemper, locked up her dead child, brought home the prophet, who restored it to life. She is not as Delilah, who bringing Samson into a sleep upon her knee, betrayed his life saying, *The Philistines be upon thee.* She is a Michal, who when her husband was escaped from Saul, laid an image in the bed to while the pursuers as if he had been in bed, but thereby preserved his person from

2.
Soul.

Job 2.9

Acts 5.5

1 Kings 21

3.
To his health
of body.

slaughter. She is a like preserver to his soul (a little to harp again upon this string) suggesting wholesome counsel to it. Her voice is quite contrary to that of Job's wife, not *curse God and die*: but, Continue (dear husband) in your integrity! Be your crosses what they will be, still trust and wait, deny not the Almighty! We shall see a good end one day. She is not as Jephthah said of his poor daughter, among them that trouble him, that damn him, and lay a snare to entrap him in sin, or consenting to him in sin, as Sapphira to Ananias: nor yet careless which end goes forward, so she may compass her wicked contentment, as Jezebel in Naboth's death made way for her own, and her husband's ruin. If she can keep him close to God she will: but she will never bid him curse God, renounce obedience, and die. Next, she is a helper to his bodily health (next under God), by keeping the precious castle of his body in good estate, for the health, strength, and vigor thereof. It is a proverb made in favor of a good wife, that if the husband looks well they say he has a good wife. She is his nurse to dress and provide him savory meat, such as his heart loves: she knows his body, to what ails he is subject, his diseases and distempers are known to her chiefly. She must order his diet, she must dissuade him from what is hurtful, present what is wholesome, and that not in a seeming curiosity, but in a real and cordial carefulness. She must be his welcomer to entertain him from his wet and cold journeys with warmth, with harbor, with comforts and refreshing: for his heart trusts to her for it, and no colds, wets, heats, or ill journeys can be wearisome to him, having so helpful a yokefellow at home to receive him. If he is sick, she is his best messenger to the physician, best and most tender keeper under his physic, best cook for kitchen physic at home, and must be the best instrument for recovery. For why? She took him not only for health and prosperity, wherein he can provide for himself, but for sickness and disasters, wherein he relies upon her helpfulness.

Again, she is as the shield of his precious name and good report. Suffers no fly of her own to light upon that ointment, is impotent to endure or put up any base aspersions upon it; honors it and the merit and repute of it, has a special faculty to commence and procure a high esteem of his virtues in the hearts of all, especially in the hearts of such as are worthy to honor a man, and shuns all occasions which might cause the basest to defame him. She has always a covering ready to carry backward upon his nakednesses and blemishes: such I say as are to be covered. And such, as she is forced to confess (as Nabal's churlishness and folly by Abigail) she is rather haled thereto by necessity than prone to it with delight. She abhors them whose fingers always itch at the disgrace of their husbands. She chooses to come between his folly and his shame by catching the wound upon her own flesh, and leaving her own bleeding rather than violate his, for enduring others to derogate therefrom: she puts no great odds between the one or the other: knowing that her own cannot be entire, if his is hurt, much less thinking his loss to be her gain. Fifthly, to his family she is an absolute helper by necessity, and cannot be spared: not only in point of housewifery, but also in the dispensing the affairs of it within. She crosses not her husband in any labor and education of children; she trains and instructs the tender fry (fittest for her hand) till more meet for his oversight: joins with him in his reproofs and corrections (knowing that Satan reigns in the children by the division of parents), holds not his hand from due strokes, but bares their skin with delight, to his fatherly stripes; defends neither hers, nor his children in their sin. And yet, as the case requires, plays the kind mediator, alienating the extremity of both words and blows lest they be discouraged, yet by consent, for the breaking of their hearts. She counts it her glory, by her lenity and love, with all innocency to keep accord between the children of diverse broods, indifferently ensuing both their welfare; if not with equal nature, yet with the same conscience; not seeking to drive the current of her husband's heart to her own, but

4.
His good name.

5.
His family.

letting it have free passage to them who are equally his. She is not in words but in truth, not a stepmother unto them: as loath to betray the one as the other to their father's wrath, or to God's: rejoicing when they are furthest off the dint of either. Not as Eve, who first had inevitably betrayed all her posterity to ruin, together with herself, before her husband knew it, and then himself. Not looking at her own maintenance, and holding the rein in her own hand, without respect to what becomes of them, or after the death of her husband, unnaturally suffering them to perish while her cruel eyes look on.

6.
In all difficulties.

Moreover she sticks close to him in all difficulties (moreover most then, that like to God, she may be most seen in the mount), as well as when his successes are most prosperous. In the affront of any ill news, losses, discontents, and injuries she keeps off the dint of sorrow from his spirit, wipes away the tears trickling down his cheeks, turns off what might incense, ensues what might satisfy and give him contentment, and putting under her helping shoulders to bear any common burden, which must be borne. Although her own neck lies upon the block, and she suffers under any special vexation lying on her spirit, yet she abhors to be moaned or eased by outcries and sorrows: rather taking it to herself, and biting it in to her own regret, than willing that for the sake of one, the whole family should be in disquiet, saying with that wise Shunammite, God can reconcile all disproportions, be quiet my soul, bite not upon the bridle, but wait and all shall be well. And as

7.
Bearing hardship.

a branch hereof, add this in the last place, that if God frowns upon their estate, she makes no mutiny nor clamor against heaven or husband, her lot and ill chance (for she knows no such goddess as fortune), but rather by her own example in submitting to providence, to fare hardly, to be attired homely, when better supply fails; she draws her husband's spirit from impatience and inequality to equanimity and subjection. In submitting of her soul to God, even when his hand is sad, and the rod is sharp, she finds sensible ease: waiting meekly until God turns the wheel, and (with Naomi) brings her home to her wonted welfare. And this shall serve for a draught of the third branch of the woman's helpfulness in the conjugal conversation.

Use 1.
Reproof.

Now it is time to finish the chapter with some use.

And first of sharp reproof. For to this end has the Lord framed woman as I have said; but she has found out new inventions; and indeed she was the first that set her wits on work in this kind. Alas! How many women have we, helpful to others with the hurt of their husbands? Others, helpful to their husbands, with the hurt of others. A third sort, helpful to themselves, whatsoever hurt befalls their husbands. And lastly, some neither helpful to themselves, nor to their husbands, but hurtful to all: but still the helpful wife is rare to come by. And, as we see that first helper of man, created most perfect, yet instantly degenerated and became the greatest hurt to him and his, so her grandchildren still tread in her steps, so that few husbands there are, but may say with Adam (and much more justly) the woman you gave me has undone me. If it had been a stranger, an enemy, I could have borne it: but behold, she that is with me out of one dish, drank out of one cup, dipped her morsels in the same vinegar, lay in my bosom, and was one with me, she has been as rottenness to my bones, as smoke to my eyes, and as a continual dropping. Oh! If the eye is blind, how great is that darkness? And, if she who was made for the choicest helper (for what earthly comfort is like her who is like herself) proves a plague and hurt to a man, how great must that wound prove? As the discord of brethren is therefore like the brazen bars of a palace (because they are in place of nearest lovers), so the hurt of a wife is unspeakably intolerable because she breaks that law in pieces, which ordained her to the contrary. For there is a cursed generation of women, out of measure sinful, whose chief revenge is to whet their misery upon their husbands and to kill their hearts, not only with despiteful tongues, but also malicious attempts, professing they do it to cross them.

Such as these I deny not to be helpers, for they help their husbands to a sad heart, to a weary life, to bitter complaints to such as they dare trust (for if they had no bosoms to empty it into, their hearts would break), to an empty purse, to a rotten name, to a ragged coat, they help them (before they are done) to the sheet, to the stocks, to the gallows, and to hell itself, without mercy, by their several hurtful inventions. Thus was not Abigail to Nabal (though a beast), if she had scorned him so far as to renounce helpfulness; she would not have en-

What kind of helpers wasteful wives are.

dangered her life for his safety; but left him to shift for himself. But such precedents as Delilah, Jezebel, Job's wife, and the like, helpless, hurtful wives, joying rather in their husband's harms, and thrusting them forward when they are falling, better suited to many of our wives than that outworn end of Abigail's. Alas! Such a pattern serves rather for wonderment than honor and imitation. Do we not see how jolly and proud dames set up a private wealth to themselves with neglect of the common good of husbands and families? Have we not coy pieces that affect a singularity of diet, apparel, company, and lofty carriage above and apart from their husbands? Public shame (which yet now restrains most abuses) not curbing these! Are those helpers that jolly it out and ruffle it in the misery, debts, bankruptcy, and dejection of their husbands, brave in their ruffs and clothes when they are all ragged, costly in their fare when they are fain to bite short, sit at the upper end of the table when Tom fool must stand with finger in hole behind the door? Are these helpers or harlots, think you! How else should it be verified of women, which is foretold of all sorts by Paul, in these latter days, they should be lovers of themselves, proud, unnatural, and treacherous? What traitor is like a bosom one?

And well might these proverbial speeches arise, that a man may thrive if he has his wife's good will: or, a man that marries a second wife with children need take no thought to purchase house and land. These argue that although the case may be otherwise in many wives, yet generally it is dangerous, especially in second marriages with widows.

Use 2.
Exhortation.

Secondly, be it exhortation to all that would be good wives, that they be helpful ones. As once that worthy divine Master Perkins wrote upon his study door: You are a minister of the Word, that do: so should a good wife upon her palms and fringes, for a helper you were made, this look to, mind the end of your creation, carry it with you as your charge, I was made for a helper. Not for a helper one way, and a hurter, ten: but only a helper. So that, as law is the soul of the state, the soul is wholly and in each fringe of the body, so should my helpfulness begin at husband and animate to all the family. But especially it should be the life of my husband; his soul I am bound chiefly to help, by godly counsel: his spirit I must help,

by my cheerful behavior: his body I must cherish with my best
benevolence; his name I must tenderly honor, his sorrows I
must wisely mitigate; his joys, I must sympathize; his dangers,
I must prevent, his health and state I must uphold: and when
I have thus done, as the bee gathering honey, as the sheep
bearing a fleece, as the ox plowing the ground, as the builder
framing the house, not for their own uses, but the commodity of others; so must the helpful wife, all these I have done,
not for myself, but for my husband. Truly, look what instinct,
nature, and art have put into these creatures, that have grace
and helpfulness put into me. A helper I was made for, this
oh Lord, let me look to! If I do it of a willing, virtuous mind
there is praise! If not, yet a necessity is laid upon me, and, woe
to me if I am not a helper! Whoever shunned or waived the
end of their creation, but vengeance pursued them as traitors
to nature, to heaven! I was not made for myself, but for another: each part of the house claiming a part of me. As he said
once to a coy virgin, Your virginity is not all yours to dispose
of: in part it is your parents', father has a stroke in it, mother
another, and kindred a third. Fight not against all, but be his,
whom they would have you. So say I to you being a wife and
a helper: your womanhood, your helpfulness is not yours, it
is your husband's, his body, state, and posterity claim it from
you: he lays claim to all, not as that tyrant did, all your wife's
silver and gold is mine: but as one that is invested in all you
have by peculiar providence. I live not by rule or examples:
the unhelpful shall not teach me to be a hurter: the helpful
shall not so teach me as if I followed for their sakes only, but
for his, who has subjected me to helpfulness.

  Lastly, it is an encouragement to all good wives, to
look off from the degenerate practice of this world, which
might pull them from this virtue. If she is such a helper to
you, oh husband, as I have said, comfort yourself in her, comfort and encourage her yourself against all dismays. And if
she is so towards a lewd companion who has not the grace to
prize her: let me here from God encourage her. God requite
you poor soul, for the world cannot, your husband will not.
God make his way the strength of the upright, in the thankfulness of both. You can do no more than you can. If a bad husband will yet ruin all, well, yet as long as you could, you have

Use 3.
Encourage-
ment to help-
ful wives.

held cart on wheels. The Lord shall be your helper, the strong helper of a helpful wife. Others shall help you. You shall not be forsaken in your greatest straits. And touching this second duty of the wife, namely helpfulness, so much.

CHAPTER XV

Concludes with the third and last several duty
of the wife, namely, her gracefulness.

I conclude now the discourse about the several duties of the woman to the man: whereof this is the last, namely her gracefulness. The former alone without this, will make a good drudge, but this added thereto will make a good wife. They say, He who has gotten both profit and pleasure together (for they are not always joined) has hit the nail on the head. But in a wife, I am sure it is so: if she is useful by her housewifery and cheerful by her graceful amiableness, she is right and straight indeed, and well accomplished. Some, yet none of the worst housewives are none of the most graceful creatures: their droil always hangs about them, as an ague in the bones: and others amiable and cheerful enough, are yet none of the most housewifely and helpful: as the apples of Sodom, if they are but touched with a finger to be useful, they molder to ashes. The former are good droils to dispatch business, the other pretty idols to look on. But the compound of these two has no fellow to reconcile into one a helpful gracefulness, and a graceful helpfulness. Of all other duties, I need least insist in proving that this woman makes her marriage honorable: and therefore, that she is bound to improve herself in this kind to the uttermost, for the attaining of it. This virtue of itself speaks (as Abel being dead) without words. This third gift is nothing else, save that complexion and luster which arises and rebounds from the mixture of the graces of a woman, duly compounded. As from the well mixed elements arises bodily temperament, and from the blood well mixed in the face arises beauty: so from a well tempered spirit in a woman arises this gracefulness. As once that philosopher said, If virtue could be seen with the eye, it would ravish a man with admirable loves of her: so the graces of a woman breaking through her, and appearing in the conversation, are able to ravish any spirit that is not a stoic, a Nabal. A little then first of the materials, then

The third
peculiar duty
of the wife,
gracefulness.

Wives must be
gracious and
graceful.

What graceful-
ness is.

of the true form and temper itself of this gracefulness.

Two things in
this.

1.
Matter of it.
Grace.
1.
Humility.
1 Pet. 3.4

For the former: grace must be the matter of it. But what grace? Surely graces fly together as birds of a feather, and link as the pieces of a chain: yet there are pearls which shine more than their fellows: and some graces do more befriend and beautify a good wife than others. The first may be humility and a meek spirit, for what is more unwomanly, unpleasing than a mannish heart of stoutness and stomach, and what so decks a woman as that whereby she is of great esteem with God himself? So is she that walks in a due and daily sense of her infirmities, a modest concealment of her graces. Not Saul's tallness, but hiding himself away from honor did most grace him. Not a scholar's art, opened all at once, but the concealment of it, most graces him. So, not a woman's part, but that so frail a creature should be above all that is in her, is as the varnish which makes all the picture so amiable. Why do we think Greek and Hebrew ill bestowed upon a woman except that it is above her ordinary sex to know it, and to know herself too: yet if I should behold a woman of excellent parts of learning, and yet to be as one that knew not her own knowledge, but drowned all in the spiritual sense of her corruption, I should think I saw a rare object. She is little in her own eye: yet that littleness makes her greater in God's eye, more precious in man's eye than that great gift with which she is furnished.

A second grace is self-denial. A mere scholar is grown into a character of disdain: and so is every other thing that is mere: a mere woman is a homely sight because ordinary. But a woman above a woman, her wits and abilities: and especially a woman above her wrath, envy, self-love, and passions: a woman above her gains, pleasures, and earthly contents: having all and yet above all: pestered with all and yet overcoming all, is an object of admiration. The Spirit of God, to affect our spirits, presents strange objects in his Word, women captains, warriors, and conquerors: what a pretty thing it is to see Jael to master a great general of the field with her hammer and nail? Deborah to sit and judge Israel? What a miracle was our maiden Queen Elizabeth to the world? Why? But because we think we see, and can scarce believe our eyes in seeing those virtues which were admirable in the man, to reside in a weak sex, as it were out of place. So, the Lord presents to us in his Word his masterpieces, an Abigail without sword or bow, conquering a conqueror, and leading him captive with her self-denial and wisdom. And in experience we see here and there one (as a berry or an olive, left behind) who can master a fierce husband's anger by her longsuffering and self-denial: one that can rule her passions, which rule all sorts. Why, save that we might admire our God as much in the ant's sagacity, as the elephant's strength? If he who can overcome himself, then much more she who can do so, is greater than he who has overcome a city! Oh not always in great things is goodness: but always in good is greatness, especially when that good is also little!

A third grace of a woman is faith, both for the truth of it and for the life of it. For the former, what is of more worth than precious faith? Paul says it is not of all, women or men: it is a flower growing in the gardens, a precious jewel worn in the bosoms of very few of this sex. What can calm the soul save pardon and grace from the promise of a Father, the blood of a Mediator? What can make a woman peaceable and of a quiet frame, save because all is well between God and herself? And what is that grace which settles the soul in this grace save faith, the fruit of the lips and mother of peace? They say there was once a famous lady in the English court that calmed the differences of all the courtiers, and therefore they called her Jane-Makepeace. This lady faith is that lady Jane: a meet ornament, not for court only but country also. Jane-Makestrifes each house is full of, but of Makepeaces, very few. Oh this grace's absence makes all amort! Women's unquietness of nature, wrath, scolding, and distempers, come not so much from outward causes, or inward humors, as for lack of this lady faith. Their hearts are wicked, casting up mire and dirt in the family, like the raging sea, casting up her own foam and all, because the peace of God which passes understanding, and settling the soul by faith, is wanting. Some, what they once had in creation, have lost it by corruption, cannot recover it by faith, and this disquiets them: the loss of a pig, a chicken will vex by consent, because there is a worse vexer within. But, as we know, if a woman had found a pearl worth a hundredth pound, she would be overjoyed (Christ speaks but of a groat), so that if she should hear she had lost one of her goslings, it would little affect her: so if this faith was within the bosom,

3.
Faith.
1.
For the truth of it.
2 Pet. 1.2
2 Thess. 3.2

the losses of toys, the occasions of common anger in the family would cease. That would change all, as Christ calmed the sea.

And secondly, for the life of it, what gold is so precious as is the trial of faith: marriage is as full of troubles, as a crown of cares. Sorrow there is sufficient to each day: to a woman by name, breeding, bearing, and bringing forth: many losses she meets with, false aspersions, fear of debts, wrong of ill neighbors and enemies, deprival of health, her dearest children, sundry diseases, and ill successes: what was then the life of a woman under all these but misery, if she believed not in the son of God and hoped for a good end? That although she cannot say, all is, yet she may say, all shall be well, when

the hour of redeemed ones is come. This life of faith will make the bush though it burn, yet not to consume, and will bring the Son of God to walk with her in the hot furnace, who will keep away the savor as well as the power of fire from them. Therefore Sarah and the widow of Zarephath, and of Shunem, and Rebecca, are brought in as believers in that cloud of witnesses, as well as Abraham, and Isaac, and Jacob. So base is

that speech of some atheists, that women must meddle with no faith, but wrap themselves up in their husband's.

A fourth grace is innocency and truth. A compound of two in one. The one is a breastplate of defense, the other a golden girdle to gird all other graces of God's Spirit close to her. These I grant are pieces of armor for champions: but I understand myself to speak of women captains and conquerors, as I told you before: and you know faith is no effeminate grace (though feminine) but overcomes the world. And why should a shield of faith (which serves to defend both the body and the armor of it too) go without a breastplate and a girdle? Deborah if she will go into the field, she must be armed, and a woman is not free from assaults and peril, shot and darts, as well as a man in this field of the world: therefore must learn to put on this armor. God has no other for men than women: though women must not put on men's apparel, yet they must be clad in the same armor of light. That will make them shot-free. The Emperor Charles the Fifth went among the thickest of his soldiers and told his men that a true emperor was never shot with a bullet. But I am sure of this, that this breastplate is armor of proof. An innocent, harmless, quiet woman, shall not be ashamed to meet her enemies in the gates, even though it were of hell; when things come to be debated, her uprightness and righteousness shall deliver her: innocency shall be her defense against evil tongues abroad, and truth against an ill conscience within; whereas the guilty and treacherous woman will betray herself and lose the day. That very harlot, true in nothing but that she was the infant's mother, by her truth escaped the sword's censure. A mischievous woman, or a woman-liar, who can endure? And who would not go or ride a far journey to see this other warlike woman? Those heroines of whom story and poets so talk, as Penthesilea and the like, were not so graceful a sight, nor those Amazons that seared off one dug that they might shoot, were no such spectacles as these women, clad in innocency and truth. Their name is more fragrant than sweet ointment, and there is no dead fly to make it stink.

    A fifth grace is zeal and piety. For the former, it serves to make the woman a stirring housewife for God, as diligence makes her so for her husband. Meekness in her own matters well becomes her who is earnest in God's. If a woman would be hot and fiery, let her turn it to God, and for his cause, and this will make her cool and calm in her own. As bleeding on the arm by art stops unnatural bleeding by flux: so zeal for God cools the heat of corrupt passion to man. This grace becomes this sex, the rather because it argues truth of grace: for else calmness of her frame naturally carries her to flatness and fulsomeness. It must be with a Christian woman as it is in nature with the female sex of the creatures. Nature has put a fierceness into the female because of the impotency thereof: therefore the she-bear, the lioness, are the most raging and cruel. But grace makes that natural impotency of the woman turn impotency for God: as to provoke her husband with sweet affections for his servants and worship. It was a great praise for the sex that God would send his prophet in the famine, rather to try the piety of the widow of Zarephath, a heathen, than any of the sons of Israel. And it was the honor of those wealthy women, Joanna the wife of Herod's steward, and other the like to be the pious supporters of the Lord Jesus' body, when he had not whereon to lay his head. And at this

5.
Zeal and piety.

1 Kings 17.9

Luke 8.3

day, if estimation is made, God is as much, if not more honored with the forwardness of women than of men: their nature (being fearful) has ever been more prone to superstition: as in Ezekiel, those women that wept from Tammuz, those devout Grecian gentlewomen stirred up by the Jews against Paul: and where they are out of the way, none are worse: but grace overruling corruption, turns superstition into zeal and devotion, into religion, and then it is comely.

Men's hearts not generally so tender and zealous as women's, if they are right.

Men's spirits are hardier, do not so easily fear majesty, tremble at judgments, believe promises, shun sin, and love good, as women: so that when they are in the way, none are better: none sooner embrace the gospel, if it comes anew to a place, none more readily join together in communion, none more tender hearted to the distressed, and such as suffer for Christ's name. God has his women that wove scarlet and twined linen for his tabernacle, as Manasseh had for his idols. Oh! How sweet a sight is it to see these votaries, not of the Pope, but the Lord Jesus! Who can think of that honorable Countess of Richmond and Derby without admiration: the founder of so many colleges and hospitals? I omit to speak of all: whose praise is in the gospel. We have many worthy women in our days, exceeding men in these pieties and zealous duties. Oh go on! Hold your daily intercourse with God! Keep quarter with heaven, have your conversation where your treasure is: and with that famous piece of devotion, old Anna, a widow who for above sixty years dwelt in the temple and ceased not to fast and pray: go on, some of you had need to do it for your husbands and yourselves too, for surely they do it but little! The closet of a good woman graces her more to frequent than her still-house, kitchen, or parlor: for therein she plays the good housewife for her own soul; being much in meditation there, in prayer, in brokenness of heart, confession, and renewing of covenant. As for Michal, who scorns zeal in her husband, has none in herself. Oh let not your soul come into her counsel.

6. Grace, mercy, and compassion.

Suitable to this piety to God is mercy and compassion to his saints, when the former, Psal. 16.2, falls short of God, let the latter be tendered to his assignees and attorneys, the saints. So says Bathsheba, she stretches out her hand to the poor, truly reaches it far to the needy. Some women clothe their own with scarlet, but suffer the poor to go in rags. Surely cotton or coarse cloth, or canvas is due to these, if scarlet to them. Turn scarlet rather to common cloth than the poor go naked. Women, especially ministers' wives (who if bad, of all other commonly are worst) must think themselves meant, when Christ says, I was naked, hungry, in prison, poor, and sick; and you clothed, fed, visited, and relieved me! Be blessed women if you are wise. Your husbands make you their almoners and stewards, beware you prove not thieves, that the poor should curse you. A gift comes more tenderly from you to a poor soul than from your husband. What sight of the basest miser is so irksome as of a hard-hearted woman? And what ornament so becoming a tender sex as a merciful heart, to give, and to give tenderly in compassion, abundantly to six and seven? Both are bowels: and a woman should have more (by right) than men. Tabitha began betimes, God would not have her die, perhaps lest wives might lose the honor and example of mercy. If being a maid she had so many good works to show, of linen clothes made for the poor, what did she being a wife? And especially let women be harborers to all which belong to the household of faith, but above all to poor of her own sex, women or widows. It is no ill sight to see you in prisons: but if you cannot go to others, send not them away empty who come to you!

Mat. 25.36

Acts 9.36

And to make an end, what grace should a Christian wife think strange? But say as he once did, A man I am, and I deem no gift of a man unbecoming me. So you woman speak: I see not but it becomes me to be loving, patient, wise, wary, prudent, and thankful. These are ingredients into the conversion, as those spices reckoned up by Moses to make the holy ointment, and to cause you to smell sweetly in the nostrils of God, your husband, and all sorts! One other Peter mentions, confidence in God, the sister of faith even now mentioned. They trusted in God, and walked without amazement (he means such carnal and distrustful fears as that sex is full of). Their daughters you are, if you tread in their steps. As the eye of your own handmaid is always awfully carried to you, waiting for acceptance, and then she is safe: so let her teach you (as God's handmaid) to carry yours towards him: for the support of your spirit in the whole wheel of your conversation,

7. Confidence with others.

1 Pet. 3.5,6

for all other gifts as well as these, to make it strong as the staves
do the cart wheel, that it cracks not into pieces. More spices
might have been brought forth: but by these you may guess
whereof a woman's sweet powder is made: let us have to the
confection.

2.
Form is
temperature of
them.

For, as not the single spices, but the apothecary's skill
made God's ointments, so not only these mere graces, but the
medley of them, the temper of that spirit arising from them, is
that thing which makes the wife so graceful. This must come
from that wise and all sufficient skill of the Spirit of grace,
which must teach her reins in the night season and put into
her the spirit of gracefulness. He who has given a gift to the
bee to dispose that honey she has gathered from all flowers,
in so wise a manner that her workmanship makes all the beholders to admire it; must in a higher kind teach her to make
her graces into one compound and temper; I say must enable
her to lay them all so sweetly together and order her whole
marriage course by the help of them; that both every one may
afford her special influence into it, and all of them together
may make her face to shine, and the beauty thereof to appear
graceful to all the beholders. She must beg of God this spirit
by prayer: and as all the loose flowers of the bouquet must be
wisely ordered and put together and then bound together with
a thread, that they scatter not: so the spirit of wariness and
wisdom must gird the loose loins of her soul closely together,
and teach her to accommodate herself to every occasion offered, in a suitable correspondence, that there is no gulf nor
interruption, no inequality nor disproportion in her carriage.
No man shall need to paint an exact beautiful face: nor teach
her that is fair, to show it forth, it shows itself to all naturally
without trouble. As Paul told the chief captain that he was
born a free man of Rome, it cost him nothing: so where a heart
is furnished with grace, it will without any difficulty express
it, and cast her savor abroad. That which will make a hypocrite to toil and sweat, comes from grace with sweetness and
facility; yet I deny not but as that Glyceris showed great skill
in compounding the flowers of her posies, and the jewels of a
crown must be skillfully set into it to make it glorious: so, the
more careful the woman shall be to mark the circumstances,
the seasons, and all the occasions of her life, so much the more

Is the sweet
union of all
into one com-
pound.
Acts 22.28

wisely she shall be able to apply each of these graces to their objects, and show forth the luster of all in her general carriage. And such as are the ingredients, such must the compound necessarily be, if skill and discretion order it well. Now, the expression of all these in one is amiableness: that is the way whereby she utters herself, and in it, the lovely blush of them all appears: humbly amiable, mercifully amiable, amiable in the comely carriage of all (as her body is in the wearing of the most costly and best suited attire), most comely and pleasing. Especially when the grace of this grace is added to it, that this is not in a pang or good mood, when all goes well, but comes from a principle within, which causes her to go on in a uniform course: so that look how you see her at one time, you see her at another: she is always herself: and as a virgin of a comely face, although she is all blubbered with tears, she loses not her beauty, but by the contrary does commend it: so, although the occasions of her life are sad as well as cheerful, yet the cloud does not disannul the sun, but causes it to shine through with a more acceptable grace. So far I say as weak flesh mixed with much corruption will admit. And this for the latter.

What shall I then say for conclusion of this former part of my text, that the married wives must honor their marriage by this amiable behavior? Surely it instructs us in and about the variety of couples in marriage. The differences are as great as the difference of the prophet's baskets of figs, very good and very naught, so that they could not be eaten. The gracious wife is not only a helper to the estate of her husband; but she is a comfort and contentment to his mind and spirit: she lies in his bosom as a bag of sweet spices under his arm-holes, as a perfumed garment to his nostrils, as the spikenard of the spouse in the Song of Solomon which gave her savor to the beloved, when he lay upon his bed. Hence it is that Solomon compares her not only to the most costly, but especially to the most comely things which nature has made. All her teeth, her forehead, lips, neck, bosom, thighs, legs, even her very goings are pleasing in his eye: he compares her to the lilies, to the washed sheep, to the roes of the mountains, to the doves, to the cedars, to the curtains of Solomon, and every lovely, amiable thing. All to show that amiableness and gracefulness is that principal excellency which commends a wife

Use of this point.
1. Instruction. Difference of couples wherein it stands.

Song of Sol.

to her husband's esteem and affection: without the which the rest is worth little. In other things she has a mixture of herself: but in this she resembles him who has restored her to her first order and comeliness in her creation. A creation which no outward wealth or price can purchase; nothing in the world can equal the reflection of those graces, and the savor of that report which came from her. They are in her, not for her: as the flowers of a garden serve to garnish the house, so these grow in her for his use (her husband's) to adorn and grace his person, that he may be known in the gates. All that city, which knew Ruth to be a virtuous woman, knew Boaz to be a happy man in her: himself thinking no less when he told her so. Her virtues indeed shine within her own sphere and center chiefly: yet, the influence thereof, is as that oil of Aaron, which stayed not where it was first laid upon his head, but wet the whole attire, and earth about. And, as that box of costly ointment, though only poured upon the feet of Christ, yet made the whole house savor of it: so the temper which arises of the simplicity, meekness, and modesty of a good wife, makes her amiable to such as never saw her face. It is as the vices of the bad wife, which like oil in the palm of one's hand, cannot be hid.

What a bad graceless wife is.

Contrariwise, an unhappy husband falls alone, not in himself so much as in his vicious wife: who creates abroad dishonor, at home discontent to him. The best man thus plagued shall hardly avoid one of these imputations, either that he is unworthy of a good one because he makes her no better: or unhappy, because she is no better: the one is his sin, the other his shame, both his sorrow. She is neither comfort to him at home, because he is an eyewitness of what he would not, nor abroad, being forced to stop his nose at the ill savor of the vices, as Abigail at Nabal's churlishness. Neither can he be but as the body sitting upon a rolling stone, which is never at rest but always in conflict with himself, with wrath and despair; yet there is no way to be rid of such, either in the getting or having, except God show a man favor, that a man fall not into her hands. So much for information. But from this another use arises.

Admonition.

And that is admonition to good wives and happy husbands, thus much: to the good wife this, if God has thus graced you, enjoy it not yourself, but set a crown upon your husband, express the temper of your inward virtues in the amiableness of a loving and sweet carriage. Forget it not even in afflic- tion; utter it even in the midst of bodily weakness. Let your pleasing influence break through all opposition and sorrows, as the sun breaks through the thick mist or dark clouds, truly although eclipsed in part, yet shine in part, and let a glim- mering appear. Remember, you are a true friend, made for the day of adversity; it is not so thankworthy for you to cheer your husband when he can cheer you or himself without you while the day of prosperity lasts; but then to play the sweet orator, and to make him merry, when all other comforts have forsaken him in the sad season of sickness, of sorrow; this is better than all music and melody. Every base bird (while sum- mer lasts) will chirp and chitter: but to sing upon the bare bow or thorn bush when the leaves are gone, and the cold winter approaches, this argues a wife truly graceful, truly amiable and cheerful, and (next to the soul's peace with God) is the great- est contentment under the sun. I exhort no woman to play the hypocrite (neither indeed can gracefulness be long acted by any apish imitator) but, I entreat her, whom God has thus graced, to understand the use she serves for, not concealing herself, but to the uttermost to apply herself to the comfort of her husband. And for himself, this I say, If God has thus honored you with such a wife, understand (oh man) your own happiness and digest it seriously with thanks to him who has framed her so, and brought her so framed into your bosom! Let her find by good experience, there is no love lost; but let your heart rest in her and trust to her: seal her a bond of your sure and faithful respect, again, and let her see, she has not a wearisome Nabal to do with, who cannot value that which is precious in her at a due rate. Set her as a signet on your right hand, and let her be nearer your heart than your costli- est jewel. Let it not be enough that you can love one who has honored you more than all your wealth or birth could do, but procure her honor in all places, and suffer none to eclipse her worth. Give her of the work of her hands, and let her works praise her in the gates. And, so much is spoken for the use of this third branch, and so touching the mean, to preserve the honor of marriage by the duties which concern each party in

Graceful wives must express it to their husbands.

Husbands that are happy in the grace of their wives, must return the same.

several.

And thus having at last absolved this task which I undertook, to wit, to show how matrimonial honor may both be purchased and preserved entire, namely, first by a wise entrance marrying in the Lord, and aptly in the Lord; as also by wise watching to the duties, both of common nature, reaching to them both; and in special, pertaining to either; let me conclude the whole treatise with an item to both sorts. First,

all that are apt, religious, joint worshippers of God, who love each other, are chaste, and consenting in the general: also who especially are understanding, provident, respective husbands,

subject, helpful, graceful wives: let me say this unto you both, I doubt not but in the reading of my former treatise, you willingly hear of other unhappy couples; yourselves better married: but which of you in thus reading look up to God, or acknowledge such a blessing with due thankfulness? Which of you do but suppose (as it is not amiss to suppose what might have been or what may be), or say within yourselves, If the Lord had not provided better for some of us than we deserved,

Look out and
compare your
lot with others.

than we desired, given us good companions, before ever we knew what the misery of bad, or the worth of good ones meant: truly, if he had not been better to us most unworthy, than he has been to more worthy than ourselves (whom he saw fitter to bear, to profit by the cross, than ourselves were), oh, what would have become of us? Oh! Nabals, Lamechs, Zipporahs, and Jezebels would have swallowed up our souls, spirits, peace, welfare, thrift, and all! The continual vexations of bad heads, daily dropping of bad wives would have oppressed us! Alas! And why has the Lord done this? Surely not for any good he saw or foresaw in us, but because he knew how unmeet we were to honor him, under such a chain!

Why then, do we not more magnify his providence and wonder at his love, who has so guarded us! There being so few apt couples in the world, that our lot should be to light upon none more unapt; there being so many bad ones, that we should light upon none that are worse. Is not this mercy? Was it a golden blessing at first, in our own sense and confession, and has it become a leaden one now, after ten, twenty, and thirty; indeed forty years of experience? Do rich pearls fall in price? Could such mercy be better spared now than it might thirty years ago? Have we had the stock of good marriage now twenty years, and come far shorter in the tribute of praise, thanks, and fruit than when we first entered? There are four ages of each marriage, through the sin of the married, the first golden, the next silver, the third brass, and the last iron! At first couples begin with precious affections to God, to each other, join much in duty, cleave closely each to other, mutually excite each other to zeal and good works, and pay their vows: well then, next God's part weakens and decays, and they hold mutual marriage-love hardly. Then thirdly, both God's part and their own fail too, and they wax fulsome and formal in both: but lastly, and before they die, the Devil will fail of his will but he will make them both loose, carnal, profane, and scandalous! Consider this! How many marriages of great hope and solemnity have by these declensions proved stark naught at last, when indeed they should have proved best, and by degrees come to perfection? Let it be a sad item to such as enter well, to beware, lest they trust too much to their own wisdom and strength, which will lay them in the dirt before they are aware.

Again, how little do we condole the unhappiness of mismatched couples? Truly, even Christians better than ourselves? Rather ready to disdain and scorn them than to condole and pity them. As those two Aaron and Miriam, fell a caviling at Moses for his Ethiopian wife. Why? Had he not sorrow enough before? Was this to mourn with him, or rather to add more burden thereto? Was it not from God? And were they to quarrel at it? Even so it fares with many. That which should provoke tenderness, love, fellow-feeling, and compassion in men rather causes disdain, indignation, alienating, estrangement of heart, and deserting of fellowship! Why I pray? Do they stoop under their burden so deeply that they are often ashamed to complain, and do you trample upon them? Do you judge them afflicted of God, and humbled for sin, knowing your wisdom and choice was no whit better? Your success only was happier in providence. No: but as yourself in the like affliction would be handled, so deal you! Bear their burden, associate their persons, use all means to reconcile their spirits, to compound their differences, to reduce them to mediocrity and indifference of affections! Many couples had proved hap-

2.
Condole the unhappiness of others.

pier, if even such as were nearest them had not rather made them objects of abhorring, than of compassion! A great sin! And means to aggravate, even exasperate those seeds of evil, which disproportion at the first was like to kindle too much! Pray, pray rather for mercy and strength to guide, and carry them through! For how hardly could you digest those morsels once, which must be their daily diet? Will you eat your sweet bits alone, and so little wish them to such as want them wholly! Once a man enjoying sweet marriage, thought seriously of another friend that never married: aviling himself as base in respect of him that seemed to be above the need of that

R.R. of I.K.

which he could neither well want, nor thankfully improve! How much more should you then pray for such as would fain enjoy that which no creature can help them with?

3.
And be
humbled.

    Moreover, if not our worth, but rather our weakness has moved the Lord to show us this mercy, how does the sense of our weakness humble us? How do we esteem of the grace of God in such, as although but ill married, yet do walk more wisely under that cross, and do grow daily more humble and wary, and purge much dross out of themselves which perhaps the blessings of God purge not out of us, but rather make us sleep securely in the love of them, as pride, hypocrisy, self-love, and sensuality? What if we, whose portion is better, do yet make a slighter matter of it, and turn it into wantonness? How just would it be for God to bereave us of our sweet companions, leaving us to pass the rest of our days either in solitariness with snares so that we should bring our gray heads to the graves with dishonor (as many have done), or in marriage more sad and sorrowful the latter part of our life, than ever it was comfortable in the former part thereof? Could we well brook such sauce and sour herbs, yet fit for such as have eaten our former dainties with such unthankfulness? Verily, the experience I have had of second or third matches which have befallen some husbands has made me to think of our Savior's

John 21.18

words to Peter, When you were young you girded yourself, and went at your pleasure: but when you are old, another shall bind you and lead you whither you would not! Surely when you are old it is ill ending, it was better beginning with it in your youth, if God would! Yet so it is, many have been fain to hang up the harps of their youth upon the willows of sad marriage in old age, and sing, this new life requires other manners, other behavior: before, I was carried upon eagles wings, now I must shift for myself: my battles were once accustomed to be fought to my hand, but now, I must know war and fight my own. Now I am tried indeed, what is in my heart, what patience, what self-denial is in it, even my best wits to please, to conceal what I cannot amend, and all too little! Do you wonder? Who should have told you that a good wife was worth the thanks while you had her, or that she was any better jewel than you thought you deserved, till she was taken away? If nothing, but wanting can convince your folly, why should not medicine cure your malady?

To end this former branch. If you have sped well in a business of such hazard, why do you not guide others by your experience to make a good choice? You will say, Marriage makings are thankless offices! I grant it, that if all I have premised is true, I think some may con them small thanks, who have helped them to their marriages: but, as hard as the world goes, and although all hopes must rest upon proof, yet by your leave, some may give a shrewder guess than others, and say more touching aptness or unaptness: howsoever, I say to you as those lepers, having stored themselves with victuals and booty: we do not well to suffer our brethren to starve! And although the best care may miscarry: yet the care is in no fault, but rather much worse it must be where counselors are wanting. *4. Guide others to good choice.* *2 Kings 7*

Secondly, I say to all such good couples, be wise: live, love, and leave. What has a man of all his sore labors under the sun, or what profits it to spend our life in needless toil and vexation? Live first in the joyful improvement of all those graces and blessings wherewith God has endowed you. Take and mutually possess each other's virtues: grow by the help of others more inward, holy, and useful in the communion of saints. Let your streams flow to others, enjoy not all to yourselves. Love secondly: endear your hearts in each other mutually. Suffer not Satan to come between bark and tree, and through a satiety of blessings, to turn all to weariness and fulsomeness: to grow estranged in your affections: indeed, ready to take offenses at each other, forgetting God's love to you both. If some had those advantages we have *Branch 2. Exhortation to live, love, and leave.*

(should you say, of consent and peace) oh, what a close walking with God would it produce, without separation, whereas we vanish. How would they settle religion and government of family, which they would and cannot, we might and will not? Leave lastly, each other willingly and contentedly when God shall determine your short pilgrimage; which will be so much easier if you have lived and loved before! The parting will be bitter however: yet much worse if all is to be done at death. Sweeter will the parting be upon experience of former marriage improvements; than upon guilt of remediless errors! But I say, the time is short, use the world as if you used it not,

1 Cor. 7.21

buy as if you bought not, marry as if you married not; do all moderately: knock off before, unloose in season. There has been a time of embracing, there must come another far from

Eccles. 3.5

it. By that rejoicing you have had in Christ, die daily; and tell it to each other in your best rejoicing. I bid you not do as heathens, set a scull before you on your marriage day with a motto: What I have been, you are: and, what I am you shall be! But know, marriage happiness is but the liberty of a prison. Squeeze it not too hard, lest you force blood: use it slightly and it will comfort you. Say not it is good being here, build not tabernacles, Mat. 17.4. Let not death knock unawares. It is a pity, a man should be in love with shells on the shore, as to forget the ship, and be swept away: or love the husband here, forgetting Christ: a carnal relation, renouncing an eternal!

Use 3.
Instruction.

Marriage is a shadow of that spiritual union of Christ and the church.
1.
In their meetings and marriage.

This point also (to conclude all) is instruction to shadow out the privilege of them who are united to Christ by the marriage of faith and the spirit. It is a mystery, as Paul calls it. And, as sometimes he teaches married persons their duties by the mutual union of Christ and the church: so also, another time he describes the true union and amity of Christ and the spouse, by the sameness of flesh, which marriage causes between husband and wife. A word or two of both: and first, how Christ and his spouse meet. For, look how Eliezer was a spokesman between Isaac and Rebecca, to draw her into a marriage knot with him: and as he carried the bracelets and tokens sent in Isaac's name, to allure her to him: also declared the abundant wealth of Abraham in cattle, gold, and jewels, all to bestow upon his only son Isaac: that so the richness and contentment of the match might persuade Rebecca. So does the Lord by his spokesmen the messengers, reveal to his church by his Spirit, all his wealth and treasures of wisdom and knowledge: all put into the flesh of the Lord Jesus, and tells her, 1 Cor. 1, all the goods which he has given us in him: that he may thereby surprise her heart, and gain her to be his; he sets out his son from head to foot in all amiableness of person and graces, that his eyes and looks might wound her, and steal her heart away from trash and toys of the world.

It is he who not only so, but whereas he found her *And how.* unapt for himself, an Amorite, a Hittite in her blood, a base captive: he shaves off her hair, pares her nails, washes her, and makes her clean: he bestows her dowry upon her (not as men upon their wives), for they look for it from them, thinking them little without it: he discovers the miserable, desolate, and forlorn life of her woeful virginity, wherein as an orphan, she lays open to all enemies, all wrongs and injuries: convinces her that her support and welfare is merely from himself. Moreover, he tells her that she was engaged before to a most cursed husband, who would have undone her: he undertakes to stab him and to make her way clear for the marriage of himself, the old contract being dissolved. He becomes an earnest suitor, a hot lover of hers, and refuses no patience to win her: even till his locks are full of the dew of the night. All to make her his own, his only one: that having renounced (not only base qualities, but) her own father's house, herself, her name, and all her own happiness, he may be happy in her, and she in him alone (for he can endure no rival), and so be married without any fear of ever being divorced. He causes her heart, by this attractive and these cords of a man, to resolve upon the match. She then inclines to him, she can say neither more nor less, save that it is from the Lord; she begins to chide herself for her so long ignorance of his worth, lack of acquaintance with his excellencies: little enquiring after such a person: now he needs no arguments, for she cannot pardon herself that she knew him no sooner, she casts off all her colors and covers of shame, and resigns up herself fully, freely, and forever to be his: abhorring herself and wondering that such a person can *2.* love such a sorry spouse, she counts all others as dung, they *Their mutual* all stink unto her in comparison of him alone: and therefore *converse.* consents to his motion, believing she shall find no other of him, than she has apprehended him to be. This touching the meeting.

What Christ is to the church.

And upon this her consent, Christ and his spouse live and love together: for Christ takes her to himself from that day forward, even home to himself, and shows her his dwelling, making her glad in the tents of her mother, as Isaac did Rebecca in Sarah's tent: he marries her to himself in righteousness, compassion, faithfulness, and love: he puts a robe about her and a ring upon her hand, a tire upon her head, shoes upon her feet: furnishes her with all his treasure: kills the fat calf, makes her a royal feast of all fat things, of refined wines; even his sacraments: he endows her with all he has, takes her both for better, to rejoice in her graces: and for the worse, to cover all her infirmities, to make a great praise of her poorest virtues, judging her by them, and not the other: undertakes for all her debts: none may sue her, but in his name, who answers all suits and quarrels: gives her himself, his heart and love, and all which is meet for her for need and comfort, for this life and a better, for why? She is his Hephzibah and Beulah. In all her sicknesses, he assists and stands by her; he is afflicted in all her afflictions, and his right hand saves, sustains, and redeems her: charges the daughters that they wake her not till she pleases. His love is her banner and defense: and let none touch his beloved, for he touches the apple of his eye: no wrong she receives of any, but he makes it good a hundred fold, till she is past all danger.

What she is to him.

And suitable (in measure) is the spouse's carriage towards Christ (if she is not degenerate). She again most dearly loves him, she is in all things helpful to him, to his glory, to his contentment, even as a wife of his desires. She is reverently and meekly subject to him, under all his commands with most loyal awe, and yet with delight as under an easy yoke; is most tender of his welfare, truly is glad, and thinks not herself too good to wash the feet of his poorest servants: if her goodness cannot reach to him, she reaches it to his children, whom (in his absence) she nourishes, solaces herself in, beholds him in them, visits, clothes, and relieves them in their needs; thinking them happy who may stand as servants in his presence: she thinks herself more happy in him than if married to the greatest potentate upon earth. The spokesmen who treated with her about this marriage, are precious in her eyes; indeed their feet are beautiful to her for the glad tidings they brought her. She counts no labor too much, no cost too dear for him. Even the costliest ointment is not good enough for his feet. The reproaches of them that upbraid him go into the bowels of her belly, and dart to her heart: she walks not only not rebelliously and contumeliously, but not uncomely, not slightly: but decks herself with all the gifts of the Spirit, humility, wisdom, and sweet tenderness of spirit, truly the spirit of grace is in her lips, that in all her behavior and converse she may walk in and out gracefully and amiably in his sight, in all longsuffering and well pleasing: she is faithful to him in all his secrets, keeps his counsel: dares not prostitute herself to any, not only lusts, but even liberties or companies which she thinks may be distasteful to him, even but suspicious. The tokens he sends her as pledges of his favor, are most dear unto her. She seeks no private welfare of her own besides his. She distrusts not his provision, but trusts him confidently, knowing she shall not want: denies herself for his sake, and rejoices that by this, her loyal heart may be tried. Thinks never the worse of him because she suffers for him, but rather the more he costs her, the dearer he is to her. No husband of other women can stain hers, for hers is above all, the chief of ten thousand; the fashions, garish and whorish attires, paintings and spangles of harlots come not about her neck or wrists, but she frames herself to his contents, in all chastity she knows his voice but abhors a stranger's. Nothing grieves her but his absence. All her longings, desires, and tears are that she might be with him, where nothing may ever divide her from him!

Let it teach us in the midst of our marriage contentments to raise up our affections to the joy of this spiritual union: and in the midst of our discontents here, to make supply with the happiness of this!

And this may serve for these two general uses also, belonging to the whole discourse: in a word therefore, to conclude all. If that which I have at large said about marriage duties, seems to discourage any weak ones, as if their oil and meal could not reach out so far; they shall never attain to this measure. I will not answer them as once a poet answered one that asked him why he always brought in women as very vir-

Conclusion of the treatise.

tuous, always commending them: but another presented them (on the stage) as vicious, always traducing them. Oh says he, I present them as I would have them, as they should be: but he brings them in as they are commonly. So I might say, my discourse does not presuppose either all husbands or wives as they are, but as they should be. Aim at it as a mark: but I will answer as a learned heathen in his epistle to his friend speaks, when he had received a very short letter from him, I have read over your very short letter very often, and so often, that I have made it a very long one. So here: my large discourse may dismay some for coming so short of practice as they do. Beseech the Lord therefore to behold your defects with a merciful eye, to read the short lines of your obedience often over in the glass and perspective of the Lord Jesus: and so, by his large interpreting and much looking upon your honest endeavor, it shall be esteemed as full and large. God help! Our discourses of these matters are far larger than the practice of the most is. Ourselves who write and ours are poor, and unsuitable to our rules! Howbeit, not contrary, not willfully opposite, and where there is but endeavor, God will accept. Give, Lord, power to do as you direct, and command what you will! Speak and spare not upon these terms: for your servants, handmaids (mourning for their deaf ears and dead hearts) desire to hearken and to obey. Look not at what is ours, it is vile, but at that which is yours in us, which is precious! In which happy desire, I conclude the treatise.

The End of the Treatise.

THE APPENDIX

to the treatise : discovering the
just vengeance of God upon all
unclean ones, especially defilers
of marriage.

Hebrews 13.4
but whoremongers and adulterers
God will judge.

It was no part of my purpose (good reader) to have used this text any further than as I have already treated upon it. The occasion of adding this discourse upon the latter part was the private request of a friend to utter my mind unto him, and to satisfy his spirit, touching the heinousness of uncleanness: whereof he desired his soul might thoroughly be convinced (as blessed be God it was, through mercy concurring both with this and other helps used to that purpose), which service I considering seriously of, took the latter part of my text as a ground of my project: even then purposing (since God brought it by that occasion to hand) to annex it to my marriage treatise: as foreseeing not only that it would satisfy some to have the equal handling of both members of the text: but that it might not be impertinent, as a spur, to help the application of the former treatise; and as a dissuasive to as many in this debauched age (who shall haply come to the reading of it), if they are not obstinate and hardened in the sin, to weigh well their estate and repent: that so God speaking peace to them, they may no more return to folly. In which hope, I begin.

Preamble to the Appendix: why the latter part of this text is handled.

The words (as you see) are, *but whoremongers and adulterers God will judge.* Which addition and denunciation fitly attends the words going before. I have opened the

Doctrine 2. Explication.

words in the beginning: all comes to this effect: God will bless them that honor marriage, but such as violate and defile it, by what means soever, God will judge them. The course may seem strange (perhaps) which here God takes, speaking to his church, so to threaten, and to work rather by downright strokes than by oil and promises of love, to allure to obedience. But even our God (mark the words, he says not the wicked man's revenging God, but even our God) is a consuming fire. And our God sees it meet, even to appear to his own sometimes in this hue, and in bloody colors when their spirits grow base and sensual: as this sin of uncleanness of all other, infatuates the spirit most, and makes it insensible of commands, except the Lord should take up weapons, and flash hellfire in men's faces. That stupor of spirit wherewith David was led a whole year together, after he had committed this sin, notwithstanding it was accompanied with such killing circumstances, as to make a man drunk, and to murder him because he would not cover the sin: these might alone have wounded him to death, if the sinful sweetness of it had not bewitched him so deeply: and the like we see in Sampson with Delilah: and we know how terribly God threatens both and pursues them. Elijah himself, if stout, must have thunders and lightning: Jonah must have a tempest mingling heaven and sea in one, and the jaws of a whale to gape for him, Job must have affrighting by Leviathan and Behemoth: and Nahum and Habakkuk must present God to the hard-hearted Jews, in jealous wrath, fierce rending the rocks: in such a voice as makes the lips to quiver, the bones to be blasted with rottenness; and all too little: Who is a God like to our God (says Micah sweetly), who passes by the sins of his remnant? But if all should use such pleasing words, cursed flesh would say that God is like them. There is use of sweetness when the heart is wounded with sin and terrified with fears; but rare is the man who is always fit to feed upon such honey without overindulgence. Too propense is, not only a base heart of the godless, but the baser part of a godly heart to turn grace into wantonness. There is a slave within us which must have a whip, although the free born is drawn by love. Each must have her diet: the one, lest it grows too rank of presumption, the other lest it is overwhelmed with despair. The apostle Paul mixes threats and promises to the choicest that he

---

Marginal notes:

God deals with his own by judgments.

Heb. 12.end

Nah. 1.3
Hab. 3.19
Micah 7.end

The godly have a slavish part in them and free.

Eph. 5.6

writes unto. For this cause comes the wrath of God upon the children of disobedience? Be not deceived, no whoremon-gers, adulterers, etc. shall inherit the kingdom of heaven. And such were some of you! Why adds he this? To show us that even God's people had need to be put in mind what they were, what they have still a disposition to, to keep them thereby in some awe. So again, let no man defraud his brother, for the Lord is the avenger of all such. Many other such places there are. All to show us that God must sometimes whip us to duty and gaster us from evil, as well as entice and draw us to or from. Therefore, even so he urges these Hebrews to chastity saying, *whoremongers and adulterers God will judge.* 1 Cor. 6.9-11 1 Thess. 4.6

The sin of adultery then is hence concluded to be a great one. But here, some may object that charge of God to Hosea the prophet: bidding him to take to himself a fornica-tress to wife, and so defile himself by getting children by her. But I answer; it was only done in vision, and in protestation before the Israelites. It was only typical and parabolic: nei-ther agreeing to the Lord who charged, nor the prophet who obeyed. By the prophet's assuming to himself such a person, in God's stead, he would teach the Jews what woeful adultery they were guilty of, in forsaking God for idols. The liberty taken by the patriarchs in the point of many wives and concu-bines was for a time, in the first furnishing of the church with posterity. Else, from the beginning (as Malach. 2 speaks) it was not so. Furthermore, this command against pollution has herein a peculiar restraint from some other: that whereas in some cases it was lawful to take the goods of Egyptians from them by dispensation; in this no such is granted, it being in no case or respect lawful to commit uncleanness, no more than murder. (Adultery a great sin. Objection. Answer.)

And we see this point verified in Scripture at large. Read these places, Lev. 20.10; Deut. 22.22, for temporal plagues and for eternal to all sorts of impure ones, Rom. 1.29-32; 1 Cor. 6.9,10; Gal. 5.19,20; 1 Tim. 1.9,10. Truly the greatest de-linquents in these kinds, even kings and great persons, are not spared, as appears, 2 Sam. 12.7; Mat. 14.4, even such as have attempted it ignorantly, as Abimelech, Gen. 20.3, even priests, 1 Sam. 2.22,23, and all sorts, Num. 25.1; Jer. 5.7; Judg. 20.4. The which have their several judgments there applied. And

more of them read, as of the old world, Gen. 6.1,2, the Sodomites, Gen. 19, the sin of self-pollution (which I wish may be
observed well), that of Er and Onan, Gen. 38.9, and Shechem,
Gen. 34.2. All summed up by the apostle, Col. 3, Mortify your
earthly members, fornication, uncleanness, effeminateness,
unnatural lust: for which the wrath of God comes upon disobedient men.

Doctrine.
God will have
all unclean-
ness laid open
in her colors,
as odious.

The point to be treated of, is that God would have
all sorts of uncleanness so laid open in their colors that they
might appear as they all are, odious and terrible! But, what
odious colors are here? I answer. Here is one terrible one,
which imports all the rest. That which God himself will in
person appear against, and sit upon the judgment seat to enquire of, that must be a terrible crime; but God himself (not
his deputies only, for all men are liars) will in person sit to
judge it. Kings (we know) and princes, come not ordinarily to
the Star Chamber or to the King's Bench in person, for slight
crimes, but remarkable and notorious. When King Henry the
Eighth, to please that bloody tiger Gardiner, came in person
to sit upon that holy man and meek lamb of Jesus Christ, John
Lambert, how terrible was his appearance, and how frowning a brow cast he upon that innocent martyr? What then is
the brow of that God that must sit upon King Henry himself?
Only the difference is, princes make a long and deep inquisition of matters, either really or for show, to bolt out the truth;
but, the Lord proceeds *ex officio mero*, he needs no inform-
ers, no evidence, but is witness, accuser, judge, and all in one,
because he knows all without enquiry. A short count shall he

Mal. 3.5

make upon the earth; how much more upon this or that man,
and his crimes? By name he will be a swift witness against
the adulterer, as Malachi speaks; and where the delinquent is
his own accuser, what need is there for a long process of law?
Such is the conscience of each sinner, and of this by name! The
Judge then, coming in person, making a swift work of it, and
having the sinner himself arraigned by his own conscience,
must necessarily set a terrible face upon the sin of uncleanness.

Digression
showing that
fornication is a
great sin.

Before I go any further, since I wrap all uncleanness
up in one bundle of wrath, I foresee that in this loose and lascivious age many will tax me for speaking so indistinctly of all

sorts in this kind, fornicators and adulterers; for the former of these had at the writing of this text, have still, and will have their patrons, not Papists only, but Protestants, to alienate and qualify them as less sinners, if not to bolster them as none. And surely in vain do I urge God's judgments upon that which is no sin: therefore observe; first, for heathens who (as Hierom says) only condemned adultery, suffering youths and maids to defile themselves without restraint, as if not will but worth made the sin, I say with him, Christ's law is one, and Caesar's another. Alas, that weak relic of light which was in heathens was soon overshadowed. It caused the apostles to forbid the Acts 15 converted Gentiles the sin of fornication and idols, as equally promiscuous among them. Their very lawgivers permitted it as lawful, and therefore Peter says, that they wondered at the 1 Pet. 4.3,4 Christians, that they ran not with them into the same confusion of uncleanness. And no wonder if pagans thought thus, when Papists openly write thus. For not to speak of their most unclean casuists, who by their base particularizing of the circumstances of filthiness, noisome to all chaste ears, do show themselves what tribe they are of; one of them expressly writes thus: He is no heretic that says, fornication is no mortal sin, because there is no text of Scripture that says so. Is there not? What means that then of Paul, Col. 3.5, are not the words plain, that wrath comes upon men for this? Other Papists add, that light of nature condemns it not; and indeed, in such as themselves who by custom have lashed out their eye, it is true, but none else? And their canonists write likewise.

But let these masters of misrule go: let us attend what the God of order speaks in his Word, of which partly I have spoken in the proof of the doctrine: add thereto that Deut. 17.18; 1 Cor. 6.18. Doubtless they who drive out the Spirit out of their souls and bodies sin mortally. So do they who shall burn in the lake of brimstone. Rev. 21.8. The fathers are all of this mind. Chrysostom, So oft as you have played Homil.22. in the fornicator, you have damned yourself. He also tells us the 2.ad Corinth. law of nature and conscience does evince it; we need not be taught what evil, incontinency is and fornication: for we know it from the beginning. I do not much desire to load my reader Homil.12. with quotations save in cases controversial, to put all out of ad popul. doubt. And the same father, Lo (says he) Paul says not abstain Antioch.

from fornication, but fly from it. Another of the fathers makes a beadroll of the reproaches of fornicators, A fornicator is a filthy ignominious slave of sin, in whom the Devil does knead in and imprint his loathsomeness. He is to be eschewed in the

house, to be abhorred in meetings, he is the reproach of such as come near him, the opprobrium of his enemies, the shame of kindred, the execration of neighbors, the sorrow of parents, etc. If he offers to marry, all reject him. So it was then, but now it is no matter, so he has land or money. So another,

Whoredom and fornication are not counted among common sins. And Cyprian, That fornication is a great sin, Paul shows to the Corinth. He names that text, all other sin is out of the body. To conclude, Gregory (a Pope himself), Single persons must be warned, that they mix not themselves with harlots. Endless it would be to mention the rest.

And is there not great reason? How woeful a mischief does it reach to? For the bastards begotten by such vagrant lust are wholly neglected in point of education, wanting the care of a father, and the cohabitation of parents, and so both an accursed posterity is begotten and beggary increased. Vagrant lust being justly plagued with a vagabond posterity. But the main reason is taken from another ground. True it is that the fornicator sins against his own body, the bastard he begets (an innocent patient, necessarily miserable), the commonwealth, and society: all bands of honesty: but especially he sins against that everlasting decree of the seventh commandment of a most holy and pure God. And so much by the way for this point.

But (it will be said) how may this wrath and justice of God against these whoremongers appear? Answer. By a particular induction of those punishments which he has inflicted upon all unclean ones. Which by and by I shall number up: but in the meantime, let me not forget to premise some reasons why the Lord strives to put so odious an outside upon this sin of uncleanness: and these reasons, I desire may be marked for the whetting up of the reader's edge, upon the matter ensuing. I will be short in all, remembering that I am now only adding a little to the former argument. First then, this sin is a

very near, natural, and familiar corruption to our nature, and as much nourished and cherished as any one, a true Reuben,

the eldest child of old Adam's strength, bearing name of the
mother, which is called in general lust or concupiscence. Heathens esteem those virtues which carry the name of the kind,
to be eminent ones: as fortitude because it is called virtue, it is
to be supposed to be eminent, and to have most of the kind of
good in it. So has uncleanness the name and most of the kind,
because it is called lust eminently. The mother and daughter
are bawds mutually to each other. Now then, the Lord seeing
how hardly those evils are shamed and abhorred, which lie so
near our heart, and are so fomented by the influence of continual corruption as the stream by her spring: seeing that this
sin is bred and steeps in our bosom, as our son: does so much
the more set himself to deface and make it odious. As a father beholding some more natural evil lurking in the spirit of
his child, pride, drunkenness, does all he can to unmask it, to
discover that blindfolding self-love which maintained it, and
does all he can to bring it out of conceit with him, and make
him loathe it.

Secondly, men are marvelously given (although they
do see and grant it to be evil) to blanch it over, and make it
as none, or very small by their slighting and extenuating of
it. So much the more does the Lord strive to point it out in
lively colors, and to aggravate it. The heathens (such as all
were, to whom Paul directs his epistles) had by ill custom so
far dashed out that dim twilight of conscience left in them,
that they deemed this sin, among others, a mere natural, necessary appetite, and (in a manner) made as common of it as
of eating and drinking: in so much that in that epistle to the
Corinthians, Paul has much ado to persuade them to see any
shame in it. Furthermore (that they might add drunkenness
to thirst), behold, they began to make the more bold with
God in this kind, under pretended privilege by the gospel, as
if Christ had come to proclaim liberty to all petty sins, for opposition to which unsavory baseness, the apostle is fain to allege the wrath of God against it, even upon them who were his
peculiar people, the Jews. The more we slight sin, the more is
God fain to cast us in teeth and upbraid us with it.

Thirdly, although we should come so far, as in words
to confess it a sin, yet the sensuality of our spirit, and the tick-
ling pleasure of the flesh (being as the belly which has no ears)

Reason 2. Men are prone to blanch over this sin.

1 Cor. 10

Reason 3. This sin enchants and bribes the judgment.

inflaming and bolstering up itself by the lewd general practice of base times, and the baits and objects of uncleanness in every corner, spread as snares by Satan: is very propense, is very apt to forget that face thereof, which in the glass of a royal law and the terror thereof, was presented unto us. Our carnal affections (I say) are so apt to take fire (as dry gunpowder) and to flash up, that they do bribe our judgments dangerously from a convinced persuasion of the loathsomeness of it. And the Devil is never far off: but presents this butter in so lordly a dish that the soul spies not the hammer and nail in his hand until he has driven it into the temples. Who should have persuaded David or Samson that those amiable objects and delights of their eyes were so baneful and odious, as they found them?

Jude 10

Jude tells us that those idol teachers were so defiled with the flesh that they bore down their conscience in that which they knew to be evil: and like sensual brute beasts, poured out themselves to their lust with greediness. Such a charming siren there is in the soul, by this sin, lulling it asleep as upon Delilah's knees, lest it should admit a thorough convincement thereof. The dead flesh then of this sore being so great, the corrosive must be strong which should eat it out.

Reason 4. Adultery is very full of colors and excuses to hide itself under.

Fourthly, no sin is so ready to hide itself under cloaks and excuses as this: none so fruitful in devising shifts and tricks that it might not be discovered; or evasions that it might not be punished. Whether we look at the tricks and inventions, which the committers themselves devise to cover it; even the many desperate ways which they have to cloak it from the sight of men: or whether we look at the covers which the Devil has fitted for these cups: how many ways of commuting, how many ways of recrimination and turning the crime upon the accusers, so that they are more snarled than the accused (for vice is manifold, virtue is simple)? How many ways of overthrowing witnesses for lack of narrow testimony? How much commuting, dispensing, and pardoning of this sin (a very mocking of God, and adding oil to the flame)? Look into the nature of the sin itself, it is a work of darkness, and therefore as deep as hell in the devising of ways to conceal itself. Sleidanus has a story of an adulterous duke in Germany, who falling in love with his duchess's handmaid, and thereof had in deep jealousy by his wife, devised a course politically to embark himself more deeply into his uncleanness, and to elude his wife's suspicion. He sent the harlot to a castle (as if he meant to cast her quite off), appointing a strait watch (as he gave it forth) that she might not be thought to escape, and after some time caused a report to be given forth in the country that she was deadly sick (whether of discontent or other disease). After this had awhile possessed his duchess, he caused it shortly after to be reported that she was dead: and left that might be suspected, he took a solemn course for her interment. He hired women for the occasion to conduct the corps, appointed an image (such was the manner of the burial) to be laid above the hearse, openly to be seen, which should resemble to the eyes of the beholders, the pale and consumed face of his mistress, as she looked as though she was dead: also witnesses he suborned such as had tended her, to swear it, a solemn funeral and a sermon, with a large dole to the poor; all framed to give demonstration and assurance to the world, and his duchess, of her death, that she might no more be looked after. But still the harlot lived, prospered in health; still the duke (pretending other journeys) haunted her company, burning in his lust much the more. Who sees not uncleanness to be as ingenious as the poet describes the parrot when she is hungry, or as the belly, which he calls a master of arts? Therefore I say, the Lord deals accordingly with it; that which we commit in secret, the Lord will revenge in the open view of the world, and reveal in the tops of houses (as at the last this duke's villainy): and by how much this sin escapes the judgment of man, the more cunningly, and smoothly, by so much, God sets himself to meet with it, the more terrible, that so his method might make it the more hated: for his colors are in grain, laid in oil, and will soon wash out our false paint.

Fifthly, that either by this discovery the Lord might teach his people the prevention of this sin, beforehand, rather than they should learn repentance too late; having before polluted themselves (and this he chiefly intends) or else, if (notwithstanding all his ways) men will still try conclusions with him, their mouths may be stopped, and themselves put to silence, either from ability to excuse the fault, or decline the punishment. They cannot then pretend that they were the bolder to commit it, because they thought it slight. They

Reason 5. Either for prevention or stopping of mouth.

cannot (with any forehead) deprecate the punishment of that which is so confessedly odious.

Sixthly, that those men who are prone to live by sense in a course of sensuality; might have as well, real and sensible pullbacks from this sin (by God's abhorring and opposing it), as by the beholding the examples of loose and dissolute offenders, to be tickled, and as it were to stand on thorns till they are like them. The Lord tries us with this bittersweet, that is whether his bitter or the world's sweet is chief with us: if not, yet we shall not have all our will, nor all the sweet of our lust, but with it we shall have some sting and prick in our flesh to make us sit uneasy upon our cushion, especially in this woeful world, degenerated to all licentiousness, as in other sins, so in this of uncleanness; which so overflows the banks of countries and towns in this declining age, that if examples may prevail, there shall not want enough to corrupt the bodies and defile the manners of the most. Just it is that such as defile the ordinances with the scurf of their own inventions, should be given over with Papists to the pollution of their bodies by all kinds of lust; the outward uncleanness having been always a brand of the spiritual. So much for reasons.

Now, I return where I left, to make fuller answer to that question, how it may appear that God is such a judge of this sin? I say therefore, if we shall consider these passages following, it may. First, if we shall consider that the Lord has not spared to set his own dearest people on the stage for this sin of uncleanness.

Mat. 1.19
God's dearest
servants not
exempt from
this general
sentence.

It is said that Joseph (Mary's husband) was a just man, and was loath to defame her openly, when he perceived her to be with child, but meant privily to rid his hand of her. But the Lord is not as man, he is a just and jealous God, not sparing to exemplify and traduce his best servants, that their blur and penalty might scare all from venturing. A just king will begin with some servant or favorite of his own, by making him the spectacle of his severity: when he would have all his subjects put it out of question, that if they transgress in the like, they shall not go guiltless. And, if this is done in the green tree, if the fire so easily kindles upon that, what shall be done in the dry? If the very righteous are not free from being stigmatics in the court of this justice, what shall become of the

ungodly and wicked? And, if judgment begins at the house

of God, what shall be done with the rest, the stubble who are ready to be burned? I say, what then shall become of the common rout of sodomites, adulterers, and fornicators? Tremble oh you unclean wretches! Do you see Lot, David, Solomon, and Sampson shoaled out from their fellows for this, and look you to escape?

Secondly, see what a judgment appeared upon the bastard offspring of the adulterer. It might seem unjust that an innocent should be so plagued for the father's uncleanness, as to be shut out and cut off from the congregation to the tenth generation. Surely the taint was deep and the iron moll canker-fretted, which could so hardly be washed out: what did this argue, but that by so severe a sentence (not to be expiated by blood or any other cleansing), the Lord would deter men from such filthiness? That, if they dare not thus offend, they might tell themselves, they must cut off the fruit of their sin, from ever coming, where God and his people had to do. Who should dare to be so profane, if yet the heat of his lust would permit him to think seriously, either of the hell which himself, or the excommunication and blasting curse which his bastard child should incur! But, alas! It is to be feared that these thoughts are the first of those which these last think of.

Branch 2. The offspring of the adulterer excluded from the tabernacle, many ages. Deut. 23.2

Thirdly, the penalty inflicted upon adultery was death without remedy. There were diverse sorts of death inflicted upon malefactors by the law; and some learned men question what this death was. The agreed tenet is, that it was stoning, although strangling and burning were used for some excesses in this sin, when it came to incest, or the unnatural sins of sodomy and bestiality. The thief was not hanged, but spared by making restitution (and in single fornication, fewer penalties might be allowed), but in these cases the Lord would allow none: as if the offer of requital in such cases was most unseasonable. No, but gave way to the jealousy of the husband, and he admits no pecuniary mulct to redeem that, which jealousy counts to be above ransom; truly, so terrible a law he ordained for the unclean harlot (upon the instance only of a jealous husband), that if she stood upon her trial, and gainsaid the accusation, she should be set before the priest and there drink a cursed water, and if she were guilty, she was found out by the providence of God, and plagued with rotting of her belly and

Branch 3. Old penalty of adultery, death without remedy.

Num. 5.18,19

thigh, and so perished. So she got nothing by her concealment, for instead of the peoples' stoning, God's hand seized upon her. And what is this, save God's coming in person to judge a whore?

Branch 4. Severe judgments executed upon adulterers.

Fourthly, what severe judgments has God executed upon unclean persons? Let first Scripture, then experience speak; for Scripture, how did the Lord pursue David for his adultery? First with the rape of Tamar, then the murder of Amnon, then the treason of Absalom (both whom he should have slain and taken from the earth), together with his just execution by Joab (the child itself conceived in adultery should have been the first): the open defiling of all his concubines in the face of the sun, as he had defiled others in secret. The perpetual unhappiness of his course all his life to his dying

Both in Scripture.

day, never free from sorrow, and even then in the usurpation of Adonijah, what godly man ever suffered so in his children, himself living to see it, as he? Why should God sit in judgment upon his own favorite for this sin, save to scare all to whom this story should come, even to the world's end? And, what became of Solomon's glory? Was it not all blasted by this sin of uncleanness? Although he lived not to see it, yet what a spectacle of ruin did the Lord make Rehoboam? Stripping him of the ten tribes, and of the richest kingdom in his father's days, making it the poorest that it had ever been before. What made Sampson of a judge in Israel, truly a giant, a conqueror to become a fool in Israel: a blind slave to grind in a mill, save

Num. 25.7,8

the besotting of himself with lust? How dealt God with those Israelites at Peor? Did he not set his vicegerent Phinehas on work, to thrust through the chief ringleaders, before he could be pacified? And when the heat of wrath seemed to be slaked, did it so vanish? Did not the tail of that plague sweep away four and twenty thousand? Could their privilege of being God's people save them? Where is now your mouth (as he said), who calls adultery but a trick of youth? Instead of one cloak which men used to put upon it, of slightness; what cloak does the Lord put upon it? Surely a cloak bathed in the blood of so many thousand adulterers, and was not this enough to drive men from such dalliance? Who might not thenceforth call it by the name of a bloody sin, of a scarlet dye? What shall say of our own experience? How many have we heard of, struck dead by the hand of God, taking them in the act? Not suffering them to go out of the bed of uncleanness, whether has God come in person to judge such or not.

And although many have been suffered to escape such judgments, yet how many missing the bear, have met with the lion? Out of the horror of their conscience some dashing their brains against the walls, others stabbed, drowned, and hanged themselves. To pen out of several writers who have written theaters of God's judgments, the examples of such as God has plagued is not my scope! Alas! These are days wherein men will rather sit upon God himself and scorn him to his face, than tremble at God's sitting in judgment upon adulterers. But there are books which do at large supply us in this kind, if our hearts are not quite sunk into a senselessness of them. Even while I was writing this, lest I should want unsought precedents, a report came to my ears of a blacksmith near Colchester (whose wound is as it were yet bleeding), who having made a chain to hang a woman that had murdered her husband, fell into such sudden terrors by God's hand oppressing his conscience for his adulterous life, that he cried out saying that he was as wicked as she for whom he had made the chain; so, that he could not rest, until by cutting his own throat, he had made an end of himself. So the Lord pulls out some to be spectacles of reproach and detestation to the world, though thousands escape. All are not dragged out by the hand of God openly as that bawdy bishop at the Council of Trent, whom Sleidanus mentions, who creeping out of his window along the leads to the wife of the next house, was watched by her husband, and caught in a grin or snare laid for him in his passage, and there hung by the neck as a ridiculous object to all the beholders. But, I say, because men object that thousands escape to some odd persons, whom vengeance intercepts: tell me, what better portion have they who survive than the other. *And in experience.*

What one sin has so manifold marks of wrath upon it, as this, upon the soul, body, or person sinning (as by the sequel may appear)? First, for soul, what sin has found less place for repentance than this? Closeness, secrecy, and shifts always attending it, which keep the heart from all tenderness, truly defile and disable the soul from repenting, moreover the curse of God sealing up that soul to impenitency: some walking ten, *Branch 5. Marks of wrath upon, 1. Soul.*

some twenty, some more years in the guilt hereof, yet with a smothered conscience: and although they are wounded, yet hardly healed in a kindly manner, but suffering their hearts to rankle inward, and outbidding all ordinances to their destruction. How can it be, but such a sore must break forth all at once with such a forcible outcry, that nothing can still or satisfy it? Secondly, what sin has so foul a blemish and dishonor cast upon the name of the committer as this? With what a blot do we think or speak of Sampson to this day? And how many divines (though amiss) have deeply questioned Solomon's salvation? Touching the outward name, what a blot and infamy do they forever procure? What an infectious plague has it proved in the stock of the adulterer? No space of time has purged it; it has been as the fretting leprosy in the walls, which nothing could heal save pulling down the whole race and family from the very foundations. Jeroboam's name not being more prodigious and odious in Israel than an adulterer's in the church of God: as if such or such a family had bought the staple of the trade! So that it is observed that this sin has so defiled the blood of some families that they are no sooner named, but their kind is offensive, scarce any in such families being noted to be chaste. What a stench might such cause, and even a taint to a whole country? How just was it for God to pull down the whole houses of such, stick and stone, no memory of such to be left behind? How just was it having first moth eaten their name by dishonor, to come upon their persons as a lion and tear them in pieces?

2.
Name.

Is not the finger of God here (as they told Pharaoh) when men on earth, who should have censured them, suffer these nasty creatures to lurk in their stys and dens, poisoning the country with their breath? Has the Lord let them alone? Has he not been fain to step in himself, and by sudden vengeance to cut them off? And, if such censures were in force as we are bidden to pray for in the church of God, such discipline I mean in the church, could such a sin as this escape the dint of excommunication, the greatest dart of wrath? Should we have had such notorious whoremongers brought forth in the most famous places in the land, to their penance, with such impudence or disdain? Not to speak of such great ones as for their villainy in some kinds, not to be named, with their own

When men have failed, God has struck in.

flesh, and forcers of their wives to yield to the lust of their servants, have been brought to open execution. Is it not a pity that through the insolence of offenders, the sacred censures of God's church should be vilified and exposed to scorn? To end this reproach of the name, it is a usual saying, that the sins of seed and pollution are punished in the seed: one way or other, a tainted seed, betraying itself. Peter speaks of some sins, de- 1 Pet. 1.18 rived by tradition from the fathers to their children; among which this is one (none of the precious legacies), as Jericho was built, so is adultery plagued, both in the eldest and young- est, it goes through the race till it has wasted all, and made an utter consumption. Some notorious monster in this kind, being as he, who puts a burning torch into a stack of straw, so violently burning that there is no quenching of it.

    Thirdly, God accurses this sin with beggary and rags, 3. wasting of state, open, or secret: no man can tell how, save that Beggary. so it is, and by this privy plague God has discovered many wretches, in the eyes of them, that else never should have sus- pected such. One of them upon his death confessed both of this and of other evils, I have spent many thousand pounds to damn my soul. Alas poor soul, it need not have cost you a penny, save that the Devil loves to have his bored slaves outvie God's servants, and (as one says) do more for him that will shed their blood than Christ's servants will do for him that shed his blood for them. When no cause, I say, has appeared of such a man's wasting, but yet wasted he is, parsonage added to parsonage, great portion in marriage to former inheritance, great befalling of legacies by this means, and that yet none will serve the turn, but a canker fretting out the marrow of all; no thriving in estate; what does it argue but that moth that eats out the abundance of all, and that fire that melts all, as fat before the sun! The sluggard and adulterer being commonly joined in one, partake of one plague of penury. Go over towns and countries, tell the choice buildings, lands, and inheritanc- es of them, and ask whose these were, all will tell you such a name, such a house enjoyed them; but now all is gone and embezzled away, not one acre remaining of four or five thou- sand pound lands by the year! And how? Oh the fire of lust and burning concupiscence has wasted all, and driven them out of their dwellings, as dogs or swine, so that all who come by may say, drunkenness, riot, whoring, idleness, or malicious persecution of the church of God, have been the means to root out the most families of this greatness and wealth. Truly it seems to me, that when I pass by them, they are as theaters of vengeance and judgment of God against adulterers and fornicators.

4.
Coherence of uncleannesses.

Fourthly, the judgment of God appears in the snaring of the sinner by this sin. As is the whore, so is the adulterer: she is a deep ditch to devour, and he is a vast gulf of lust and concupiscence. He is so drowned in his own perdition, and cannot get out: snarled as a bird, so that the more she struggles, the worse she is hampered, would unwind herself, but cannot. Oh! Then what a judgment is this, neither to be able to be chaste, nor endure to be unchaste? As the poet said of the paramour to his harlot, neither can I live with you, nor without you! So of this lust: I cannot endure it, it is so dogging, so insatiable that it wastes my marrow in my bones, and causes a perishing daily without death: it is a tyrant to me, forcing me to serve it beyond my strength: and yet, I cannot be without it either, it has so prevailed against me by the false, sweet, and cursed habit of it that I cannot lack it. One in this kind was so addicted to it that even when he was spent to the very pith, yet had appointed his harlot to meet him when death approached: and could not believe he should die, till want of breath intercepted his thoughts and trade. The soul in this plight sinks deeper and deeper. One harlot makes way for another; one insatiable stallion in this kind having three, four, even seven harlots to exhaust him. As he said merrily, so I here, such need no gout, dropsy, ague, or consumption to bring them to their end, they have provided a speedier course. There is no end of sinning, and he must go whom the Devil drives.

5.
It is the Devil's nest egg.
2 Sam. 11.etc.

Fifthly, it is the Devil's nest egg, and causes many sins to be laid, one to, and upon another. Look upon the woeful chain of David's lust, how did one follow another, the act urged the concealment; the eagerness thereof provoked a suborning of Uriah: that brought on the making of him drunk, when that will not serve turn then the innocent must be murdered: any one of these is odious in a wretch, how odious then are all in a saint? How many secret murders of infants have been caused by Popish votaries, let the vaults, privies, and fish-ponds belonging to their lawless houses testify; furthermore their own Pope Gregory, who took an order with them upon the observation of such villainy! Oh the lies, shifts, perjuries, and purging by forsworn men, bribes given and taken, policies and tricks to cover, defend, and make off such abominations! So it must be. I wonder that a man should be so debauched as to be a whoremonger, but being one, I wonder not that he is as such a one must be: for can a bowl rolling down the hill stop her own course? No more can he who is in the power of his lust do as he would, but as the force of ill custom, and the prevailing sweetness of his lust necessitates him unto. No sin goes alone, but to be sure, uncleanness cannot avoid many to accompany it. Once over the shoes in this puddle, rarely will Satan leave off, till he has by degrees got you over head and ears.

Sixthly, what woeful consequences follow this sin? As Solomon of the drunkard, whence are red eyes? To whom are wounds, black and blue cheeks? So say I here, to whom are quarrels, broils, bloodshed, duels between rivals of harlots, with a raging heart never at peace: to whom? To those whom the fury of harlot's discontent has incensed: what will not such do to gratify their mistress? Moreover, where do robberies by the highways and murders and burglaries begin? Surely in the love of harlots, as much as in any other root: it must be so, love will not be maintained with nothing; this sin is and must be desperately wasteful. The old speech is, Venus must be nourished with Ceres and Bacchus: infinite is the luxury and riot of such, no end of expenses in each kind: and as the grave, so the harlot insatiably cries, give, give, else she thinks herself scorned and scorns her bankrupt lover. Now, then what does Satan drive them to? To all violent, hideous ways rather than want oil for this lamp. A harlot must be fed with the rapine of all sorts, and when she is rich upon the price of the soul of a man, she is most content. How many come to untimely, shameful ends this way (especially of those gentlemen thieves as we call them) by the just intercepting hand of God's instrument, the magistrate? So that many have said with him, finding God to pursue them, Just oh Lord are your judgments! Many have been executed for crimes, which they never com-

6.
Consequents
of mischief
upon it.

mitted; but yet confessed that God has plagued them for such as man knows not, such as the law cannot take hold of: secret sodomy, adultery, or other uncleanness, which I never looked to have discovered. I did under a false title and crime, but not without due and just desert: man has done me wrong, but God has done me right. Oh what a just hand of God is here? Vengeance will not suffer them to live.

7.
The body.

Seventhly, the body of the unclean is judged: seldom is it free from diseases and distempers. Whence are such maladies, as poison wife, child, and each one that drinks in their cup? Who but God plagued that army of the French with that loathsome disease, never before heard of? Whence are inflamed, swollen, spotted faces, puffed flesh, stinking breath, disguised body, putrefaction of the blood, rottenness of the carcass, unsound health, speedy age, and infinite infirmities? Whence is that outcry which Solomon speaks of, when your liver is darted through with an arrow, when your strength is given to the cruel, and you mourn when your flesh and body are consumed, then shall you cry out, how have I

Prov. 5.10,11

hated instruction? Oh fool, and beast that I am, how am I led to the shambles as an ox, and how to the stocks like a drunkard? When all your honor is laid in the dust, your friends are ashamed of you, your conscience flies in your face, and your harlot has forsaken you, and all is gone, then must you say, God is departed from me also, and leaves me hardened, and woe be to him that is alone! And yet all which I have said is but as the adulterer's prison and chain, the chief bar of judgment which he must take sentence at, are death and the last day: then will God judge whoremongers indeed, then he will be a swift witness to purpose; all his delaying and reprieving of adulterers shall be recompensed with sweetness in kind: then shall flames revenge flames, and one fire punish another, and there shall be an eternal heat of wrath for the short and sweet pleasures of lust. For, without shall be sorcerers, murderers, dogs, idolaters, thieves, liars, and adulterers; this is the second death. This death shall be the reward of this sin, and this is the last judgment from which no escape, no appeal shall be admitted. And this is said for answer to the question.

Use 1.
Terror to the
unclean.

It is now time to hasten to use. And first, let this be terror to all such as thwart and contradict God in his course;

does God all he can to terrify adulterers, and to make this sin odious? Woe be to them then that make an honorable thing of it; I shall not need to seek out as far as Spain, Italy, or France to find out matter hereof, such as make bastardy a title of honor, covering it with greatness, so that a term of dishonor with God, is with them a name of renown; woe be to them, who honor that which God abhors! To these add the Papists (touched before), who honor whores and concubines far above lawful wives in the clergy, setting up open brothels, out of the which the Pope draws an exceeding yearly tribute (for you must note, he is not so holy, but he will take the price of a whore into his treasury, and savor it well), justifying the lawfulness of such practices and tolerations of harlots, to the end indeed, that the chastity of matrons may be preserved! Are not these wise proctors, think we, for God and for his seventh command; to make the plaster of the rankest poison? But who wonders that the great mother of spiritual whoredoms, that old bawd Circe, who has poisoned the entire world with her double cup of doctrine and practice, should so tenderly nurse up the brothels? Oh you harlots' children, and seedplots of bastards, are you so careful of matrons and the safeguard of their chastity! No, rather your banner and buckler is for whores, than matrons! You care as much for your chastity, as Judas did for the poor, whose successors you are, while for the filling of your bags, you suffer any villainy, and live upon the sins of the people.

Once a young spark son to an emperor told his father, he wondered at him that he would be so base as to exact tribute of the city for urine! But he took a piece of that golden tribute, and put it to his nose, bidding him smell to it. Which he doing, he asked him how it smelled. He answering, well for all he felt, yet (says he) it comes from the city urine. A base speech for a man of so incomparable worth! But this tributemonger of souls is ten times worse; for hellfire and all, do smell sweet in his nostrils, the smell of gain from anything favors well to him; so he has it. To these add such as slight this sin, calling it but a trick of youth: such as blanch and color these sins of all sorts, not to be named: never so rise in all estates, as now in this debauched age! Such as play the bawds to their own children, their own wives, such as make a sport of it, and lay their

Prov. 26.19

bastards in their own wives' bosoms, forcing them to nurse them, or else turning them out of doors. Casting darts and mortal things, and asking, am not I in sport? Such as make a trade of this sin, serving the turns of their commanders, as that hang-by Hirah the Adullamite did the turn of Judah. Do these, or such as these (for they are infinite) believe these terrors of God? Or do they take notice that God will have this sin made odious and terrible, to frighten all from it? Oh woeful rebels and traitors to the edicts of Christ, beware, lest God come upon you, and tear you in pieces, and there be none to deliver you for so impudent a forehead of brass, and daring to resist him in his own way! If he aggravates, dare you alienate? Surely he shall add unto you all the plagues of his book, and diminish your names from that other of life!

Use 2.
Admonition
to all unclean
ones.

Secondly, if God so strives to make this sin odious consider in the fear of God, both upon what ground, and to what end he does so. Surely it is not for nothing that he does so. The ground is, that it opposes his ordinance; the end to prevent sin. For the former, beware of defiling any ordinance of God! That which he has put honor upon, put not you contempt upon! Marriage is honorable, and the bed undefiled by an ordinance. It is like the decree of Medes and Persians, which alters not. Take not away the honor thereof, either by

Branch 1.
Deface not
God's way.

willful abandoning of marriage to live in lust unbridled; or defiling marriage, to cover your filthiness (it was not made to such an end)! God will be surely avenged upon all such! It is the practice of Satan and Antichrist, his eldest son, to be God's opposite to thwart an ordinance. What is so holy an ordinance as the ministry of the Word, the use of sacraments, and the use of the keys? And, what does he more purposely contradict? How basely speaks all this rabble from top to toe, of a minister, of preaching, of our sacraments, and our communion table! They jeer all, and oppose their priesthood, mass, sacrifice, and altar! What so sacred a civil ordinance, as magistracy? They abhor it; tread under feet all kinds that cross their own government: cursing, destroying, excommunicating, and murdering them at pleasure, if they can come by them! What is so pure an ordinance as marriage? But what uncleanness is there, which they prefer not before it? Beware you rebels! You fight against God, one that is stronger than

you! Hearten not one another against this ark that is come
into your camp, lest he plague you, and makes it too hot and
too heavy for your keeping! Call not those things common
and carnal, which he has called pure; honor that which God
has stamped: discern the solemnity, the sacredness of it; defile
not my ordinance, lest I make you your sacrilege!

    Secondly, the end is to stop and prevent the sin itself. **Branch 2.**
Beware then of all riot and excess this way: you who formerly **To prevent the**
during your dissolute youth, have defiled your bodies, or since **sin.**
marriage have adventured to do so: look back and consider
what you have done! Tremble to think that you dared to presume to sin in that kind, which God has frightened you from.
Should Adam have ventured to break into the garden again,
upon the shaken sword of a cherubim? But behold, the shaken
sword of a greater than cherubims are, is here! How just were
it that God had struck you dead in the act? Still to strip you of
all at once, and bring you into the pit of despair! To accurse
your posterity, and to transmit your sin through your race, to
make you a byword as Jeroboam! Oh wonder that ever you
got out of this pit (if yet you are), and take heed lest he who
delights to see dogs and swine turn to their mire and vomit,
pull you not into this ditch again! Tax not God for his severe
and hard sentence against such unclean wretches, whose bodies have rotted in prison, persons that have been ruined with
penury, souls perished in impenitency! It were just with God,
your own should have suffered no less, for such as despise his
terrors, go on still as the forlorn rank in the mouth of the canon, wrath has always swept them away as a man who is angry
will smite him that is next, so has he smitten some in their
souls, in their names, bodies, estates, and posterity, to affright
others. Else had he been unjust. Now then, take warning:
God aims at the preventing of sin. If you by these examples
repent not, you shall go in the drove, and be made examples,
that others may repent by yours.

    And to conclude, to both sorts, I say, knowing the ter- **Conclusion**
ror of the Lord, desist from your unclean course! Who shall **of it.**
stand when God shall come in person to judge? It is said that
when Jehu sent to the princes of Samaria, tutors of Ahab's chil- **2 Kings 10.3-5**
dren, to set up one of their master's children and fight for him,
they trembled and said, Two kings could not stand before him,

and can we? Therefore they chose to cut off the heads of them, and send them in to him, rather than to try it out! I tell you, though the son of Nimshi was a furious marcher, the son of God is more! Not two or ten, but ten thousand kings could never stand before his revenge. Hell is prepared for kings, if unclean and adulterous. Stand not out, cut off the heads of these lusts, and thereby make way for pardon and atonement to yourself, if yet ever this woeful spot and crock of spirit may be washed out (for there is but one thing, even the blood of this judge which can cleanse it) and forgiven. Think not by peeking out of God's sight for a while, to wind out, and be for-

Rev. 2.14

gotten! So did Balaam, that bawd of Peor, who cursed Israel more by this stumblingblock than otherwise! Oh! He went to his place, and lurked in his nest, until the Lord in person came upon Midian, and then both the five kings of it and all those enticing fornicatresses, and then Balaam himself was dragged out of his hole to execution; verifying his own prophecy, who shall stand when God does these things! Will an innocent lamb tremble before a lion, and shall not guilty adulterers, when God sits upon them? Shall this be the fruit of God's scaring of men, that with the new built house they settle the more upon the frame when the wind most shakes them; to run to sin, to snort in it with so much the more impudence, securely? What is this save to mock God, and play the giants against heaven? To dare him with a Babel, and try whether he can confound us! As those Philistines cried, now play the

2 Sam. 10.12

men, kill both Israel and the God of Israel, if you can! Be not so mad! Time will make you think God is like yourselves, and he will neither do good nor evil! Because judgment is deferred, your hearts are set in you to play the whores and villains still: but your damnation sleeps not! He shall come upon you, and set your disordered ways in order before you, and bring (as Solomon did Shemei's) all your pranks, old and new at one view into your eyes, and then shall it not be possible for your shoulders, your consciences to stand under your load, nor endure those terrors that shall sting you, as the handsels

Use 3.
Instruction to
be subdued by
the terrors of
God.

of hell which are ready to devour you!

Lastly, let us all learn to be of God's mind; and so convince our hearts of the judgments of God against uncleanness; as not to dare to think of committing it. I have seen many

wretches, and one the other day who was affrighted in his conscience by the fear of sudden death, unloading his guilty spirit
into the bosom of God's minister, even his filthy haunts with
many close queans, unsuspected: and under this he lays as
long as the dint lasted: but having found no further favor with
God, relapsed to his old course, as a rabbit though taken in her
hole, yet if let go, has no shift but to run to her old burrow and
harbor! If Christ is not the cover from the storm and rain, sin
must be; and although it is but a sorry one, which will one day
wet to the skin, yet it must serve the while. Subdue therefore
your soul with these terrors: as Christ says, let them sink deeply into your heart! It is yourself, it serves to keep you from the
paths of death. As our Savior then when he bids watch: tell us, Mark 13.37
he says it to the disciples, and to all: so, I wish that this watch-
word might reach to all, none excepted, even forward profes- Forward pro-
sors themselves. I much fear this sin is rising among many fessors beware
even of such: for profession cannot alone quit us of secret pro- of this snare.
faneness. So near is the flesh, so sly is Satan, so copious is a
false heart of evasions, that no sort of people is free. There
want not fearful examples at this day of each degree of men
and women. I need not silence that which all tongues jangle,
and the ears of the good might tingle with: what debauched
varlets there are of late brought forth from among them, who
have crept in amongst the zealous servants of Christ, and tak-
en upon them to be the most forward. To conceal, is now too
late, too late to say, tell it not Gath: for it is all over the places
about their dwelling. One being reproved for attempting the
maids (who came to his house) to folly: answered, though I
may not covet my neighbor's maid, yet for his own maids, or
those that offered themselves, he thought he might. It is time
now (my brethren of all sorts) to cease striving, to hold oil in
your palm; it is rather time to apply corrosives. The best way
now is in taking notice of these, to say, they were among us:
they were not of us, if they had, they would not so foully have
gone out of us. And yet (were it not that I fear doing hurt) I
would add that I must not, nor dare finally to censure everyone as lost, who is guilty of this sin: but I know, ten to one of
these are hypocrites; though for causes, God may leave some
odd person, whose repentance he purposes to make as eminent as ever his sin was: and moreover, to use this sin in others

as a forcible occasion to convert them from all sin. But of this after. Of the hypocrites I say, let him that is filthy be filthy still; of the other, the Lord give them grace with Achan in the midst of their reproach, to give glory to God: woeful creatures the while weltering in their misery from whom the unclean spirit seemed to be cast out, and they to have escaped the pollution of the world through lust: but through their looseness, the Devil has returned into their hearts, and brought seven spirits with him, worse than the former: so that if that stronger man throw not out this strong, the end of such will prove worse than the beginning.

Profes-
sion cannot
dispense with
this sin.

Consider all such, profession cannot dispense with you, rather it shall make your sin triple, and heat hell seven times hotter! If we never found any other effect of the sins of our ignorance, save shame and death: what are we like to find for sins against knowledge! Truly, men are strangely impudent and hardened in these days! This makes me insist as I do! Fear not him who can destroy the body only and not the soul: but him who can cast both bodies and souls into hell, I say, fear him! Get we our spirits truly molded into this terror of God! Those Corinthians pretended the liberty of the gospel against the terror of the law: but, how does Paul answer them? Surely by a fit instance of the Israelites in the wilderness, committing filthiness at Peor. Are you better then they? Had not they the Word, the ordinances, the cloud, the manna, and rock, but God was never the better pleased with them for that! Their carcasses all fell, and were made dung in the wilderness. Therefore deceive not yourselves; be not fornicators as they were, and were destroyed of the destroyer! Their angel of presence turned their destroyer for their uncleanness. If this is all the privilege of your bare profession, let who will venture, but venture not yourselves! Well (may some say), we would fain be of God's mind, but our hearts are so giddy and slight in this point that we cannot get them to be seriously awed by God's judgments. I answer. I shall refer it to the exhortation following in the next chapter: in the meantime, consider what has been said in this.

1 Cor. 10.10

CHAPTER XVII

*And last; containing the use of exhortation, with
counsels and motives to preserve chastity,
and avoid uncleanness.*

I finish the whole use of the point with exhortation; to this effect, that all who truly tremble at this judgment of God against adulterers and fornicators, do preserve their vessels with as much holiness and honor as is possible. To all such (as in the end of this point I shall touch) belongs consolation: but let it lie by a while, until you are able to apply it to yourself by the experience of what I shall now say. Wherefore, I exhort all such, be chaste and pure in body and spirit, passing the whole time of their conversation here in holy prevention and caution against uncleanness. A solemn duty, to bring a clean body to the marriage bed: to maintain it so, and bring it so to the grave! But how (will some say) may this be effected? I answer, by observing three counsels: and first, to abhor somewhat. Secondly, to meditate upon somewhat. Thirdly, by practicing. Touching the first, abhor somewhat within and somewhat without. In the prosecution of which three, if I shall haply trench upon anything before touched, through the nearness of the argument, let the reader consider that when I wrote that before upon the point of chastity, I intended not the handling of this latter part of the verse: but I hope I shall avoid any purposed repeating of anything, which the necessity of the order does not enforce upon me, for the avoiding of any interruption. For the first of abhorring: first, with David, abhor yourself, that inward original corruption of nature, the foment of this flame: he begins at the right end of the staff with that poison wherewith his mother had warmed him in her womb. Abhorring of some outward acts or penalties of this sin, may go without any loathing of the fountain. Had it not been (says David) for my natural stain, I had never committed such an actual abomination as this. Alas! As the field of a poor man vanishes in the map of a whole town, so does this evil of con-

*Use 4.
Exhortation.*

*Counsels
three.*

*First counsel.
Abhorring
somewhat.*

*1.
Your own self.*

cupiscence vanish in most men's eye, when they take a survey of sin; whereas this inward is the body: and that which we see breaking out is but a member, as it might be here a toe, there a finger of defiled old Adam. Till then the mother is abhorred, the daughter will never be renounced. Suppose you could bitterly inveigh, even incense your heart, against some actual filthiness, yet, till this inward dunghill is raked, which is able to steam forth into a hundred adulterers, indeed sins without number; I say till this furnace kindled by hell, as ready to defile you again (when you have seemed to wash out many stains as they appear) with tenfold more wickedness; look for no redress of your disease. It is a running sore, an issue of uncleanness, and must first be drained, before the passages dry up. The silly man who saw the stream of the river run very swift, sat him down upon the bank and slept, thinking by that time all would be run out, and he might go over dry shod! Poor soul! For that river ran still, ever did, and ever will. So is it here: till God dry up or turn the current, it cannot be otherwise. The due sight of this your bent of heart, your frame of spirit, always inclining one way, never to purity, first tiring you as a traveller, worry you as a dog, pursue you at heels, as the avenger of blood did the manslayer; is one of the best ways to quit you of this mischief. Get an inward abhorring of yourself, see what a huge heap of filth lies there; mark how it is like the door rolling the same way on his hinges; and this wearisome sight may (perhaps) drink up your spirit, and dismiss all your daubing, colors, and excuses. I say, this may raise your fort itself, and shake it from the foundations, and then the outworks will soon yield and fall to the ground. Look upon this sin in that glass with that eye, which Paul looked in, when he beheld lust forbidden: and (if anything) this shall swallow your ship wholly up in the quicksand of self-abhorring. Say to your soul thus, Was I washed with niter, even scoured with soap, yet the clothes I wear will defile me as fast. Alas! I get nothing by all my outward abhorring; lust will not be scared away with holy water. I have a bosom orator within, which will draw me to lust twenty times, one after another, and pull me faster to filth than all my own, or other's dissuasion can withdraw me from it. Lord then, drain this flood and overflow! Teach me to abhor myself in dust and ashes, if ever I get victory over my actual corruptions!

Secondly, abhor your inward, actual thoughts of contemplative uncleanness. A workman proceeds according to an idea and platform in his mind, set before him, in all his projects and attempts: so does the adulterer. The heart (says our Savior) is the adulterer, all the mischief is hatched there. What contemplations of villainy does the forlorn sty of thoughts nourish in many? What unclean man or woman is there whose thoughts do not plod and contrive their meetings, the places, the time, manner, and circumstances? What a thoroughfare of such scurf is that defiled spirit of theirs, which they carry about them? Once, a learned man was called a walking library: but of these, it may be said, they are walking brothels. It is as easy to pull their hearts out of their bellies, as to alter and turn the course of these suggestions: the Devil being the presenter, and the fancy the receiver. Mortify then and nip these thoughts, which have the whole man at command. Senses do not so much hurt to thoughts, as thoughts to them and to the bodily performance. The loathing of base, vain, wanton, and capering thoughts in this kind is half the cure. These vaporing up from the heart to the brain, do so possess and beleaguer it that the affections are fired, and on thorns, till they come to practice. Now, when the fuel is gone, or lessened, the fire must cease: let original corruption be once abhorred truly, and this will follow. Think that God speaks to you in James in his phrase, *Cleanse your thoughts ye sinners, and purge your hearts, ye wantonly minded.* How long shall your unclean thoughts abide with and within you? Know you not that imaginations are the first mover of the whole frame of corrupt nature? If they move, must not all inferior ones dance after their pipe? And tell me, when Satan fires the whole man, where does he inject first his fireballs? Is it not into the thoughts? If he would tempt, accuse, or terrify, how goes he to work but by raising up a commotion in the thoughts? And in what part is hellfire kindled in the damned? Is it not first in the thoughts? Keep then your thoughts with all diligence! Forestall Satan and uncleanness by good thoughts, chaste, pure, and contrary thoughts; let the chambers of the thoughts be prepossessed with these guests: and they will spare the door from such encroachers, especially if the pure Spirit is the

2.
Things to be abhorred, thoughts of contemplative uncleanness.

James 4.8

usherer of them in, by the Word.

3.
Things to be
abhorred,
colors and
excuses of it.

Thirdly, abhor all those cursed colors and mufflers of this sin: which the fertile heart can devise abundantly to alienate and lessen this sin! The heart is the forge of all these tricks and evasions. If the Lord has called this sin so terrible; let it be enough to you; abhor the Devil's fig leaves; and behold the filth of this skirt with detestation. Blanch it not over with your nature (that worst of all), the propensity of your constitution, the strength of allurements, the difficulty of preserving yourself, the generality of the sin, the slight opinion of the multitude. Abhor these cordially, or else the sin abides still, under dispensation and connivance. Then fourthly, as touching other inward fomenters of lust (of which I briefly speak because I have prevented myself in the point of chastity before), abhor your covers and shelters, hope of impunity, hiding your uncleanness under the shroud of a married whore, or of your wicked friends and abettors; such as the Devil will raise up to stick to you, or any such as for a base bribe will aid you and keep you from open shame. Such impunity being forecast in the mind is a hardener of the adulterer in his sin: abhor a luskish, lazy heart that delights in ease and idleness, loathe softness, effeminateness, and impurity of spirit (a thoroughfare for lust); also unarmedness of the soul, lying open and exposed to occasion, empty, swept, and garnished, fit for the next Devil that comes. Abhor rashness and unsteadiness, which will on the sudden betray you to the occasions of lust. Renounce all self-confidence and venturousness upon your strength, as rather scorning to be snared than humbly fearing snares (for alas! poor worm, who are you, if left to yourself?). Know this that lust will give small warning, it comes as a torrent: as the necessity of an armed man. There is the same mettle in you which is in others; and they are soonest snared, who fear least.

Beware of self-love, which gives itself allowance of the largest size, as loath to deny itself nothing which it covets, and counting nothing too precious, no liberty or delight too dear for itself. Abandon inconstancy and giddiness of spirit, which cannot stand its own ground, nor rest in one place, cleave to one task. For the bent of spirit to one settled object, study, calling, or lawful object will divert the vain mind from frothy fancies, and ideas of unclean thoughts, companies, and allurements. A spirit whose banks run full of employment will hardly be unsettled: but holds Satan at stave's end. Ask your gadding, roving heart where she will, when she comes, and what is her business (as watchmen do rogues). Examine the ground and warrant of your journeys, travels, errands, and wanderings up and down, forsaking your station and family. Set your knife to your throat, if you are an Athenian, daily lusting after new places, companies, pleasures, meetings, and delights. And whatsoever savors of carnal and sensual desire, know it cannot but threaten mischief, and dispossess you of your watch: I speak still of such, as in appearance have given their names to Christ, even these (for I judge none, let every man judge himself) have so far taken liberties to themselves, in the brink, that they have fallen into the water. One of them once much pleasing himself in admiring the features and beauties of women, and stroking the cheeks of one with wantonness, was by his wiser neighbor warned thereof, saying, These crimson faces (so he called them) will sadly cost you the setting on, one day: and so it fell out soon after; for such an aspersion was soon after cast upon him (whether true from man, or just with God), as brought his hoary head to the grave with sorrow; to teach all such gnats to beware how near they fly to the candle, lest they be burnt.

And thus much for inward abhorring: as touching outward, I will repeat nothing before said, in the chastity of prevention; only, whatsoever occasion threatens any affront to the fort of chastity, and the preserving of the whole man in integrity and honor, renounce it. And so much for the first of the four heads of counsel against this sin of uncleanness, namely, abhorring of somewhat, is spoken.

5.
All outward
temptations.

The second counsel is to meditate of somewhat. And whereof? Surely of such things as might help to quash and quell lust: and that partly concerning the sin itself, and partly the penalties thereof. And both these, especially of meditation, must be attended with two properties in general. First, that this meditation be wise, and secondly, that it be deep. First I say, wise: for I would have this noted that some things are of that nature, that some kind of musing of them, is rather an incensing of the heart unto the sin than any checking thereof. As are all such evils, as border upon the sensual appe-

Second counsel.
Meditate of somewhat.

Two properties of it.
1. It must be wise.

tite and concupiscible faculty: of which sort especially is this sin of uncleanness. Many complain, that they muse much, of the odiousness thereof, that so they might abhor it. But they find it more and more to follow their hand: and to snare their spirit. And so the remedy proves much worse than the disease. And it fares with such, as it does with two men at variance: who put their quarrels to compromise: but when wise men should set them at one, they fall on ripping up all circumstances of unkindness offered to each other that they part worse enemies than they met, and so make the wound incurable. So here, men meditate of the sensual and carnal occurrents of this sin, their base meetings, words, gestures, unchaste looks and acts, under pretense of a purpose more fully to detest and abhor them: but by this means the Devil casts fire into the dry powder of their concupiscence; and inflames them to it the more. The reason is, because the sense and fleshly familiarity of the thoughts do prevail against the spiritual hatred thereof. So it fares in other temptations of a hideous nature, as atheistical thoughts against the majesty of God, or blasphemous thoughts against the Scriptures, or the essence and attributes of God: the baseness whereof the more we plod upon (especially while Satan's wild fire is in the spirit), the more we are snared therewith. Therefore in such cases as these, the practice of Elisha to the servant of Jehoram is to be followed: we must pray against the tenacity thereof, and force ourselves to handle such thoughts roughly at the door; and in no sort to give place to them: as knowing their master's feet are not far behind them. Toss not thoughts off and on, about passages, which tickle the fancy, and wind in more deeply into it, than it can be rid thereof, indeed though they were most irksome to it: but take up the sin in the whole lump and bundle:

Psal. 51

muse of the bitter root from where it comes, as David did in his meditations. Incense your soul against the body of corruption, from where it flows, that wherein your mother conceived you; and from there descends to the fruits of it, as the wound which it leaves upon the conscience, the wrath of God, which it pulls upon itself; the curse of it, how it makes all the soil barren, blasts and wastes the grace of God, or the least show of any. Keep it thus at stave's end, but tamper not much with pitch, lest we be defiled. Such unwise meditation is not water to quench, but oil to increase the flame.

     Secondly, let this meditation be deep and solemn, both about the properties and the penalties of this sin. Touching the former, the first meditation about it is how spiritual a wickedness it is, especially under the gospel. It is like Absalom's incest committed shamelessly in the sight of the sun; before all Israel. It does not only sin against moral light of the natural conscience, but also against the grace of God; and the remedy offered thereby. For the grace of God has appeared to all, and teaches them to deny all ungodliness and fleshly lusts, and to live soberly, godly, and purely in this present world. David's adultery was a moral act; but yet inseparable from spiritual wickedness: for he resisted conscience in point, not of moral light only, as any heathen might do, but of grace and mercy from God, teaching him to abhor it. Truly, this very thing was the thing that made the Lord so severely punish it, both then and after; even because he fought against his spiritual light, embracing a lust, and the sweet of a base heart, with the loss of that sweet mercy of God, which he had tasted. Truly, against that sweet communion with God, which he had formerly enjoyed: both which he knew would be wasted hereby, as also that hereby the spirit of God was displeased and vexed with this rebellion, and the effects thereof, and his conscience gulled down and defiled with sensuality and security, even hardened by the deceitfulness of sin: and hereby the enemies of God were caused to blaspheme God, his worship, and the generation of the righteous. For our better conceiving of this point (in my judgment the weightiest of all to frighten a soul from such abominations), let us observe how the Holy Ghost has described it. Read and ponder that Heb. 3.12, where the apostle in effect tells us that this is the nature of all sin committed against the light, and it has these degrees: as the words do express. *Take heed, lest there be in any of you, an evil heart of unbelief, to depart from the living God, but exhort one another, lest you be hardened by the deceitfulness of sin.* Mark: first there is an evil heart of averseness from God, and enmity or alienation from God, in each child of old Adam. Thus David confesses himself guilty hereof, in committing adultery. Secondly, this being not subdued in the soul by the Word, breaks out into outward and moral evils, as ill humors in the body,

2. Property. It must be deep about the properties and penalties.
1.
Of the spiritualness of this sin.

Steps of spiritual sin.
1.
An evil heart.
2.
Evil works.

into sores and botches. So says our Savior, An evil man, out of the evil treasure of his heart brings forth evil things; for out of the heart proceeds all such refuse: that is the nest and forge of them all. Both these make the heart an evil heart.

3.
Unbelief.

Thirdly, this evil heart and these evil works, become evil works of unbelief! That is, whereas God has ordained a blessed remedy of pardon and cleansing of both, behold, the love of an evil heart to her evil works will not suffer it to part with them, but chooses rather to forsake mercy itself. They that embrace lying vanities, forsake their own mercy. And our Savior plainly, This is the condemnation of the world, that light came into the world: but loved darkness rather than light, because their works were evil. Jesus Christ received by faith, would have destroyed such works. But men loving them, and that darkness which nourished them, more than light, they added drunkenness to thirst, that is unbelief to moral sins. And so sins which at the first were but dipped in the color of nature, being dyed in grain by contempt of light, became spiritual evils, consisting in a treacherous refusal of grace, that it might nuzzle itself in sin more and more, which by embracing of grace, it might have been rid of. So that this unbelief, defending itself in the practice of darkness, causes the soul to be guilty of horrible villainy against the grace of God and that Spirit of Christ, which offers itself to purge and wash it from sin.

Jonah 2.8
John 3.19

4.
Delusion and
defilement.

Fourthly, by this means there follows a delusion and defilement of the soul: by the sweetness and deceitfulness of sin. That is, a desertion of the soul, whereby it is left by the just hand of God to the error of its own way and choice: to be as it desired to be: so that it becomes of a voluntarily, a necessarily seduced heart, thinking evil to be good, feeding upon ashes, as a perverted appetite will do upon coals or chalk; it suffers conscience to be blindfolded and baffled, and the accusing power thereof to become a defiled power; so that though it knows sin to be sin, as this of adultery; yet being lulled asleep upon Delilah's lap, it feels no sting, but dreams of ease, as Samson and David, who differed not in this from Balaam, save only in this, that the Spirit sustained and reserved their judgments, that they sinned not upon the last practical understanding and choice of free will, but by prevention and temptation; but to their own sense, they had shaken off the Spirit.

Fifthly, from here proceeds hardening of heart in the sin, against the recourse and checks of conscience. Thus David, being once defiled and snared, so that he could go neither backward nor forward, grew so hardened that he resolved upon all those ways whereby his sin might be concealed, extenuated, and defended, and that with odious circumstances; which what was it save (as much as in him lay) to put off the Spirit of God, and to fulfill his lust, providing that he might not be unsettled. And lastly (in some unclean ones, although the elect cannot go so far), from here proceeds a departing from the living God, a disabling of the Spirit from returning back to him again, through a heart which cannot mourn, relent, and repent: and so finally a pouring forth of the heart to all other sin, without control or restraint; even some go so far herein that they fight not only against the revealing light of the Spirit, but against the Spirit itself, out of malice: and what wonder, if the restraining power of the Spirit is taken from such as have despised the saving power of it? Now, to gather up all into one, how woeful a hazard do all they run, as play the unclean beasts under the clear light of the gospel? How do they lay the stumblingblock of their own iniquities before themselves? For although I deny not a possibility of returning, so long as the Spirit is grieved only, except it is despised also, yet who knows how far he may go in his descent, being not able to stop himself? And as for the elect, how many bear themselves upon it, till they prove errant hypocrites? This meditation therefore, let all such ponder deeply, who are given to slight this sin! What God may do for ignorant ones (as Paul speaks) I say not (though we see but few of these repent), but for them that sin willfully after light, it is far worse.

A second object of meditation, against this sin, is the peculiarity of it from other sins. That of the apostle is notable for this, flee fornication: why? All other sins are apart from the body, this abides in it: what is that? Other sins of wrath, theft, swearing, and the like abide not in, but pass away from the instrument acting them. I say not in guilt but in act of cleaving: but this of uncleanness as it leaves no less scar in the body than they (rather more), so it leaves a far greater and more loathsome stain in the body: causing it to be a more irk-

5.
Hardness of heart.

6.
Departing from the living God.

1 Tim. 1

2.
Things to be meditated of, the peculiarness of this sin.

some dwelling for the Spirit of God, to be more loathsome to itself, and bears mark in the open sight of others of its own filthiness. If God then has set such a mark of this sin upon the body, as upon no other: and now much more than when Paul speaks; if other sins (in comparison) are without, but this within it: others by the body out of the body, this by it and in it: that is, it is a more real and bodily sin, requiring more of a sinner for the perfecting of it than others, even forfeiting a piece of the body, in the committing of it; how odious is it? Again, if it is a more fulsome vice, and more difficult to be washed out (as before has been said), if it shuts God out of his temple, indeed, out of porch and all: I conclude, it behooves all to beware lest they conceive that a more slight sin than others, which God has branded with more distinctness than others. I do not here speak of that loathsomeness which follows the act: of that before; but I say, the Lord loathes these leprous walls. What should such a one have to do with prayer, reading, hearing, and sacraments, whose lips, eyes, hands, and whole flesh is defiled with this sin? Who sees not the unsuitableness hereof? So that as the leper was accustomed to be shut out of company, to have his lips sown up, scarce suffered to breath, and to try out, unclean so here. This sinner shuts out himself from God, in that he cannot approach to him with any member without loathsomeness. I speak not this to exclude any penitent from the free grace of God (though God who gives each penitent grace, gives not each sinner to be penitent), for Rahab, Bathsheba, Tamar, even a worse than a Mary Magdalene found mercy, and sore covered the honor of each member: but I speak how odious the sin is, in peculiar. Let it therefore be a second meditation against it.

That other sins are out of the body, but this is (as it were) within it.

Thirdly, meditate of that woeful separation, which it makes inwardly, between God and the soul; few see this. But if union with God is the root of all other privileges, and a restoring us to our integrity: what then is separation from him, and cutting off from the fountain, save a curse? Now, who so is one with a harlot is cut off from God: for how can a man be at once a member of a harlot and a member of Christ? Know you not, that who so is one with Christ is one spirit? And what is he then, who is one with a harlot? Can he, with and in the same spirit, be united to one and to other at the same

*3.
Separates from God.*

time? Does he not, what lies in himself to disjoint himself forever from God, who is joined with a whore? Is it so easy to unlink the chain of uncleanness, and to be knit to God, who is once enchained in the band of this sin? Or, can there be communion and influence maintained with God while fellowship continues with harlots? Is pureness and filthiness so easily reconciled; a spirit of holiness, with a spirit of adultery? What communion is there between Christ and Belial? Or, how can two walk together, except agreed? If then the Spirit is saddened and grieved, what joy can it have to walk with the soul? What had become of David's fellowship with God when he had defiled himself? With what a conscience (think we) did he walk? What peace, joy, and going in and out with God, had he? Or, why does he so crave for the Spirit and for washing and renewed grace, save that he felt them withdrawn from him? And, if the Spirit of Christ is gone, what is the name of Christ and of communion worth? Perhaps many an adulterer pleases himself in this, that he is not yet cast out from the church! But why is he not cast out? Is God's judgment changed? Where then is that censure become, of which Paul speaks of, that you being gathered together with my spirit in the name of the Lord 1 Cor. 5 Jesus, deliver such a one (an unclean wretch) unto Satan, for the destruction of the flesh, that his soul may be saved in the day of the Lord Jesus. Is not here solemn excommunication against uncleanness urged? Neither let any cavil and say, This was in a case of high degree of this sin. For God's nets take And from all open sinners, in foul kinds, be the degrees whatever they the church by are. What else does that speech mean, Withdraw yourselves excommunica- from every brother, who walks inordinately? How? Except tion, either by the censure, excommunicating him from communion of deserved. sacraments and secret fellowship. Thus once it was: but the sin of man interverting the censure, disannuls not the ordinance. If such are not cast out, the greater is the shame of neglecters, and the offender has the greater wrong.

And say that he is not formally cast out by discipline: has he not really cast out himself by his desert? As he once said of his books, that they were published, and they were not, in effect: for none could understand, or be the better for them: so say I. They are in communion, and they are not: locally, by intrusion, not spiritually, not by acceptation, so that (save for his pleasing himself sinfully) he is never the better for it. For why? Does not conscience within tell him, all who would thrive by the ordinances, must cast up their gorge? So says Peter, Casting out all superfluity, as newborn babes, covet the sincere milk of the Word to grow by? And, are not all things unclean to the unclean? Does not such a man's spirit say to him, as God to Elijah, *What doest though here, Elijah?* Why do you take my Word (pure as I am) into your mouth, hating to be reformed; minister into your mouth, hearer into your ears, being both in your body and spirit polluted? Can wrath or doubting (as the same apostle speaks) hinder the lifting up of pure hands, and must not an unclean conscience much more? Can such a swine, coming into the assembly to a sermon, or sacrament, think himself to be in his place? Does he not tell himself, a brothel, a whore's bosom is fitter for you than such a place as God's house? Now, if outward communion (which yet many a sinner will buy with his money or thrust himself into boldly) is so improper for him, what then is communion with the graces of God, with his saints, with the duties of both tables? Has such a one any joy in his soul, peace with God, delight in his service, exercise of graces, as seal, faith, meekness, compassion, and patience? Or can he lay claim to a holy example? Are not these irksome objects to such, more fit to tear them in pieces to think themselves cut off than to comfort them! So then let this be a meditation of great weight, to frighten the soul from all uncleanness, or to humble it being fallen, to consider what a gulf it sets between the Lord and the soul, so that one cannot come at the other. And woe is to him that is alone! All ordinances, all duties, all graces, speaking thus to him, If God helps you not, how can I help you, with the barn or the winepress? Influence being wanting, presence gone, what can second comforts avail? Do not all issue from union with the head? Do not all conduit-comforts rise and fall with the fountain? Except then, you care not for God, for his Spirit, or Christ, beware of uncleanness. For that lays all channels of the Spirit dry, empties the soul of all heavenly savor: making it as careless to have it, as it is empty of it. And these three may serve for a short description of the nature of this sin, and how we may derive arguments from that place to deter us from it. Now to the penalties.

The Spirit of God excommunicates him in the court of his own conscience.

Touching which, they are either spiritual or outward. For the former, the reader may partly gather what the spiritual burden is, which God lays upon it, by that which before I said of the nature of it: for, if it is so defiling and hardening a sin, and so seldom is found in the way of repentance, who should not be afraid of it? Who is so stupid, as, seeing a drove of adulterers going towards the den of the Dragon (the Devil I mean) with their foresteps, and observing so few backsteps coming from that place, would think any other, save that there they were devoured? And who would dare to hazard himself upon such a point, as whether he should come back from that pit from which it is ten to one, if any at all return? That heathen philosopher Xenocrates may teach us wisdom herein: who was a Stoic of most exact chastity and morality. He, having read to his scholars deep lectures of austerity, and abstinence from all pleasures; seeming to his scholars to speak more than he had strength to perform: was attempted by them, what he was: they got a harlot of exquisite beauty, and laid her in his bed to provoke him to folly. But he, according to his rules, abhorring the temptation, answered them, he would not buy repentance at so dear a rate. Surely, if he who had no more to lose, save his moral conscience, and feared, lest the forfeit thereof, would prove so irrecoverable; what should we Christians say who have our souls to lose, what should it profit to win the world and lose them, or what shall be given in exchange of them? And, having no hope of recovering repentance anymore, how should they tremble at so great a loss? In one word, this I say, that this sin has a woeful spiritual giddiness and drunkenness annexed unto it, disabling the sinner from laying it to heart, except strange mercy prevents him; so that as Solomon speaks, in comparing the two sexes, so may I say, in comparing these with other sinners, I have seen of them, one of a thousand to repent, but of this, scarce one of a thousand. It is the Lord's course to give over these sinners to their haunt and custom. It is said of Queen Tomyris, that having overcome Cambyses, a bloody tyrant in battle, and surprised his person, she cut off his head, and soused it in a barrel of blood, saying, Satiate yourself with that whereof you have been always so insatiable. So says the Lord to the adulterers, since fleshly pleasure has been that which you have always so hunted after: fill yourself

Secondly, he must meditate on the penalties of this sin.

1. Inward. A woeful giddy drunkenness disabling the sinner from repenting.

with it forever. Split your soul against the rock and stone wall of my seventh command, at which you have so stumbled; let that grind you in pieces. This curse of God, sealing up the heart of the adulterer, gives him over to his own sinful sweetness; so that, the surfeit thereof, does so waste and embezzle the spirit of such a one, that he walks up and down staggering in the drunken pleasure of his uncleanness: he is quite asleep as Jonah under the hatches. If any of God's mariners (ministers I mean) cry out, Arise you adulterer, call upon God and pray, if possibly this tempest of wrath may be prevented. Alas! He is as that fellow upon the top of the mast, ready to topple into the sea, and yet neither awakes, nor fears any danger.

A fearful example of a debauched adulterer, urged.

Once I knew (and still there are some alive who will bear me witness) a most odious adulterer of seventy years old, who having long consumed his strength with harlots (as he in the proverbs), wasted himself and all; at last being laid in a barn (good enough for him) for no man could endure the vermin and savor which came from his rotten body, was requested thus, Potter (so was his forename) call upon God. He replied with his ordinary oaths, calamity, and wounds, is this a time to pray? Thus he spoke at death: all his life long, the season of prayer and repenting was not come. And now at his death, behold, it is gone! As he merrily said of marriage, either it is not yet time, or past time! Oh! It is just with God to bereave such of all desire to apprehend any sound notion of their misery! They are held off, from capableness to mourn after God: and in a following deceit of sin, even to death. I heard

Mr. Bol.

once an Oxford man of worthy memory in a sermon relate of two students of eminent parts in that university, who were sunk in a brutish custom of tobacco and sack, and then into a loathsome habit of unclean pleasures, and in time, grew into such a slavish impotency of spirit in those ways; that when necessity urged them to return to their chambers, they could not there rest till they had pitched a new meeting, and so another; till in time they grew so enfeebled and past all sense of sobriety, that with their pipes and pots at their mouths, they were fain to be had into their beds, and so miserably died. Alas no wonder! If drink and riot alone can do it, how much more when lust is added to it, as a threefold cord not easily broken; both streams meeting in one channel to overflow the

banks? This is that arrow of God shot through the liver of all
such unclean ones; to be so enthralled to their lust that all sap
of the spirit is dried up, and a kingdom of uncleanness is set
up in their hearts and bodies to carry them beyond all hope of
repenting. Muse of this seriously if you would root up the love
of lust and kindle a deadly feud with it, never to be razed out.

Touching the outward penalties, what should I say
or what can I add to that I have already said of God's judgments against this sin? Look to the former doctrine. Only I
add this exhortation, suffer not yourself (when you read the
judgments of God against the name, body, and person of an
unclean wretch) to pass away without meditation, till they
have wrought your heart to a due abhorring thereof: yet, lest
I might seem to mention this point for nothing, let me add
one outward penalty to all the former, and that is, that even
repentance itself is not able wholly to wash off the stain of this
sin, from the committers of it. Such is the wound that those
men give to the name of God; his religion and truth do suffer so deadly by their means that God in justice suffers them
to expiate it by an outlasting infamy. This was God's threat
to David, You have made the enemies of God to blaspheme,
therefore, behold, the sword shall never depart from your
house, nor reproach from your name. That same text which
shall most eternize you for a man according to God's heart:
shall again crock you, saying: save in the matter of Bathsheba.
That is a back blow: yet just, for he thought his secret convey-
ance would cover all, but he saw not this; that the thing he
had done, displeased the Lord. Therefore he must feel it to
his smart! His repenting God knew: but yet that must not
serve to quit him of a work of sorrow, as before I noted. He
that commits folly with a woman is destitute of understanding: his blot shall never go out. Courts of men, absolve such
from all aspersions, but when they are white and fair in them,
they are foul and black in God's. No time, no concealment of
witnesses, no dwelling far off, no oaths of purging, no bribes
must ever look to do it, when as repentance cannot do it. Who
should imagine a possibility of it, seeing what the name of
David, Lot, and Solomon till this day, suffer for it! As a blur
in fair cambric, so this is always cast upon him as his shame.
God does not usually upbraid his people: but this he always

Meditation of
the temporal
penalties of
uncleanness.

casts him in the teeth with: yet this caution I add by the way, it is not lawful hereby to condemn whom God has justified: but to cover it rather for our parts: but for caution to others, the Lord will rather make a record of it, and hang it on the file, than it shall be forgotten. And when we hear the uncharitable imputations of men, fret not at them, but say, God is in it, he will keep it on foot: he will check the soul with it, and cause the guilty thereof to possess the sin of their youth, as Job did. If God shall conceal the shame of any, guilty of this sin, let them praise him, and make an end of all in his privy chamber of mercy and repentance, that so his open judicial proceeding in court may be stopped. Let this also add some weight of terror, and divorce you from this sin: whip the slaves back with this rod: but the son will be drawn by love. So much for this second of meditation.

Third counsel. Practicing it somewhat.

Whom this concerns especially. Two sorts. 1. Such as are guilty of it only.

Branch 1. Adulterers ought to humble themselves for it.

Luke 1

The third and last is, to practice somewhat. And this is the main of all other helps, to rid us of this mischief. And it consists of sundry particulars. Touching all which, let the reader understand, that they properly concern such as have been actually defiled with uncleanness in one kind or another. And these men are either guilty of their crime, during their estate of ignorance and unregeneracy; or else, such as have revolted from that grace, which they have (either soundly or seemingly) received. To both, I would give some advice; and first to the former. To that then, which has been abundantly spoken of the terrors of God against this sin, let this only be added, that all those men, whose hearts God shall touch for it, do lay them close to their hearts that as that perking presumptuous Asahel was met with and pierced in the fifth rib by Abner's spear; so may these wild creatures be, in their venturous provoking of God. Surely, such a giddy lightness is in every unclean heart: even the religious: they cannot be solid, when as they would (they are so drunken with this sin), except the law, or else that old Simeon speaks of, which must open and let out the thoughts of many hearts, do let out these wild and unbridled affections. And, as that Asahel, 2 Sam. 2, being once darted through, was tame enough, and stopped in his wantonness; so let your soul be earnest with God to step out of his ordinary way, to make a high fence and sharp hedge of thorns (which he does but for few in this kind), even to set an angel before the door of that harlot, shaking a sword, that you may no more venture to return. This will not be, till a fire is thrust into your soul, to feel the intolerable wrath of God, upon all whoremongers; which may so sting you, that, as a man scalded or burnt, has small joy or mirth, so the feeling of yourself in the suburbs of hell, may cause you to feel small desire or edge, to your former occupation! Hell (my friend) is no painted fire on the wall (such as you see in alehouses to make drunkards merry), but is kindled with the breath of God, who has vowed to be a terrible judge, and consuming fire to all defilers of themselves with whores or harlots, single, or married: yet, entreat him, that this terror of his may not be extreme and desperate (as his was of whom I last spoke), ending in violent laying of hands upon himself, and preventing of repentance; but rather break the force of lust, pull down your jollity, that it may be as sad an object to you as was the murdering of the Lord of life to Peter's hearers, Acts 2.37.

And not only so, but stoop and quail under this terror of God; we see, prisoners at the bar do not descant or quarrel with the judge; all their language is confession and supplication; for why? They know the judge has them at advantage, their lives stand at his courtesy. Do likewise. Will God judge adulterers? Stoop then at his bar; he can save or destroy. Other judges admit appeal, themselves may, and must be judged: their judgments may be questioned or disannulled, they sit but upon the breath and life of a man. Not so with the Lord: he is judge of the high court, a Sovereign, King, and Judge. If he once passes sentence, no revocation, it touches the life of your precious soul! This should affright all unclean persons! What suing and seeking is there, to the judges of spiritual courts, if they threaten but the sheet? Oh! But here is a greater judge that can damn you in hell forever! No bribes prevail here: he is like that enemy of Babel, who should scorn all gifts, and be above gold and silver. Submit therefore under his hand: confess your damnation is just: lie prostrate upon the earth with your mouth in the dust, and say, Oh sovereign God of the creatures, enemy of all unclean wretches, if you send me to hell, I have nothing to allege, if I perish, I may thank myself, you have power to destroy! Tremble at this sovereignty, do not quarrel, nor shift, with him; there is nothing to be pleaded

An abasement under the mighty hand of God.

save mere favor, I can say nothing, why the sentence of death should not be pronounced against me.

Branch 2.
They must
gather hope
out of the
promise to
pardon it.

Secondly, seeing all repentance stands not in a preparative, go on, be earnest with God to give you a glimpse of hope in the Lord Jesus, who was made all sin, and this by name (not only for David, but for the nature of man, and for yours) and has satisfied the wrath of this judge, that he might say, Deliver him, I have accepted a ransom. The law of Moses knew no such atonement: stoning and strangling was the end of it. As the judge tells some felons that the law has no mercy for them: their sins exceed it, so here. But the gospel affords more grace: refuses to pardon no sin, no offence, which the soul can be humbled for: I grant this will not easily enter so debauched a spirit, to dream of a possibility of such a grace. For, when that conscience which was so deeply benumbed, is once stirred to the bottom, it becomes as sensible as ever it was senseless before; and while conscience holds under bondage, it is no easy thing to see such a hope of grace by the gospel. But yet, in this your amazement, utter loss and despair in yourself, you must wait upon God, who can sustain your

See and con-
sider.
Jer. 3.2,3

bottomless spirit from sinking altogether; till in due time, he opens a crevice of light into your dark dungeon. And, when it shall please him, to turn your eye towards some likelihood of finding mercy in the way of promise; follow this work hard. It belongs to the hopeless: not to such as turn this hope to a snare. Beg of the Lord to turn a terrified heart into a melting one: that it is, which must mold an unclean soul, to a clean and chaste one: no hammer can do this: mercy must dissolve it in the furnace of grace. Cease not, till you feel that heart, which has been drenched in the sweetness of lust, to be steeped in bitterness, over head and ears, for your wounding the Lord of life, and his virgin-pure flesh, to death, by your uncleanness. Look not upon other sinners: you were a murderer sufficient of his sacred person: you sought to destroy his Godhead as well as his flesh, if it had been in the power of your sin! Though there had been no other sinner in the world, you were enough. And should you not care (for your base lust's sake) to kill not a man only, an innocent Uriah, but the person of the Son of God? If this melting spirit is wrought in you by the Spirit of grace, you shall behold him as pierced willingly and

of his own accord for you; who did as little deserve it as Judas
the traitor, but yet, seeing you have a melting heart, which he
wanted, and can with Peter, weep bitterly, it is a sign that the
curse shall turn to a blessing; truly you shall see God so ordering the matter for you, and Christ so giving up his soul to
the spear's point of wrath for you, that your eye shall behold
another sight that is an enwrapped hope of forgiveness in this
satisfaction of his: and of life in his resurrection: so that now
your horror shall turn to hope. And know it, only this glimpse
of sunshine in your dungeon of fear can dissolve your hard
heart, and prepare you for pardon.

Thirdly, let this hope, rip up all the seams of your **Branch 3.**
unclean heart; and all that filth which lay hid in the entrails **Glorify God in**
thereof, never like to have come to light, had not God revealed **the confession**
it and uncased you. Let, I say, this seed of hope discover that, **of it.**
which a habitual love of your sin would have smothered forever. For, this opening and ingenuous confessing of your sin
will make way for further mercy. It is none of your work, but
the Spirit of grace, that makes way for it. Now a frank heart is
put into you, to be as open as ever you were close before, and
to take as much pains with yourself, how you must give glory
to God, in a full confession, and turning up that cursed poak
of falsehood from the bottom, pouring out all your sin, as ever
you took care before to swear your heart to a hellish secrecy. It
is with you, as with a woman who has many old pieces of gold
and jewels lying by her, which she is loath to forgo, although
she might thereby make a sum for the purchase of fair house
and land, yet perhaps rather than quite forgo the purchase, she
will fetch them all, and pour them down upon the table. So,
when hope of mercy offers itself, oh the pearl thereof (exceeding all petty shreds) will make you freely disburden your soul
of whatsoever loads it, your most beloved lusts (I speak not
now of abandoning the habits of them, that is mortification
following after; but of the clear intention and meaning of your
heart to abandon without any base hollowness). Oh! You desire now to spare God a labor of proclaiming your sin before
men and angels! And, if it were meet (as it is, where God's
ordinance may prevail) you would choose that place rather
to shame yourself in, where the solemn presence of God, his
angels, and church are gathered together. Still I speak with

caution, if your sin has broken out publicly: but if you have kept it secret, you are not tied to make yourself public: nor to take witness, except your hard heart requires it, to confess to others, for the breaking thereof; the reason is, because the way of church correction for open sins, is one, and the evangelical correction of the Spirit of Christ in private is another. But usually these sins are open: and therefore openly to be proclaimed in confession, as in the committing. If mercy has touched you at the heart never so little it will work in you, as God's voice in the whale, when she vomited up Jonah, upon the dry ground. You shall no more take care what becomes of your lust, so you must be rid of it: nor who shames you, so you be shamed, and sin have her due! You take more care, how God may be honored in the abhorring of your rebellion: how others may be frightened from the like; how your own heart may be melted upon melting: not, how you may escape in a whole skin, and lie hardened in your sty of uncleanness! No, rather shall litter and whelps, and all, be raked together, and cast to the dunghill. I tell you of a solemn thing, rarely seen: yet I will not say, I have not seen such a confessing spirit: Ephraim had it when she smote upon her thigh, the publican, the prodigal, the thief on the cross: and here and there (as a berry left upon the bush). I have seen such as sincerely penitent, but, when I did so, I never pleased myself with any object like it, I was almost ravished with it and took it as a real mark of the Lord's pardoning of it, in heaven, which was so performed on earth.

This is as their bringing of their curious books, and burning them. Acts

And good cause, for, what should you care to nourish that in yourself, which you purpose forever to be divorced from! Therefore, here oh Lord (say you) comes the most tainted adulterer that ever lived! These were my first allurements to filthiness, such and such companies, I haunted, such baits for my lust I maintained, so many base harlots, married or single, I clave unto! Such were the places I frequented, the filthy sonnets I sang, the music, dancing, reveling, and wantonness I was defiled with! Indeed, such and such were the colors whereupon I hardened my heart in sin, such fees, such bribes, such perjuries, such friends in courts and proctors I corrupted with money: and in this confusion I had lain forever had not mercy cast an eye upon me! No day, no Sabbath, or season of

And why?

Aggravation of sin needful for unclean penitents.

worship came amiss: no light of conscience could bear down my sin; no shame of world, no patience of yours, long winking at me, no good education, no hope of my friends, and no terror by your judgments could dissuade, I sinned against all. Here therefore, I uncase myself oh Lord! Against you, you Lord, have I done this villainy, in itself moral, in me spiritual, and in a high degree! I was ever tainted, even from the womb, and this my sin is but one of a thousand, which the forge of my heart has sent forth. If for this you had drowned me in perdition, even in the act, burying me up in the bed of my lust, you had been just; truly your deserting of my spirit, cutting off my days, and sending me into the hottest place of hell, had been little enough for me! But oh! If you shall wash this spot away, and cleanse me with hyssop, I shall be whiter than the snow: what I am is not the thing, confusion belongs to me for it, it is all I can plead. But there is mercy with you, that you may be feared: and some little hope has opened my heart to confess my sin, as, rather relying upon your Word than upon my own fears, that you will deal rigorously, and of my own mouth (as you might) condemn me!

Fourthly, you must not thus walk only with your penance fagot upon your shoulders, and the sheet of your shame upon your back, as one shut out, and excommunicated from the assemblies, upon whose face your father has spit: but you must set before your eyes a double promise; one this. That if the Lord shall once accept you, all your former sins shall never be so imputed, as to cast you off. Look at that place in Jeremiah, full of comfort, If a harlot is divorced from her husband, shall he return to her anymore? Certainly not. But behold, you adulterer, you harlot, you have defiled the bed which I made honorable; yet, I will deal better with you; return, and I will accept you, says the Lord! And what upon that? Surely it shall be with you in my account as if you had never sinned. The Lord will open to such a fountain for sin and uncleanness. This may seem as a cable to the eye of a needle! Such mercy for so graceless a wretch! Yes, be encouraged: for the Lord looks not at the greatness of the sin (if your traitor's heart distrust him not), but at the expression of his own grace, and getting himself a name, in pardoning it; that, where sin has abounded, grace might abound much more. A dog will

Branch 4. Set before your eyes the promises.

Jer. 3.1,2

catch at this morsel, and poison himself, for he will sin, to try a conclusion: but this must not cast off a poor penitent soul, who has sinned already, and been carried by the stream of his sensuality. Neither must a hypocrite be bolstered: nor yet the grace of God to his own frustrate. And secondly, consider what you have been, the Lord looks not at: he beholds you in his Son, as washed and purified, therefore will be honored, even by these members, which have most served the lusts of your uncleanness. The Lord delights to see it so, if once the property is altered. Witness Mary Magdalene, so highly honored by Christ to be the first witness of his resurrection, and so enrolled in the book of God that wheresoever the gospel should come, her name should be honorable. How did our Lord Jesus admit her to come to his body, and with those eyes, hands, wherewith she had beheld, embraced, those tresses and forelocks which had allured so many unclean lovers, yet he was content to be washed, anointed, and wiped! What exceeding love is this, thus to restore an adulterer to his blood, and to entertain him to that dignity and service, which he had forfeited? Try your own heart in this case; no other medicine save this made of the blood of Christ can satisfy for your sin, or wash off the guilt and stain of it!

The second.

Believe this promise, apply this blood, and this will be a true seed of abhorring it forever. Faith will carry you to the cross of the Lord Jesus, tell you in this manner, I have seen him bleed and breathe out his last conflict with wrath, and overcome it, for the full expiation of your uncleanness: if it could have overcome him, you had lost the day, forever: but seeing he got the victory, your sin shall not damn you, so long as he prevailed against death and hell for you. Christ only, can make a divorce between you and your sin, till he shed his precious blood in the defiance of sin, the soul and sin could never be made enemies. Only death, which separated his soul and body asunder, can divide them. If then, you seek no other moral shifts or carnal, Popish ways of abhorring this sin (at least does rest in no other), all is well. You take a sure course to part with it forever. I Come in therefore, and clasp to this pardon, offered you in the promise, sue it out, and apply it to your soul. Perhaps your base heart will choose rather to lose it than to take it God's way: but consider, since God

3.
Believe the promise.

will not stoop to your way, and there is but one way to come to him, be it never so unwelcome, stoop to that way, and come in. Any way of your own daubing with untempered mortar will please your flesh better than this. But seeing, in them you must perish, by this you must be saved, to use Isaiah's words, in the promises there is continuance; in the other, lying vanity: cleave to this and know, this only can satisfy God, and change your leper's skin, therefore venture upon this. If you can possibly perish in believing this, perish: yet know, much surer it is that you must perish, except you believe. If you (like those nasty lepers) sit still in the city, die you must, no shift of it; here you may live; value your life at no greater rate than the life of a desperate man is worth: if elsewhere there were hope, you might shrug at it: but, worse than you are you cannot be! If you find more favor than you deserve, count it for a vantage. But howsoever, do not prefer assured death before hope of recovery: nor lose it for venturing.

Fifthly, rest not here either, but if more mercy is shown to you than you looked for (for God is best to a sinner when he is past pleading), then let this persuade you to follow him for further grace. I mean, when the guilt of your conscience is gone, sue to him for repentance; for the mortifying and subduing the rage, power, defiling, and snaring property of your sin: and begin with the root, kill there first, begin not with Adonibezek, at the fingers' ends: Christ stabs the old man at heart first. As he told the Pharisee, nothing which comes from without can defile the man: but that which defiles the man comes from within. From the heart proceed, as other sins, so uncleanness, and all the fruits. Therefore, either purge the root first, or else let all alone. You shall find this a new work. Yet that faith, which has washed your conscience and inner man from guilt and fear, and hell: can purge you a second way, from all slavery to your lust. Mercy will act the part of a priest; it will both set an eternal conflict between you and your lust: and it will mortify your concupiscence daily, till it is quite dead. It will truly set you on mourning; truly work you to a hearty indignation against yourself. It will teach you the art of sin detesting; which no wit of man, no skill of hypocrites can teach you. It will intercept all your succors of lust, your provision to fulfill your lusts. When the Court is pulled

Isa. 64.5

4. Hereby your heart must be changed from it and part with it.

Branch 5. Sue out the destroying power of sin from Christ.

down who needs to fear suits in it? It will cause you (not morally, but from a principle of grace) to shun all means, motives, provocations, and snares of uncleanness, which the Devil shall straw in your way! That so, the oil being gone, the flames may vanish. It shall change your unclean thoughts, affections, eyes, and ears into clean and pure ones. If your harlot meets you and says, It is I: you shall answer, But I am not I, not myself. Another is become that in me which my cursed self used to be.

The sign is pulled down, the alehouse is let to a man of trade, no more harlots or adulterers come there; new lords, new laws, all old things are done away, behold all things are become new. I am redeemed with a price, not to be my own: if my Lord and Master will endure lust, if any accord between Christ's body and a harlot ask him leave, and I obey: else, I am not my own. Oh! This grace shall bring your lust to the horns of the altar, bind it thereto with cords, and cut the throat of it with the sacrificing knife of the priest. Your priest will teach you to do that office very handsomely, to let out the rank blood of your lust, and the strength and sway which it bore in you. Indeed, it shall drag your unclean heart to Golgotha, and nail it to the cross of your priest, with the same nails which nailed the body of Christ. It is happier to find out those implements, cross, blood, nails, tomb, and all, than ever Helen was, or any Popish relic-monger: and to make use of them too, to better end than at this day that Popish monastery of friars do, who have hired those places of the Turk, built temples, altars, and silver floors in honor of the Passion. It shall cry in your soul, oh lust, I will be your death! Oh concupiscence, I will be your destruction! The sting of sin is death, and the strength of lust is the law: but thanks be to God in Jesus Christ, who has condemned sin in the flesh, and mortified it by the flesh of his holy body, that neither guilt nor dominion might prevail! Pursue the victory, the Lord is with you, you valiant man, and in this your strength, fight and rest not while through your captain, both sin and lust die in you.

Branch 6. Return to the Lord, in chastity forever.

Sixthly, return to the Lord with full bent of soul to renounce all cleaving to the flesh, and to cleave to him without separation. That grace which has killed lust, will quicken the life of pureness in your soul; it will indeed make you a true penitent, not only to renounce uncleanness, but to embrace a chaste spirit, and live a chaste life; to return to God in a contrary practice of unblameableness all your days: so far as weakness will permit. As he took off from your jaws the yoke of servitude: so he shall make his own yoke easy, and his burden light. He shall be as one that lays meat before you! You shall be so preserved by the sweetness of grace that all the sweetness of lust, of adultery, and of lasciviousness shall stink before you; so that they shall never have hope to recover you into their possession any more. And what then remains? But when lust knows not what to do with you; then your ear is bored with God's awl, that so you must be his servant, and walk in pureness and holiness all your days! The Lord bless this main direction with all others unto you, and remember, none but Christ can heal this sore. And so much for the former branch of counsel, to them, who are only guilty of the sin. I pass lastly to the others, who have revolted from this grace once obtained.

Lastly therefore, if your uncleanness is yet of a deeper dye, as being a revolt from the grace of God, and the vow of your spiritual baptism, once made; then know, the cure is somewhat different from the former. Here then remember that the seed of God in his, dies not. Therefore, if once God has awakened you out of this your relapse, and the dead sleep of security under it, which if he loves you, he will do by some three stringed whip or other which he shall make for you (as once he did for those defilers of his temple), by some cross or stirring terrors of the Word in your soul, then take David's course. Beseech the Lord first that the despair and extreme horror which an ill conscience (sick of a relapse) might work in you, through unbelief added to it, may graciously be kept off, and so your heart may be staid from utter departing from the living God, upon fear that he is wholly departed from you. *The second general in practice for such as have revolted to it again.* *1 Counsel. What such are to do.*

Secondly, remember that the covenant of God cannot be repealed: it comprehends you, when you cannot it. Therefore apply those mercies of old, and be comforted. *2 Counsel.*

Thirdly, take heed, lest Satan confound and oppress your spirit by the conscience of your base revolting, sinning against such mercies, and snarling your soul with so many successive evils as you have heaped upon one another, without a heart to get out. For it is an easy thing to lose a man's spirit *3 Counsel.*

and self in the Devil's maze.

4 Counsel.

Fourthly, with a penitent heart for your treachery, that you should kick up your heel against former mercies and covenants; behold that promise, of which I formerly spoke, and apply it unto your soul as you are able, knowing that (whatsoever Satan has to gainsay) the Lord Jesus was made all sin, both of rebellion against, and also revolt from God, that you might be his righteousness, and recover it, having lost it.

5 Counsel.

Fifthly, let the affliction of your soul so deeply seize upon you, till (through mercy) it has soaked into you, and pierced you as deep as your sin has pierced God: as the tent must go as deep as the sore is festered, and fetch out the bottom scurf. Content not yourself with such a humbling as your slight heart would admit. For this is one attendant of this sin, to be light and wanton, and not to be able to be serious. Therefore, set your heart to it, mock not God: make not the remedy worse than the disease, that you should even be fetched in again by Satan's claws before your repentance is finished, which is to unsettle the work of God in you, and work your heart to a despair of recovery. It has been the portion of many unclean ones, never to get a serious spirit. If therefore your heart is once down, hold it, as if you should keep cork under water, and trust it not: pray thus, withdraw from me all objects of vanity, and teach me your law graciously! Arraign, accuse, condemn yourself, and judge yourself lest God judge you: and till God raise you, be content to lie low, bear the indignation of the Lord, because you have sinned: and be glad if any such vein of wrath may be let into your soul, as may truly subdue you under the mighty hand of God, that he may raise you up. Think not the time long, take leisure; a heart long defiled, a vessel once fusty, will hardly change her hue, or be sweetened.

6 Counsel.

Sixthly, let faith always come between your sinning and your repenting: solder not up a repentance of your own: it is bad in any sin, but deadly in this: such sudden leaping out of one contrary to another, may admit as easy a relapse from this to the former. And so you must make your fall, to become a falling sickness; if the power of pardon and purging come between your sin and your redress, then is the cure from God, and from Christ the sure physician, whose healings are sound and perfect. Let his blood come into your nasty soul, come between your sin and your spirit, loosening the sweetness and the defilement thereof from you, or else it will return. Moral plasters may hold while the soul is in fear: but when sensuality returns, she breaks all such cords in sunder.

Seventhly, when God has healed you, go your ways: and think you meet with him that said, Sin no more, lest a worse thing happen to you, even an impenitent spirit. Let the experience of your revolt bind you to a double care and fear of time to come: as that incestuous Corinthian, a kindly convert (and as fit an object as any, to be set before a relapsing adulterer's eye) approved his repentance, so do you yours! How rare a sight is it in these days to see such a one, so swallowed up with sorrow that the Church has need to comfort him, in all haste, for fear of despairing? Oh! Mourn for the wasting of the Spirit of grace, by an unclean spirit of your own! Count yourself cut off, moan your condition in the ears of God, and beseech him to set you so in joint again, that your heart may be stronger than ever, to resist: think yourself unworthy to be restored to the communion of saints: be as an excommunicate in your own eyes: as those offenders in the ancient times, who were hardly and by degrees admitted to the assembly. Then the judgments of the ministers were so harsh, as if such might not be admitted (as Cyprian and others erroneously thought); but to be sure, they were admitted with great difficulty, for fear of second relapses. But now our discipline is in a contrary extreme: you are a law to yourself.

7 Counsel.
John 5.14

2 Cor. 7

Eighthly, if your revolt has been open and public, let your repentance be so. Think not that remarkable offences will be huddled up in the court of heaven, without open repentance, and more than ordinary humiliation. Most men's plasters are too narrow for their sores. But if we observe God's penitents, you shall see that their revolts were never so famous, as their repenting has been eminent. You have sinned with David: repent also with him, and let the church be well satisfied, she has not lost a member.

8 Counsel.

Ninthly, be content to bear the reproach of your sin forever, as a burden, upon your back: even to carry it written in great letters upon the forehead, if God think meet to exercise you in that kind. Not you, but he, must judge of the

9 Counsel.

breadth of your offence. It is to keep down your heart, which would ever be perking up, and floating aloft, and running to the like excess. Better to have your fagot always upon your back.

10 Counsel.

Tenthly, return to a much closer and narrower walking with God, watching to a chaste and inoffensive course not only against open evils, but even secret-suspicions; and learn to sanctify the marriage bed against such foreign provocations. But, if any desire to read more of this argument, I refer him to my Treatise of the Sacraments, part 2 and the Chapter of Sacramental Repentance. So much here may suffice.

Use 5.
Caveat.
Magistrates to whom this work belongs must look strictly to the censure of God.

Fifthly, if God himself is so severe a witness and Judge of adulterers, thundering out such threats against them; let it be a caveat to all magistrates and governors, both civil and ecclesiastical, who take upon them the censures of such delinquents, to look to themselves: you are in the place of God's officers, you should execute the authority of God. Do in these cases as the great Judge would do. If he sat in judgment, he would verify this threat here in my text. Perhaps it is not in your power to do as he would do, if he sat in commission against whoremongers; but yet, as far as lies in your power, show yourselves swift witnesses against this crew, which does now so swarm in cities, great towns, and generally everywhere, and among all sorts, that they will make the land rue it, and spew out her inhabitants, as once Canaan did hers. Consider what a vengeance this one sin (not to speak of others, both spiritual and moral) might justly bring upon this our land, which groans under it as much as ever Israel and Judah did, to which God does threaten such terrible plagues by Isaiah, Jeremiah, and other prophets, for their fullness of bread, the sins of Sodom, and their neighing like horses after their neighbors' wives, or else after other harlots, which perhaps in England is the more frequent. Suffer not vile adulterers (making open profession of it) to live with their harlots and bastards, under their noses, and moreover in the beds of their wives, expelling them, and harboring the others in their bosoms, with despite. Do not through bribes and flattery, or an ill conscience (privy to the like evils) through sloth and ease, or love of sin, seek pretenses to shift your hands of censuring such, and so connive at them! But by what means possibly you can, vindicate

the honor of God, atone the land of the just plagues which
she is liable unto, for hatching such vipers in her bosom. Be
vicegerents of God! Will you not judge them? Yes, judge these
sinners, I say not stone them (for it is beyond your power, and
the long impunity of this sin has hardened the hearts of men
in their impudence) but send them to the cart, to the house
of correction, to the sheet and shame of their uncleanness; to
excommunication from the sacraments, and the fellowship of
Christians. Post not off these men from one magistrate to the
other, as if neither were willing to brand them with shame.
They have sinned both against church and commonwealth, let
them pay for both. But in no wise harden them by allaying,
releasing, or exchanging of censures. If you discharge those,
whom God holds guilty, turning such heinous sins to mere
pageants, huddling up that which the Lord would have proclaimed on the tops of houses, know it, your lives shall go for
theirs. God will call you over himself, and when he punishes
adulterers themselves, he will judge you, for not executing his
judgment upon them: which has prevented it, and spared their
souls.

Lastly, let this point be also encouragement and consolation to all such as are pure in heart and body: without shall
be dogs and swine, sensual epicures, unclean persons: within
shall be all clean and chaste ones. And this conclusion, I cannot omit, as having before grounded it in the text. Marriage is
honorable, and the bed undefiled, and God will bless all that so
preserve it: but whoredom and adultery are odious and base in
God's esteem, and he will judge all such as pollute themselves
thereby: you see that the parallel of the two members of the
text does necessarily import it. Blessed are you that fears the
Lord in this particular. Your wife shall be as the vine about
your house: your children as olive plants about your table.
The Lord shall bless your stock and store, your goings out and
coming in: you shall eat of the fruit of your labors, and see the
travail of your hands: with peace and prosperity to Israel. As
all the plagues of the unclean shall pursue the former, so shall
all the blessings of the clean follow you. Your body shall be
clean, your health continued, your posterity shall be pure and
be free from pollution, as a holy seed: your estate shall prosper: your name shall be savory, and as an ointment poured

out. You shall see God, for so shall all pure in heart do: and the Lord shall bring you forth with honor one day with chaste Joseph, whom God released from all false aspersions; behold here are they that have washed their garments in the blood of the Lamb, walk undefiled, have not touched any unclean thing, therefore I will be a father unto them, and they shall be sons and daughters of the Lord Almighty: truly your foul garments shall be all taken from you, and the clean linen of the saints shall be put upon you, and you shall walk with Christ in white, for he has counted you worthy! Only, preserve your soul in suitable purity with your body: keep both in holiness and honor: and you shall inherit all the promises of God made to such.

The Papists do not so much magnify their vestal virgins, because they are not defiled with men (though many of them are), as the Lord shall honor you before men and angels, as his chaste and undefiled spouse, and set a crown of glory upon your head. Your marriage shall not prejudice or stain this virginity, fear it not, such as have abused this honorable estate, calling it a life of the flesh, shall not come where you have to do, to interrupt, to disturb your happiness. Enjoy your comfort here: separate yourself from all uncleanness of body and spirit; indeed hate the garment spotted with the flesh. Separate the precious from the vile and you shall be honorable! Oh you ministers of the Lord that carry his vessels in your hands, and draw near to him, be clean, and handle not his matters with unclean hands: defile not his Bible, his church, sacraments, and ordinances with polluted hands, bodies: and the Lord shall say to you as to his prophet, you shall be precious! Finally, to conclude, all his people, who have gotten out of this depth of uncleanness, be truly thankful to God, never cease to magnify him, for so narrow an escape, and so great a deliverance; it is a thousand to one that ever you got out of this pit: do not try conclusions, put it not to the venture by sinning again, whether God will pluck you out the second time. If you will try, know that if ever at all you get to heaven, you shall find it a hard work. Play not the mountebanks, to thrust your flesh through, because you have balm at command to thrust after it: you may perhaps miss of it when you would have it: and if God save you, it shall be as through fire:

Jer. 15.19

though God cannot repent, if ever you were his, yet he shall make every vein in your hearts to ache before you come to feel it: and that kingdom of God, which else might have afforded large entrance unto you shall now become a narrow passage. If you love your souls, bring not such a needless sorrow upon yourselves. It is enough, too much, that you spent so much of your former days in the vanity of the flesh, and the service of your lusts: spend the rest in holy awe, and godly fear! Say with Hezekiah and David, the living shall praise you, the dead will not; cannot. But I will sacrifice to the Lord with the voice of thanksgiving. Salvation is of the Lord. To him, Father, Son, and Spirit, unity in Trinity, and Trinity in unity be all honor and praise forever! Amen.

Jonah 2.8,9

A table of the principal things of this
treatise alphabetically framed

A.

D.

E.

F.

G.

H.

I. and J.

L.

N.

O.

P.

Q.

R.

Y.

FINIS.